ASTER FAMILY FLOWER

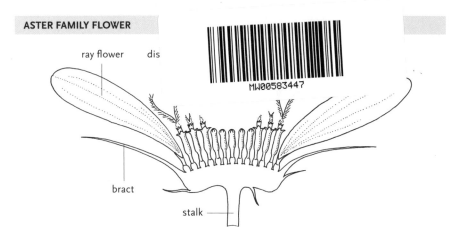

ray flower   dis

bract

stalk

INFLORESCENCES

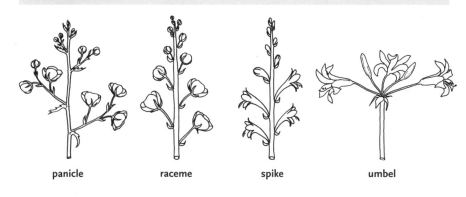

panicle   raceme   spike   umbel

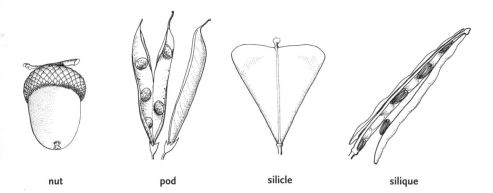

nut   pod   silicle   silique

WILDFLOWERS
of NEW ENGLAND

Ted Elliman &
Native Plant Trust

TIMBER PRESS FIELD GUIDE

Dedicated to my mother and
to the memory of my father.

Page 1: Mt. Katahdin, Maine. Pages 2–3: *Centaurea jacea*. Page 5: *Sparganium eurycarpum*. Page 6: *Lupinus perennis*. Pages 58–59: *Rubus flagellaris*. Pages 172–173: *Bidens laevis*. Page 253: *Aquilegia canadensis*. Page 319: *Campanula rotundifolia*. Page 365: *Heuchera americana*. Page 387: *Lilium philadelphicum*. Page 391: *Lechea intermedia*. Page 396: *Lobelia cardinalis*.

Photo and illustration credits appear on pages 404–411.

Published in 2016 by Timber Press, Inc.

The Haseltine Building
133 S.W. Second Avenue, Suite 450
Portland, Oregon 97204-3527
timberpress.com

Printed in China
Second printing 2020
Cover design by Anna Eshelman
Text design by Susan Applegate

Library of Congress Cataloging-in-Publication Data

Names: Elliman, Ted, author. | Native Plant Trust, author.
Title: Wildflowers of New England / Ted Elliman and Native Plant Trust.
Other titles: Timber Press field guide.
Description: First edition. | Portland, Oregon : Timber Press, 2016. | Series:
    Timber Press field guide | Includes bibliographical references and index.
Identifiers: LCCN 2015029231| ISBN 9781604694642 (flexibound) |
    ISBN 9781604697407 (e-book)
Subjects: LCSH: Wild flowers—New England—Identification.
Classification: LCC QK121 .E45 2016 | DDC 582.130974—dc23
    LC record available at https://lccn.loc.gov/ 2015029231

A catalog record for this book is also available from the British Library.

CONTENTS

FOREWORD

The New England flora has been studied by botanists, both amateur and professional, for more than three hundred years, yet our knowledge of the region's plants continues to evolve as new species are discovered and others move into (or out of) our region. In 2011, the scope of our region's flora was compiled in the manual *Flora Novae-Angliae*, written by Arthur Haines and published by Native Plant Trust. Writing a flora is a monumental work, but creating a field guide from that information presents additional problems for the author. Consider the following three issues:

1. **How many.** In a field guide it is impossible to cover all of the plants contained in a flora (that would make it too cumbersome), yet a guide should include those species that the reader is likely to see or should at least be familiar with. The reader is relying on the author's experience to present those species the reader may find (be they common or rare), and leave out others.

2. **How to.** What system of identification should the author use? Should a dichotomous key to all plant groups be included? Is it sufficient to rely on color photographs or drawings for identification? This gets to the heart of an educational debate on how to identify plants: rely on color or other easily seen characters requiring little or no botanical knowledge, or use botanical terms which may seem arcane, but once learned become part of the user's vocabulary forever? While this may seem a small point, at the extremes the methods used can produce either a coffee table book or a functional field guide.

3. **How much.** The information presented about each species must be concise, but complete enough so that the reader can be sure the plant being identified is the one he or she thinks it is. The author also must present those characteristics of plants or habitats that are most important and/or interesting to both professional and nonprofessional plant enthusiasts without much space for elaboration. We want the field guide author to give us those little details learned over the years, those little hints that demonstrate the author's knowledge and command of the flora.

Luckily for Native Plant Trust and plant enthusiasts in the region, Ted Elliman has balanced all of these issues beautifully in this field guide to New England wildflowers. His decades of experience with the

New England flora have produced a book that is thorough and concise, as well as interesting to professional and amateur alike. Based on *Flora Novae-Angliae*, this field guide continues Native Plant Trust's efforts to promote knowledge about native plants so that all may come to appreciate the plants that make up the biologically diverse landscapes across our region. As readers become aware of the astounding beauty and breadth of our plants, they will also come to value their conservation. I am sure that this book will be a catalyst for conservation of our flora.

Bill Brumback
Director of Conservation Emeritus
Native Plant Trust

ACKNOWLEDGMENTS

I owe a great debt of thanks to many people who have helped in many ways with this book. The writing would have been far more difficult and much less enjoyable without their generous contributions of time, knowledge, and expertise.

At Native Plant Trust, my colleagues Bill Brumback, John Burns, Elizabeth Farnsworth, Arthur Haines, and Dan Jaffe have provided many photographs, reviewed and commented on drafts, and helped immeasurably with their extensive knowledge of the wildflowers and natural communities of the New England region. Bonnie Drexler, former education director, has devoted a lot of time, thought, and energy into helping with the selection and organization of photographs—my thanks to her for her enthusiasm and persistence. Debbi Edelstein, Native Plant Trust's executive director, has provided continuing moral and administrative support throughout the project.

Many others connected to Native Plant Trust as staff, instructors, guides, volunteers, board or committee members, and certificate students have given very generously of their time, skill, and knowledge. For photographs, reviews of drafts, discussions, ideas, research, and much else, I am deeply appreciative of the kindness, contributions, and insightful critiques of Mimi Chandler, Frances Clark, Deb Fountain, Andrea Golden, Barbara and Charles Grunden, Sandra Henderson, Kelly Kerrigan, Bruce Patterson, Nancy Savage, Dick Snellgrove, Gray Wexelblat, and Betty Wright. Any errors of fact or interpretation are my responsibility.

For years it's been a pleasure to work with the Massachusetts Natural Heritage and Endangered Species Program on many botanical and ecological field projects, and I am very grateful to past and present Program staff members Bryan Connolly, Melissa Cullina, Karro Frost, Jennifer Garrett, Paul Somers, and Patricia Swain for their knowledge, advice, guidance, and photographs, which have meant so much for this book.

My thanks too, for contributions both direct and indirect, to long-time colleagues in the field David Huang, the late Les Mehrhoff, Charles Quinlan, Kent Schwarzkopf, and Wang Zhijun.

My wife, Alice, has not only very patiently accommodated my preoccupation with this book over two plus years, she has also helped greatly in reviewing and critiquing manuscript drafts.

Many photographers have contributed images for the book—their names are given on the illustration credits pages, but I also wish to acknowledge here their photographic skill, botanical acumen, and generosity. Many photographers spent a lot of time selecting and sending photographs with a particular eye towards what would work well for this book. My thanks to them all.

Juree Sondker and Linda Willms of Timber Press have been patient and skillful editors; I thank them for conversations, encouragement, prodding, and attentive reviews and critiques of the manuscript.

Finally, I want to express my gratitude for the friendship and support of Native Plant Trust's Sanctuary Committee, with whom I worked closely for many years and because of whom this book became a possibility: Pam Durrant, Bruce Patterson, Doug Payne, Bonnie Potter, Jim Wickis, and the late Rob Held.

INTRODUCTION

This field guide describes 1100 wildflowers and small flowering shrubs that occur in Connecticut, Maine, Massachusetts, New Hampshire, Rhode Island, and Vermont—the six New England states. Most of these plants are herbaceous, that is, they are species with conspicuous flowers whose stems die back in winter. Others are small, woody-stemmed shrubs, primarily those that grow no more than 3 feet in height and also have conspicuous flowers. Trees and large shrubs are not included; neither are grasses and grasslike plants, nor non-flowering plants such as ferns, horsetails, and club-mosses.

The selected plants represent a high proportion of the region's flora that we think of as "wildflowers." Most grow in natural habitats—in the forests, meadows, wetlands, hills, mountains, valleys, and coastlines throughout the region. Others have found favored niches along roadsides, railway beds, and in pavement cracks. Many of them are common in the region and some are rare. A number of species are distributed throughout New England, while others are found only within a small area of a single state. Some grow only in particular conditions, such as an alpine meadow or sphagnum bog, while others flourish in a

Wildflowers and grasses dominate saturated soil in an open wet meadow.

wide variety of habitats. Most of these wildflowers occur in other parts of the northeastern United States and in southeastern Canada as well as in New England. Only a few species are entirely limited to New England in their range.

Plants that are native to New England and plants that are nonnative to the region are described. The common thread is that all of them grow in self-sustaining populations independent of human cultivation. A native species is one that has continuously grown in the northeastern landscape since before the time of European colonization. A nonnative or introduced plant has been brought here, accidentally or deliberately, from outside the region, and now grows here in natural conditions. Today, approximately two-thirds of the species growing in natural conditions in New England are native, and one-third of them are nonnative, introduced species.

The book is intended to be a handy reference to wildflower identification in the field. It is designed for beginners as well as experienced naturalists, indeed for anyone who is curious about exploring the beauty and variety of wildflowers in the natural landscape. The primary goal is to provide the reader with a reliable, nontechnical means of correctly identifying the wildflowers that he or she encounters in New England.

To this end, the book uses a key system based on flower and leaf characteristics. By following the key, which starts with flower color, the reader will be able to track down the plant that he or she is observing in the wild to a group of species that share its flower and leaf features. Then, by reading the individual species descriptions and looking at the accompanying images of that similar-looking group of plants, the reader will be able to find the one that matches the plant that he or she is observing.

Parts of a Plant

The plant descriptions discuss the flowers, leaves, stems, and fruits of each species in nontechnical language, but a working knowledge of these plant parts is very helpful for identification. The following definitions, along with the illustrated glossary and endpapers, explain these terms.

Flower

The flower is the reproductive part of the plant and consists of sepals, petals, stamens, and pistils.

The sepals are the outermost part of the flower, generally occurring in a spreading, reflexed, or tubular pattern beneath the petals. The sepals are usually green and obscured by the petals, but in some plants they are brightly colored and larger than the petals. Collectively, the sepals are known as the calyx.

The petals are generally the most conspicuous part of the flower, attracting pollinators and human attention with their bright colors and their scent. Collectively, the petals are known as the corolla. Note that in the key, the term "petals" is not always used in its technical sense. In cases where petals are inconspicuous or absent, "petals" may refer to sepals or, more rarely, to flowerlike bracts, when either of these features is more conspicuous than the petals. Yellow water-lily (*Nuphar variegata*) is an example of a plant with large, petal-like sepals, which in this case surround and hide the much smaller petals. Anemones (*Anemone* spp.) lack petals altogether; their showy flowers are composed of sepals.

The stamens, or male parts of the flower, occur at the base of the petals in the interior of the flower. A stamen is composed of a very slender stalk known as the filament, and a tip known as the anther. The anther holds the pollen that is dispersed to, and fertilizes, the female part of the flower, known as the pistil.

The pistil is located at the center of the flower. It consists of a swollen basal portion known as the ovary; a slender stalk, known as the style; and a tip, known as the stigma. Pollen is received by the stigma and ultimately grows down the style to fertilize the egg cell(s) in the ovary.

Many species have flowers with both stamens and pistils. In other species, the flowers are segregated into male flowers (with stamens but lacking pistils) and female flowers (with pistils but lacking stamens).

Pollen is dispersed by wind, by insects, or, for some brightly colored, tubular flowers, by hummingbirds. Insects of many kinds—bees, butterflies, moths, beetles, ants, and flies—are especially important for pollination. An individual flower often can self-pollinate, but cross-pollination, with dispersal from the anthers of one plant to the stigmas of another plant of the same species, is the more common process of fertilization.

Flower Shapes and Petal Arrangements

Flowers are characterized by the symmetry of their petals and sepals. There are two basic patterns: radially symmetrical flowers and bilaterally symmetrical flowers.

Radial flowers have petals of similar size and shape, arranged in an entirely symmetrical pattern like spokes on a wheel. The flower can be divided into equal halves along both vertical and horizontal planes.

In the key, radial flowers are further categorized by their number of petals: two, three, four, five, six, and seven or more. Note that in the infrequent cases where the actual petals are absent or tiny, as in *Nuphar variegata* and *Anemone* species mentioned previously, the petal-like sepals or bracts compose the radial aspect of the flower and are treated as "petals" in the key. Some radial flowers are very small (the 5-petaled flowers of the parsley family, or Apiaceae, for example), and close inspection is necessary to see the arrangement and number of petals.

Bilateral flowers have petals that are not all of equal size and shape. The flowers can be divided into symmetrical halves

The radially symmetrical flowers of *Sium suave* (water parsnip), a member of the parsley family (Apiaceae), require close inspection to see the 5 petals.

along one plane, but not along both planes, much like a human face. Examples of bilateral flowers include members of the pea (Fabaceae), mint (Lamiaceae), and orchid (Orchidaceae) families. Bilateral flowers are not further categorized in the key by their number of petals.

The key has a third general category, for flowers with indistinguishable parts. Their flowers may be radial or bilateral, but because the petals and sepals are miniscule, closed, or absent, their symmetry is not apparent. Examples include the tiny flowers of species such as the amaranths (*Amaranthus* spp.) and the closed flowers of many members of the smartweed family (Polygonaceae).

Like other members of the aster family (Asteraceae), *Solidago simplex* (Rand's goldenrod) has a flower head with numerous individual ray and disk flowers.

Inflorescences

The inflorescence is the arrangement of the flowers on an individual plant. There are many kinds of inflorescences, condensed in this guide into a smaller number of general types. Plants with solitary flowers have just a single flower, not an inflorescence. Those described as few-flowered have a small number of flowers. Most plants, however, have numerous flowers in a variety of arrangements and branching patterns. The term "branching clusters of flowers' is used for a number of inflorescence types with multiple flowers, but in many cases a specific term is used to describe the type of arrangement: panicle, raceme, spike, and umbel.

A panicle is an elongated, branching inflorescence, roughly pyramidal in shape. A raceme is a long, narrow inflorescence where the individual flowers are held on short stalks from the central stem. A spike is a long, narrow inflorescence similar to a raceme, but the individual flowers are not stalked—the flower bases are attached directly to the stem. An umbel is a rounded or flattish, often dense, inflorescence in which the flowers are held on the ends of spreading stalks that originate from the same point, like the ribs of an umbrella.

The flowers of the aster family (Asteraceae), which includes asters, goldenrods, thistles, the common daisy, and many other wildflowers, differ in structure from the flowers of other plant families. The most conspicuous part of many aster-family flowers, the straplike "petals" that radiate at the top of the flower, are in fact all individual flowers, known as ray flowers. The central disk to which the ray flowers are attached is densely composed of many very small flowers, known as disk flowers.

So, what appears to be a single flower is in fact a head of numerous individual ray and disk flowers. The term "flower head" is used instead of "flower" in descriptions of aster-family plants.

Other terms found in the flower descriptions are "bract," "axillary," and "terminal." A bract is a modified leaf, usually small, that is located immediately below the flower or the inflorescence. Axillary refers to the location of a flower in the axil of the leaf. The axil is the point of junction between the stem and the base of the leaf stalk (petiole), or of the base of the leaf if there is no petiole. Terminal refers to the uppermost part of a plant. In a terminal inflorescence, for example, a group of flowers is found at the top of the stem.

Leaf

The primary unit of the leaf is the expanded outer section, known as the blade. The leaf blade is the part of the plant that is primarily responsible for photosynthesis. In most species, the blade is attached to the stem by a stalk, known as the petiole. The veins of the leaf, visible as a network on the blade's upper and lower surfaces, are the tissues that transport the products of photosynthesis to other parts of the plant.

Leaf Form

Leaves have two general forms: simple and compound. A simple leaf is undivided. The edges of the leaf may be toothed or lobed, but the leaf is not divided into distinct, smaller units. A compound leaf is composed of two or more distinct, individual leaflets that are clearly separated from each other.

Compound leaves may be either palmate, with the leaflets spread like the fingers of the human hand, or pinnate, where the leaflets are arranged on two sides of a central axis. The leaves of wild lupine (*Lupinus perennis*) and common cinquefoil (*Potentilla simplex*) are examples of palmately compound leaves. The leaves of vetches (*Vicia* spp.) and garden valerian (*Valeriana officinalis*) are examples of pinnately compound leaves.

The compound leaves of some species are further divided into secondary or tertiary leaflet segments. These leaves are known as doubly or triply compound leaves and often look lacy, or fernlike. Many members of the parsley (Apiaceae) family, such as Queen Anne's-lace (*Daucus carota*), have doubly or triply compound leaves.

A deeply segmented leaf that is cut into segments more than half-way from the leaf margin to the middle vein can appear to be compound even though technically it is a simple leaf. In contrast to a truly compound leaf, the segments are not completely divided into separate leaflets. Winter cress (*Barbarea vulgaris*) and the common dandelion (*Taraxacum officinale*) are examples of plants that have deeply segmented leaves. For the sake of simplicity, compound and deeply segmented leaves are combined in the key, collectively called deeply divided leaves.

Leaf Margins and Stem Patterns

The margin of the leaf (or the leaflet margin for compound leaves) may be entire, toothed, or lobed. An entire leaf has a smooth, uniform edge without teeth or lobes. A toothed leaf has sharp-pointed serrations on the margins. A lobed leaf has blunt or rounded projections along the margins, interspersed with indentations known as sinuses.

Leaves have particular arrangement patterns in relation to the stem. The four primary patterns are alternate, opposite, whorled, and basal. Alternate leaves are arranged singly along the stem. Opposite leaves are arranged in pairs along the stem. Whorled leaves refer to three or more leaves originating at the same point on the stem. Basal leaves occur at the base of the stem and are used as an identification feature in the key when the plant only has leaves at the base, that is, when there are no leaves on the stem. A clump or whorl of leaves at the base of the stem is called a basal rosette.

In some species, the leaves are reduced to scales pressed close to the stem, as in an asparagus shoot, or to clusters of tiny needles, similar to the needles of a spruce or fir tree. Some plants, such as wild leek (*Allium tricoccum*), do not have leaves during the blooming period.

The leaves of some species lack petioles; instead, the base of each leaf is in contact with the stem. Leaves without petioles can be sessile, or clasping, or perfoliate. In sessile leaves, the leaf base touches the stem. In clasping leaves, the leaf base touches the stem and has small, often paired projections that partially surround the stem. In perfoliate leaves, the base of a single leaf, or the fused bases of a pair of opposite leaves, completely surrounds the stem, so that the stem appears to pierce the leaf or leaf pair.

Leaf Shapes

Leaf blade shapes are extremely variable, from very narrow to rotund. Linear leaves are extremely narrow, with parallel sides. Lance-shaped leaves are broadest at or below the middle, tapering narrowly to the tip; the blade is generally at least four times longer than wide. Oval leaves

The compound leaves of *Oxalis violacea* (violet wood sorrel) are broadest at the tip and narrowest at the base.

are broadest at or below the middle, narrowing to the tip, the blade generally 1½–4 times longer than wide. Elliptical leaves are broadest in the middle, tapering to both ends. Spoon-shaped leaves are broadly rounded at the tip and narrowed at the base. Heart-shaped leaves have a broad, slightly notched base, gradually tapering to a pointed tip. Arrow-shaped leaves are shaped like an arrowhead. Rounded leaves are approximately as wide as long, with a round or blunt tip.

Stem

The stem is the primary, supporting structure of the plant that holds the flowers and the leaves. The stem may be simple (single-stemmed) or branching. The stems of most species are erect, but some are semierect, reclining, mat-forming, creeping, or climbing.

Smooth stems have no or virtually no hairs. Hairy stems are partly or entirely covered with hairs. On some species, the hairs may be very fine and sparse, and on others coarse and dense. The type of hair on a stem (spreading hairs versus pressed-in hairs, for example) can be important in distinguishing two similar-looking species. Hairs that are gland-tipped, a feature of a number of species, have small, sticky protuberances at the tip of the hair stalk.

"Stalk," in contrast to "stem," refers to a secondary, supporting structure, such as the stalk of an individual flower or a fruit.

Fruits

The fruit is the tissue of the fertilized ovary that encases the seed. Fruit comes in many sizes, shapes, and forms, from large and fleshy to tiny and hard. There are a great variety of fruits and technical names for them. In this guide, fruit types have been condensed into achene, berry, capsule, follicle, nut, pod, silicle, and silique. Fruits that are not technically one of these kinds but have features that resemble them are given the suffix "-like," as in "berrylike" or "capsulelike," in the species descriptions.

An achene is a dry, usually very small, one-seeded fruit that does not separate or split open at maturity. A berry is a fleshy fruit with a juicy or succulent wall that encloses two or more seeds. "Berrylike" is also applied to other fleshy fruit forms, such as cherries (which are technically drupes and have one seed) and strawberries (which are an aggregation of tiny achenes set within a soft, succulent body that develops from the base of the flower).

A capsule is a dry fruit that opens along two or more seams, pores, or teeth to release two or more seeds. "Capsulelike" is applied to other types of dry fruit that split open at maturity.

A follicle is an often-elongate fruit that splits along a single side to release the seeds. A nut is a dry fruit with a hard wall that does not split open when mature. It usually contains one seed. "Nutlike" or "nutlet" is applied to other small, rounded, hard-shelled fruits. A pod is a dry fruit enclosing a hollow space with one or more seeds; it splits open along the edges.

A silicle is a fruit less than three times as long as wide, often broad in shape; it opens along two sides. This type of fruit is only found in members of the mustard family (Brassicaceae). A silique is a fruit more than three times as long as wide, often very narrow and elongate; it opens along two sides. This type of fruit is also only found in the mustard family.

Plant Names

The scientific names in this guide follow those in Native Plant Trust's *Flora-Novae-Angliae: A Manual for the Identification of Native and Naturalized Higher Vascular Plants of New England*, by Arthur Haines (2011).

The scientific name of a species consists of the genus, the first letter of which is capitalized, followed by the specific epithet. The scientific name of the common dandelion, for example, is *Taraxacum officinale*. Species within the same genus are closely related and usually are similar in appearance. Some plant species have variable forms and are further classified into subspecies and varieties.

Related genera (plural of genus) are classified into larger groups called families. The names of plant families usually end with the suffix "-aceae." The characteristics of the different plant families that appear in the guide are summarized elsewhere in this book.

With new research leading to an increased understanding of the genetic relationships among plants, many family, genus, and species names have changed in recent years. The species descriptions in this guide use the current scientific names, as provided in Arthur Haines' work. Older, alternative scientific names are given in parentheses, following the current name.

A wildflower may have several (or even more) common names, often varying by region. Common names in this guide are those in general use, including names that appear on Native Plant Trust's GoBotany website and in other field guides to the Northeast.

HOW TO USE THIS BOOK

The plant descriptions are organized first by flower color. White, yellow, red, blue, green, orange, and brown flowers are presented in different chapters. Each chapter includes wildflowers with these "standard" colors and also those with tones and shadings of these colors. The chapter on white flowers, for example, includes flowers that are cream-colored as well as white. The yellow flower chapter covers flowers with shadings from pale to bright yellow. The red flower chapter includes blossoms that are pink, scarlet, magenta, and red-purple as well as red. The blue flower chapter covers violet, lilac, and blue-purple flowers as well as various shades of blue. The same pattern pertains to the green, orange, and brown flower chapters.

It is possible to flip through the pages of a particular color section to find a flower, but because there are many flowers of any given color, some of which appear similar, this approach can be time-consuming. A more direct approach to identification is to use the key (starting on page 26).

After the initial division by flower color, the plants are further subdivided according to a combination of flower and leaf characteristics. Plants with similar-looking flowers and leaves are grouped together. The individual plant descriptions and the accompanying images highlight the distinctions between these similar-looking species.

The key may seem complicated at first, but in fact it relies on only a small number of flower and leaf features. Once these are learned, the key becomes a quick and reliable method of narrowing down the range of choices for a particular identification.

Using the Key

Step 1. Determine flower color: white, yellow, red, blue, green, orange, brown

Step 2. Determine flower symmetry: radial, bilateral, petals indistinguishable

Step 3. Determine number of petals (for radial flowers only): 2, 3, 4, 5, 6, 7 or more

Step 4. Determine leaf type: simple or deeply divided

Step 5. Determine leaf arrangement: alternate, opposite, whorled, basal, scaly/needlelike/absent

Step 6. Determine leaf margin: entire, toothed/lobed

How do these steps lead to identifying a flower? Say you're in an oak and pine woods in spring and see a small plant with a solitary white flower (wood anemone, *Anemone quinquefolia*, although you haven't identified it yet). You notice that the petals are of equal size and shape, arranged in a radially symmetrical pattern. You count five "petals" (or apparent petals—these are actually petal-like sepals). The leaves are on the stem, and each leaf is palmately divided into three to five leaflets. The leaves are in a single group of three, all originating at the same point on the stem. The leaflet margins have teeth. You have made these six observations:

Flower color: White

Flower type: Radial

Petal number: 5

Leaf type: Deeply divided

Leaf arrangement: Whorled

Leaflet margins: Toothed or lobed

You turn to the key, which directs you to the pages in the white flower chapter for the plants with those characteristics. In this example, you will see six wildflower species described under that heading. By looking closely at the photographs, reading the descriptions, and matching the image and text with the wildflower, you should arrive at the right identification.

To take another example, in the same oak and pine woods, you notice a large, entirely pink flower on a leafless stem. The stem is 16 inches tall, with a pair of leaves at the base. You see that the flower is bilateral, that is, the petals—in this case, a large, rounded, pouchlike lip, and two narrow, spreading, slightly twisted wings just above the lip—are unequal in size and dissimilar in shape. The flower could be divided into equal halves only in one plane. The leaves are simple, at the base of the stem, and their margins are entire. You have made the following observations:

Flower color: Pink (in red flower chapter)

Flower type: Bilateral

Petal number: (not used for bilateral flowers)

Leaf type: Simple

Anemone quinquefolia: white radial flowers with 5 petals, deeply divided, toothed leaves in a whorl.

Leaf arrangement: Basal

Leaf margins: Entire

You go to the key, and, turning to the pages in the red flower chapter for those characteristics, you see five species described under that heading, all in the orchid family. A glance at the images and descriptions should quickly take you to pink lady's-slipper (*Cypripedium acaule*).

Or, taking a third example, you are walking along a weedy roadside in late summer. You notice many tallish, leafy plants with erect, narrow clusters of tiny green flowers. The flowers are without discernible petals, the leaves are finely divided, arranged in an opposite pattern on the stem, and the leaflet margins are toothed or lobed. You have made these observations:

Flower color: Green

Flower type: Petals indistinguishable

Petal number: (not used for "petals indistinguishable" flowers)

Leaf type: Deeply divided

Leaf arrangement: Opposite

Leaflet margins: Toothed or lobed

You go to the key, turn to the pages in the green flower chapter that show plants with those characteristics, and see two species, common ragweed and giant ragweed (*Ambrosia artemisiifolia* and *A. trifida*). The very fine divisions of the leaf, shown in the image and described in the text, will take you to common ragweed.

Cypripedium acaule: pink bilateral flowers, simple leaves with entire margins arranged at the base of the stem.

Ambrosia artemisiifolia: green flowers with indistinguishable petals, deeply divided leaves with lobed margins arranged in an opposite pattern on the stem.

Note that in each of these three examples, there is more than one choice under the specific heading. Plants are organized under each heading alphabetically, first by its family name, and then by genus and species. In the first example (of the wood anemone), two of the six species under the heading are in the Apiaceae (parsley family). These two species are listed first: *Panax quinquefolius* and *P. trifolius*. They are followed by four species in the Ranunculaceae (buttercup family): *Anemone canadensis*, *A. cylindrica*, *A. quinquefolia,* and *A. virginiana*. Listing the plants alphabetically by family means that closely related species with similar features are adjacent to each other in the guide, allowing for a convenient comparison between the plants that most closely resemble one another.

Species Descriptions

To identify the species within the group where the key has taken you, carefully read the descriptions, look at the photographs, and match them with the actual plant. Focus on the characteristics that distinguish the plant from similar-looking species. These characteristics include the physical features (height, stem, and fruit as well as flower and leaf), and also its flowering period, habitats, and distribution in New England.

Plant Names

Each entry begins with the current scientific name of the species. The name consists of the genus (for example, *Potentilla*) and the specific epithet (for example, *simplex*). If there is an older, alternative name, it follows, in parentheses. An asterisk (*) next to the scientific name indicates a non-native, introduced species.

The plant family to which the species belongs follows (for example, Rosaceae). If there is an older, alternative family name, it follows in parentheses.

The common name or names of the plant are provided in the third line.

Headnote

The first paragraph provides the blooming period for the species, its typical height range in inches or feet, its life cycle, and its habitats.

Bloom time is self-explanatory as is plant height. For vines and low, scrambling plants, the measurement is length, not height, and the word *long* is used with the measurement range.

A plant's life cycle may be annual, biennial, perennial, or shrub. Annual plants live for only one year, reproducing entirely by seed production. Biennial plants live for two years, generally producing only leaves the first year, and flowers and seeds the second year. Perennial plants live for two or more years. Annual, biennial, and perennial plants are all herbaceous plants; their stems die back in winter. Shrubs are woody species whose aboveground stems live throughout the year.

Typical habitats are listed next. Some plants are restricted to specific habitat types, while others occur in many habitats. Not all of the habitats may be shown for plants that occur in multiple habitat types. Habitat is a significant part of plant identification. If the key takes you to two similar species, check their respective habitats. If you're looking at a plant in a swamp, and the habitat described for one of your choices is "fields and thickets" and the other is "swamps and floodplains," that is a valuable clue to the identity of the species.

Potentilla simplex   ROSACEAE ┤————————— Plant names
Common cinquefoil, old-field cinquefoil ┘
Spring to early summer, 4–16 in., perennial. ┤————— Headnote
Thickets, fields, lawns, and roadsides. ┘

Flowers yellow, ½ in. wide, solitary on long stalks
from upper leaf axils, usually produced from the
axil of the second well-developed stem leaf; the petals longer than the sepals. Leaves divided into 5
lance-shaped leaflets, ¾–3 in. long, the margins ┤————— Description
sharply toothed about ¾ of their length; terminal
leaflet more than twice as long as wide. Stems hairy,
initially erect, later arching or trailing. Fruit an
achene, ¹⁄₁₆ in. long. CT, MA, ME, NH, RI, VT

Potentilla canadensis (dwarf cinquefoil) is similar,
with the flower produced usually from the axil of the
1st well-developed stem leaf, and with the terminal ┤————— Related plants
leaflet of the leaves usually less than 2 times as long
as wide.

At the end of the first paragraph, the term "invasive" may appear. This is a designation given to those nonnative plants that have become nuisance species in natural landscapes. These species have been identified as invasive by state environmental agencies and by the Invasive Plant Atlas of New England Program (IPANE).

Description

The main paragraph in each description gives the physical characteristics of the plant in the following order:

flower: color, dimensions, arrangement, and other features

leaf: length, shape, arrangement, and other features

stem: simple or branching, hairy or smooth

fruit: type, shape, and dimensions

All of these terms have been discussed in the Introduction.

At the end of this paragraph are listed the New England states where the species is known to occur:

CT = Connecticut

MA = Massachusetts

ME = Maine

NH = New Hampshire

RI = Rhode Island

VT = Vermont

When a species is rare in a particular state, the state abbreviation is followed by the word "rare" in parentheses. Rarity within a state is determined by that state's Natural Heritage Program, based on the number of populations known to occur there. Plants listed by the state as endangered, threatened, special concern, or watch-list are considered to be rare plants.

When the text says of a species that it "only occurs in ME" or "only occurs in RI," this refers to its presence in the six New England states. The same plant most likely grows in other areas of the United States and/or Canada. Only a small number of native North American plants are limited in their distribution to New England.

For nonnative species, the region of origin (for example, Europe, Asia) is given just before its New England distribution.

Photographs

Many photographers have contributed images for this book (see Illustration Credits page). The images have been selected for their clarity in presenting key species identification features, particularly flowers and leaves. The photographs show the plants in natural light and in natural conditions. For most species, there is one photograph; for others there is also an inset showing an important identification feature.

Tips for Identifying Plants

When you are identifying a plant, be patient and look carefully. The flower and leaves are the primary elements of identification, but it is important to have a sense of the entire plant: height, growth habit, and habitat. What is the appearance of the sepals and stamens as well as the petals? Do the leaves have petioles, or are they sessile? Are there hairs on the stem, and, if so, are they fine or coarse?

Get a good feel of the surroundings. Is the plant in light or shade, in moist or dry soil? What are some of the other plants here? Do all the features you are observing correlate with the description in the guide? If there is more than one individual of the plant you are trying to identify, look at other individuals to get a better overall impression of the plant.

As with all living things, plants are variable. Flower colors can vary between individuals of the same species, and leaf shapes can vary as well. The key is based on the typical patterns of the species, but keep the possibility of differences in mind, especially with flower colors. In most cases, a plant will be a particular color, but the flowers of some species have more than one color. If you don't find a given species in a particular chapter, it may be because its flower has more than one color and so is shown in another chapter. Follow the key for the other characteristics of the flower (besides color) as well as the leaves, and look for the species in another chapter. The guide only has space to show a given flower in a characteristic color form, but the species descriptions state whether the flowers of that particular species have more than one color.

A 10× hand lens is very helpful for identifying plants, enabling the observer to see features of flower, leaf, stem hairs, and so on, which may not be distinct to the naked eye. Recognition of very fine features is sometimes essential for distinguishing similar-looking species.

If identification is elusive, take photographs of the entire plant and closer shots of its flowers, leaves, and any other key features. Then, back home, look at your images and match them again with the descriptions and images in the guide. The guide has a great number of New England's wildflowers, but it does not have all of them. If you don't find the species in the guide, you can check the keys and images on Native Plant Trust's GoBotany website, which has images and information for all (or nearly all) of New England's vascular plants.

Range information can be helpful for identification. If you are looking at a plant in Maine, and the key has led you to a plant listed only in Connecticut, your identification is probably mistaken. By taking another look at the plant, the key, and the descriptions, you may arrive at a different result. The same applies to rarity: if you have narrowed your choice in the key to two or three similar-looking species, one of which is listed as rare, you have probably found one of the more common species (but it is certainly possible that you have found the rare one). Take another look at the plant and the descriptions.

If you think you have identified a rare plant, photograph it, taking shots of the entire plant and closer images of flowers, leaves, stem, and other visible plant parts.

Match your photos with the text and description. For further confirmation, you may send your photo and a message to "Ask the Botanist" on the GoBotany website's PlantShare feature, at gobotany .nativeplanttrust.org/plantshare.

If your observation is a rare plant, the state's Natural Heritage Program will appreciate information about it. Links to the six State Natural Heritage Program websites are given on the References page.

As you look for and identify wildflowers in their natural habitats, keep in mind the importance of their conservation. Many wildflower populations have disappeared due to collection or damage to their habitats from overenthusiastic naturalists and photographers. Unless you have a permit to do so, please do not collect the plant, and take special care not to trample or damage the ground around the plant. Remember that plants on public and private conservation lands are legally protected. Take photographs, make sketches, and observe and appreciate the plant, but leave the flowers, and their habitat, in the condition in which you found them. As the adage goes, plants grow by the inch and die by the foot.

KEY TO WILDFLOWERS

WHITE FLOWERS

YELLOW FLOWERS

RED FLOWERS

BLUE FLOWERS

LANDSCAPE AND NATURAL COMMUNITIES

The six New England states of Connecticut, Maine, Massachusetts, New Hampshire, Rhode Island, and Vermont have a total area of 72,000 square miles. Maine, by far the largest of the six states, comprises almost half of New England's land area. The region's natural landscape is a varied mosaic of coastal shoreline, mountains, hills, valleys, rivers, lakes, and offshore islands, and this mosaic creates habitats for a high diversity of plants. Most of New England, including the densely populated states of Connecticut, Massachusetts, and Rhode Island, is covered by deciduous, coniferous, and mixed deciduous-coniferous forests.

The coastline, from Connecticut's border with New York on Long Island Sound north to Maine's border with New Brunswick in the Bay of Fundy, is almost 600 miles in length. Most of the shoreline from Connecticut to southern Maine features sandy or stony beaches, dunes, and salt marsh meadows, which support plants adapted to saline habitats. The upper (Down East) Maine coastline is rock-bound, with boulders, headlands, and cliffs abruptly meeting the sea.

The White Mountains of New Hampshire, the Green Mountains of Vermont, and the mountains of western and north-central Maine are the highest in the region and support rare communities of alpine and subalpine plants. At 6288 feet, Mount Washington in New Hampshire's White Mountains is the region's highest; the White Mountains have 47 more peaks with elevations of 4000 feet or higher. Mount Katahdin, at 5268 feet, is the highest mountain in Maine, and Mount Mansfield, at 4393 feet, is the highest in Vermont. Other prominent ranges include the Taconic Mountains in western Connecticut, Massachusetts, and Vermont, and the Berkshire Hills of western Massachusetts and northwest Connecticut. Mount Monadnock, a well-known and much-climbed mountain in southern New Hampshire, is an isolated summit on a broad plateau extending from north-central Massachusetts to southwestern New Hampshire.

The interior of southern and central New England is lower in elevation, with rolling hills interspersed with valley lowlands. Connecticut, Rhode Island, and most of Massachusetts are hilly rather than mountainous. The coastal and near-coastal areas of New Hampshire and Maine are also hilly, with elevations increasing with distance from the coast. The Metacomet ridge, a range of rugged, reddish hills extending for 100 miles from the Connecticut coast to northern Massachusetts and flanking the Lower Connecticut River Valley for much of its length, is an especially prominent series of hills.

Rivers, lakes, and ponds are abundant throughout the region, supporting communities of wetland and aquatic plants. The Connecticut River is the region's longest river, flowing for 410 miles from its headwaters at the New Hampshire–Quebec border south to Long Island Sound.

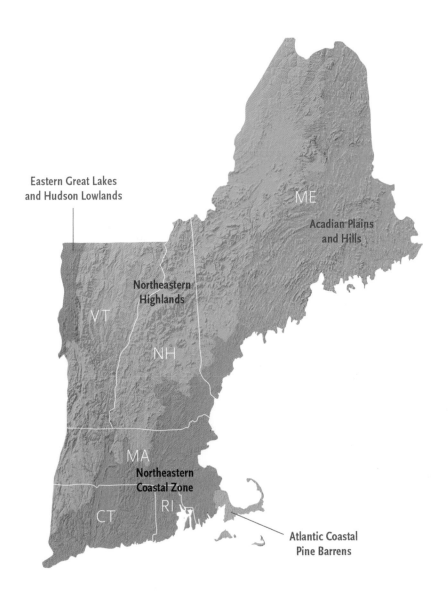

Eastern Great Lakes
and Hudson Lowlands

ME

Acadian Plains
and Hills

Northeastern
Highlands

VT

NH

MA

Northeastern
Coastal Zone

RI

CT

Atlantic Coastal
Pine Barrens

Ecoregions of New England.

Other major rivers include the Kennebec, Penobscot, and St. John Rivers in Maine; the Androscoggin River in New Hampshire and Maine; the Merrimack River in New Hampshire and Massachusetts; the Housatonic River in Massachusetts and Connecticut; and Otter Creek in Vermont. Lake Champlain, shared by Vermont and New York, is the region's largest lake, followed by Moosehead Lake in Maine and Lake Winnipesaukee in New Hampshire. Western Maine has an especially large number of lakes.

For hundreds of millions of years, geologic forces have shaped the New England landscape through continental plate collisions and separations, volcanic activity, and repeated glaciations. The oldest dated rock in the region, located in the southern Green Mountains, is one billion years old. Between 300 and 500 million years ago, the Taconic, Green, and White Mountain ranges were created by two major mountain-building events, the Taconic and Acadian Orogenies. The mountains, which stood much higher than they are today, resulted from collisions between volcanic island arcs and the proto-North American continental plate. The broad valley from Long Island Sound through central Connecticut and west-central Massachusetts, defining much of the Lower Connecticut River Valley, is the result of a rift, or separation, of the African from the proto-North American plate about 200 million years ago.

In the last 1.6 million years, the New England region has experienced at least four periods of glaciation. The most recent glacial period, known as the Wisconsin, reached its maximum extent about

Tuckerman Ravine on the east side of Mount Washington in the White Mountains of New Hampshire is an example of a glacial cirque.

21,000 years ago, covering the entire area with a mile-thick sheet of ice. By the time the ice sheet receded, 12,000–14,000 years ago, it had left a deep and lasting imprint on the land, scooping up and moving bedrock many hundreds of miles, eroding hills and mountains, and creating broad valleys and basins in areas of softer, more erodible rock. In the White Mountains and at Mount Katahdin, the glacial ice sheet formed U-shaped valleys and deep, bowl-like depressions, known as cirques, on the upper slopes. In its southward movement, the ice sheet also plucked up, carried, and deposited vast quantities of rock, grinding and eroding it in the process. The glacial depositions, known as till, consist of rocks, stones, and other sediments that now cover much of the region's land surface.

Glacial erratics are large boulders that the ice sheet transported long distances before dumping them onto the landscape. The 85-foot long, 23-foot high Madison Boulder in New Hampshire is the largest known erratic in New England.

Near its terminal point, the glacier deposited jumbles of "rock debris"—unsorted accumulations of boulders, rocks, gravels, and finer sediments—in low hills known as moraines. Later, meltwater from the retreating ice sheet deposited sands and gravels onto the moraines. Cape Cod, Martha's Vineyard, Nantucket, Block Island, and other, smaller islands off the southeastern Massachusetts and the Rhode Island coastlines were formed by this process of deposition.

Other glacier-molded features of the landscape include drumlins, which are low, clayey, rounded hills, often occurring in clusters, or "swarms," and eskers, which are long, sinuous ridges of sand and gravel deposited by glacial streams running through a tunnel of ice. Kettle holes are ponds originally formed by great blocks of ice that separated from the main body of the retreating glacier; the ice block was surrounded and covered by sands deposited by glacial meltwater. Then the ice block melted, creating the pond. Walden Pond in Concord, Massachusetts, made famous by Henry David Thoreau, is an example of a kettlehole pond.

New England's varieties of bedrock and surficial rock have resulted from this complex geologic history. A region's bedrock is a determining factor in the nature and quality of its soil. The type of soil, in turn, strongly influences the species of plants that can grow in that region.

Much of New England is underlain by volcanic or metamorphic rocks such as granite, schist, and gneiss. Soils derived from these rocks are generally acidic and low in nutrients, producing communities less rich in species that those growing on soils with higher pH.

The basalt and sandstone ridges along the Lower Connecticut River Valley produce a higher pH soil, which yields nutrients to plants more easily and fosters their growth. A variety of plant species scarce or absent elsewhere in the region occurs along these ridges. In Vermont and western Massachusetts, the valleys and slopes to the west of the Green Mountains and the Berkshire Hills are underlain by limestone and marble, which produce very fertile, calcareous (high-pH) soils. The forests and wetlands of the limestone and marble zone generally are richer in species than physically similar habitat types on the more acidic rock in most of New England. In contrast, the sandy soils in many coastal regions are coarser and drier than the soils in other parts of the region. These dry conditions, naturally conducive to fire, are reflected in the types of plants that grow here: pitch pine, scrub oak, and a variety of grasses and wildflowers only found in sandy, coastal habitats.

This generalized picture of the region's geologic features does not do justice to the variety in the landscape. Pockets of calcareous rock with rich forest stands occur throughout New England. Dry, sandy soils with pitch pine occasionally occur inland as well as along the coast. In any landscape, there are gradations in the nature of the rocks and soils, in soil moisture, and in patterns of light and shade. It is useful to know the prevailing patterns, but keep in mind the subtleties that are present in all landscapes.

Ecological Communities

Most of the New England landscape is forested. Even the densely populated states of Connecticut, Massachusetts, and Rhode Island have over 50 percent forest cover; for the region as a whole, forests cover about 75 percent of the landscape. New England's forests are in the northeastern section of a broadly defined forest region known as the Eastern Deciduous Forest. This forest covers most of the eastern United States as far west as the Mississippi River, and includes the southern portions of adjacent Canadian provinces. It is bounded to the north by the evergreen, boreal forest that covers most of Canada, and to the west by the grasslands and prairies of the midwestern United States.

The term "Eastern Deciduous Forest" is somewhat misleading as a description of New England: the forests of the six New England states include both broad-leaved deciduous (also known as hardwood) trees, such as aspen, ash, basswood, beech, birch, cherry, oak, maple, and hickory, and coniferous (softwood) trees, including pine, spruce, cedar, and hemlock.

The region's current extent of forest cover is a result of its humid, cool-temperate, four-season climate, with annual precipitation of 35–50 inches, and of its historical pattern of land use. By the 1850s, most of New England had been cleared for croplands and pasture, but the hilly, stony landscape and relatively infertile soils have long been a challenge for agriculture. During the latter half of the 19th century and continuing into the 20th, New England farms were largely abandoned. With the fields left fallow, forests recovered and steadily increased in extent until the start of the 21st century, when pressures from development caused a slight reversal in the region's forest cover. In a longer-term perspective, New England's forests have been recovering ground since the retreat of the Wisconsin Glacier 12,000 years ago.

New England's forest communities and plant species distributions vary significantly from north to south, and from lower to higher elevations. The variation is in large part due to climatic differences. Presque Isle, Maine, in the region's far northern interior, has an average annual temperature of 41° Fahrenheit, and a total of 105 consecutive frost-free days. Presque Isle receives 35 inches of total precipitation per year, with 89 inches of snow. In contrast, Hartford, Connecticut, in the southern interior of the region, has an annual average temperature of 50° Fahrenheit and about 160 consecutive frost-free days. The city receives 45 inches of precipitation per year, with 45 inches of snow.

Even at similar latitudes, tree species vary from the coast, where winter temperatures are milder, to the interior, where winters are colder. This pattern also holds along the valleys of major rivers, where warmer temperatures foster narrow bands of more "southern" forest types within a matrix of a more typically northern type of forest in the surrounding hills. Microhabitat conditions, such as location on a north-facing slope with cooler and moister conditions, or on a south-facing slope with warmer and drier conditions, also influence forest composition.

The following summaries of the region's primary forest communities, ranging from north to south, or, in terms of elevation, from upper to lower slopes, focus on the dominant trees. The forest types vary and intergrade, affected not only by climate and elevation but also by the quality of their soils, position on the landscape, wildlife relationships, and past and present patterns of human use. Descriptions of the region's nonforested communities, including upland, wetland, and aquatic habitats, follows the discussion of the forests.

Forests

Spruce-fir forests. Red spruce and balsam fir forests grow in the coldest and snowiest areas of the region: the northern half of Maine, and the northernmost parts of New Hampshire and Vermont. These coniferous forests also occur on the middle to upper slopes of the region's higher mountains as far south as northwestern Massachusetts. Spruce and fir stands that grow at high elevations are also known as subalpine forest. New England's spruce-fir forest is a southward extension of the boreal forest that covers much of Canada.

Subalpine spruce-fir forest.

Northern hardwoods–white pine–hemlock forest. South of the spruce-fir zone, and sometimes intergrading with it, is a mixed deciduous-evergreen forest of beech, yellow birch, and sugar maple, often sharing the canopy with white pine and eastern hemlock. This forest grows in much of Maine, New Hampshire, Vermont, and western Massachusetts, extending south to the hills of northwestern Connecticut. A variant of this forest, dominated by sugar maple and white ash, grows on slopes with high-pH soils. This rich, deciduous forest is most common in the marble and limestone bedrock regions of Vermont and western Massachusetts. The moist, high-nutrient soils in this forest produce an exceptional diversity of spring wildflowers.

Mixed (or transition) hardwoods–white pine–hemlock. South of the northern hardwoods region, red and white oak, and also shagbark hickory, join beech, birch, maple, white pine, and hemlock in the canopy. This forest type ranges from southern Maine, New Hampshire, and Vermont, through much of Massachusetts, to northern Connecticut and Rhode Island.

Oak-hickory-hemlock forest. An oak- and hickory-dominated forest is the southernmost major forest type in the region, most common in eastern Massachusetts and much of Connecticut and Rhode Island. Canopy trees include red, white, black, and scarlet oaks, and shagbark, pignut, and mockernut hickories. Hemlock, sometimes forming almost pure stands, grows on cool, moist, rocky slopes and flats. American chestnut was a dominant tree in this forest until its decimation by blight in the 1920s. Chestnut saplings still sprout from old root systems, occasionally

Oak-hickory glade forest.

a German word meaning "crooked wood." **Cliffs, ledges, and talus slopes.** Cliffs and exposed ledges have sparse plant growth, but some plants, such as pale corydalis (*Capnoides sempervirens*), harebell (*Campanula rotundifolia*), and early saxifrage (*Micranthes virginiensis*), make their home on the rocks. Cliffs and ledges at high elevations or on a high-pH rock type may harbor very rare plants.

Talus slopes are steep, boulder-covered slopes that form below sheer cliff faces. Trees, shrubs, vines, and wildflowers grow among the boulders, mostly near the base of the slopes.

Wetland Habitats

Wetlands represent a transitional state between upland communities and truly aquatic systems such as lakes, ponds, rivers, and streams. Wetland soils are frequently saturated or inundated and low in oxygen; plants that grow in wetlands are adapted to these conditions.

Wetlands of many kinds occur throughout New England, on mountains, on the borders of rivers and lakes, in low basins, and along the coast. Wetland community types are differentiated by their vegetation and by their type of soil or substrate.

Swamps. Swamps are dominated by trees or shrubs. Commonly occurring trees include red maple, yellow birch, black gum, swamp white oak, and black ash. Trees in coniferous swamps, which are more common in northern New England, include northern white cedar, red and black spruce, balsam fir, and occasionally white pine and hemlock. Atlantic white cedar swamps are mostly near the coast in southern and central New England. Highbush blueberry, maleberry, common winterberry, sweet pepperbush, alder, and buttonbush are common swamp shrubs.

A deep marsh of emergent and floating plants on a pond margin.

Marshes. Herbaceous plants such as broad-leaved cattail (*Typha latifolia*), grasses, sedges, rushes, and a diversity of wildflowers dominate marshes, which are more open than swamps and have more standing water. Deeper marshes have emergent plants, such as arrowheads (*Sagittaria* spp.), pickerelweed (*Pontederia cordata*), and bur-reeds (*Sparganium* spp.), whose roots and lower stems lie under water. Wet meadows, which often develop on low-lying, abandoned pasture lands, are also herbaceous communities, with sedges, grasses, and wildflowers, but have little or no standing water.

Floodplain forests. Forested wetland communities that grow on terraces above the banks of large rivers are known as floodplain forests. They are subject to periodic flooding and silt deposition, and their soils are rich in nutrients. Silver maple, cottonwood, green ash, and sycamore, often growing to a very large size, are characteristic floodplain trees.

Bogs. Bogs are very acidic, low-nutrient wetlands that often develop on lake and pond edges. Sphagnum moss forms the base of the bog plant community. Due to the lack of microbial activity in these harsh conditions, the sphagnum decomposes gradually, forming thick layers of peat that support the living vegetation. Many bog shrubs, such as leatherleaf (*Chamaedaphne calyculata*), bog laurel (*Kalmia polifolia*), bog rosemary (*Andromeda polifolia*), and large-leaf cranberry (*Vaccinium macrocarpon*), are shrubs in the heath family (Ericaceae) and have leathery, evergreen

Marsh

Floodplain forest

Philbrick-Cricenti Bog, New London, New Hampshire.

leaves. The well-known pitcher-plant (*Sarracenia purpurea*) and sundews (*Drosera* spp.) trap insects and absorb nutrients from their bodies. Black spruce and several other tree species grow in bogs, but heath family shrubs usually dominate bog communities.

Fens. Like bogs, fens grow on peat, but sedges and grasses rather than sphagnum moss form the peat layer. In contrast to bogs, which depend on precipitation for water inflow, fens occur along seepages, where groundwater flows over the soil surface. The acidity or alkalinity of a fen is conditioned by the surrounding bedrock; fens, even those associated with acidic bedrock, generally have a higher pH and faster decomposition rates than a bog. Rich fens have high pH and nutrient levels and very often a striking diversity of rare wildflowers. Fens may be forested or open, sloping or flat. Tamarack and northern white cedar are two trees that occur in fens.

Aquatic Communities

Aquatic communities include freshwater ponds, lakes, rivers, and streams. Many of the plants that grow in these communities have submerged stems, floating leaves, and flowers stalked just above the water surface. The aquatic species described in this guide are mostly those with conspicuous flowers, such as yellow pond-lily (*Nuphar variegata*) and fragrant water-lily (*Nymphaea odorata*).

Coastal Communities

Coastal communities are directly influenced by proximity to the ocean. They include tidal habitats such as salt marshes, estuaries, and beach fronts. Plants in these environments are adapted to high salinity.

Cordgrasses (*Spartina* spp.) along the Lower Connecticut River.

Other coastal environments include dunes, rocky headlands, and (freshwater) coastal plain ponds.

Salt marshes. Inundated twice daily by high tides, salt marshes range in size from pocket-sized habitats tucked into narrow coves to expansive meadows covering hundreds or even thousands of acres. Salt marshes are dominated by two species of grass: cordgrass (*Spartina alterniflora*) and salt hay (*S. patens*). A number of wildflowers occur in openings and mudflats among the grasses.

Estuaries. Estuaries are tidally influenced stretches of rivers that flow into the ocean. Estuaries can extend a long distance upriver: the tidal influence of the Connecticut River extends for 60 miles from Long Island Sound to Windsor Locks, Connecticut. Water in upper estuaries may be all fresh. At low tide, the exposed estuary shorelines are muddy. The brackish, lower stretches of estuaries have plant species similar to those found in salt marshes; the upper reaches of estuaries can have some extremely rare species that grow only in these tidal freshwater systems.

Beach fronts, or strands. A small community of plants, including beach pea (*Lathyrus japonicus*), sea rocket (*Cakile edentula*), saltwort (*Salsola kali*), goosefoots (*Chenopodium* spp.), and seabeach dock (*Rumex pallidus*), occurs at the high tide or wrack line on sandy and stony beaches.

Dunes. Dunes often have little if any vegetation, but beach grass (*Ammophila breviligulata*) and a scattering of wildflowers, such as the golden-heathers (*Hudsonia ericoides* and *H. tomentosa*) and seaside goldenrod (*Solidago sempervirens*), do grow on

Storm-eroded dunes

foredunes and are adapted to withstand burial by wind-blown sand. Shrub thickets and a greater variety of plants often occur on the lee side of dunes.

Rocky coastal headlands. Cliffs and rock faces fronting the ocean have a scattering of plants, such as yarrow (*Achillea millefolium*) and seaside plantain (*Plantago maritima*), that are tolerant of salt spray. Dense shrub thickets often grow at the top of these headland communities.

Coastal plain pond shores. Coastal plain ponds are sandy freshwater ponds near the coast. Pond water levels fluctuate widely in response to changes in the water table. In summer, exposed shorelines have a unique association of plants, including a number of rare wildflowers such as Plymouth gentian (*Sabatia kennedyana*). In high water summers, the shorelines may be entirely inundated. Coastal plain ponds occur in southeastern Massachusetts and southern Rhode Island.

Disturbed Sites

Certain hardy plants find footholds on disturbed sites such as roadways, railroad beds, vacant lots, and pavement cracks. A number of these species are considered weeds, but they show a remarkable ability to thrive in conditions of minimal soil and of exposure to many kinds of impact. Many of these plants are nonnative, but a number of natives also grow in these conditions.

Changes in New England Plant Composition

The plant species that occupy the New England landscape have been in a constant process of movement and change since the retreat of the last glacial ice sheet. Forests and other natural communities are not static or permanent entities. They change in the process of natural succession, in response to natural disturbances (such as fire and hurricanes), to the infestations of invasive species, to warming global temperatures, and to continuing human alterations of the landscape. The decline in New England's total forest cover in the early 2000s is attributable primarily to residential and commercial development. This pattern is likely to continue, with suburban encroachment into open landscapes and further incremental reduction of the region's total forest cover.

Invasive pests, pathogens, and plants have had a major impact on the region's natural communities. Most of the invasive species in New England come from temperate areas of Europe and East Asia, regions with climates similar to the northeastern United States. The ability of invasive species to spread rapidly is due to a number of factors, among them an absence of predators and other natural controls on these newly arrived species (controls that exist in their area of origin), and a lack of natural defenses in native, host plants. These advantages allow the invasive organism to quickly exploit its new environment.

Within the last 100 years, the chestnut blight (American chestnut), Dutch elm disease (American elm), gypsy moth (oaks and other hardwoods), beech bark disease (American beech), and the hemlock woolly adelgid (eastern hemlock) have killed millions of forest trees in New England. The emerald ash borer, which has devastated ash trees in the Midwest, has been discovered in Massachusetts and New Hampshire, and the Asian long-horned beetle, destructive to maples and other hardwoods, has had localized outbreaks in Worcester,

Massachusetts, and near Boston.

Invasive plants spread rapidly, proliferate, and persist in natural habitats, displacing native plants. Approximately 100 of the more than 1000 introduced plant species in New England are listed as invasive by the Invasive Plant Atlas of New England Program. Examples include garlic mustard (*Alliaria petiolata*), Japanese barberry (*Berberis thunbergii*), oriental bittersweet (*Celastrus orbiculatus*), purple loosestrife (*Lythrum salicaria*), and water chestnut (*Trapa natans*). Conservation organizations and volunteer groups are making vigorous efforts to control invasive plants, but many have spread widely and become a fixed feature of the landscape.

The climatic pattern of warming temperatures will change plant distribution patterns. It is not clear how quickly these shifts are taking place, but with higher temperatures and longer frost-free seasons, plant species can be expected to migrate northward. Some plants at the southern end of their range in New England, and those inhabiting colder, more northern habitats, are at risk of reduction and possible disappearance. Warming temperatures may also encourage the spread of more nonnative, invasive species on the landscape.

Notwithstanding these issues, the New England landscape has a thriving diversity of upland, wetland, aquatic, and coastal plant communities. Over 8 million acres in the six New England States is in public or private conservation, at scales ranging from large national forests and parks to town-protected lands. Baxter State Park and Acadia National Park in Maine, White Mountain National Forest in New Hampshire, Green Mountain National Forest in Vermont, and Cape Cod National Seashore in Massachusetts are among the largest and most spectacular landscapes in the region, but efforts to conserve land and protect forests, wetlands, meadows, river corridors, and ridgelines are ongoing at many levels all across New England. Individually and collectively, these lands contain a diverse and delightful array of wildflowers.

PLANT FAMILIES

Scientists used to classify angiosperms (flowering plants) as either monocots (having one seed leaf) or dicots (having two seed leaves). Today, using information obtained through genetic studies, the traditional classification has been modified. Scientists now refer to the two main groups of angiosperms as monocots and eudicots ("true dicots"), or tricolpates. The few remaining flowering plants comprise a third group, basal angiosperms, of which magnoliids are an important group. Note that the genera listed here within the family groups are only those that are discussed in the guide, so many of the genera that occur within these families, in North America and elsewhere in the world, are not included.

Magnoliids

Magnoliids have two seed leaves, floral parts in multiples of three, and leaves with branching veins. Unlike the pollen grains of "true dicots" (tricolpates), which have three germination pores, the pollen grains of magnoliids have a single germination pore.

ARISTOLOCHIACEAE—PIPEVINE FAMILY. Perennial herbs. Flowers are bilaterally or radially symmetrical, solitary, cuplike, green-brown or maroon, with 3 triangular sepals, no petals, 6 or 12 stamens, and one pistil. The single flower is borne from the leaf axil. Leaves are simple, entire, usually heart-shaped, with palmate veins. Fruit is a capsule.

Genera: *Asarum, Endodeca.*

NYMPHAEACEAE—WATER-LILY FAMILY. Aquatic, perennial herbs, with submerged stems that root in mud. Flowers are radially symmetrical and solitary, with 3 sepals and 3 petals or with many petal-like parts. Leaves are floating, entire, and notched at the base. Stems and leaves have air chambers to help with flotation. Fruit is a berry or achene. Genera: *Brasenia, Nuphar, Nymphaea.*

SAURURACEAE—LIZARD'S-TAIL FAMILY. Perennial wetland herbs. Flowers are tiny, numerous, and arranged in dense spikes or racemes. There are no petals or sepals and usually 6 or 8 stamens and 1–5 pistils. Leaves are heart-shaped, simple, entire, and alternate. The stems are jointed. Fruit is a capsule. Genus: *Saururus.*

Monocots

Monocots have one seed leaf, floral parts in multiples of three, and leaves with parallel veins. They are differentiated from the other groups of angiosperms by the number of seed leaves. The flowers of many monocots have tepals, which are petals and sepals indistinguishable from each other in appearance.

ACORACEAE—SWEET-FLAG FAMILY. Aromatic, wetland perennial herbs. Flowers are tiny, with 6 stamens and 6 petal-like sepals, numerous, crowded on a spadix which projects at an angle from the flat, leaflike stem. Leaves are long and narrow with parallel veins; the basal leaves overlap. Fruit is a berry, shaped like an inverted pyramid. Genus: *Acorus.*

ALISMATACEAE—WATER-PLANTAIN FAMILY, ARROWHEAD FAMILY. Aquatic or wetland perennial herbs. Flowers are radially symmetrical, with 3 petals and 3 sepals, and 6 to many stamens. The inflorescences are wide-branching or in whorled clusters close to the stem. Leaves are variable, with shapes ranging from linear, to lance-shaped, to arrow-shaped, to oval; they stand erect or float on the water. Fruit is an achene. Genera: *Alisma, Sagittaria.*

ALLIACEAE—ONION FAMILY. Perennial herbs with onion- or garlic-scented leaves. Flowers are radially symmetrical, with 6 tepals and 6 stamens; they are arranged in umbels at the top of the stem. Leaves are long, simple, narrow, and either alternate or basal. Fruit is a capsule with black seeds. Genus: *Allium.*

ARACEAE—ARUM FAMILY. Perennial herbs found in wetlands or moist uplands. Flowers have very small (or no) petals and 4–6 stamens; they are clustered in a cylindrical spadix often underlain by or enclosed in a spathe. Leaves are alternate and usually smooth and glossy. Fruit is a berry. Genera: *Arisaema, Calla, Orontium, Symplocarpus.*

ASPARAGACEAE—ASPARAGUS FAMILY. Perennial herbs of meadows and fields, with edible shoots. Flowers are tiny and inconspicuous, with 6 stamens and 6 petal-like sepals, crowded on racemes. Scalelike leaves are alternate along the stem. Fruit is a berry. Genus: *Asparagus.*

BUTOMACEAE—FLOWERING RUSH FAMILY. Perennial aquatic or marsh plants, often with triangular stems. Flowers are radially symmetrical, solitary or several in an umbel, with 6 pink to pinkish green tepals, 6 or 9 stamens, and 6 to many pistils. Leaves are basal and swordlike. Fruit is a follicle. Genus: *Butomus.*

COLCHICACEAE—COLCHICUM FAMILY. Perennial herbs. Flowers are radially symmetrical, with 6 distinct tepals, and 6 stamens; the flowers are held singly on stalks drooping from the leaf axils. Leaves are entire and alternate along the stem. Fruit is a capsule. Genus: *Uvularia.*

COMMELINACEAE—SPIDERWORT FAMILY. Annual or perennial herbs that often have soft stems. Flowers are radially or bilaterally symmetrical, with 3 petals and 3 sepals, arranged in a branching inflorescence. There are 6 stamens and a long, curving style. A pale green spathe sometimes surrounds the inflorescence. Leaves are alternate, simple, and entire. Fruit is a capsule. Genera: *Commelina, Tradescantia.*

DIOSCORACEAE—YAM FAMILY. Perennial herbs or vines. The flowers are radially symmetrical, with 6 tepals in 2 whorls of 3, forming a tube. They have 6 stamens and 3 pistils and are arranged in long, branching inflorescences. Leaves are simple or sometimes lobed, usually alternate, but may be opposite or whorled. Fruit is a capsule. Genus: *Dioscorea.*

ERIOCAULACEAE—PIPEWORT FAMILY. Perennial wetland herbs. Flowers are tiny and inconspicuous, with 2 or 3 petals, 2 or 3 sepals, and 2–4 stamens; they are clustered in a buttonlike head. Leaves, in a basal rosette, are grasslike. Fruit is a small capsule. Genus: *Eriocaulon.*

HAEMODORACEAE—BLOODWORT FAMILY. Perennial herbs with red or orange sap in roots and stems. The flowers are radially symmetrical, with 6 tepals and 3 or 6 stamens. They are arranged in an umbel-like cluster at the top of the stem, and are covered with white hairs. Leaves are mostly basal, with swordlike blades. Fruit is a capsule. Genus: *Lachnanthes*.

HEMEROCALLIDACEAE—HEMEROCALLIS FAMILY. Perennial herbs. Flowers are radially symmetrical, red-orange or yellow, large and branching, with 6 tepals and 6 stamens. Leaves are simple, basal, and swordlike. Fruit is a capsule. Genus: *Hemerocallis*.

HYACINTHACEAE—HYACINTH FAMILY. Perennial herbs. Flowers are radially symmetrical, with 6 distinct tepals and 6 stamens; the flowers are arranged in a branching inflorescence. Leaves are narrow, fleshy, and basal. Fruit is a capsule. Genus: *Ornithogalum*.

HYPOXIDACEAE—STAR GRASS FAMILY. Perennial herbs. Flowers are radially symmetrical, with 6 tepals and 6 stamens, arranged in branching clusters that are overtopped by the leaves. Leaves are linear or lance-shaped, with white hairs. Fruit is a capsule. Genus: *Hypoxis*.

IRIDACEAE—IRIS FAMILY. Perennial herbs. Flowers are radially symmetrical and usually multicolored, with 3 petals, 3 petal-like sepals, and 3 stamens. Leaves are long, straight, and swordlike. Fruit is a capsule. Genera: *Iris, Sisyrinchium*.

LILIACEAE–LILY FAMILY. Perennial herbs. Flowers are radially symmetrical, with 3 petals, 3 petal-like sepals, and usually 6 stamens. The flowers are often showy and may be solitary, paired, or clustered.

Leaves are often basal. When stem leaves are present, they can be alternate, opposite, or whorled. Fruit is a capsule or berry. Genera: *Clintonia, Erythronium, Lilium, Medeola, Streptopus*.

MELANTHIACEAE—BUNCHFLOWER FAMILY. Perennial herbs. Flowers are radially symmetrical, with 3 petals and 3 sepals. The flowers are solitary (*Trillium*) or densely clustered (*Veratrum*). Leaves are simple and variably shaped; stem leaves are alternate or whorled. Fruit is a berry or capsule. Genera: *Trillium, Veratrum*.

NARTHECIACEAE—ASPHODEL FAMILY. Perennial herbs. Flowers are radially symmetrical, with 6 tepals, 6 stamens, and one pistil. They are arranged in a spike. Leaves grow from the base and overlap in a dense whorl. Fruit is a capsule. Genus: *Aletris*.

ORCHIDACEAE—ORCHID FAMILY. Perennial herbs. Flowers are bilaterally symmetrical with 3 petals and 3 sepals; 2 of the petals are lateral and the third forms a lower lip (technically known as a labellum). There are 1–3 stamens and 3 united pistils. Leaves are entire. Fruit is a capsule. Genera: *Amerorchis, Aplectrum, Arethusa, Calopogon, Calypso, Coeloglossum, Corallorhiza, Cypripedium, Epipactis, Galearis, Goodyera, Isotria, Liparis, Malaxis, Neottia, Platanthera, Pogonia, Spiranthes, Tipularia, Triphora*.

PONTEDERIACEAE—PICKERELWEED FAMILY. Aquatic, annual or perennial herbs. Flowers are bilaterally symmetrical, with 6 blue, purple, or white tepals and 3 or 6 stamens; they are arranged in a dense spike. Leaves are simple, alternate, entire, arrow-shaped, and rooted in mud. Fruit is an achene. Genus: *Pontederia*.

RUSCACEAE—BUTCHER'S-BROOM FAMILY. Perennial herbs. Flowers are radially symmetrical, with 6 tepals and usually 6 stamens, arranged in various types of inflorescences. Leaves are entire and commonly alternate, although some may be basal. Fruit is a berry. Genera: *Convallaria, Maianthemum, Polygonatum.*

SCHEUCHZERIACEAE—POD-GRASS FAMILY. Perennial wetland herbs. Flowers are radially symmetrical, with 6 yellow-green tepals and 6 stamens; they are arranged in racemes. Leaves are linear, overtopping the flowers; they have an open sheath at the base and a small pore at the apex. Fruit is a follicle. Genus: *Scheuchzeria.*

SMILACACEAE—CAT-BRIER FAMILY. Herbaceous vines. Flowers are radially symmetrical, greenish yellow, with 6 distinct tepals and 6 stamens; they are arranged in racemes along the stem. Leaves are alternate, broad, with 3 main veins radiating out from the leaf base. Fruit is a berry. Genus: *Smilax.* (Note that woody-stemmed members of this genus, not covered in this book, have prickles.)

TOFIELDIACEAE—FALSE ASPHODEL FAMILY. Perennial wetland herbs. Flowers are radially symmetrical, with 6 tepals; the flowers are borne in clusters of 3 along the stem. The stems have short, sticky hairs and may be leafless, or have 1–3 grasslike, alternate leaves near the base. Fruit is a capsule. Genus: *Triantha.*

TYPHACEAE—CATTAIL FAMILY. Perennial wetland herbs. Flowers are tiny, arranged in dense spherical or cylindrical heads. Leaves are long, linear or lance-shaped, with sheathing bases; in some species, the leaves are floating. Fruit is a an achene or follicle. Genera: *Sparganium, Typha.*

XYRIDACEAE—YELLOW-EYED GRASS FAMILY. Perennial wetland herbs. Flowers are radially symmetrical, yellow, with 3 petals, 3 sepals, and 3 stamens; they are borne in conelike heads at the tip of the stem. Leaves are long, alternate, and sometimes twisted. Fruit is a capsule. Genus: *Xyris.*

Tricolpates

Tricolpates are "true dicots." They have two seed leaves, floral parts in multiples of four or five, and leaves with netted veins. Unlike "primitive dicots" (magnoliids), which have one germination pore per pollen grain, tricolpates have pollen grains with three germination pores (hence their name).

AMARANTHACEAE—AMARANTH AND GOOSEFOOT FAMILY. Annual or perennial herbs. Flowers are tiny and inconspicuous, with 1–5 sepals and 4 or 5 stamens; there are bracts beneath the flowers. Leaves are simple, and either alternate or opposite. Fruit is tiny and seedlike. Genera: *Amaranthus, Atriplex, Chenopodium, Dysphania, Kochia, Salicornia, Salsola, Suaeda.*

APIACEAE—CARROT FAMILY. Perennial herbs. Flowers are radially symmetrical and very small, with 5 petals, 5 sepals, and 5 stamens; they are arranged in umbels. Leaves are compound, with a sheathing base. Fruit is usually dry and seedlike, but fleshy and berrylike in *Aralia.* Genera: *Aegopodium, Angelica, Anthriscus, Aralia, Cicuta, Conioselinum, Conium, Cryptotaenia, Daucus, Heracleum, Hydrocotyle, Ligusticum, Osmorhiza, Panax, Pastinaca, Ptilimnium,*

Sanicula, Sium, Taenidia, Zizia.

APOCYNACEAE—DOGBANE FAMILY. Perennial herbs and vines, mostly with milky sap. Flowers are radially symmetrical with 5 petals, 5 sepals, and 5 stamens. Leaves are simple, usually opposite, but sometimes whorled. Fruit is a long follicle; the wind-dispersed seeds have tufts of hair. Genera: *Apocynum, Asclepias, Cynanchum, Vinca.*

ASTERACEAE—ASTER FAMILY. Annual or perennial herbs. The flower heads are composed of spreading, straplike ray flowers and/or tiny, densely packed, tubular disk flowers. The flowers are aggregated above a whorl of small, pointed bracts. Leaves are variable. Fruit is an achene, often with hairs attached. Genera: *Achillea, Ageratina, Ambrosia, Anaphalis, Antennaria, Anthemis, Arctium, Arnica, Arnoseris, Artemisia, Bidens, Centaurea, Chrysopsis, Cichorium, Cirsium, Coreopsis, Crepis, Doellingeria, Echinacea, Erechtites, Erigeron, Eupatorium, Eurybia, Euthamia, Eutrochium, Galinsoga, Gnaphalium, Grindelia, Helenium, Helianthus, Heliopsis, Hieracium, Hypochaeris, Inula, Ionactis, Jacobaea, Krigia, Lactuca, Lapsana, Leucanthemum, Liatris, Matricaria, Mikania, Mycelis, Nabalus, Oclemena, Oligoneuron, Omalotheca, Onopordum, Packera, Petasites, Pityopsis, Pluchea, Polymnia, Pseudognaphalium, Rudbeckia, Sclerolepis, Scorzoneroides, Senecio, Sericocarpus, Silphium, Solidago, Sonchus, Symphyotrichum, Tanacetum, Taraxacum, Tragopogon, Tripleurospermum, Tussilago, Vernonia, Xanthium.*

BALSAMINACEAE—TOUCH-ME-NOT FAMILY. Annual herbs. Flowers are bilaterally symmetrical with 5 petals, but give the appearance of 3 because the lower 4 petals are fused in pairs; the upper petal is hood-shaped. There are 3 sepals, the uppermost projecting into a spur behind the flower. Leaves are opposite, alternate, or occasionally whorled. Fruit is a capsule that splits open to explosively disperse seeds. Genus: *Impatiens.*

BERBERIDACEAE—BARBERRY FAMILY. Perennial herbs, often occurring in rich soils. Flowers are radially symmetrical with 6–9 petals, 4–6 sepals, and 6 stamens. Leaves are alternate and may be simple or compound. Fruit is a berry. Genera: *Caulophyllum, Podophyllum.*

BORAGINACEAE—BORAGE FAMILY. Annual, biennial, or perennial herbs that frequently have rough-hairy stems. Flowers are radially symmetrical, funnel- or trumpet-shaped, with 5 petals and 5 sepals, often arranged in coiled clusters which uncoil as they mature. Leaves are simple and alternate, but sometimes may be basal. Fruit is very small, hard, and 4-parted. Genera: *Cynoglossum, Echium, Hackelia, Hydrophyllum, Lithospermum, Mertensia, Myosotis, Onosmodium, Symphytum.*

BRASSICACEAE—MUSTARD FAMILY. Annual, biennial, or perennial herbs. Flowers are radially symmetrical, with 4 petals, 4 sepals, and 6 stamens; they are arranged in racemes. Leaves are simple or divided, often basal as well as located along the stem. Fruit is long and thin (silique) or short and broad (silicle). Genera: *Alliaria, Arabidopsis, Arabis, Armoracia, Barbarea, Berteroa, Boechera, Brassica, Cakile, Capsella, Cardamine, Draba, Erysimum, Hesperis, Lepidium, Lunaria, Nasturtium, Raphanus, Rorippa, Sisymbrium, Thlaspi, Turritis.*

CACTACEAE—CACTUS FAMILY. Succulent perennials with swollen, fleshy stems. Flowers are solitary and large with many petals and sepals. Spines grow from a specialized area (areoles) of the plant, which is the equivalent to branches in other plants. Fruit is a berry. Genus: *Opuntia*.

CAMPANULACEAE—HAREBELL FAMILY. Annual or perennial herbs. Flowers are radially or bilaterally symmetrical. There are 5 petals united at the base forming a tube or bell, 5 sepals, and usually 5 stamens. Leaves are usually simple, entire, and alternate. Fruit is a capsule. Genera: *Campanula, Jasione, Lobelia, Triodanis*.

CANNABACEAE— CANNABIS AND HOP FAMILY. Perennial vines. Flowers are radially symmetrical, with no petals, and 5 sepals fused at the base. The branched flower arrays grow from the leaf axils. Leaves are lobed or palmately compound. Fruit is an achene or drupe. Genus: *Humulus*.

CAPRIFOLIACEAE—HONEYSUCKLE FAM-ILY. Perennial herbs. Flowers are either radially or bilaterally symmetrical with 4 or 5 sepals and 4 or 5 petals fused into a tube or funnel shape. There are 4 or 5 stamens. Leaves are opposite. Fruit is a capsule or berry. Genera: *Dipsacus, Knautia, Linnaea, Triosteum*.

CARYOPHYLLACEAE—CARNATION FAM-ILY, PINK FAMILY. Annual or perennial herbs. Flowers are radially symmetrical with 5 petals, sometimes divided or notched, 5 sepals, and usually 5 or 10 stamens; the flowers may be solitary or arranged in branched inflorescences. Leaves are usually simple and opposite,

but sometimes alternate or whorled. Fruit is a capsule. Genera: *Arenaria, Cerastium, Dianthus, Honckenya, Lychnis, Minuartia, Moehringia, Myosoton, Paronychia, Sagina, Saponaria, Silene, Spergula, Spergularia, Stellaria*.

CISTACEAE—ROCKROSE FAMILY. Perennial herbs or shrubs. Flowers are radially symmetrical, either single or in branched inflorescences; and may only be open for a few hours before withering. The flowers have 3 or 5 petals and 5 sepals; 2 of the sepals are much narrower than the others. Leaves are alternate, simple, and sometimes scalelike. Fruit is a capsule. Genera: *Crocanthemum, Hudsonia, Lechea*

COMANDRACEAE—BASTARD TOADFLAX FAMILY. Perennial herbs. Partially parasitic (hemiparasitic). Flowers are radially symmetrical with 4 or 5 sepals and no petals. Leaves are simple, entire and either alternate or opposite. Fruit is fleshy, berrylike. Genera: *Comandra, Geocaulon*.

CONVOLVULACEAE—MORNING GLORY FAMILY. Annual or perennial vines. Flowers are radially symmetrical, typically with 5 petals fused to form a funnel or tube. Leaves are usually simple and alternate. Fruit is a capsule. *Cuscuta* species do not produce chlorophyll, obtaining nutrients by parasitizing other plants; these plants have very tiny flowers. Genera: *Calystegia, Convolvulus, Cuscuta, Ipomoea*.

CORNACEAE—DOGWOOD FAMILY. Perennial herbs. Flowers are tiny, radially symmetrical, with 4 or 5 petals and 4–15 stamens; the tight flower clusters are surrounded by 4 large, white, petal-like bracts. Leaves are simple, entire, and usually opposite. Fruit is berrylike. Genus: *Chamaepericlymenum*.

CRASSULACEAE—STONECROP FAMILY, ORPINE FAMILY. Fleshy, succulent herbs. Flowers have 4 or 5 petals and sepals and 4–10 stamens; they are arranged in branched inflorescences. Leaves are simple, entire or toothed, and succulent. Fruit is a dry follicle. Genera: *Hylotelephium, Rhodiola, Sedum*.

CUCURBITACEAE–CUCUMBER FAMILY, GOURD AND PUMPKIN FAMILY. Annual or perennial vines with coiled tendrils. Flowers are radially symmetrical with 5 petals, 5 sepals, and 5 stamens. Leaves are alternate and may be entire, lobed or divided. Fruit is a berry or capsule, often with a tough rind and prickly. Genera: *Echinocystis, Sicyos*.

DIAPENSIACEAE—DIAPENSIA FAMILY. Small, evergreen shrubs that occur in alpine zones. Flowers are radially symmetrical with 5 petals, 5 sepals, and 5 or 10 stamens. Leaves are opposite, and densely packed, forming cushionlike mounds. Fruit is a capsule. Genus: *Diapensia*.

DROSERACEAE—SUNDEW FAMILY. Perennial herbs. Flowers are radially symmetrical, with 5 petals, 5 sepals, and 5 stamens; they are arrayed in coiled racemes. Leaves are basal, covered in mucilaginous hairs to attract insects, which are digested for nutrients. Fruit is a capsule. Genus: *Drosera*.

ERICACEAE—HEATH FAMILY. Perennial herbs or shrubs, often found in acidic soils. Flowers are radially symmetrical, with 5 or sometimes 4 petals and sepals, and 8–10 stamens. Leaves are usually simple and usually alternate, but may be opposite or whorled. Fruit is a berry,

capsule, or drupe. Genera: *Andromeda, Arctostaphylos, Calluna, Chamaedaphne, Chimaphila, Corema, Empetrum, Epigaea, Gaultheria, Gaylussacia, Harrimanella, Hypopitys, Kalmia, Moneses, Monotropa, Orthilia, Phyllodoce, Pterospora, Pyrola, Rhododendron, Vaccinium*.

EUPHORBIACEAE—SPURGE FAMILY. Annual or perennial herbs, often with milky sap. Flowers are radially symmetrical, very small and inconspicuous, and 5-parted; the 3 styles are branched or forked. Bracts underlie the tight clusters of flowers. Leaves are usually simple and alternate, but may be opposite or whorled. Fruit is a capsule. Genera: *Acalypha, Euphorbia*.

FABACEAE—PEA FAMILY, LEGUME FAMILY. Annual or perennial herbs or vines. Flowers are usually bilaterally symmetrical with 5 petals and sepals. Typical flower arrangement has a large upper petal, 2 lateral (wing) petals, and 2 lower (keel) petals that are often fused. Leaves are usually alternate and compound. Fruit is a pod. Genera: *Amphicarpaea, Apios, Baptisia, Chamaecrista, Crotalaria, Desmodium, Hylodesmum, Kummerowia, Lathyrus, Lespedeza, Lotus, Lupinus, Medicago, Melilotus, Securigera, Senna, Strophostyles, Tephrosia, Trifolium, Vicia*.

GENTIANACEAE—GENTIAN FAMILY. Annual or biennial herbs. Flowers are radially symmetrical, single or clustered, and bell-shaped or tubular with 4 or 5 petals that are fused at the base and, in many species, also closed at the tip. Leaves are usually opposite, simple, and entire. Fruit is a capsule. Genera: *Bartonia, Centaurium, Gentiana, Gentianella, Gentianopsis, Halenia*, and *Sabatia*.

GERANIACEAE—GERANIUM FAMILY. Annual or perennial herbs. Flowers are radially symmetrical with 5 petals and 5 sepals; they are solitary or in branching clusters. Leaves are variable, opposite or alternate, simple or compound. Stems frequently have sticky hairs. Fruit is dry, capsulelike, 5-parted. Genus: *Geranium*.

HALORAGACEAE—WATER MILFOIL FAMILY. Aquatic herbs. Flowers are radially symmetrical, very small, 3- or 4-parted, often without petals, and arranged in a spike. Leaves are simple and lance-shaped or finely divided; the submerged leaves are feathery. Fruit is an achene. Genus: *Proserpinaca*.

HYPERICACEAE—ST. JOHN'S-WORT FAMILY. Annual or perennial herbs or shrubs. Flowers are radially symmetrical and have 4 or 5 petals, 4 or 5 sepals, and 5 or more stamens; they are arranged in a branching inflorescence. Leaves are simple, entire, and opposite and have tiny translucent dots. Fruit is a dry capsule. Genera: *Hypericum*, *Triadenum*.

LAMIACEAE—MINT FAMILY. Annual or perennial herbs. Flowers are bilaterally symmetrical, usually united into a 5-parted corolla with a 2-lobed upper lip and a 3-lobed lower lip; there are 5 sepals. Leaves are opposite and often aromatic. Fruit is tiny, dry, and 4-parted. Genera: *Agastache, Ajuga, Blephilia, Clinopodium, Collinsonia, Dracocephalum, Elsholtzia, Galeopsis, Glechoma, Hedeoma, Lamium, Leonurus, Lycopus, Mentha, Monarda, Nepeta, Origanum, Physostegia, Prunella, Pycnanthemum, Scutellaria, Stachys, Teucrium, Thymus, Trichostema*.

LENTIBULARIACEAE—BLADDERWORT FAMILY. Carnivorous perennials found in ponds and wetlands (*Utricularia*) and ledges at high elevations (*Pinguicula*). Flowers are bilaterally symmetrical and solitary or in racemes. There are 5 fused petals, comprised of a 2-lobed upper lip and a 3-lobed lower lip; sepals are united. Leaves are basal (*Pinguicula*), often floating or submerged and feathery (*Utricularia*). Fruit is a capsule. Genera: *Pinguicula, Utricularia*.

LIMNANTHACEAE—FALSE MERMAID FAMILY, MEADOW-FOAM FAMILY. Herbaceous, aquatic perennials. Flowers are tiny and inconspicuous, radially symmetrical, 3-parted, bowl- or bell-shaped, and long-stalked. Leaves are pinnately compound, usually with 3–5 leaflets. Fruit is a warty capsule. Genus: *Floerkea*.

LINACEAE—FLAX FAMILY. Annual or perennial herbs. Flowers are radially symmetrical, with 5 petals, 5 sepals, and 5 or 10 stamens, and usually grow in clusters. Leaves are typically simple, alternate, and entire. Fruit is a 5-parted capsule. Genus: *Linum*.

LINDERNIACEAE—FALSE PIMPERNEL FAMILY. Annual herbs. Flowers are small, solitary, bilaterally symmetrical, with 5 petals, 5 sepals, and 4 stamens. Leaves are simple, opposite, and entire or finely toothed. Fruit is a capsule. Genus: *Lindernia*.

LYTHRACEAE—LOOSESTRIFE FAMILY. Annual or perennial wetland and aquatic herbs. Flowers are either radially or bilaterally symmetrical, with 4 or 8 petals and sepals fused to form a tube. Leaves are usually simple and opposite, but occasionally are alternate or whorled. The fruit is a capsule. Genera: *Lythrum, Rotala, Trapa.*

MALVACEAE—MALLOW FAMILY. Perennial herbs. Flowers are radially symmetrical, with 5 petals and 5 sepals; there are also calyx-like bracts just below the true calyx. The flowers are solitary or in clusters. The stamens form a central tube that surrounds the pistil. Leaves are alternate, simple, and lobed. Fruit is a capsule. Genera: *Abutilon, Hibiscus, Malva.*

MELASTOMATACEAE—MELASTOMA FAMILY. Annual or perennial herbs. Flowers are radially symmetrical, with 4 petals, 4 sepals, and 8 stamens; they are clustered at the top of the stem. Leaves are simple and opposite, usually with 1–4 side veins running from the base to the tip. Fruit is an urn-shaped capsule. Genus: *Rhexia.*

MENYANTHACEAE—BUCKBEAN FAMILY. Perennial wetland herbs. Flowers are radially symmetrical, with 5 petals and 5 sepals united into a funnel shape with spreading lobes. Leaves are basal or alternate, simple or compound. Fruit is a capsule. Genera: *Menyanthes, Nymphoides.*

MOLLUGINACEAE—CARPETWEED FAMILY. Annual or perennial herbs, with creeping, fleshy stems. Flowers are radially symmetrical, very small, often lacking petals, and with 5 petal-like sepals. Leaves are simple, entire, and may be opposite, alternate, or whorled. Genus: *Mollugo.*

MYRSINACEAE—MARLBERRY FAMILY. Annual or perennial herbs. Flowers are radially symmetrical, with 4–9 fused petals that spread horizontally, and 4–9 sepals. Flowers grow in branching arrays at the end of the stems or from the axils. Leaves are simple and may be opposite, alternate, or whorled. Fruit is a dry capsule or fleshy and berrylike. Genus: *Lysimachia.*

NELUMBONACEAE—LOTUS FAMILY. Perennial aquatic herbs. Flowers are radially symmetrical, large, solitary, with many petals and sepals and 13 or more stamens. Leaves are simple, large, and long-stalked. Fruit is a nut embedded in a cylindrical floral cup with a pitted surface. Genus: *Nelumbo.*

NYCTAGINACEAE—FOUR O'CLOCK FAMILY. Perennial herbs. Flowers are radially symmetrical, bell- or funnel-shaped, with 5 petal-like sepals and colorful bracts beneath the flower; the flowers are arranged in branching, umbel-like arrays on the upper stem. Leaves are simple, entire, and opposite. Fruit is an achene. Genus: *Mirabilis.*

ONAGRACEAE—EVENING-PRIMROSE FAMILY. Annual, biennial, or perennial herbs. Flowers are radially symmetrical with 4 petals and 4 sepals. Petals, sepals, and stamens are fused at the base to form a tube. Leaves are simple, and may be opposite or alternate, and toothed, lobed, or entire. Fruit is a 4-parted capsule. Genera: *Chamerion, Circaea, Epilobium, Ludwigia, Oenothera.*

OROBANCHACEAE—BROOMRAPE FAMILY. Annual, biennial, or perennial herbs. Some species are parasites lacking chlorophyll. Other are partial parasites which photosynthesize and have green foliage. Flowers are bilaterally symmetrical with a hoodlike upper lip, 4 or 5 petals fused at the base and 2–5 fused sepals. Leaves are variable, from small and scalelike to green and leafy. Fruit is a dry capsule. Genera: *Agalinis,*

Aureolaria, Castilleja, Conopholis, Epifagus, Euphrasia, Melampyrum, Orobanche, Pedicularis, Rhinanthus.

OXALIDACEAE—WOOD SORREL FAMILY. Annual or (usually) perennial herbs. The radially symmetrical flowers are solitary or in clusters, with 5 petals and 5 sepals; the 10 stamens are united at the base and are in 2 sets of unequal lengths. Leaves are basal or alternate, typically compound with 3 leaflets that are rounded and notched at the tip. Fruit is a capsule. Genus: *Oxalis.*

PAPAVERACEAE—POPPY FAMILY. Annual or perennial herbs. Flowers are large and are radially or bilaterally symmetrical. Petals are in multiples of 4, with 2 or 3 sepals that fall off early. Leaves are basal, opposite, alternate, or whorled; they are simple or compound. Stem has a colored sap when broken. Fruit is a capsule. Genera: *Adlumia, Capnoides, Chelidonium, Corydalis, Dicentra, Fumaria, Glaucium, Sanguinaria.*

PARNASSIACEAE—GRASS OF PARNASSUS FAMILY. Perennial herbs. Flowers are radially symmetrical, solitary, with 5 veined petals and 5 sepals, borne on slender stalks. The flowers have 5 true stamens and 5 smaller, infertile stamens (staminodes), which have 3-pronged tips. Leaves are entire and primarily basal. Fruit is a capsule. Genus: *Parnassia.*

PENTHORACEAE—DITCH STONECROP FAMILY. Perennial herbs. Flowers are radially symmetrical with 5 petal-like sepals fused at the base and no petals; the flowers are arranged in branching clusters at the top of the stem. Leaves are simple, toothed, and alternate. Fruit is a dry 5-parted capsule. Genus: *Penthorum.*

PHRYMACEAE—LOPSEED FAMILY. Perennial herbs. Flowers are bilaterally symmetrical, paired, with 5 petals fused into an upper and lower lip, and 5 sepals. Leaves are simple and opposite with toothed margins. Fruit is an achene or capsule. Genera: *Mimulus, Phryma.*

PHYTOLACCACEAE—POKEWEED FAMILY. Perennial herbs. Flowers are radially symmetrical with no petals, 4 or 8 sepals, and 4 or 8 stamens; the flowers are arranged in drooping racemes. Leaves are simple, alternate, and entire. Fruit is a berry. Genus: *Phytolacca.*

PLANTAGINACEAE—PLANTAIN FAMILY. Annual or perennial herbs. Flowers in this family are variable. They may be radially or bilaterally symmetrical, either inconspicuous and lacking petals, or with 5 distinct petals and 4 or 5 sepals. The flowers may be arranged in slender spikes, or paired, or in open clusters. Leaves are usually simple and opposite. Fruit is a capsule. Genera: *Chaenorhinum, Chelone, Gratiola, Linaria, Nuttallanthus, Penstemon, Plantago, Veronica, Veronicastrum.*

PLUMBAGINACEAE—LEADWORT FAMILY. Perennial herbs. The flowers are radially symmetrical with 5 petals and 5 sepals united at the base; they are arranged in a panicle. Leaves are in a basal rosette, and are simple and entire. Fruit is a capsule. Genus: *Limonium.*

POLEMONIACEAE—PHLOX FAMILY. Annual or perennial herbs. Flowers are radially symmetrical with 5 petals joined at the base and 5 united sepals. Flowers are often showy and borne in heads, clusters, or singly. Leaves are basal, alternate or opposite, and simple or pinnately compound. Fruit is a capsule. Genera: *Phlox, Polemonium.*

POLYGALACEAE—MILKWORT FAMILY. Annual or perennial herbs. Flowers are bilaterally symmetrical, with 3 petals that are often fringed, and 5 sepals, 2 of which are petal-like and winged. Leaves are simple, entire, and usually alternate but occasionally are opposite or whorled. Fruit is a capsule. Genus: *Polygala*.

POLYGONACEAE—BUCKWHEAT FAMILY, SMARTWEED FAMILY. Annual or perennial herbs or vines. Flowers are radially symmetrical, very small, often closed, with 2–6 tepals, usually in a slender cluster. Leaves are usually alternate, simple, and entire, but may be in a basal rosette. Stems have swollen joints and a papery sheath at the point of leaf attachment. Fruit is an achene. Genera: *Fallopia, Persicaria, Polygonum, Rumex*.

PORTULACACEAE—PURSLANE FAMILY. Annual, biennial, or perennial herbs. Flowers are radially symmetrical, usually with 5 petals, and 2 or more sepals; they are solitary or arranged in a raceme. Leaves are simple, usually opposite, and entire. Plants are small and fleshy with red to purple hairless stems. Fruit is a capsule. Genera: *Claytonia, Portulaca*.

PRIMULACEAE—PRIMROSE FAMILY. Annual or perennial herbs. Flowers are radially symmetrical, with 5 petals and 5 sepals, borne singly or in clusters, sometimes on long, leafless stems (*Primula*). Leaves are basal and lance-shaped or oval (*Primula*), or finely divided and feathery (*Hottonia*). Fruit is a capsule. *Hottonia* is aquatic. Genera: *Hottonia, Primula*.

RANUNCULACEAE—BUTTERCUP FAMILY, CROWFOOT FAMILY. Annual or perennial herbs and sometimes perennial vines. Flowers are radially symmetrical and are either solitary or arranged in branched clusters. Petal numbers are variable or occasionally absent; the sepals are often showy and petal-like. Numerous stamens and pistils are clustered in the center of the flower. Leaves are generally alternate or basal, and either simple or compound. Fruits are variable and include achenes, berries, capsules, and follicles. Genera: *Actaea, Anemone, Aquilegia, Caltha, Clematis, Coptis, Ficaria, Hydrastis, Ranunculus, Thalictrum*.

ROSACEAE—ROSE FAMILY. Perennial herbs and shrubs. Flowers are radially symmetrical, often showy, with 5 petals, 5 sepals, and numerous stamens, all attached to a floral cup; the flowers are solitary or arranged in a variety of inflorescence types. Leaves are alternate, toothed, simple or compound, often with a pair of stipules at the base. Fruits are variable and include achenes, capsules, and drupes (a berrylike fruit). Genera: *Agrimonia, Argentina, Comarum, Drymocallis, Fragaria, Geum, Potentilla, Rubus, Sanguisorba, Sibbaldiopsis, Spiraea*.

RUBIACEAE—MADDER FAMILY, BEDSTRAW FAMILY. Perennial herbs. Flowers are radially symmetrical, with 4 petals and 4 sepals, borne singly or in clusters. Leaves are simple, opposite or whorled, and entire. Fruit is a capsule, capsule-like, berry, or drupe. Genera: *Diodia, Galium, Houstonia, Mitchella*.

SARRACENIACEAE—PITCHER-PLANT FAMILY. Perennial, carnivorous bog herbs.

Flowers are radially symmetrical, with 5 broad petals, 3 or 6 sepals, and a large umbrella-shaped style; the flowers are solitary and nodding. Leaves are basal, heavily veined, pitcher-shaped, red or green, with hoodlike flaps covered by downward-pointing hairs. Leaves collect rainwater to trap insects. Fruit is a capsule. Genus: *Sarracenia*.

SAXIFRAGACEAE—SAXIFRAGE FAMILY. Annual, biennial, or perennial herbs. Flowers are radially symmetrical, small, solitary or clustered, with 5 petals (sometimes absent), 5 sepals, and 5 or 10 stamens; the sepals and petals are attached to the rim of a floral cup. Basal leaves are frequently in rosettes, and stem leaves are usually alternate. Fruit is a capsule. Genera: *Chrysosplenium*, *Heuchera*, *Micranthes*, *Mitella*, *Saxifraga*, *Tiarella*.

SCROPHULARIACEAE—FIGWORT FAMILY. Annual, biennial, or perennial herbs. Flowers are bilaterally symmetrical, usually united into a 5-parted corolla with a 2-lobed upper lip and a 3-lobed lower lip. Leaves are simple, alternate, opposite, or whorled, and either toothed or entire. Fruit is a capsule. Genera: *Limosella*, *Scrophularia*, *Verbascum*.

SOLANACEAE—NIGHTSHADE FAMILY. Annual or perennial herbs and vines. Flowers are radially symmetrical, with 5 petals and 5 sepals, which are fused at the base. Leaves are usually simple, alternate, and toothed or entire, sometimes with flaring basal lobes. Fruit is a capsule or berry. Genera: *Datura*, *Physalis*, *Solanum*.

THEOPHRASTACEAE—THEOPHRASTA FAMILY. Perennial herbs. Flowers are radially symmetrical with 5 petals fused into a tube; the flowers are arranged in open panicles. Leaves are simple, alternate, and entire. Fruit is a hard berry. Genus: *Samolus*.

URTICACEAE—NETTLE FAMILY. Annual or perennial herbs. Flowers are inconspicuous, with 4 or 5 sepals and no petals; they are often clustered in the leaf axils. Leaves are simple, toothed, and opposite or alternate. Stems of some species (*Laportea*, *Urtica*) have stinging hairs. Fruit is a small achene. Genera: *Boehmeria*, *Laportea*, *Parietaria*, *Pilea*, *Urtica*.

VERBENACEAE—VERVAIN FAMILY. Perennial herbs. Flowers are small, bilaterally or radially symmetrical, with 5 petals united into a slender tube and 5 sepals fused into a base; the flowers are arranged in spikes. Leaves are simple, with entire, toothed, or lobed margins, and are opposite or whorled. Fruit is 4-parted, capsulelike. Genus: *Verbena*.

VIOLACEAE—VIOLET FAMILY. Low annual or perennial herbs. Flowers are bilaterally symmetrical, usually solitary, with 5 petals, the lowest one often larger and spurred. Lateral petals usually have interior hairs. There are 5 sepals, and the stamens are fused around the style. Leaves are variable among the many species; they may be entire, toothed, lobed, or deeply divided. Fruit is a 3-valved capsule. Genus: *Viola*.

WHITE FLOWERS

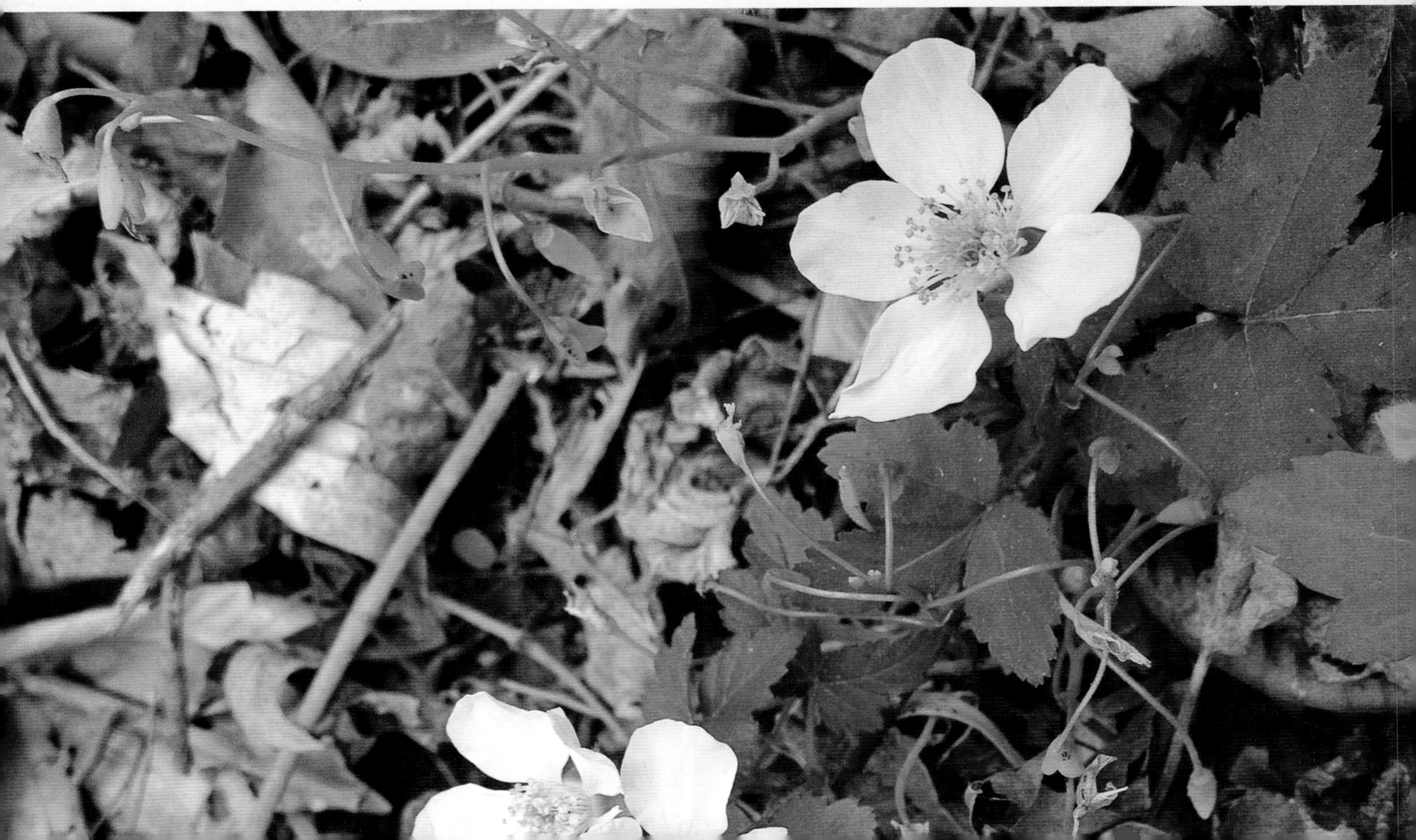

Circaea alpina   ONAGRACEAE
Dwarf enchanter's nightshade, small enchanter's nightshade
Late spring to summer, 3–10 in., perennial. Cool, moist forests, seepages, and streambanks.

Flowers white, ⅛ in. wide, stalked, arranged in a sparse, terminal raceme; the 2 petals deeply notched, appearing to be 4. Leaves ¾–2 in. long, triangular or oval, the lower long-petioled. Stems weak, the upper part with gland-tipped hairs. Fruit a flattened, hairy capsule, ⅛ in. long. CT, MA, ME, NH, RI (rare), VT

Circaea canadensis (C. lutetiana, C. quadrisulcata)
ONAGRACEAE
Common enchanter's nightshade, broad-leaved enchanter's nightshade
Late spring to summer, 10–30 in., perennial. Forests and woodlands.

Flowers white, ⅛–¼ in. wide, stalked, arranged in many-flowered racemes to 8 in. long; the 2 petals deeply notched, appearing to be 4. Leaves 2–4 in. long, oval, long-petioled. Stems with scattered, glandless hairs. Fruit a rounded, bristly capsule with a ridged surface, ⅛–¼ in. long. CT, MA, ME, NH, RI, VT

Trillium cernuum   MELANTHIACEAE
Nodding trillium, nodding wake-robin
Spring, 8–20 in., perennial. Moist forests and woodlands, often on sandy or peaty soils.

Flowers white, 1–2 in. wide, solitary, nodding below leaves, with dark-tipped stamens and recurved petal tips. Leaves 2½–4 in. long, broadly oval, sessile or short-petioled. Stems smooth. Fruit a broadly oval, dark red berry, about 1 in. wide. CT, MA, ME, NH, RI, VT

Trillium grandiflorum   MELANTHIACEAE
Large-flowered trillium, white trillium
Spring, 6–20 in., perennial. Rich, moist forests.

Flowers white, 3–5 in. wide, solitary, upright, with
yellow-tipped stamens; fading petals turn pink. Leaves
3½–7 in. long, broadly oval, sessile or short-petioled.
Stems smooth. Fruit a rounded, pale green berry, ½ in.
long. Native in VT; introduced in CT, MA, NH.

Trillium undulatum   MELANTHIACEAE
Painted trillium
Spring, 8–20 in., perennial. Cool, moist
forests and swamp edges.

Flowers white with crimson-streaked centers, 1½–2½
in. wide, solitary, upright. Leaves 2–5 in. long, oval, on
distinct petioles. Stems smooth, reddish green. Fruit a
bright red, oval berry, ½ in. long. CT, MA, ME, NH, RI, VT

Galium tinctorium   RUBIACEAE
Stiff three-petaled bedstraw, Clayton's bedstraw
Summer to early fall, 6–30 in., perennial.
Swamps, marshes, and wet meadows.

Flowers white, ¹⁄₁₆–⅛ in. wide, in branching clusters of
2–4 on short, straight stalks. Leaves ¼–¾ in. long, linear,
blunt-tipped; the lower in whorls of 5 or 6, the upper in
whorls of 4 or 5. Stems square, prickly, erect or sprawling.
Fruit round, ¹⁄₁₆–⅛ in. wide, on a straight stalk. CT, MA,
ME, NH, RI, VT

Galium trifidum   RUBIACEAE
Three-petaled bedstraw, small bedstraw
Summer to early fall, 2–16 in., perennial. Swamps,
marshes, wet meadows, and tidal wetlands.

Flowers white, 1/16–1/8 in. wide, in branching clusters
of 1 or 2 on arching stalks. Leaves 1/4–3/4 in. long, linear, blunt-tipped; the lower and upper mostly in whorls
of 4. Stems square, prickly, weak, sprawling and often
mat-forming. Fruit round, 1/16–1/8 in. wide, on an arching
stalk. CT, MA, ME, NH, RI, VT (rare)

Alisma subcordatum   ALISMATACEAE
Southern water plantain, smaller water plantain
Summer to early fall, 1–2 ft., perennial.
Swamps, marshes, pond shores, ditches.

Flowers white, 1/8–1/4 in. wide, arranged in an open,
wide-branching panicle to 12 in. long; petals and
sepals about equal in length. Leaves 4–6 in. long, oval,
long-petioled. Stems smooth. Fruit a disk-shaped achene,
1/8–1/4 in. wide. CT, MA, ME, NH, RI, VT

Alisma triviale   ALISMATACEAE
Northern water plantain, larger water-plantain
Summer to early fall, 1–3 ft., perennial. Swamps,
marshes, pond shallows, and ditches.

Flowers white, 1/4–3/8 in. wide, arranged in an open,
wide-branching panicle to 2 ft. long; petals longer than
the sepals. Leaves 6–14 in. long, oval, long-petioled.
Stems smooth. Fruit a disk-shaped achene, 1/16–1/8 in.
wide. CT, MA, ME, NH, RI, VT

Sagittaria filiformis ALISMATACEAE
Narrow-leaved arrowhead
Summer, leaves to 8 ft. long, perennial. Rivers,
tidal estuaries, sandy or peaty pond shallows.

Flowers white, ½ in. wide, arranged in 1–4 whorled clusters stalked just above the water surface. Leaves 1–8 ft. long, floating or submerged, linear, threadlike. Flower stems erect or floating just above water surface. Fruit a tiny achene, aggregated in rounded heads ¼–⅜ in. wide. Only plants growing in deeper water produce flowers. CT, MA, ME (rare), RI

Sagittaria graminea ALISMATACEAE
Grass-leaved arrowhead
Summer to early fall, 1–3 ft., perennial. Marshes,
pond and river shores, and estuaries.

Flowers white, ½–1 in. wide, long-stalked, arranged in 1–12 whorled clusters, forming a raceme, 1–8 in. long. Leaves linear or narrowly lance-shaped, submerged or erect; the above-surface leaves 2–6 in. long, often with narrow, flat blades. Stems erect. Fruit a tiny achene, aggregated into rounded heads ¼–⅜ in. wide. CT, MA, ME, NH, RI (rare), VT

Sagittaria latifolia ALISMATACEAE
Common arrowhead, broad-leaved arrowhead
Summer to early fall, 1–3 ft., perennial. Marshes,
pond and river shallows, and estuaries.

Flowers white, 1–1½ in. wide, stalked, arranged in 2–15 whorled clusters; the male flowers with 25–40 stamens in center (female flowers with rounded disk in center). Leaves variable, 2–12 in. long, narrowly to broadly lance-shaped, with narrow or broad basal lobes (lobes sometimes absent). Stems erect. Fruit a tiny achene, aggregated into rounded heads ¼ in. wide. The most common arrowhead species. CT, MA, ME, NH, RI, VT
 Sagittaria engelmanniana (Engelmann's arrowhead) is similar, but the leaves are linear or narrowly lance-shaped, often with very slender basal lobes, and the male flowers have 15–25 stamens in the center. Grows in marshes and pond shores. CT, MA, RI, VT

3 radial petals; leaves simple, basal, entire

Sagittaria rigida   ALISMATACEAE
Sessile-fruited arrowhead
Summer to early fall, 4–30 in., perennial. Tidal
and freshwater marshes, pond shores, and
floodplains, often in high-pH conditions.

Flowers white, ¾–1¼ in. wide, arranged in 2–8 whorled
clusters; the upper whorls (of male flowers) usually
stalked, the lowermost whorls (of female flowers) sessile.
Leaf blades 2–6 in. long, oval or lance-shaped, lacking
basal lobes, on long petioles, overtopping flower stems.
Stems erect. Fruit a tiny achene, aggregated into sessile,
bristly balls, ½ in. wide. CT, MA (rare), ME (rare), VT

3 radial petals; leaves deeply divided, alternate, leaflets entire

Floerkea proserpinacoides   LIMNANTHACEAE
False mermaid weed
Spring, 2–15 in., annual. Swamps, river
shores, floodplains, forest seeps.

Flowers ¼–½ in. wide, stalked from leaf axils, the green
sepals larger than the tiny white petals. Leaves divided
into 3–7 narrow leaflets, ¼–¾ in. long; the petioles ½–1¼
in. long. Stems smooth, weak, often prostrate. Fruit capsulelike, ⅛ in. long. CT (rare)

4 radial petals; leaves simple, alternate, entire

Arabidopsis thaliana⁎   BRASSICACEAE
Mouse-ear cress, mouse-ear thale cress
Spring, 4–16 in., annual. Fields, roadsides, and lawns.

Flowers white, ⅜–½ in. long, sparsely clustered at the
tips of spreading, divergent branches. Leaves ½–1½ in.
long, linear or lance-shaped; the basal leaves longer and
wider than stem leaves, hairy, occasionally toothed on the
margins. Stems hairy, grayish green. Fruit
a linear silique curving upwards, ½–¾ in.
long. Native to Eurasia and North Africa.
CT, MA, ME, NH, RI, VT

Arabis pycnocarpa (*A. hirsuta*) BRASSICACEAE
Hairy rockcress, hairy eared-rockcress
Spring and early summer, 6–24 in., biennial
or perennial. Dry rocky woodlands, ledges,
and outcrops with high-pH bedrock.

Flowers white, ⅛–¼ in. wide, arranged
in small, stiffly ascending clusters along
upper stem. Basal leaves ¾–3 in. long,
oval, hairy, usually entire; stem leaves
smaller, linear, overlapping, sessile or
short-petioled. Stems hairy. Fruit a linear
ascending silique, 1½–3½ in. long. CT,
MA, ME, NH (rare), VT

Berteroa incana ⁎ BRASSICACEAE
Hoary alyssum, hoary false alyssum
Summer, 1–3 ft., annual or perennial. Dry fields,
thicket edges, and open, disturbed habitats.

Flowers white, ⅛–¼ in. long, short-stalked, arranged
in narrow, erect, stiffly branched racemes; the petals
notched. Leaves ½–1½ in. long, lance-shaped, covered
with fine hairs. Stems grayish downy. Fruit an oval, hairy
silique, ⅛–¼ in. long, tapering to a short beak. Native to
Eurasia. CT, MA, ME, NH, RI, VT

Gaultheria hispidula ERICACEAE
Creeping snowberry, moxie, creeping spicy-wintergreen
Summer, 4–6 in., trailing shrub. Bogs, mossy
hummocks, and moist coniferous and mixed forests.

Flowers white, ¼ in. wide, bell-shaped, often hidden by
leaves. Leaves ½ in. long, oval, crowded, with a wintergreen fragrance when bruised. Stems hairy, creeping,
mat-forming. Fruit a snow-white
berry, ¼–⅜ in. long. CT (rare), MA,
ME, NH, RI (rare), VT

Maianthemum canadense RUSCACEAE
Canada mayflower, wild lily-of-the-valley
Spring, 2–6 in., perennial. Forests and forest edges.

Flowers white, 1/8–1/4 in. wide, clustered in a short terminal raceme; the stamens protruding and the petals reflexed. Leaves 1½–4 in. long, oval, with a clasping, heart-shaped base. Fruit a red berry, 1/4 in. wide. CT, MA, ME, NH, RI, VT

*Alliaria petiolata**** (*A. officinalis*) BRASSICACEAE
Garlic mustard
Early spring, 1–3½ ft., biennial. Woodlands, thickets, floodplains, field edges, and roadsides. Invasive.

Flowers white, 1/4–1/2 in. wide, arranged in small, dense racemes. Stem leaves 1–3 in. long, triangular, sharply toothed, long-petioled; basal leaves to 4 in. long, rounded, with scalloped edges; the crushed foliage smells of garlic. Stems hairy or smooth. Fruit a linear, stalked, ascending silique, 1–2½ in. long. Native to Eurasia. CT, MA, ME, NH, RI, VT

Armoracia rusticana (*A. lapathifolia*)
BRASSICACEAE
Horse-radish
Summer, 2–3 ft., perennial. Moist fields and open, disturbed sites.

Flowers white, 1/4–1/2 in. wide, arranged in a dense, wide-branching raceme. Leaves 6–24 in. long, broadly oblong or elliptic, the basal and lower leaves long-petioled, often with undulating margins; the upper leaves short-petioled or sessile. Stems smooth, thick. Fruit an oval or elliptic silicle, 1/8–1/4 in. long. Roots pungent with horseradish scent. Native to Eurasia. CT, MA, ME, NH, RI, VT

Boechera canadensis (*Arabis canadensis*)
BRASSICACEAE
Sickle-pod, sicklepod rockcress
Spring to early summer, 1–3 ft., biennial.
Rocky forests and woodlands.

Flowers white, ¼–½ in. long, partially closed, stalked, spreading or nodding in a narrow raceme. Leaves 1–4 in. long, oval or lance-shaped, sessile, with shallow teeth. Stems hairy below, usually smooth above. Fruit a linear, flattened silique, arching downward in a sickle shape, 2½–4 in. long. CT, MA, NH (rare), RI, VT

Boechera laevigata (*Arabis laevigata*)
BRASSICACEAE
Smooth rockcress
Spring to early summer, 1–3 ft., biennial. Rocky woods, ledges, cliffs, and talus slopes, often on high-pH bedrock.

Flowers white or greenish white, ¼–½ in. long, partially closed, stalked, drooping in a narrow raceme; the petals equal to or slightly longer than the sepals. Leaves 1–6 in. long, lance-shaped, clasping, entire or with shallow teeth; about 13 stem leaves below lowermost flower. Stems smooth, with a whitish bloom. Fruit a linear, spreading or drooping silique, 2–4 in. long. CT, MA (rare), ME (rare), NH (rare), VT

Boechera missouriensis (*Arabis missouriensis,*
A. viridis) BRASSICACEAE
Green rockcress
Early spring, 8–20 in., perennial. Rocky woodlands, ledges, cliffs, and bald summits in areas of high-pH bedrock.

Flowers white or greenish white, ½–¾ in. long, partially closed, stalked, nodding in a narrow raceme; the petals about twice as long as sepals. Leaves 1–4 in. long, lance-shaped, clasping, entire or toothed; about 25 stem leaves below lowermost flower. Stems smooth, green. Fruit a linear, green, spreading or drooping silique, 2½–3½ in. long. CT, MA (rare), ME (rare), NH (rare), RI (rare), VT

Cardamine bulbosa   BRASSICACEAE
Spring cress, bulbous bitter-cress
Early spring, 6–24 in., perennial. Wet meadows, floodplains, and streambanks.

Flowers white, occasionally pink, ½ in. wide, stalked, arranged in an open raceme along upper stem. Basal leaves ¾–2 in. long, rounded, long-petioled, entire or with a few blunt teeth; stem leaves ½–1½ in. long, broadly lance-shaped, bluntly toothed, the uppermost sessile. Fruit a linear, long-stalked, spreading silique, ½–1 in. long. CT, MA (rare), NH (rare), VT

Lepidium campestre✷   BRASSICACEAE
Field peppergrass, field pepperweed
Spring to fall, 8–18 in., annual or biennial. Fields, lawns, and roadsides.

Flowers white, ⅛–¼ in. wide, on hairy, spreading stalks, arranged in a terminal raceme. Basal leaves oval, shallowly toothed or entire; stem leaves 1–1½ in. long, oval or lance-shaped, clasping, toothed or sometimes entire. Stems densely hairy. Fruit an oval, flattened, narrowly winged silicle, indented at tip, ¼ in. long. Native to Eurasia. CT, MA, ME, NH, RI, VT

Lepidium latifolium✷   BRASSICACEAE
Broad-leaved pepperweed, perennial pepperweed, dittander
Early to midsummer, 2–6 ft., biennial. Salt marshes and sea beaches; occasionally inland along salted roadways. Invasive.

Flowers white, ⅛ in wide, clustered in leafy, branching racemes. Basal leaves to 12 in. long, long-petioled, slightly toothed or entire, often withered by flowering time; stem leaves 3–8 in. long, thick, often sessile, entire or sparsely toothed. Stems and leaves smooth, grayish green. Fruit a rounded silicle, 1/16–⅛ in. long. Native to Eurasia. CT, MA, ME, NH

Lepidium virginicum BRASSICACEAE
Wild peppergrass, poor-man's pepperweed
Spring to fall, 4–20 in., annual or biennial.
Fields, lawns, and roadsides.

Flowers white, 1/16–1/8 in. wide, arranged in dense,
branching racemes. Basal leaves 1–4 in. long,
lance-shaped, sharply toothed; stem leaves 1/2–2 1/2 in.
long, lance-shaped, short-petioled, entire or with blunt
teeth. Stems smooth or with very fine hairs. Fruit a
broadly oval silicle, with a tiny indentation at tip, 1/8 in.
long. CT, MA, ME, NH, RI, VT

Thlaspi arvense* BRASSICACEAE
Field pennycress
Spring and summer, 4–20 in., annual.
Fields, lawns, and roadsides.

Flowers white, 1/8 in. wide, on smooth, ascending stalks,
arranged in narrow racemes. Leaves 1/2–4 in. long,
lance-shaped, bluntly toothed, the upper sessile, sometimes entire. Stems smooth. Fruit a rounded silicle,
winged on the margins, notched at tip, 1/4 in. long. Native
to Eurasia. CT, MA, ME, NH, RI, VT

Draba reptans BRASSICACEAE
Carolina whitlow-grass, Carolina whitlow-mustard
Early spring, 2–8 in., annual. Sandy
and rocky fields, open ledges.

Flowers white, 1/4–1/2 in. wide, arranged in a sparse terminal raceme; the petals slightly notched. Basal leaves
1/4–1 1/4 in. long, rounded, densely hairy; stem leaves tiny,
few, oval, sessile, only on lower stem. Stems hairy. Fruit a
narrow silique, 1/4–3/4 in. long. CT (rare)
   *Draba verna** (whitlow grass), a widespread, nonnative
with white flowers, has deeply notched petals and only
basal leaves, no stem leaves.

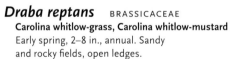

4 radial petals; leaves simple,
alternate, toothed or lobed

4 radial petals; leaves simple,
opposite, entire

4 radial petals; leaves simple, opposite, entire

Mitchella repens   RUBIACEAE
Partridge-berry
Early to midsummer, 4–12 in., trailing perennial.
Forests and woodlands.

Flowers white, ½ in. wide, paired at stem tips; the petals coated with fuzzy hairs. Leaves ½–1 in. long, evergreen, oval or rounded, leathery, with a prominent white midvein. Stems prostrate, creeping, woody. Fruit a red berry with a pair of eyelike indentations, ¼ in. wide. CT, MA, ME, NH, RI, VT

4 radial petals; leaves simple, whorled, entire

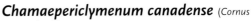

Chamaepericlymenum canadense (Cornus canadensis) CORNACEAE
Bunchberry, Canada dwarf-dogwood
Spring and early summer, 4–8 in., perennial. Moist forests and swamp edges; subalpine and alpine meadows.

True flowers tiny, greenish white, surrounded by 4 white, conspicuous, spreading, petal-like bracts, 1 in. long. Leaves ¾–3½ in. long, oval, in whorls of 4–6. Stems trailing at base, often colonial. Fruit berrylike, bright red, clustered above leaves, ¼ in. long. CT, MA, ME, NH, RI, VT

Galium aparine   RUBIACEAE
Cleavers, scratch bedstraw
Late spring and early summer, 6–40 in., perennial.
Fields, thickets, woodlands, and wetland edges.

Flowers white, ⅛ in. wide, arranged in short-branching, axillary clusters. Leaves 1–3 in. long, linear, prickly, bristle-tipped, in whorls of 6–8. Stems weak, prickly. Fruits round, bristly, ⅛ in. long. CT, MA, ME, NH, RI, VT

70

Galium asprellum RUBIACEAE
Rough bedstraw
Summer and early fall, 1½–6 ft., perennial.
Swamps, floodplain forests, and streambanks.

Flowers white, ⅛–¼ in. wide, arranged in sparse,
short-branching, axillary clusters. Leaves ½–¾ in. long,
narrowly oval, prickly, bristle-tipped, in
whorls of 6 on main stem, 4 or 5 on side
branches. Stem reclining, prickly, often
mat-forming. Fruit round, smooth, ⅟₁₆
in. long. CT, MA, ME, NH, RI, VT

Galium boreale RUBIACEAE
Northern bedstraw
Summer, 12–30 in., perennial. Rich fens and wet
meadows; fields and woodlands in high-pH soils.

Flowers white, ⅛ in. wide, arranged in dense terminal
and upper axillary clusters. Leaves 1–2 in. long, narrowly
lance-shaped, finely hairy along margins, in whorls of 4.
Stems smooth, erect. Fruit round, smooth or with short
hairs, ⅟₁₆ in. long. CT, MA (rare), ME, NH, RI (rare), VT

Galium labradoricum RUBIACEAE
Labrador bedstraw, northern bog bedstraw
Summer, 4–16 in., perennial. Cool, rich
fens and forested swamps.

Flowers white, ⅟₁₆ in. wide, arranged in
sparse, 3-flowered clusters branching
from upper axils. Leaves ½ in. long, oval
or oblong, often tilted downward, prickly
on margins, in whorls of 4. Stems erect,
mostly smooth but hairy at leaf nodes.

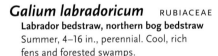

Fruits round, smooth, ⅟₁₆ in. long. CT, MA, ME, VT (rare
in all)
   Galium obtusum (blunt-leaved bedstraw) is similar
but has hairy fruits and slightly broader, blunt-tipped,
upward-tilting leaves with hairs on lower surface as well
as on margins. Grows in swamps and floodplain forests.
CT, MA, RI, VT (rare)

Galium mollugo⁎ RUBIACEAE
Wild madder, whorled bedstraw
Late spring and early summer, 1–3 ft.,
perennial. Meadows, thickets, and fields.

Flowers white, 1⁄16 in. wide, in many branching clusters,
often forming a dense inflorescence. Leaves 1⁄2–11⁄2 in.
long, narrowly lance-shaped, sharp-tipped,
smooth, mostly in whorls of 7 or 8. Stems
smooth, erect or sprawling. Fruit round,
smooth, 1⁄16 in. long. Native to Eurasia. CT,
MA, ME, NH, RI, VT

Galium palustre RUBIACEAE
Marsh bedstraw
Summer, 8–24 in., perennial. Swamps,
marshes, and wet meadows.

Flowers white, 1⁄16–1⁄8 in. wide, in many branching clusters along upper stem. Leaves 1⁄4–3⁄4 in. long,
lance-shaped or narrowly oval, slightly prickly on margins, with a blunt tip, in whorls of 2–6 (mostly 4). Stems
weak, semierect or sprawling, usually with scattered
prickles, occasionally smooth. Fruit round, smooth, 1⁄16
in. long. CT, MA, ME, NH, RI, VT

Galium triflorum RUBIACEAE
Sweet-scented bedstraw
Summer, 6–30 in., perennial. Forests and rocky slopes.

Flowers greenish white, occasionally purple, 1⁄16 in. wide,
in forking, 3-flowered clusters branching from the leaf
axils. Leaves 1⁄2–2 in. long, lance-shaped or narrowly oval,
tapering to a sharp tip, in whorls of 6. Stems weak or
reclining, usually with scattered prickles. Fruit round,
with hooked hairs, 1⁄16 in. long. CT, MA, ME, NH, RI, VT

Trapa natans* LYTHRACEAE
Water chestnut
Summer, to 12 ft. long (below water surface), annual.
Lakes, ponds, slow-moving rivers and estuaries. Invasive.

Flowers white, ½ in. wide, short-stalked, scattered among
the floating leaves. Leaves in floating rosettes, 1–2 in.
wide and long, diamond-shaped, on long, swollen petioles. Stems submerged. Fruit a brown nut, 1–1½ in. long
and wide, with 4 spiny, triangular lobes. CT, MA, NH, VT

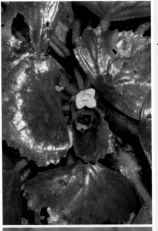

4 radial petals; leaves simple,
whorled, toothed or lobed

Draba verna* BRASSICACEAE
Whitlow grass, spring whitlow-mustard
Early spring, 2–6 in., annual. Lawns, fields, and roadsides.

Flowers white, ⅛ in. wide, arranged in sparse racemes;
the petals deeply notched. Basal leaves ¼–1¼ in. long,
oval, densely hairy; stem leaves absent. Stems smooth or
hairy. Fruit an oval silicle, ⅛–¼ in. long. Native to Eurasia. CT, MA, ME, NH, RI, VT

4 radial petals; leaves
simple, basal, entire

Cardamine parviflora BRASSICACEAE
Small-flowered bittercress
Spring, 4–12 in., annual or biennial. Dry
woods, ledges, sandy fields.

Flowers white, ⅛ in. wide, arranged in a sparse terminal
raceme. Basal leaves few, usually withered by flowering
time; stem leaves ½–1½ in. long, entirely smooth, deeply
divided into 5–8 pairs of linear leaflets. Stems smooth.
Fruit a linear, erect silique, ½ in. long. CT, MA, ME, NH,
RI, VT

    *Cardamine hirsuta** (hairy bittercress) is similar, but
has numerous, persistent basal leaves, and hairs at the
base of the leaf petioles. Grows in fields, gardens, and
roadsides. Native to Eurasia. CT, MA, ME, NH, VT

4 radial petals; leaves deeply
divided, alternate, leaflets entire

4 radial petals; leaves deeply divided, alternate, leaflets entire

Nasturtium officinale✻ (Rorippa nasturtium-aquaticum) BRASSICACEAE
Water cress, nasturtium, two-rowed water-cress
Late spring and summer, 6–40 in., perennial.
Streams, springs, and ditches. Invasive.

Flowers white, ⅛–¼ in. long, arranged in compact, branching racemes. Leaves 2–8 in. long, deeply divided into 3–9 pairs of rounded or oval leaflets, terminal leaflet usually largest. Stems succulent, floating or submerged, sometimes reclining in mud. Fruit a linear, erect silique, ½–¾ in. long, on branching stalks. Native to Europe. CT, MA, ME, NH, RI, VT

4 radial petals; leaves deeply divided, alternate, leaflets toothed or lobed

Arabidopsis lyrata (Arabis lyrata) BRASSICACEAE
Lyre-leaved rockcress, lyre-leaved thale-cress
Spring and early summer, 4–12 in., biennial or perennial.
Cliffs, open ridges, and ledges with high-pH bedrock.

Flowers white, ¼ in. wide, arranged in a sparse, branching raceme. Basal leaves 1–1½ in. long, deeply divided into sharp segments, the terminal segment often largest; stem leaves ¼–½ in. long, linear, entire. Lower stem hairy, upper stem usually smooth. Fruit a linear, ascending or spreading silique, 1–2 in. long. CT, MA (rare), VT (rare)

Capsella bursa-pastoris✻ BRASSICACEAE
Shepherd's purse
Spring to fall, 6–20 in., annual or biennial.
Fields, roadsides, and lawns.

Flowers white, ⅛–¼ in. wide, stalked, arranged in a terminal raceme. Basal leaves 2–4 in. long, deeply divided into sharp, narrow segments; stem leaves ½–2 in. long, lance-shaped, clasping, toothed or almost entire. Stems smooth. Fruit a triangular silicle, notched at the tip, ¼ in. long. Native to Eurasia and North Africa. CT, MA, ME, NH, RI, VT

Cardamine impatiens* BRASSICACEAE
Narrow-leaf bittercress
Late spring and summer, 6–30 in., biennial. Woodlands,
thickets, streambanks, and fields. Invasive.

Flowers white, ⅛ in. wide, arranged in leafy racemes.
Basal leaves divided into 2–6 pairs of oval, lobed leaflets; stem leaves sharply divided into 6–9 pairs of narrowly lance-shaped leaflets; the petioles of stem leaves
have thin, lobelike projections that
clasp the stem. Fruit a linear, stalked
silique, ½–¾ in. long. Native to Eurasia. CT, MA, ME, NH, VT

Cardamine maxima (Dentaria maxima)
BRASSICACEAE
Large toothwort
Spring, 6–16 in., perennial. Rich deciduous
forests, seepages, and floodplains.

Flowers white, occasionally pink-purple, ½–¾ in. wide,
arranged in short racemes at the top of the stem. Leaves
3, alternate, 3–7 in. long; each leaf deeply divided into
3 coarsely toothed or lobed leaflets with tiny, spreading hairs at the margins. Stems smooth. Fruit a linear,
long-stalked, spreading silique, ¾–1½ in. long. CT, MA
(rare), ME (rare), NH (rare), VT

Cardamine pensylvanica BRASSICACEAE
Pennsylvania bittercress
Spring, 2–24 in., annual or biennial. Wet meadows,
swamps, streambanks, and lake shores.

Flowers white, ⅛–¼ in. wide, arranged in short racemes
on upper stem. Leaves ½–1½ in. long, divided into 3–12
oval or lance-shaped leaflets, the terminal leaflet largest.
Upper stems sparsely hairy or smooth; the lower stems
hairy. Fruit a linear, spreading silique, ½–1 in. long. CT,
MA, ME, NH, RI, VT

4 radial petals; leaves deeply divided, alternate, leaflets toothed or lobed

4 radial petals; leaves deeply divided, opposite, leaflets entire

4 radial petals; leaves deeply divided, opposite, leaflets toothed or lobed

Cardamine pratensis✻ BRASSICACEAE
Cuckoo-flower, pink cuckoo bitter-cress
Spring, 8–20 in., perennial. Wet
meadows, lawns, and pastures.

Flowers white or pink, ¾–1 in. wide, arranged in ascending racemes; the petals tips rounded. Lower leaves to 12 in. long, long-petioled, pinnately divided into 5–30 oval, bluntly toothed or entire leaflets; the upper leaves smaller, short-petioled, with narrow leaflets. Stems smooth. Fruit a linear silique, ¾–2 in. long. Native to Eurasia. CT, MA, ME, NH, RI, VT

Clematis terniflora✻ (*Clematis dioscoreifolia*)
RANUNCULACEAE
Sweet autumn clematis, yam-leaved clematis
Late summer to fall, 6–10 ft. long, perennial
vine. Roadsides, fields, riverbanks.

Flowers white, ¾–1¼ in. wide, arranged in ascending, flat-topped clusters stalked from the leaf axils. Leaves palmately divided into 3–5 leaflets; the leaflets lance-shaped or oval, 2–3 in. long, with entire margins. Stems smooth, climbing, often densely colonial. Fruit a beaked achene covered with long, silvery hairs. Native to East Asia. CT, MA, NH, RI, VT

Cardamine diphylla (*Dentaria diphylla*)
BRASSICACEAE
Common toothwort, two-leaved toothwort
Spring, 6–16 in., perennial. Rich deciduous forests.

Flowers white, occasionally pink or purplish, 1–1½ in. wide, arranged in short racemes at the top of the stem. Leaves 2, opposite, 4–6 in. long; each leaf broadly divided into 3 coarsely toothed or lobed leaflets with tiny, flattened or ascending hairs on the margins. Fruit a linear, spreading or ascending silique, ¾–1½ in. long. CT, MA, ME, NH, VT

Clematis virginiana RANUNCULACEAE
Virgin's bower, Virginia virgin's-bower
Summer, 6–10 ft. long, perennial vine. Thickets,
forest edges, swamps, and pond shores.

Flowers white, ½–¾ in. wide, ascending from leaf
axils in long-stalked, flat-topped clusters. Leaves palmately divided into 3 leaflets; the leaflets 1½–4 in. long,
coarsely toothed, stalked, long-pointed. Stems hairy,
climbing or scrambling, the lower part woody. Fruit a
cluster of tiny achenes with long, feathery plumes. CT,
MA, ME, NH, RI, VT
  Clematis ternifolia (sweet autumn clematis) is similar
but has entire leaflet margins.

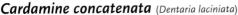

Cardamine concatenata (*Dentaria laciniata*)
BRASSICACEAE
Cut-leaved toothwort
Early spring, 4–22 in., perennial. Rich, deciduous forests.

Flowers white, occasionally pink or light purple, ½–¾
in. wide, arranged in a long-stalked, nodding, terminal raceme. Leaves 1½–4 in. long, in a solitary whorl of
3; each leaf deeply divided into 3–5 saw-toothed leaflets.
Stems smooth or slightly hairy. Fruit an ascending, linear
silique, ¾–2 in. long. CT, MA, ME (rare), NH (rare), VT

Sericocarpus linifolius (*Aster solidagineus*)
ASTERACEAE
Narrow-leaved white-topped aster
Summer, 8–24 in., perennial. Sandy
fields, woodlands, and clearings.

Flower heads ½ in. wide, with 3–6 white rays (usually
4 or 5) in a sparsely flowered, flat-topped cluster. Leaves
¾–3¼ in. long, narrowly oblong, sessile or short-petioled.
Stems smooth. CT, MA, NH (rare), RI

4 radial petals; leaves deeply divided,
opposite, leaflets toothed or lobed

4 radial petals; leaves deeply divided,
whorled, leaflets toothed or lobed

5 radial petals; leaves simple,
alternate, entire

Hackelia virginiana   BORAGINACEAE
Virginia stickseed
Midsummer to early fall, 1–4 ft., biennial.
Rocky woodlands, talus slopes, and cliffs.

Flowers white or pale blue, 1/16–1/8 in wide, arranged in branching, divergent, one-sided racemes. Lower leaves 2–6 in. long, to 3½ in. wide, lance-shaped or oval, with petioles; the upper leaves smaller and sessile. Stems hairy. Fruits oval, burlike, 1/8 in. long, the margins and faces covered with small prickles. CT, MA, NH (rare), VT
 Hackelia deflexa (northern stickseed), a rare species, is similar. The best distinguishing feature is the fruit, which is prickly on the margins but smooth or with only a few prickles on the faces. The flowers are sometimes a deeper blue, the leaves are narrower (to 1¼ in. wide), and the bloom period is late spring to late summer. Grows in high-pH talus slopes, rocky woodland clearings, and cliff bases. ME, VT

Lithospermum officiale∗   BORAGINACEAE
European gromwell
Spring and summer, 1½–3 ft., perennial. Fields, roadsides, and open, disturbed sites.

Flowers creamy, yellowish white, ¼ in. wide, crowded in upper leaf axils. Leaves ½–3 in. long, lance-shaped or narrowly oval, sessile. Stems downy. Fruit capsulelike, white or brown, often shining, 1/8–¼ in. long. Native to Europe and western Asia. CT, MA, ME, NH, RI, VT

Myosotis verna   BORAGINACEAE
Spring forget-me-not, early scorpion-grass
Spring, 3–16 in., annual or biennial. Dry fields, ledges, and woodland openings, often in sandy or rocky soils.

Flowers white, 1/8 in. wide, arranged in coiled clusters on upper stem; the hairy sepals beneath the petals uneven in length (3 longer, 2 shorter). Leaves ½–1 in. long, oval, hairy. Stems downy. Fruit capsulelike, less than 1/8 in. long. CT, MA, ME, NH (rare), RI, VT (rare)

Comandra umbellata COMANDRACEAE
Bastard-toadflax
Spring and early summer, 4–12 in., perennial.
Cliffs, ledges, fields, and woodlands.

Flowers white, ⅛ in. wide, arranged in flattish or rounded
clusters at the top of the stem. Leaves ½–2 in. long,
lance-shaped or oval, sessile or very short-petioled, pale
green. Stems smooth. Fruit berrylike, rounded, ⅛–¼ in.,
brown when ripe. Semiparasitic on roots of other plants.
CT, MA, ME, NH, RI, VT

Calystegia spithamaea CONVOLVULACEAE
Upright bindweed, low bindweed
Late spring and summer, 4–18 in., perennial.
Fields and sandy grasslands.

Flowers white, 1½–2 in. wide, funnel-shaped, stalked
from lower leaf axils. Leaves 1–3 in. long, oval or
lance-shaped, often hairy, heart-shaped at base, without
basal lobes. Stems semierect, hairy. Fruit a rounded capsule, ½ in. long. CT, MA, ME, NH, VT (rare in all)

*Convolvulus arvensis** CONVOLVULACEAE
Field bindweed
Summer and fall, to 3 ft. long, perennial vine.
Fields, thickets, and disturbed, open sites.

Flowers white or pink, ¾ in. wide, funnel-shaped, stalked
from leaf axils; the 2 bracts below the flower tiny, linear,
on flower stalk beneath the sepals. Leaves ½–2 in. long,
triangular, with flared basal lobes. Stems smooth or
hairy, climbing, forming a dense, twining growth. Fruit a
dry, oval capsule, ¼–⅜ in. long. Native to Europe. CT, MA,
ME, NH, RI, VT

Arctostaphylos uva-ursi   ERICACEAE
Bearberry, kinnikinnick
Spring and early summer, to 3 ft. long, shrub. Sandy or rocky fields and thickets, open ridges and summits.

Flowers white or pink, ¼–⅜ in. long, bell-shaped, nodding in small, stalked clusters. Leaves ½–1 in. long, oval or paddle-shaped, leathery, evergreen. Stems creeping, mat-forming, with reddish, shredding bark. Fruit a round, bright red berry, ¼ in. wide. CT, MA, ME, NH, RI, VT

Epigaea repens   ERICACEAE
Trailing arbutus, mayflower
Early spring, 8–16 in., perennial. Woodland openings, trailsides, and ridgetops in sandy or rocky soils.

Flowers white or pink-tinged, ½ in. wide, fragrant, in small, stem-tip clusters close to ground. Leaves 1–3 in. long, oval, leathery, evergreen. Stems trailing, densely hairy. Fruit a round capsule, ¼ in. wide. CT, MA, ME, NH, RI, VT

Gaylussacia bigeloviana (*G. dumosa*) ERICACEAE
Dwarf huckleberry
Spring and early summer, 8–20 in., shrub.
Bogs, fens, and sandy thickets.

Flowers white or pink-tinged, ⅜ in. long, bell-shaped, arranged in dangling clusters; the sepals and flower stalks with gland-tipped hairs. Leaves ¾–2 in. long, oval or elliptic, shiny, gland-dotted, with a pointed tip. Fruit a black berry with scattered hairs, ¼ in. long. CT (rare), MA, ME, NH (rare), RI (rare)

Rhododendron groenlandicum

(*Ledum groenlandicum*) ERICACEAE
Labrador-tea
Midspring to early summer, 1–3 ft., shrub. Bogs,
swamps, river and lake shores, and mountain ridges.

Flowers white, ⅜ in. wide, with protruding stamens,
arranged in dense, radiating clusters at tops of stems.
Leaves 1–2 in. long, lance-shaped, with inrolled margins
and a thick coating of white or rusty hairs on the undersurface. Stems densely hairy, wide-branching. Fruit an
oval capsule, ¼–⅜ in. long. CT (rare), MA, ME, NH, VT

Vaccinium myrtilloides   ERICACEAE

Velvet-leaf blueberry
Spring and early summer, 1–3 ft., shrub. Forests,
woodlands, thickets, and mountain summits.

Flowers white, occasionally greenish or pink-tinged, ¼
in. long, bell-shaped, arranged in small, nodding clusters
at stem tips. Leaves ¾–2 in. long, oval, with entire margins, downy on the undersurface. Stems branching, the
new growth densely hairy. Fruit a sour blue berry with a
whitish bloom, ¼ in. wide. CT (rare), MA, ME, NH, VT

Vaccinium pallidum   ERICACEAE

Hillside blueberry, early lowbush blueberry
Spring and early summer, 1–3 ft., shrub. Forests,
woodlands, ledges, thickets, and fields.

Flowers white, sometimes pink, ¼ in. long, bell-shaped,
arranged in small, nodding clusters at stem tips. Leaves
¾–2 in. long, oval or rounded, pale and smooth underneath, usually entire but occasionally with a few fine
teeth on the margins. Stems branching, the new growth
smooth or slightly hairy. Fruit a sweet blue berry, ¼ in.
wide. CT, MA, ME, NH, RI, VT

5 radial petals; leaves simple, alternate, entire

Euphorbia corollata EUPHORBIACEAE
Flowering spurge
Summer and fall, 1–3 ft., perennial. Open
woodlands, fields, and roadsides.

True flowers tiny, yellow-orange, enclosed by 5 conspicuous, white, petal-like bracts, ¼ in. wide, arranged in a
forking cluster at the top of the stem. Lower leaves 1–2½
in. long, lance-shaped; the leaves at the base of the flower
branches whorled. Stems hairy or smooth, exuding a
milky sap when broken. Fruit a rounded capsule, ⅛ in.
long. Native to much of eastern and central North America, introduced in New England. CT, MA, ME, NH, RI, VT

Nymphoides cordata MENYANTHACEAE
Floating heart, little floating-heart
Summer and early fall, slightly above water surface,
perennial. Ponds, lakes, and slow streams.

Flowers white with yellow centers, ¼–½ in. wide stalked
just above the floating leaves. Leaves ½–3 in. long, floating, rounded, notched at base; a whorl of spurlike, subsurface tubers often present just below leaves. Stems
slender, submerged. Fruit an oval capsule, ¹⁄₁₆–⅛ in.
long. CT, MA, ME, NH, RI, VT

Parnassia glauca PARNASSIACEAE
Grass-of-Parnassus, fen grass-of-Parnassus
Midsummer to early fall, 6–24 in., perennial. Fens,
seepages, and wet meadows in high-pH soils.

Flowers white, with fine green veins, ¾–1½ in. wide, solitary, long-stalked at top of mostly leafless stems. Basal
leaves 1–2 in. long, rounded, long-petioled, in a rosette;
the single stem leaf smaller than basals, clasping lower
stem. Stems smooth. Fruit a rounded capsule. CT, MA,
ME, NH (rare), VT

Phytolacca americana   PHYTOLACCACEAE
American pokeweed
Summer, 3–10 ft., perennial. Thickets,
fields, and roadsides.

Flowers greenish white, ¼ in. wide, arranged in long
racemes drooping from the leaf axils. Leaves 4–12 in.
long, lance-shaped or oval. Stems red, smooth. Fruit a
deep purple, succulent, toxic (to humans) berry, ¼–½ in.
wide. Stems and leaves are also poisonous. CT, MA, ME,
NH, RI, VT

Samolus valerandi (*S. floribundus*)
THEOPHRASTACEAE
Water pimpernel, brookweed
Late spring to fall, 4–20 in., perennial. Salt
marshes, estuaries, and tidal mudflats;
occasionally in freshwater wetlands.

Flowers white, ⅛ in. wide, long-stalked, arranged in open
racemes. Leaves 1–2 in. long, oval or rounded, fleshy,
broadest toward tip. Stems smooth. Fruit a round capsule, ⅛ in. long. CT, MA, ME (rare), NH (rare), RI, VT (rare)

Hydrocotyle americana   APIACEAE
Water pennywort, American marsh pennywort
Summer, 2–5 in., perennial. Woodland seepages,
marshes, wet meadows, and shorelines.

Flowers ⅛ in. wide, greenish white, in small, sessile,
clusters at base of leaf petioles. Leaves ½–2 in. long,
rounded, shiny, notched at base, with scalloped or bluntly
toothed margins. Stems creeping, smooth, often colonial.
Fruit capsulelike, ribbed, 1⁄16–⅛ in. long. CT, MA, ME, NH,
RI, VT

Sericocarpus asteroides (Aster paternus)
ASTERACEAE
Toothed white-topped aster
Summer, 6–24 in., perennial. Fields,
grasslands, and dry woodlands.

Flower heads ½ in. wide, with 4–8 (often 5) white rays,
arranged in a branching, flattish cluster. Basal and lower
stem leaves ¾–4 in. long, lance-shaped or spoon-shaped,
long-petioled, with a few blunt teeth; the upper leaves
smaller, often sessile. Stems hairy. CT, MA, ME (rare),
NH, RI

Hydrophyllum canadense   BORAGINACEAE
**Broad-leaved waterleaf, maple-leaved waterleaf, blunt-
leaved waterleaf**
Early summer, 6–24 in., perennial. Rich,
moist forests and river floodplains.

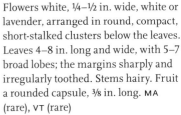

Flowers white, ¼–½ in. wide, white or
lavender, arranged in round, compact,
short-stalked clusters below the leaves.
Leaves 4–8 in. long and wide, with 5–7
broad lobes; the margins sharply and
irregularly toothed. Stems hairy. Fruit
a rounded capsule, ⅜ in. long. MA
(rare), VT (rare)

Sicyos angulatus   CUCURBITACEAE
One-seeded bur-cucumber
Summer, to 20 ft. long, annual vine. Floodplains,
thickets, woodland margins, and pond shores.

Flowers greenish white, ¼–½ in. wide, arranged in
stalked clusters from leaf axils; the stalks with glandular
hairs. Leaves to 8 in. long and wide, notched at base, with
3–5 broad, blunt lobes; the leaf margins finely toothed.
Stems climbing, sticky, hairy, with 3-forked tendrils.
Fruits spiny, oval, ½ in. long, in tight, round clusters. CT,
MA, ME, NH, RI, VT
  Echinocystis lobata (wild cucumber) is similar, but
the flowers have 6 petals, the leaves have 5 triangular,
sharp-pointed lobes, the stems are smooth, and the spiny,
oval fruits are solitary and larger (1½–2 in. long). Grows
in floodplains, wet meadows, and thickets. CT, MA, ME,
NH, RI, VT

Chamaedaphne calyculata ERICACEAE
Leatherleaf
Early spring, 2–4 ft., shrub. Bogs, acidic
swamps, and peaty pond and lake shores.

Flowers white, ¼ in. long, bell-shaped, nodding,
arranged in leafy, one-sided racemes. Leaves ½–2 in.
long, lance-shaped or oval, leathery, evergreen, finely
toothed; the undersurfaces with rusty scales. Stems
widely branching, the new growth hairy. Fruit a rounded
capsule, ⅛–¼ in. long. CT, MA, ME, NH, RI, VT

Gaultheria procumbens ERICACEAE
Wintergreen, teaberry, checkerberry
Summer, 2–6 in., perennial. Forests,
woodlands, and clearings.

Flowers white, ¼–½ in. long, bell-shaped, nodding, usually in clusters of 2 or 3, dangling below the leaves. Leaves
1–2 in. long, oval, evergreen, with a strong wintergreen
fragrance. Stems smooth or hairy, woody. Fruit a bright
red, wintergreen-flavored berry, ¼–½ in. long. CT, MA,
ME, NH, RI, VT

Vaccinium angustifolium ERICACEAE
Common lowbush blueberry, late lowbush blueberry
Late spring to midsummer, 4–24 in., shrub.
Forests, woodlands, thickets, and fields,
from low elevations to alpine zones.

Flowers white, ¼ in. long, bell-shaped, arranged in nodding clusters at stem tips. Leaves ½–1¼ in. long and
¼–¾ in. wide, lance-shaped, smooth, green underneath, with very fine teeth on the margins. Stems widely
branching, smooth. Fruit a sweet blue berry, ¼ in. wide.
CT, MA, ME, NH, RI, VT
   Vaccinium boreale (northern blueberry), a very rare species, is similar, but shorter (only to 4 in. tall), with very
narrow leaves (⅛–¼ in. wide). It blooms 10–20 days earlier than *V. angustifolium* where the 2 species co-occur. Its
distribution is limited to high elevation, alpine and subalpine zones in ME, NH, VT, and rocky coastal headlands
in ME.

5 radial petals; leaves simple, alternate, toothed or lobed

Penthorum sedoides   PENTHORACEAE
Ditch stonecrop
Midsummer to early fall, 12–30 in., perennial. Swamps, marshes, wet meadows, and river and lake shores.

Flowers white or yellowish green, ¼ in. wide, arranged in branching terminal and axillary clusters, 1–3 in. long. Leaves 2–4 in. long, lance-shaped, finely and sharply serrated. Stems green or red, smooth or slightly hairy. Fruit a 5-parted capsule, ¼ in. wide, bright red in fall. CT, MA, ME, NH, RI (rare), VT

Prunus pumila (*P. depressa*) ROSACEAE
Sand cherry, sandbar cherry, dwarf sand plum
Spring, 4–24 in., shrub. Rocky ice-scoured river shores and ledges; sandy roadsides.

Flowers white, ½ in. wide, in small, ground-level clusters. Leaves 1½–4 in. long, lance- or narrowly lance-shaped, 3–6 times as long as wide, smooth underneath. Stems prostrate, mat-forming, with short, upright branches. Fruits black, berrylike, ⅜ in. wide. MA (rare), ME, NH

Prunus susquehanae (Appalachian sand plum, Susquehanna sand cherry) is similar but has taller, more upright stems (to 3 ft. high) and broader leaves (2–3 times as long as wide). Grows in sandy or rocky clearings, thickets, fields, beaches, and roadsides. CT, MA, ME, NH, RI (rare), VT (rare)

Rubus chamaemorus   ROSACEAE
Cloudberry, baked apple-berry
Summer, 2–12 in., perennial. Alpine summits and northern, coastal bogs.

Flowers white, ¾–1 in. wide, solitary, long-stalked. Leaves 1–3½ in. long and wide, with 5–7 broad lobes and sharply toothed, crinkled margins. Stems woody, creeping at base. Fruits berrylike, red, yellow, or orange, succulent, ½–¾ in. wide. ME, NH (rare)

Spiraea alba (*S. latifolia*) ROSACEAE
Meadowsweet, white meadowsweet
Summer, 1–5 ft., shrub. Fields, thickets, wet
meadows, bogs, marshes, and alpine summits.

Flowers white or pink, ⅛–¼ in. wide, arranged in a dense
panicle, 2–6 in. long. Leaves 1–3 in. long, lance-shaped or
oval, sharply toothed, green on the undersurface. Stems
woody, smooth. Fruit a brown follicle, ¼ in. long. CT, MA,
ME, NH, RI, VT

Saxifraga paniculata (*S. aizoon*)
SAXIFRAGACEAE
White alpine saxifrage, white mountain saxifrage
Summer, 4–12 in., perennial. Alpine and subalpine
ledges and cliffs, usually on high-pH bedrock.

Flowers white, ¼ in. wide, in branched clusters; the petals sometimes with red or orange spots. Basal leaves
½–1½ in. long, oval, finely toothed, the tips whitened
with crusted lime; stem leaves few (or absent), hugging
stem. Stems hairy. Fruit a capsule, ¼ in. long. ME, NH, VT
(rare in all)

Solanum carolinense SOLANACEAE
Horse nettle, Carolina nightshade
Summer and early fall, 1–4 ft., perennial.
Dry fields and disturbed, open sites.

Flowers white, occasionally violet, ¾ in. wide, arranged
in small, erect clusters; the petals with 5 yellow
stamen-cones in center. Leaves 2½–5 in. long, triangular or oval, spiny underneath. Stems hairy, with scattered
spines. Fruit a yellow or orange berry, ½ in. long, poisonous. CT, MA, ME, NH, RI, VT

5 radial petals; leaves simple,
alternate, toothed or lobed

Solanum ptycanthum   SOLANACEAE
Eastern black nightshade
Summer, 6–24 in., annual. Woodlands, fields, beaches, shorelines, and wetland margins.

Flowers white, ¼–½ in. wide, with reflexed petals, arranged in short, drooping clusters of 1–4 flowers; the petals with a single yellow cone of fused stamens in the center. Leaves ¾–3 in. long, triangular, broadly and bluntly toothed. Stems smooth or hairy. Fruit a drooping black berry, ¼ in. long. CT, MA, ME, NH, RI, VT
   *Solanum nigrum** (black nightshade) is very similar, but has 5–7 flowers per cluster and slightly larger fruits (⅜–½ in. long). Native to Europe. Occurs in coastal shorelines. MA, ME

Apocynum cannabinum   APOCYNACEAE
Indian hemp, hemp dogbane
Summer, 1½–5 ft., perennial. Fields, thickets, river shores, and open woodlands.

Flowers greenish white, ⅛–¼ in. long, arranged in short-stalked, ascending clusters; the petals erect or spreading slightly, fused for much of their length. Leaves 2–4 in. long, oval, sessile or on short petioles, with prominent veins and a pointed tip. Stems reddish, smooth; stems and leaves exude a milky sap when broken. Fruit a linear, slightly curved follicle, 4½–8 in. long. CT, MA, ME, NH, RI, VT

Asclepias exaltata   APOCYNACEAE
Poke milkweed, tall milkweed
Summer, 2–6 ft., perennial. Woodlands, thickets, and field edges.

Flowers greenish white, ½–¾ in. long, clustered on stalked, nodding umbels; the 5 greenish petals reflexed and the 5 white hoods erect, with tiny, projecting horns. Leaves 4–8 in. long, oval, tapering at both ends, smooth or slightly hairy on the undersurface. Stems smooth or slightly hairy; stems and leaves exude milky sap when broken. Fruit a thick, long-pointed follicle, 4–6 in. long, ascending on bent stalk. CT, MA, ME, NH, RI (rare), VT (rare)

88

Arenaria serpyllifolia* CARYOPHYLLACEAE
Thyme-leaved sandwort
Spring and summer, 2–10 in., annual.
Cliffs, ledges, fields, and gardens.

Flowers white, ⅛ in. wide, loosely clustered in ascending, forking branches from the leaf axils; the petals shorter than the sharply pointed sepals. Leaves ⅛–¼ in. long, oval, sessile, with pointed tips. Stems purple, finely hairy. Fruit a dry, oval capsule, ⅛ in. long. Native to Eurasia. CT, MA, ME, NH, RI, VT

Cerastium arvense* CARYOPHYLLACEAE
Field chickweed
Spring and summer, 10–16 in., perennial.
Fields, lawns, and roadsides.

Flowers white, ½ in. wide, in stalked, branching, terminal and axillary clusters; the petals notched, longer than the sepals. Leaves 1–2½ in. long, lance-shaped, sessile. Stems hairy, sometimes creeping at base. Fruit a finely toothed, cylindrical capsule, ¼–½ in. long. Native to Eurasia. CT, MA, ME, NH, RI, VT
    Cerastium strictum (American field chickweed) is similar but on average shorter (2–8 in.), with slightly smaller flowers (¼–½ in. wide). Grows on cliffs, talus slopes, rocky beaches, and coastal headlands. CT, MA, ME, NH (rare), RI, VT

Cerastium fontanum* (C. vulgatum)
CARYOPHYLLACEAE
Mouse-ear chickweed
Spring to fall, 6–20 in., perennial. Fields, lawns, roadsides, and disturbed, open sites.

Flowers white, ¼ in. wide, erect, arranged in forking branches on upper stem; the petals notched, about equal in length to the hairy sepals. Leaves ½–1½ in. long, oval, sessile, hairy. Stems densely hairy, creeping at base. Fruit a cylindrical, toothed capsule, ¼–½ in. long. Native to Europe. CT, MA, ME, NH, RI, VT

5 radial petals; leaves simple, opposite, entire

89

Cerastium nutans CARYOPHYLLACEAE
Nodding chickweed
Mid to late spring, 4–24 in., annual. Rocky
woods, ridges, cliffs, and talus slopes.

Flowers white, nodding or erect, ¼ in. wide, arranged
in forking branches on upper stem; the petals notched,
about equal in length to the hairy sepals. Leaves ½–2 in.
long, lance-shaped, hairy. Stems sticky-hairy, weak, but
not creeping at base. Fruit a cylindrical, toothed capsule,
½ in. long. CT, MA (rare), VT (rare)

Honckenya peploides (*Arenaria peploides*)
CARYOPHYLLACEAE
Seabeach sandwort, seaside sandwort
Summer, 4–20 in., perennial. Sea beaches and dunes.

Flowers white, ¼ in. wide, solitary or in small,
few-flowered clusters at the top of the stem; the sepals
equal to or longer than petals. Leaves ¼–2 in. long, oval,
crowded, succulent, with sharp-pointed tips. Stems
fleshy, erect or creeping, often densely colonial. Fruit a
brown, broadly oval capsule, ⅛–¼ in. long. CT (rare), MA,
ME, RI (rare)

Minuartia groenlandica (*Arenaria groenlandica*)
CARYOPHYLLACEAE
Mountain sandwort, mountain sandplant
Summer, 2–6 in., perennial. Rocky alpine summits,
ledges, and cliffs, usually at elevations over 3500 ft.

Flowers white, ½ in. wide, in branching clusters; the petals slightly notched, longer than the sepals. Leaves ¼–1
in. long, linear, blunt-tipped; the basal leaves clumped
and matted, forming tufts in rock crevices. Stems
smooth. Fruit a rounded to oval capsule, ⅛–¼ in. long.
ME, NH, VT (rare in all)
   Minuartia glabra (Appalachian sandwort) is very similar but has slightly smaller flowers (¼–⅜ in. wide) and
little or no tuft-forming leaf growth. Grows on rocky
summits and ledges, at elevations less than 3500 feet. CT,
ME, NH, RI (rare in all)

Minuartia michauxii (*Arenaria stricta*)
CARYOPHYLLACEAE
Rock sandwort, Michaux's sandplant
Summer, 2–12 in., annual or perennial. Open ledges
and gravels, usually on limestone or trap rock.

Flowers white, ¼–⅜ in. wide, loosely clustered on slender, forking branches; the petals much longer than the
sepals. Leaves ¼–1 in. long, linear, stiff, pointed, with
clusters of tiny leaves tucked in axils of the paired, primary leaves. Stems smooth. Fruit a dry, oval capsule,
⅛–¼ in. long. CT, MA (rare), ME, NH (rare), RI (rare), VT

Moehringia lateriflora (*Arenaria lateriflora*)
CARYOPHYLLACEAE
Grove sandwort, blunt-leaved sandwort
Spring and summer, 2–16 in., perennial. Woodlands,
thickets, shorelines, and field edges.

Flowers white, ¼–½ in. wide, in branching, 1- to
6-flowered clusters; the petals longer than the sepals.
Leaves ½–1 in. long, oval, hairy, blunt at the tips. Stems
weak, finely hairy. Fruit a dry oval capsule, ⅛–¼ in. long.
CT, MA, ME, NH, RI, VT (rare)

Moehringia macrophylla (*Arenaria macrophylla*)
CARYOPHYLLACEAE
Large-leaved grove-sandwort
Spring and summer, 2–6 in., perennial.
Cliffs, talus slopes, and open ledges.

Flowers white, ¼–½ in. wide, solitary or in a sparse
cluster; the sepals equal to or longer than petals. Leaves
¾–2½ in. long, lance-shaped, smooth, with pointed tips.
Stems weak, hairy. Fruit an oval or rounded capsule,
⅛–¼ in. long. CT, MA, VT (rare in all)

Myosoton aquaticum⁕   CARYOPHYLLACEAE
Giant chickweed
Summer and fall, 12–30 in., perennial. Stream
corridors, floodplains, and swamps.

Flowers white, ½ in. wide, long-stalked, solitary or in
sparse clusters at the top of the stem and upper axils;
the petals deeply notched, longer than the sepals. Leaves
½–2 in. long, oval; the lower leaves with short petioles;
the upper leaves sessile. Stems hairy, erect or sprawling.
Fruit an oval capsule, ¼–½ in. long. Native to Europe. CT,
MA, NH, VT

Paronychia argyrocoma   CARYOPHYLLACEAE
Silverling, silver whitlow-wort
Summer, 2–12 in., Rocky or sandy ridges,
from lower elevations to subalpine zones;
occasionally along river shores.

Flowers whitish green, ¼ in. wide, clustered at stem tips,
camouflaged by conspicuous, silvery, petal-like bracts.
Leaves ½–1½ in. long, linear or narrowly lance-shaped,
with silken hairs. Stems silvery-hairy, branching,
mat-forming. Fruit an oval capsule, less than ⅛ in. long.
MA, ME, NH (rare in all)

Paronychia canadensis   CARYOPHYLLACEAE
Forked chickweed, smooth forked whitlow-wort
Summer and early fall, 3–16 in., annual. Rocky or
sandy woodlands and ridges with dry soils.

Flowers greenish white, 1/16–⅛ in. wide, arranged in tiny,
axillary clusters. Leaves ¼–1 in. long, oval, blunt-tipped,
tapering to the base, with dark glandular dots. Stems
smooth, with finely forking branches. Fruit a rounded
capsule, about 1/16 in. long. CT, MA, NH (rare), RI, VT
    Paronychia fastigiata (hairy forked chickweed) is simi-
lar but has hairy stems and lance-shaped, pointed leaves.
Grows in grasslands and dry woodlands. CT (rare), MA
(rare)

Sagina nodosa CARYOPHYLLACEAE
Knotted pearlwort
Summer, 1–8 in., perennial. Coastal
headlands and beaches.

Flowers white, ¼ in. wide, solitary or in sparse, forking
clusters; the petals about twice as long as sepals. Lower
leaves ¼–1 in. long, linear, clumped at the base; the
upper leaves tiny, sessile, forming "knots" at the nodes.
Stems weak, hairy or smooth. Fruit an oval capsule, ⅛ in.
long. The native subspecies (subsp. *borealis*) has smooth
stems and leaves (see photo); the nonnative subspecies
(subsp. *nodosa*) has glandular-hairy stems and leaves. MA,
ME, NH

Saponaria officinalis✳ CARYOPHYLLACEAE
Soapwort, bouncing-bet
Summer, 12–30 in., perennial. Fields,
roadsides, and disturbed, open sites.

Flowers white or pink, 1 in. wide, in dense, branching clusters; the petals slightly notched; the calyx tube
green or red-tinged, narrow, ¾–1 in. long. Leaves 2½–4
in. long, broadly oval, sessile or clasping; leaves contain
saponin, which, mixed with water, makes a soapy lather.
Stems smooth. Fruit a cylindrical capsule, ½–¾ in. long.
Native to Eurasia. CT, MA, ME, NH, RI, VT

Silene antirrhina CARYOPHYLLACEAE
Sleepy catchfly, sleepy campion
Summer, 8–30 in., annual. Sandy fields,
roadsides, ledges, and woodlands.

Flowers white or pink, ¼–⅜ in. wide, arranged in a
sparse, ascending inflorescence; the petals notched,
spreading just above the narrow, ribbed calyx sac. Leaves
1–3 in. long, lance-shaped. Stems hairy, with dark, sticky
bands beneath upper leaf nodes. Fruit a capsule, ¼ in.
long. CT, MA, ME, NH, RI, VT

Silene latifolia* (Lychnis alba) CARYOPHYLLACEAE
White campion, evening lychnis
Late spring to fall, 1–3 ft., biennial or perennial. Fields, meadows, roadsides, and disturbed, open sites.

Flowers white or pink, 1 in. wide, fragrant, open in the evening, arranged in branching panicles; the petals deeply notched; the calyx sac inflated, hairy, with 10–20 reddish veins. Leaves 1–4 in. long, broadly lance-shaped, hairy. Stems hairy, sticky. Fruit a golden-brown capsule, ¾ in. long. Native to Europe. CT, MA, ME, NH, RI, VT

Silene vulgaris* (S. cucubalus) CARYOPHYLLACEAE
Bladder campion
Spring and summer, 6–24 in., perennial. Fields, roadsides, and disturbed, open habitats.

Flowers white, ½–¾ in. wide, arranged in open panicles; the petals deeply notched; the calyx sac inflated, smooth, bulb-shaped, papery, with 20 primary veins and an intricate network of secondary veins. Leaves 1–3 in. long, oval, sessile or clasping. Stems smooth or slightly downy. Fruit a finely toothed capsule, ¼–½ in. long. Native to Eurasia. CT, MA, ME, NH, RI, VT

Stellaria alsine CARYOPHYLLACEAE
Bog stitchwort, bog chickweed
Spring and summer, 4–16 in., perennial. Streamsides, seepages, swamps, and ditches.

Flowers white, ¼ in. wide, arranged in sparse, branching clusters from leaf axils; the petals deeply cleft, shorter than the sharp-pointed, green sepals. Leaves ¼–1 in. long, oval, fleshy, sessile. Stems creeping, smooth. Fruit a slender capsule, ⅛ in. long. CT, MA, ME, NH, RI, VT

Stellaria borealis CARYOPHYLLACEAE
Northern stitchwort, boreal stitchwort
Late spring and summer, 4–16 in., perennial. Bogs,
alpine seepages, wet meadows, and forested swamps.

Flowers white, ¼ in. wide, arranged in sparse clusters
at the top of the stem; the petals notched, often absent,
when present, shorter than the sharp-pointed green
sepals. Leaves ½–2 in. long, lance-shaped, not fleshy.
Stems weak, branching, smooth, erect or reclining. Fruit
an oval capsule, ¼ in. long. CT (rare), MA (rare), ME, NH,
RI, VT

Stellaria graminea* CARYOPHYLLACEAE
Lesser stitchwort, grass-leaved stitchwort
Spring to fall, 8–18 in., perennial. Fields,
meadows, streambanks and roadsides.

Flowers white, ¼–½ in. wide, arranged in open, forking
branches on upper stem; the petals deeply cleft, about
equal to the strongly veined sepals. Leaves ½–2 in. long,
linear or narrowly lance-shaped (at least 5 times as long
as wide), broadest at base. Stems smooth, weakly erect
or creeping. Fruit an oval, greenish or straw-colored capsule, ⅛–¼ in. long. Native to Europe. CT, MA, ME, NH,
RI, VT

Native *Stellaria longifolia* (long-leaved stitchwort) is
similar, but the flowers are mostly on axillary branches
(not the upper stem), the sepals are weakly veined,
the leaves are broadest at the middle, and the stems
are roughened at the edges. Grows in moist meadows,
marshes, riverbanks, and wetland edges. CT, MA, ME, NH,
RI, VT

Stellaria media* CARYOPHYLLACEAE
Common chickweed, common starwort
Early spring to late fall, 4–16 in., annual or perennial.
Fields, roadsides, and open, disturbed sites.

Flowers white, ¼–½ in. wide, solitary or in open clusters, branching from upper stem; the petals deeply cleft,
shorter than the sepals. Leaves ¼–1 in. long, oval (less
than 4 times as long as wide), the lower on petioles, the
upper sessile. Stems weak, finely hairy, erect or reclining. Fruit an oval, greenish brown capsule, ⅛–¼ in. long.
Native to Eurasia. CT, MA, ME, NH, RI, VT

*Sedum ternatum** CRASSULACEAE
Woodland stonecrop, wild stonecrop
Spring, 3–8 in., perennial. Woodland
edges, fields, mossy rocks.

Flowers white, ¼–⅜ in. long, star-shaped, in branching,
3-forked clusters; the petal number occasionally 4. Leaves
½–¾ in. long, oval, fleshy; the leaf pattern is sometimes
alternate or in whorls of 3. Stems smooth, succulent,
creeping at base. Fruit a narrowly oval pod, ¼ in. long.
Native to much of eastern and central North America, but
introduced in New England. CT, MA, ME, VT

*Galinsoga quadriradiata** (*G. ciliata*)
ASTERACEAE
Common quickweed, shaggy soldier
Early summer to fall, 6–18 in., annual. Gardens,
fields, roadsides, and disturbed, open sites.

Flower heads ¼ in. in. wide, with 4 or 5 small white rays
around a central yellow disk; the rays with 3 tiny teeth at
the tips. Leaves 1–2½ in. long, oval, long-petioled, sharply
and coarsely toothed. Stems densely hairy with spreading
hairs. Native to South America. CT, MA, ME, NH, RI, VT
   Galinsoga parviflora* (lesser quickweed) is similar,
but the stems are mostly smooth or finely hairy with
pressed-in hairs, and the leaves are more shallowly and
evenly toothed. Native to Central America. CT, MA, ME,
NH, RI, VT

Mitella diphylla SAXIFRAGACEAE
Two-leaved bishop's-cap, two-leaved miterwort
Early spring, 6–16 in., perennial. Rich, moist forests.

Flowers white, ⅛–¼ in. wide, in a slender, leafless, terminal spike; the petals with delicate, snowflakelike fringes.
Basal leaves 1–3½ in. long, roughly triangular, with a
tapering tip, long-petioled, coarsely toothed; the single
pair of stem leaves smaller, sessile. Stems hairy. Fruit a
spherical capsule, ⅛ in. long, holding a cluster of black
seeds. CT, MA, NH, VT

Verbena urticifolia   VERBENACEAE
White vervain
Summer and early fall, 2–5 ft., perennial. Forest
edges, meadows, and river floodplains.

Flowers white, ⅛ in. wide, arranged in axillary and terminal spikes; only a few flowers are simultaneously open on
each spike. Leaves 4–6 in. long, oval, sharply toothed; the
lower leaves with long petioles. Stems hairy. Fruit brown,
capsulelike, ¹⁄₁₆ in. long. CT, MA, NH, RI, VT

Asclepias quadrifolia   APOCYNACEAE
Four-leaved milkweed
Spring and early summer, 12–30 in., perennial. Dry
woodlands and forest openings, usually on high-pH soils.

Flowers white, occasionally pink, ½ in. long, arranged
in 1–3 long-stalked, nodding umbels; the petals reflexed
and the 5 hoods erect, with tiny, projecting horns. Middle leaves 2–5 in. long, oval, in a whorl of 4; the upper
and lower leaves smaller, opposite (not whorled). Stems
slightly hairy, exuding a milky sap. Fruit an erect,
needle-thin follicle, 3–5 in. long. CT, MA, NH (rare), RI
(rare), VT (rare)

Asclepias verticillata   APOCYNACEAE
Whorled milkweed
Summer, 8–20 in., perennial. Rocky
woodlands, balds, and cliff bases.

Flowers greenish white, ¼–½ in. long, arranged in one
to several erect umbels at the top of the stem; the petals reflexed and the 5 hoods erect, with long-projecting,
awl-shaped horns. Leaves ½–2 in. long, linear, in whorls
of 3–6, with inrolled margins and a prominent central
vein. Stems finely hairy. Fruit an erect, linear follicle, 3–4
in. long. Toxic to cattle and horses. CT, MA (rare), RI (rare),
VT (rare)

Silene stellata   CARYOPHYLLACEAE
Starry campion
Summer, 1–3 ft., perennial. Dry oak forests and riverbanks.

Flowers white, ¾ in. wide, arranged in open panicles; the petals fringed with 8–12 fine incisions. Leaves 1–4 in. long, lance-shaped or oval, in whorls of 4. Stems hairy. Fruit a rounded, 6-toothed capsule, ½ in. long. CT (rare)

Spergula arvensis⁎   CARYOPHYLLACEAE
Corn spurry
Spring to early summer, 6–18 in., annual. Fields, roadsides, and disturbed, open sites, often on sandy soil.

Flowers white, ¼ in. wide, arranged in forking clusters on upper stem; the petals and sepals about equal. Leaves 1–2 in. long, needle-thin, channeled on the underside, in whorls of 10 or more. Stems hairy. Fruit an oval capsule, 1/16 in. long. Native to Europe. CT, MA, ME, NH, RI, VT

Mollugo verticillata⁎   MOLLUGINACEAE
Carpetweed, green carpetweed
Summer and fall, to 16 in., annual. Roadsides, sidewalks, and disturbed, open sites, frequently on pavement.

Flowers white, ⅛ in. wide, arranged in forking clusters of 2–5. Leaves ½–1½ in. long, lance-shaped or spoon-shaped, in whorls of 3–8. Stems smooth, prostrate, widely branching, forming mats. Fruit an oval capsule, 1/16 in. long. Area of origin unclear. CT, MA, ME, NH, RI, VT

Chimaphila maculata ERICACEAE
Spotted wintergreen
Summer, 4–10 in., perennial. Dry or moist
forests, often in sandy soils.

Flowers white, sometimes pink-tinged, ½ in. wide, fragrant, in nodding clusters of 2–5. Leaves ¾–2½ in. long, broadly lance-shaped, evergreen, with conspicuous white veins; toothed mostly near the tip. Stems smooth. Fruit a round, ribbed capsule, ¼ in. long. CT, MA, ME (rare), NH, RI, VT

Chimaphila umbellata ERICACEAE
Pipsissewa, prince's-pine
Summer, 4–12 in., perennial. Forests, often in sandy soils.

Flowers white or pink, ½ in. wide, often with a magenta interior ring, in nodding clusters of 4–8. Leaves 1–2½ in. long, lance-shaped or oblong, evergreen, dark green, sharply toothed. Stems smooth. Fruit a round, ribbed capsule, ¼ in. long. CT, MA, ME, NH, RI, VT

Hydrocotyle umbellata APIACEAE
Umbellate pennywort; many-flowered marsh-pennywort
Midsummer to fall, 3–8 in., perennial aquatic.
Sandy and muddy pond shores.

Flowers white, ⅛ in wide, clustered in solitary umbels of (usually) 10–35 (or more) flowers, borne on erect, leafless stalks separate from the leaves. Leaves ½–2½ in. long, rounded, with scalloped edges and a notch at base; the long petioles creeping or floating, attached to the center of the leaf undersurface. Fruit capsulelike, 1/16–⅛ in. long. CT (rare), MA, RI

Hydrocotyle verticillata (whorled marsh-pennywort) is similar, but the flower stalks have 2 or more sparsely flowered umbels, each with 7 or fewer flowers. Found only in sandy pond shores and bogs in coastal regions. CT, MA (extremely rare in both)

Diapensia lapponica   DIAPENSIACEAE
Diapensia, pin-cushion plant
May to June (first bloom), July to August (second bloom),
1–3½ in., shrub. Rocky alpine zones at high elevations.

Flowers white, ½ in. wide, stalked pincushion-like above
the matted leaves, often crowded in dense many-flowered
colonies. Leaves ¼–½ in. long, spoon-shaped, densely
crowded, forming cushionlike mounds. Stems prostrate,
woody. Fruit a rounded capsule, ¼ in. long. ME, NH, VT
(rare in all)

Drosera intermedia   DROSERACEAE
Spatulate-leaved sundew, narrow-leaved sundew
Summer, 2–8 in., carnivorous annual or perennial.
Bogs, fens, acidic swamps, and shorelines.

Flowers white, sometimes pink, ¼ in. wide, in one-sided
coils of about 20 flowers that open singly or 2 at a time.
Leaf blades ⅜–¾ in. long, spoon-shaped, on long,
smooth, spreading or ascending petioles; the blades
covered with glandular hairs that exude a sticky,
insect-trapping dew. Stems smooth. Fruit an oval capsule, ⅛ in. long. CT, MA, ME, NH, RI, VT

Drosera rotundifolia   DROSERACEAE
Round-leaved sundew
Summer, 2–14 in., carnivorous annual or perennial.
Bogs, fens, acidic swamps and shorelines.

Flowers white, sometimes pink, ⅛–¼ in. wide, in
one-sided coils of 3–15 flowers that open singly or 2 at a
time. Leaf blades ¼–¾ in. long and wide, round, on long,
glandular-hairy, spreading or ascending petioles; the
blades covered with glandular hairs that exude a sticky,
insect-trapping dew. Stems with fine hairs. Fruit an oval
capsule, ⅛ in. long. CT, MA, ME, NH, RI, VT

Limosella australis *(L. subulata)*
SCROPHULARIACEAE
Atlantic mudwort, mudwort
Late summer and fall, 1–2 in., matted annual.
Brackish and freshwater conditions in sands and
mudflats along tidal estuaries and tidal rivers.

Flowers white, tiny, ⅛ in. wide, borne on short stems
lower than the leaves. Leaves to 2 in. long, fleshy, in
needlelike basal clusters. Fruit a rounded capsule, ¹/₁₆ in.
long. CT (rare), MA, ME (rare), NH (rare), RI (rare)

Moneses uniflora *(Pyrola uniflora)* ERICACEAE
One-flowered pyrola, one-flowered shinleaf
Summer, 2–5 in., perennial. Cool,
moist forests and swamps.

Flowers white or pink-tinged, ½–¾ in. wide, solitary, fragrant, nodding on an arching stalk, with a straight protruding style. Leaves ½–1 in. long, rounded or oval, finely
toothed. Stems smooth. Fruit a rounded capsule, ¼ in.
long. CT (rare), MA (rare), ME, NH, RI (rare), VT

Orthilia secunda *(Pyrola secunda)* ERICACEAE
One-sided pyrola, one-sided shinleaf
Summer, 4–8 in., perennial. Cool, moist forests
and northern white cedar swamps.

Flowers white or greenish, ¼–⅜ in. long, nodding,
arranged in a one-sided raceme; the style straight, protruding. Leaves ¾–1½ in. long, rounded or elliptical,
finely toothed, occasionally entire. Stems smooth, bend-
ing just below the inflorescence. Fruit a rounded capsule,
¼ in. long. CT (rare), MA, ME, NH, RI (rare), VT

5 radial petals; leaves
simple, basal, entire

5 radial petals; leaves simple,
basal, toothed or lobed

Pyrola americana (*P. rotundifolia*) ERICACEAE
Round-leaf pyrola, American shinleaf
Summer, 4–12 in., perennial. Forests and woodlands.

Flowers white, ½ in. wide, nodding, arranged in a narrow raceme of 3–13 flowers; the styles curved, protruding. Leaves 1–3 in. long, rounded, leathery, shining, with shallow teeth and prominent veins; the petioles about equal in length to the blades. Stems smooth. Fruit a rounded capsule, ⅛–¼ in. long. CT, MA, ME, NH, RI, VT

Pyrola chlorantha (*P. virens*) ERICACEAE
Green-flowered pyrola, green-flowered shinleaf
Summer, 4–12 in., perennial. Cool,
dry forests and woodlands.

Flowers greenish white, ½ in. wide, nodding, arranged in a narrow raceme of 2–10 flowers; the styles curved, protruding. Leaves ½–1¼ in. long, broadly oval or rounded, thick, dark green, not shining, with very shallow teeth or entire; the petioles longer than the blades. Stems smooth. Fruit a rounded capsule, ⅛–¼ in. long. CT, MA, ME, NH, RI (rare), VT

Pyrola elliptica ERICACEAE
Shinleaf, elliptic-leaved shinleaf
Summer, 4–12 in., perennial. Forests and woodlands.

Flowers white, ⅜–½ in. wide, nodding, arranged in a raceme of 7–15 flowers; the styles curved, protruding. Leaves 1–3 in. long, oval or elliptic, thin, light green, not shining, with shallow teeth; the petioles shorter than the blades. Stems smooth. Fruit a rounded capsule, ⅛–¼ in. long. CT, MA, ME, NH, RI, VT

Pyrola minor ERICACEAE
Lesser pyrola, little shinleaf
Summer, 4–8 in., perennial. Cool, moist
coniferous forests and wetlands.

Flowers white, ¼ in. long, nodding, arranged in a raceme
of 5–15 flowers; the styles straight, barely protruding
from the petals. Leaves ¾–1½ in. long, rounded at both
ends, thin, with shallow teeth; the petioles longer than or
equal to the blades. Stems smooth. Fruit a rounded capsule, ⅛–¼ in. long. ME, NH, VT (rare in all)

Rubus dalibarda (Dalibarda repens) ROSACEAE
Dew-drop, robin run-a-way, false violet
Summer, 2–4 in., perennial. Cool,
moist forests and swamps.

Flowers ½–¾ in. wide, solitary, with bushy stamens,
stalked just above the leaves, infertile; the fertile flowers are closed, without petals, hidden below the leaves.
Leaves 1–2 in. long, heart-shaped, with blunt, shallow
teeth. Stems creeping, hairy. Fruit ⅛–¼ in. long, white,
berrylike. CT (rare), MA, ME, NH, RI (rare), VT

Micranthes pensylvanica (Saxifraga pensylvanica)
SAXIFRAGACEAE
Swamp saxifrage, swamp small-flowered saxifrage
Spring, 1–4 ft., perennial. Swamps, fens,
wet meadows, and forest seepages.

Flowers ⅛–¼ in. wide, greenish white,
yellowish, or purple, packed in a dense,
spikelike cone in bud, which elongates
in bloom into wide-branching clusters.
Leaves 4–10 in. long, oval, clumped at
the base, shallowly toothed, occasionally
entire. Stems thick, densely hairy. Fruit a
2-parted capsule, ⅛ in. long. CT, MA, ME
(rare), NH, RI (rare), VT

5 radial petals; leaves simple, basal, toothed or lobed

103

Micranthes virginiensis (*Saxifraga virginiensis*)
SAXIFRAGACEAE
Early saxifrage, early small-flowered saxifrage
Early spring, 4–16 in., perennial. Cliffs, talus
slopes, ledges, and rocky wooded slopes.

Flowers white, ¼–½ in. wide, arranged in small, branching clusters. Leaves ½–3 in. long, oval, hairy, with shallow, blunt teeth. Stems stout, hairy. Fruit a 2-parted capsule, ⅛–¼ in. long. CT, MA, ME, NH, RI (rare), VT

Tiarella cordifolia   SAXIFRAGACEAE
Foam-flower
Spring and early summer, 4–14 in., perennial.
Moist forests, often with rich soils.

Flowers white, ¼ in. wide, arranged in a long, terminal, spraylike raceme; the flowers with linear petals and 10 long, projecting stamens. Leaves 2–4 in. long, triangular, long-petioled, sharply and irregularly toothed, with 3–5 broad lobes. Stems hairy. Fruit a narrowly oval, flattened capsule, ¼–⅜ in. long. CT, MA, ME, NH, VT

*Aegopodium podagraria** ⃰   APIACEAE
Goutweed, bishop's-weed
Late spring and summer, 1–3 ft., perennial. Roadsides, thickets, moist woodlands, and floodplains. Invasive.

Flowers white, ¼ in. wide, clustered in flattish umbels, 2–4½ in. wide, with 25–40 spokelike branches. Leaves

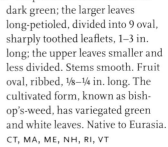

dark green; the larger leaves long-petioled, divided into 9 oval, sharply toothed leaflets, 1–3 in. long; the upper leaves smaller and less divided. Stems smooth. Fruit oval, ribbed, ⅛–¼ in. long. The cultivated form, known as bishop's-weed, has variegated green and white leaves. Native to Eurasia. CT, MA, ME, NH, RI, VT

Angelica atropurpurea   APIACEAE
Purple-stemmed angelica
Summer and early fall, 4–7 ft., perennial. Wet
meadows, streambanks, swamps, and ditches.

Flowers white, ¼ in. wide, clustered in round,
ball-like umbels 3–9 in. wide, with 20–45 spokelike
branches. Leaves pinnately compound, with sheathing,
purple-veined bases; the larger leaves divided into 9–27
oval or lance-shaped, sharply toothed leaflets, 1–4 in.
long. Stems smooth, purple or purple-blotched. Fruits
elliptical, with prominent ribs, ¼ in. long. CT, MA, ME,
NH, RI (rare), VT

Angelica lucida (*Coelopleurum lucidum*) APIACEAE
Seaside angelica, seacoast angelica
Summer, 2–4 ft., perennial. Salt marshes and
beach edges; fields and thickets near beaches.

Flowers white, ¼ in. wide, clustered in flattish,
long-stalked umbels, with 20–50 finely hairy spokelike
branches. Leaves pinnately compound, the upper with
broad, sheathing bases; the larger leaves divided into
9–21 lance-shaped or oval, sharply toothed leaflets, 1–3
in. long. Stems smooth, green. Fruit elliptical or broadly
oval, with corky ribs, ⅛–¼ in. long. CT (rare), MA (rare),
ME, NH (rare), RI (rare)
    Angelica venenosa (hairy angelica), restricted to dry,
rocky woodlands, is similar but grows to 6 ft. high, with
hairy stems and blunt-tipped leaflets. The uppermost
stem leaves are reduced to tubelike sheaths. CT (rare)

Anthriscus sylvestris⁎   APIACEAE
Wild chervil
Spring and summer, 1–3½ ft., biennial or short-lived
perennial. Fields, thicket edges, and roadsides. Invasive.

Flowers white, ¼ in. wide, clustered on flattish, spreading
umbels, to 3 in. wide, with 6–15 long, spokelike branches.
Leaves finely divided and fernlike, clasping at base; the
leaflets ½–2 in. long. Stems ridged, hairy, especially near
base. Fruit cylindrical, paired, capped by the beaked style,
¼ in. long. Native to Eurasia. CT, MA, ME, NH, RI, VT

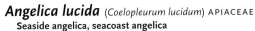

5 radial petals; leaves deeply divided, alternate; leaflets toothed or lobed

Aralia hispida APIACEAE
Bristly sarsaparilla
Summer, 1–3 ft., perennial. Dry woodlands and
fields, cliffs, ledges, and recently burned sites.

Flowers white, ¼ in. wide, clustered in long-stalked,
rounded umbels, 1–1¼ in. wide, held high above the
leaves. Leaves mostly near base, pinnately divided into
lance-shaped or oval, sharply toothed leaflets, 1–4 in.
long. Stems woody, bristly near base. Fruit berrylike,
blue-black, ¼ in. long. CT, MA, ME, NH, RI, VT

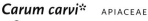

Carum carvi⁕ APIACEAE
Caraway
Late spring and summer, 8–30 in., biennial.
Fields, roadsides, and open, disturbed sites.

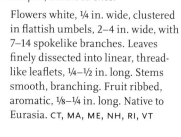

Flowers white, ¼ in. wide, clustered
in flattish umbels, 2–4 in. wide, with
7–14 spokelike branches. Leaves
finely dissected into linear, threadlike leaflets, ¼–½ in. long. Stems
smooth, branching. Fruit ribbed,
aromatic, ⅛–¼ in. long. Native to
Eurasia. CT, MA, ME, NH, RI, VT

Cicuta bulbifera APIACEAE
Bulb-bearing water-hemlock
Summer, 1–4 ft., perennial. Marshes,
swamps, streambanks, and shallows.

Flowers white, ¼ in. wide, clustered in one to several flattish umbels, 1–2 in. wide, with 5–7 spokelike branches.
Leaves finely divided into long-stalked, sparse, spreading, threadlike leaflets, ½–3 in. long, often toothed on
the margins; tiny bulblets tucked in the upper leaf axils.
Stems smooth, green. Fruit oval, ribbed, 1/16 in. long.
Plant is very poisonous. CT, MA, ME, NH, RI, VT

Cicuta maculata   APIACEAE
Water hemlock, spotted water-hemlock
Summer, 2–6 ft., biennial. Swamps, marshes,
wet meadows, and shorelines.

Flowers white, ¼ in. wide, clustered in numerous, flattish or dome-shaped umbels, 2–5 in. wide, with 15–30
spokelike branches. Leaves pinnately divided into
lance-shaped, sharply toothed leaflets, 1–4 in. long.
Stems smooth, purple or purple-spotted. Fruit oval or
rounded, ribbed, about ¹⁄₁₆ in. long. Plant is very poisonous. CT, MA, ME, NH, RI, VT

Conioselinum chinense   APIACEAE
Hemlock parsley, Chinese hemlock-parsley
Summer and early fall, 1–5 ft., perennial. Wooded swamps,
floodplain forests, wet meadows, and shorelines.

Flowers white, ¼ in. wide, clustered in one to several flattish or
dome-shaped umbels, 1–4 in. wide,
with 10–13 spokelike branches.
Leaves 2–8 in. long, triangular,
finely divided into fernlike segments; the lower long-petioled,
the upper with broadly sheathing
bases. Stems green, smooth. Fruit oval, ribbed, ⅛–¼ in.
long. CT, MA (rare), ME, NH, VT

Conium maculatum*   APIACEAE
Poison hemlock
Summer, 2–10 ft., biennial. Fields,
wet meadows and roadsides.

Flowers white, ¼ in. wide, clustered in numerous flattish,
branching umbels, 1½–2½ in. wide, with 10–15 spokelike branches. Leaves 8–16 in. long, triangular, finely
divided into many, sharp-toothed, fernlike segments.
Stems smooth, ribbed, purple-blotched. Fruit oval, flattened, ¹⁄₁₆ in. long. Plant is very poisonous. Native to Eurasia. CT, MA, ME, NH, RI, VT

5 radial petals; leaves deeply divided, alternate; leaflets toothed or lobed

Cryptotaenia canadensis   APIACEAE
Honewort, Canada honewort
Summer, 1–3 ft., perennial. Rich
deciduous forests and floodplains.

Flowers white, ⅛ in. wide, thinly clustered in sparse,
irregular umbels, 1–3 in. wide, with 2–5 spokelike
branches of unequal length. Leaves 3-parted; the 3 leaflets lance-shaped, sharply toothed, sometimes lobed,
1½–6 in. long. Stems smooth. Fruits linear or narrowly
oval, ribbed, ¼ in. long. CT, MA, NH, RI (rare), VT

Daucus carota⁕   APIACEAE
Wild carrot, Queen Anne's lace
Summer and fall, 1–3 ft., biennial. Fields,
roadsides, and open, disturbed sites.

Flowers white, ⅛ in. wide, clustered in flat umbels, 2–4½
in. wide, with 10–60 spokelike branches; a single dark
purple flower often in center of umbel. Leaves 2–10 in.
long, finely divided into lacy, fernlike leaflet segments.
Stems densely hairy. Fruit oval, flattened, bristly, ⅛ in.
long; in fruit, the umbels curl upward, forming a "bird's
nest." Native to Eurasia. CT, MA, ME, NH, RI, VT

Heracleum mantegazzianum⁕   APIACEAE
Giant hogweed
Early to midsummer, 7–16 ft., biennial or perennial. Fields,
open woodlands, ditches, and roadsides. Invasive.

Flowers white, ¼–½ in. wide, clustered in dome-shaped
umbels, 1–2 ft. wide, with 50–150 spokelike branches.
Lower leaves 8–9 ft. wide, long-petioled, deeply cut into

lance-shaped, sharply toothed lobes,
with long, sharp-pointed tips. Stems
thick, hairy, purple-blotched. Fruits
flattened, elliptical, stalked, ⅜ in.
long. Stem has phytotoxic sap that
causes severe skin burns on contact.
Native to southern Russia. CT, MA,
ME, VT

108

Heracleum maximum (*H. lanatum*) APIACEAE
Cow parsnip, American cow parsnip
Summer, 3–10 ft., perennial. Fields, floodplains,
ditches, and subalpine meadows.

Flowers white, ¼–⅜ in. wide, clustered in flattish
umbels, 4–8 in. wide, with 15–45 spokelike branches.
Leaves to 18 in. long and wide, divided into 3 broadly triangular, sharply toothed leaflets, 6–12 in. long. Stems
hairy or woolly, usually all green or purple, without purple splotches (except for
purple-veined leaf sheath). Fruit elliptical,
stalked, ¼–½ in. long. CT, MA, ME, NH,
RI, VT

Ligusticum scoticum (*L. scothicum*) APIACEAE
Scotch lovage, Scotch wild lovage
Summer and early fall, 1–2 ft., perennial. Salt
marshes and sandy or rocky beaches.

Flowers white, ¼ in. wide, clustered in umbels 2–4½
in. wide, with 10–20 spokelike branches. Leaves divided
into 3 leaflets; the 3 leaflets also 3-parted, broadly oval
or triangular, sharply toothed and often lobed, 1¼–4
in. long; the lower leaves have long petioles, the upper
leaves have a closed sheath at base. Stems smooth, red or
purple-tinged near base. Fruit cylindrical, ribbed, ¼–⅜
in. long. CT, MA, ME, NH, RI

Osmorhiza claytonii   APIACEAE
Sweet cicely, bland sweet-cicely
Spring and early summer, 1–3 ft.,
perennial. Rich, deciduous forests.

Flowers white, ⅛ in. wide, clustered in very small,
sparsely flowered umbels, ¾–1½ in. wide, with 1–4
spokelike branches; the petals longer than the styles.
Leaves triangular, divided into oval, toothed, fernlike
leaflets, 1–3 in. long. Stems densely covered with soft,
spreading hairs. Fruit linear, ¾ in. long; the persistent
styles at top of fruit 1/16 in. or less. Roots with faint odor of
anise. CT, MA, ME, NH, RI, VT

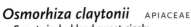

5 radial petals; leaves deeply divided,
alternate; leaflets toothed or lobed

Osmorhiza longistylis   APIACEAE
Anise-root, long-styled sweet-cicely
Spring and early summer, 1–4 ft. Rich, deciduous forests.

Flowers white, ⅛ in. wide, clustered in very small, sparsely flowered umbels, ¾–1½ in. wide, with 1–4 spokelike branches; the styles longer than the petals. Leaves triangular, divided into oval, toothed, fernlike leaflets, 1–3 in. long. Stems mostly smooth, hairy at leaf nodes. Fruits linear, ¾ in. long; the persistent styles at top of fruit ⅛ in. long. Roots and foliage have a strong odor of anise. CT, MA, ME, NH, RI (rare), VT

Ptilimnium capillaceum   APIACEAE
Mock bishop's weed; Atlantic mock bishop's-weed
Summer and fall, 1–3 ft., annual.
Salt and brackish marshes.

Flowers white, 1/16–⅛ in. wide, clustered into flattish umbels, ¾–2 in. wide, with 5–16 spokelike branches. Leaves 1½–4 in. long, finely dissected into lacy, thread-like leaflets, ¼–1 in. long. Stems smooth. Fruit broadly oval, ribbed, 1/16–⅛ in. long. Coastal regions of CT, MA, and RI (rare)

Sium suave   APIACEAE
Water parsnip
Summer to early fall, 2–6 ft., perennial. Wet meadows, swamps, river and pond shallows.

Flowers white, ¼ in. wide, clustered in flattish umbels, 1½–4½ in. wide, with 10–25 spokelike branches. Leaves pinnately divided into 5–17 sharply toothed, lance-shaped leaflets ½–6 in. long; submerged leaves, when present, finely dissected. Stems smooth, ridged. Fruit oval, ribbed, 1/16–⅛ in. long. CT, MA, ME, NH, RI, VT

110

Achillea millefolium   ASTERACEAE
Yarrow, common yarrow
Summer and fall, 1–3 ft., perennial. Fields, thickets, and ledges, from low to high elevations; also roadsides.

Flowerheads white, occasionally pink, ⅛–¼ in. wide, clustered in a branched, flat-topped, umbel-like inflorescence, 3–30 in. wide; the tiny petal-like ray flowers have 3 teeth at the tip. Leaves 1¼–6 in. long, lance-shaped, strongly aromatic, finely dissected into fernlike segments. Stems usually hairy, sometimes smooth. Fruit an achene, 1/16 in. long. CT, MA, ME, NH, RI, VT

Hydrophyllum virginianum   BORAGINACEAE
Virginia waterleaf, eastern waterleaf, John's-cabbage
Spring and early summer, 1–3 ft., perennial.
Moist deciduous forests and floodplains.

Flowers white or lavender, ¼–⅜ in. wide, in coiled clusters, stalked above the leaves, with protruding stamens and bristly sepals. Leaves 4–8 in. long, often mottled, deeply divided into 3–7 lance-shaped or oval, sharply toothed leaflets. Stems hairy or smooth. Fruit a round, hairy capsule, ⅛–¼ in. long, aggregated in bristly clusters. CT (rare), MA, NH (rare), VT

Ranunculus aquatilis (*R. longirostris,*
R. trichophyllus) RANUNCULACEAE
White water crowfoot
Summer, size, 4–20 in., perennial. Ponds and slow streams, often with a high pH.

Flowers white, ½ in. wide, solitary, stalked just above the water surface; the petals with yellow bases. Surface leaves ¼–¾ in. long and wide, broadly 3-lobed, with shallow teeth; subsurface leaves finely dissected into linear segments. Stems smooth, white, fleshy, usually floating or submerged. Fruit an achene, 1/16 in. long, aggregated into rounded heads ⅛–¼ in. wide. CT (rare), MA, RI (rare), VT (rare)

111

Drymocallis arguta (*Potentilla arguta*) ROSACEAE
Tall cinquefoil, tall wood beauty
Summer, 1–3 ft., perennial. Fields,
woodlands, cliffs, and rocky slopes.

Flowers white or creamy, ½–¾ in. wide, in a narrow,
branching cluster at the top of the stem; the sepals
glandular-hairy, about equal in length to petals. Leaves
pinnately divided into 3–11 oval, coarsely toothed leaflets;
the lower leaves long-petioled, to 12 in. long or longer, the
upper progressively smaller. Stems densely hairy, sticky.
Fruit a broadly oval, beaked achene, less than ¹⁄₁₆ in. long.
CT, MA, ME, NH, RI, VT (rare)

Geum canadense ROSACEAE
White avens
Summer, 1–3 ft., perennial. Forests,
woodlands, thickets, and swamps.

Flowers white, ½ in. wide, solitary or in few-flowered
clusters; the petals equal to or longer than the
sepals. Leaves variable; the basal leaves to 3 in. long,
lance-shaped, in a rosette, with 5–7 pinnately divided,
lobed leaflets; the stem leaves 3- to 5-parted, with sharply
toothed, oval, triangular, or diamond-shaped leaflets.
Stems smooth or slightly hairy. Fruit an achene, ⅛ in.
long, aggregated into bristly heads ½–¾ in. wide. CT, MA,
ME, NH, RI, VT

Rubus flagellaris ROSACEAE
**Common dewberry, northern dewberry, northern
blackberry**
Spring and early summer, to 15 ft. long, trailing shrub.
Fields, thickets, ledges, and open woodlands.

Flowers white, 1 in. wide, in stalked clusters of 2–5.
Leaves light to medium green, divided into 3–5 oval
leaflets, 1–3 in. long, with sharp teeth and pointed tips.
Stems trailing or scrambling, with curved, broad-based
prickles, sometimes rooting at the tips. Fruit black, berrylike, sweet, ½–¾ in. long. CT, MA, ME, NH, RI, VT

Rubus hispidus   ROSACEAE
Swamp dewberry, bristly dewberry, bristly blackberry
Summer, to 8 ft. long, trailing shrub. Fields, thickets,
woodlands, wet meadows, and swamps.

Flowers white, ½–¾ in. wide, in stalked clusters of 3–6.
Leaves dark green, divided into 3 (occasionally 5) oval
leaflets, 1–2½ in. long, with blunt teeth and rounded tips.
Stems trailing or scrambling, with weak, slender bristles,
sometimes rooting at the tips. Fruit red or black, berrylike, sour, ½ in. long. CT, MA, ME, NH, RI, VT

Rubus pubescens   ROSACEAE
Dwarf raspberry, swamp red raspberry
Spring and summer, 4–16 in., perennial.
Swamps, wetland edges, and moist forests.

Flowers white, ¼–½ in. wide, arranged in stalked clusters of 1–3; the sepals reflexed. Leaves divided into 3 oval
or diamond-shaped, sharply toothed
leaflets, 1½–3 in. long. Stems smooth,
without prickles, trailing at base, producing erect, leafy shoots. Fruit red,
berrylike, juicy, ⅜–¾ in. long. CT, MA,
ME, NH, RI, VT

Sibbaldiopsis tridentata (*Potentilla tridentata*)
ROSACEAE
Three-toothed cinquefoil
Late spring and summer, 2–12 in., perennial. Ledges,
open summits, alpine zones, and sand plains.

Flowers white, ⅜–½ in. wide, arranged in stalked,
branching, few-flowered clusters. Leaves divided into 3
narrowly oval leaflets, ½–1 in. long, toothed only at the
tips, turning bright red in fall. Stems hairy, trailing and
woody at base. Fruit a hairy achene, ¹⁄₁₆ in. long. CT (rare),
MA, ME, NH, VT

5 radial petals; leaves deeply divided,
alternate; leaflets toothed or lobed

Saxifraga rivularis   SAXIFRAGACEAE
Alpine brook saxifrage
Summer, 1–5 in., perennial. Alpine summits
and gullies, at high elevations.

Flowers white, ¼–½ in. wide, in branching, few-flowered
clusters. Leaves ¼–½ in. long, broadly divided into 3–5
tridentlike lobes. Stems hairy. Fruit a capsule, ¼ in. long.
Only in White Mountains. NH (rare)
   Saxifraga cernua (nodding saxifrage), another alpine
species only in the White Mountains, is similar but taller
(3–8 in.), with tiny bulbs in the upper leaf axils, and only
a single flower. NH (rare)

Polymnia canadensis   ASTERACEAE
Small-flowered leafcup, white-flowered leafcup
Summer and fall, 2–6 ft., perennial. Woodlands
and talus slopes in high-pH soils.

Flower heads ½–1 in. wide, with 5–8 small, 3-toothed
white rays (rays occasionally absent) around a central yellow disk. Leaves 10–16 in. long, deeply divided into 3–7
sharply pointed, coarsely toothed lobes; the lower leaves
with long petioles. Stems densely hairy. CT (rare), VT
(rare)

Panax quinquefolius   APIACEAE
American ginseng
Summer, 6–24 in., perennial. Rich deciduous forests.

Flowers greenish or yellowish white, ⅛ in. wide, fragrant,
clustered in a solitary umbel stalked from the axil of the
whorled leaves. Leaves in a whorl of 3–5, long-petioled,
palmately divided into 5 oval leaflets, 2½–6 in. long,
the 3 upper leaflets larger than the 2 lower ones. Stems
smooth. Fruit bright red, berrylike, ⅜ in. wide. CT, MA,
ME, NH, RI, VT (rare in all)

Panax trifolius (*P. trifolium*) APIACEAE
Dwarf ginseng
Spring, 4–8 in., perennial. Moist forests.

Flowers white, ⅛ in. wide, clustered in a round, solitary umbel stalked above the leaves. Leaves in a whorl of 3, long-petioled, divided into 3–5 narrowly oval leaflets, ¾–2 in. long. Stems smooth. Fruit berrylike, yellow, fleshy, ¼ in. wide. CT, MA, ME, NH, RI, VT

Anemone canadensis RANUNCULACEAE
Canada anemone, Canada windflower
Spring and summer, 1–2½ ft., perennial. Wet meadows, thickets, and river and lake shores.

Flowers white, 1–1½ in. wide, solitary, long-stalked; the apparent petals are actually sepals. Basal leaves 2–6 in. long, long-petioled, with 5–7 deeply cut, sharply toothed lobes; stem leaves usually 3-lobed, in whorls of 3. Stems hairy. Fruit a flattened, beaked achene, ⅛–¼ in. long, aggregated into round, spiky heads. CT (rare), MA, ME, NH, VT

Anemone cylindrica RANUNCULACEAE
Long-fruited anemone, long-headed windflower
Summer, 1–3 ft., perennial. Fields and dry open woodlands.

Flowers white or greenish white, ¾ in. wide, solitary, on long, leafless stalk; the apparent petals actually sepals. Stem leaves 1½–5 in. long, long-petioled, in 2 whorls of 5–9, divided into 3–5 oval or diamond-shaped leaflets, toothed only along the upper margins. Stems hairy. Fruit a woolly achene, 1/16 in. long, aggregated into narrow, cylindrical heads ¾–1½ in. long, more than twice as long as broad. CT, MA, ME, RI (rare), VT

Anemone quinquefolia RANUNCULACEAE
Windflower, wood anemone, wood windflower
Spring, 2–12 in., perennial. Forests, forest
edges, floodplains, and fields.

Flowers white, sometimes pink or purple-tinged, ½–1 in.
wide, solitary, erect or slightly nodding, stalked just above
the leaves; the apparent petals actually sepals. Leaves
divided into 3–5 oval leaflets, narrowed at base, ½–1½ in.
long, toothed on the upper margins, sometimes lobed.
Stems smooth. Fruit a narrowly oval, hairy achene, ⅛–¼
in. long. CT, MA, ME, NH, RI, VT

Anemone virginiana (includes A. riparia)
RANUNCULACEAE
Thimbleweed, tall anemone, tall windflower
Summer, 1–3 ft., perennial. Forests, woodlands,
floodplains, wetland edges, cliffs, and balds.

Flowers white or greenish white, ¾–1½ in. long, solitary, on long, leafless stalks; the apparent petals actually
sepals. Stem leaves long-petioled, in 2 whorls of 3, divided
into 3–5 oval or diamond-shaped leaflets, 1–3 in. long, the
terminal leaflet with a wedge-shaped base. Stems hairy.
Fruit a woolly achene, ⅛–¼ in. long, aggregated into
cylindrical heads ¾–1 in. long, less than twice as long as
wide. CT, MA, ME, NH, RI, VT

Menyanthes trifoliata MENYANTHACEAE
Bog buckbean, buck-bean
Spring and early summer, 4–12 in., perennial.
Wet meadows, fens, and pond edges.

Flowers white, ½–1¼ in. wide, clustered near the top of a
long, leafless stalk; the petals with conspicuous, fringing
hairs. Leaves long-petioled, divided into 3 oval, entire or
wavy-margined leaflets, 1¼–2½ in. long. Stems smooth.
Fruit a rounded, long-beaked capsule, ¼–⅜ in. long. CT,
MA, ME, NH, RI, VT

Oxalis montana OXALIDACEAE
Common wood sorrel, northern wood sorrel
Spring to midsummer, 2–6 in.,
perennial. Cool, moist forests.

Flowers white with pink veins, ¾–1 in. wide, solitary, on
slender stalks. Leaves ½–1¼ in. long and wide, 3-parted;
the 3 leaflets heart-shaped at the tip. Stems finely hairy.
Fruit an oval capsule, ⅛–¼ in. long. CT (rare), MA, ME,
NH, VT

Hottonia inflata PRIMULACEAE
Featherfoil
Spring and summer, 2–20 in., annual. Pond and
stream shallows, swamps, and muddy shorelines.

Flowers white, ⅛ in. wide, whorled at the top of the stem
and in upper nodes; the sepals sharp-pointed, longer
than petals. Basal leaves ¾–2½ in. long, feathery, finely
dissected, floating or submerged. Stems light green,
inflated, constricted at the nodes, appearing like a bonsai
baobab. Fruit a rounded capsule, ¹⁄₁₆ in. long. CT, MA, ME,
NH, RI (rare in all)

Coptis trifolia (*C. groenlandica*) RANUNCULACEAE
Goldthread, three-leaved goldthread
Spring, 2–6 in., perennial. Moist forests, bogs,
swamp edges, and mossy hummocks.

Flowers white, ½ in. wide, solitary, the 4–7 (usually 5)
"petals" actually sepals surrounding a bushy stamen
cluster. Leaves dark green, shiny, evergreen, 3-parted; the
3 leaflets ½–1 in. long, broadly oval or rounded, toothed.
Fruit narrowly elliptical, beaked, ⅜–½ in. long, in
stalked, radiating clusters. CT, MA, ME, NH, RI, VT

5 radial petals; leaves deeply
divided, basal, leaflets entire

5 radial petals; leaves deeply divided,
basal, leaflets toothed or lobed

117

Fragaria vesca   ROSACEAE
Woodland strawberry
Spring and early summer, 3–6 in., perennial.
Rocky woodlands and slopes.

Flowers white, ½–¾ in. wide, solitary or in clusters of
2–9; the flowers usually overtopping the leaves. Leaves
3-parted; the 3 leaflets 1–5 in. long, oval, sharply toothed;
the uppermost tooth of the terminal leaflet longer than
the adjacent teeth. Stems hairy. Fruit berrylike, ½ in.
long, red, yellow, or sometimes whitish; seeds on the fruit
surface, not embedded. CT, MA, ME, NH, RI, VT

The native variety (var. *americana)* has smaller flowers (½ in.) and slender fruits; the nonnative variety (var.
vesca*) has larger flowers (½–¾ in.) and rounder, sometimes whitish fruits.

Fragaria virginiana   ROSACEAE
Wild strawberry, common strawberry
Spring, 3–6 in., perennial. Fields,
thickets, and forest edges.

Flowers white, ½–1 in. wide, solitary or in clusters of
2–12; the leaves usually overtopping the flowers. Leaves
3-parted; the 3 leaflets 1–5 in. long, oval, sharply toothed;
the uppermost tooth of the terminal leaflet shorter than
the adjacent teeth. Stems hairy. Fruit berrylike, ½ in.
long, red, sweet; the seeds embedded in the pitted surface. CT, MA, ME, NH, RI, VT

Cuscuta gronovii   CONVOLVULACEAE
Common dodder
Summer and fall, 1–6 ft. long, annual vine. Meadows,
thickets, and edges of freshwater and tidal wetlands.

Flowers white, ¹⁄₁₆–⅛ in. wide, arranged in dense clusters
along the twining stem. Leaves tiny, scaly. Stems threadlike, yellow or orange, climbing, forming twining net-
works on other vegetation. Fruit a rounded capsule, ⅛ in.
long. Parasitic on numerous wild and cultivated plants.
CT, MA, ME, NH, RI, VT

Harrimanella hypnoides (*Cassiope hypnoides*)
ERICACEAE
Moss-plant
Summer, 1–10 in., perennial. Alpine
cliffs, ravines, and gullies.

Flowers white or pink-tinged, ⅜ in. long, bell-shaped,
nodding, solitary at the tips of red stalks. Leaves ¹⁄₁₆–⅛
in. long, needlelike, bristly. Stems prostrate, branching,
forming mosslike mounds. Fruit a rounded capsule, ¹⁄₁₆
in. long. ME (rare), NH (rare)

Monotropa uniflora   ERICACEAE
Indian pipe, one-flowered Indian pipe, corpse plant
Summer, 2–12 in., perennial. Forests.

Flowers white, ⅜–¾ in. long, solitary, nodding at the top
of the milk-white stem. Leaves scaly, numerous, thin,
translucent. Stems smooth, white, occasionally with
a pink tinge. Fruit a capsule, oval, erect, brown when
mature, ⅜–½ in. long. A parasitic or saprophytic plant
that obtains nutrients from fungi associated with tree
roots. CT, MA, ME, NH, RI, VT

Orobanche uniflora   OROBANCHACEAE
**One-flowered cancer-root, one-flowered broom-rape,
ghost pipe**
Spring, 2–8 in., perennial. Meadows,
thickets, and moist woodlands.

Flowers white or lavender, ¾–1 in. long, solitary, tubular, the petals broadly oval and slightly unequal in length.
Leaves scalelike, only at base of plant. Stems downy,
glandular. Fruit an oval capsule, ¼–½ in. long. Parasitic
on numerous plants, including goldenrods, saxifrages,
sedums, and sunflowers. CT, MA, ME, NH, RI, VT

Dioscorea villosa DIOSCORACEAE
Wild yam
Summer, 5–15 ft. long, perennial vine. Moist woodlands, thickets, and floodplains.

Flowers greenish white, ⅛–¼ in. wide; arranged in drooping axillary spikes. Leaves 2–5 in. long,

heart-shaped, long-pointed, on long petioles, with 7–11 pairs of veins. Stems twining, climbing, smooth. Fruit an oval, ribbed capsule, ⅜–1¼ in. long. CT, southeastern MA, RI (rare)

Streptopus amplexifolius LILIACEAE
White mandarin, clasping-leaf twisted-stalk
Spring to midsummer, 12–36 in., perennial. Cool, moist forests; also subalpine and alpine zones.

Flowers greenish white, sometimes yellowish, ⅜ in. wide, with recurved tips; the flowers dangling beneath the leaf axils on kinked stalks. Leaves 2–6 in. long, smooth, lance-shaped or oval, clasping, whitish underneath. Fruit an oval red berry, ½ in. long. CT (rare), MA, ME, NH, VT

Maianthemum racemosum
(*Smilacina racemosa*) RUSCACEAE
False Solomon's-seal, feathery false Solomon's-seal
Spring and early summer, 1–3 ft., perennial. Forests, woodlands, and floodplains.

Flowers ⅛–¼ in. long, arranged in a plumelike panicle with 70–250 flowers; the petals shorter than the stamens. Leaves 3–6 in. long, numerous, oval or broadly lance-shaped, short-petioled. Stems arching, zigzag in form. Fruit a berry, ⅛–¼ in. long, red when ripe. CT, MA, ME, NH, RI, VT

120

Maianthemum stellatum (*Smilacina stellata*)
RUSCACEAE
Starry false Solomon's-seal, starlike false Solomon's-seal
Late spring to early summer, 8–24 in.,
perennial. Moist, sandy woodlands, thickets,
and swamps; also in dunes and dry fields.

Flowers white, ¼ in. long, arranged in a terminal raceme
of 6–15 flowers; the petals exceeding the stamens. Leaves
2–6 in. long, lance-shaped, sessile or clasping, crowded (4
or more). Stems smooth or hairy, erect or upwardly arching. Fruit a berry, ¼–⅜ in. wide, at first green with black
stripes, turning red when ripe. CT, MA, ME, NH, RI, VT

Maianthemum trifolium   RUSCACEAE
Three-leaved false Solomon's-seal
Late spring, 4–16 in., perennial. Bogs, fens,
and wet, peaty woodlands and thickets.

Flowers white, ¼ in. wide, arranged in a long-stalked terminal raceme of 3–8 flowers; the petals exceeding the stamens. Leaves usually 3, 2½–5 in. long, lance-shaped, sessile. Stems erect, smooth or hairy. Fruit a berry, ⅛–¼ in.
wide, at first green, turning red. CT (rare), MA (rare), ME,
NH, RI (rare), VT

Triantha glutinosa (*Tofieldia glutinosa*)
TOFIELDIACEAE
Sticky false asphodel
Summer, 8–20 in., perennial. Riverside seeps, fens,
and wet meadows in areas of high-pH bedrock.

Flowers white, ¼ in. wide, clustered in 3-flowered heads
on upper stem; the flower stalks short, sticky, and glandular. Basal leaves 3–8 in. long, linear or narrowly
lance-shaped; single stem leaf (if present) small, bractlike. Stems sticky-hairy. Fruit an oval capsule, ¼–⅜ in.
long ME, NH (rare), VT (rare)

Ornithogalum umbellatum*
HYACINTHACEAE
Star-of-Bethlehem, nap-at-noon
Spring, 8–12 in., perennial. Roadsides, fields, thickets, and open woodlands. Invasive.

Flowers white, 1¼ in. wide, open in afternoon, arranged in a star-shaped, flattish raceme of 8–20 flowers; the petals with a green stripe on the back. Leaves 8–12 in. long and about ⅛ in. wide, grasslike, the midvein of upper surface white. Stems smooth. Fruit an oval capsule, ⅜–¾ in. long. Bulbs are poisonous. Native to Europe and North Africa. CT, MA, ME, NH, RI, VT

Aletris farinosa   NARTHECIACEAE
Colic-root, white colic-root, unicorn root
Late spring and summer, 1–3 ft., perennial. Sandy fields, thickets, and open woodlands.

Flowers white, ⅜ in. long, tubular, with granular surfaces, arranged in a raceme. Leaves 2–8 in. long, lance-shaped, forming a rosette. Fruit a beaked capsule, ¼–⅜ in. long. CT, MA, RI (rare)

Convallaria majalis*   RUSCACEAE
Lily-of-the-valley, European lily-of-the-valley
Spring, 4–12 in., perennial (often colonial). Fields, thickets, woodlands, and abandoned homesteads, spreading by rhizomes.

Flowers white, ¼–⅛ in. long, bell-shaped, nodding, fragrant, arranged in a one-sided raceme; the petals with recurved tips. Leaves 6–20 in. long, 2 or 3, lance-shaped, basal, overtopping flowers and tapering to a pointed tip. Stems smooth. Fruit a red berry, ⅜ in. long. Native to Europe. CT, MA, ME, NH, RI, VT

Allium tricoccum ALLIACEAE
Ramps, wild leek
Early summer, 4–20 in., perennial. Moist
deciduous forests and floodplains.

Flowers white, ⅛–¼ in. wide, arranged in rounded, 30-
to 50-flowered umbels on top of leafless stems. Basal
leaves withered by flowering time; leaves in early spring
dark green, shining, oval or broadly lance-shaped, 6–12
in. long. Stems smooth. Fruit a capsule that opens to
reveal round, blue-black seeds. CT, MA, ME (rare), NH, RI
(rare), VT

Doellingeria infirma (*Aster infirmus*) ASTERACEAE
Appalachian white-aster, cornel-leaved aster
Mid to late summer, 1½–3½ ft., perennial.
Deciduous, rocky woodlands.

Flower heads 1 in. wide, with 5–9 white rays, arranged
in an open, branching inflorescence of several to 45
heads (occasionally more). Leaves 1¼–5 in. long, broadly
lance-shaped or oval, short-petioled or subsessile; the
lower leaves smaller. Stems smooth. MA (rare)

Doellingeria umbellata (*Aster umbellatus*)
ASTERACEAE
**Flat-topped aster, tall white-aster, tall flat-topped
white-aster**
Midsummer to early fall, 2–7 ft., perennial. Moist
ditches, meadows, thickets, and wetland edges.

Flower heads ½–¾ in. wide, with 7–14 white rays,
arranged in a crowded, flat-topped inflorescence of
20–100 heads. Leaves 1½–6 ½ in. long, sessile; the uppermost leaves smallest. Stems smooth or hairy. CT, MA, ME,
NH, RI, VT

Oligoneuron album (Aster ptarmicoides, Solidago ptarmicoides) ASTERACEAE
Upland white aster, white flat-topped goldenrod
Summer, 4–24 in., perennial. Cliffs, ledges, bald summits, and rocky river shores.

Flower heads ¾–1 in. wide, with 10–25 white rays, arranged in a crowded, flattish inflorescence of 3–50 heads; the whorled bracts beneath the heads flat, darkened at tip, with thickened midrib. Leaves 1–8 in. long, linear or lance-shaped, rigid, 3-veined, sessile or short-petioled. Stems smooth or hairy. CT (rare), MA (rare), NH (rare), VT

Symphyotrichum boreale (Aster borealis, A. junciformis) ASTERACEAE
Northern bog aster, rush aster, rush American-aster
Summer and early fall, 10–30 in., perennial. Rich, open fens.

Flower heads 1 in. wide, with 20–50 white or pale blue rays, arranged in an upwardly branching inflorescence of 1–35 heads ; the whorled bracts beneath the heads flat, narrow, and sharp-tipped. Leaves 1–6 in. long, linear or narrowly lance-shaped, sessile, ascending, with rough, slightly inrolled margins. Stems smooth, slender. ME, NH

Symphyotrichum ericoides (Aster ericoides)
ASTERACEAE
Many-flowered aster, heath American-aster
Summer and fall, 1–4 ft., perennial. Dry grasslands and sandy fields.

Flower heads ¼–½ in. wide, with 8–20 white rays, arranged in dense, branching clusters; the whorled bracts beneath the heads recurved, bristle-tipped, green, with tiny marginal hairs. Leaves 2 in. long or less, linear, ses-

sile; the upper leaves needle-like and crowded. Stems hairy. CT, MA, ME, NH, RI, VT

Symphyotrichum lanceolatum (Aster lanceolatus, A. simplex) ASTERACEAE
Panicled aster, lance-leaved American-aster
Summer and fall, 2–8 ft., perennial. Moist and wet meadows, swamp and marsh edges, and ditches.

Flower heads ¾–1 in. wide, with 20–40 white or violet rays, arranged in an open, leafy, wide-branching inflorescence; the whorled bracts beneath the heads slender, pointed, darkened at tip. Lower leaves 3–6 in. long, linear or lance-shaped, sometimes toothed. Stems smooth or hairy. CT, MA, ME, NH, RI, VT

Symphyotrichum lateriflorum (Aster lateriflorus) ASTERACEAE
Calico aster, starved aster, calico American-aster
Late summer and fall, 1–4 ft., perennial. Fields and woodlands.

Flower heads ½ in. wide, with 8–15 white or blue rays, arranged in branching, one-sided, dense clusters; the central disks yellowish or purple; the whorled bracts beneath the heads linear, sharp-pointed, green, with a prominent central rib. Leaves 2–6 in. long, linear or lance-shaped, occasionally toothed, the uppermost leaves crowded and smaller. Stems smooth or hairy. CT, MA, ME, NH, RI, VT

Symphyotrichum pilosum (Aster pilosus) ASTERACEAE
Awl aster, awl American-aster, heath aster
Summer and fall, 1–5 ft., perennial. Dry fields, roadsides, and open, disturbed habitats.

Flower heads ⅜–¾ in. wide, with 16–35 white rays, arranged in stiff, branching, many-flowered clusters; the whorled bracts beneath the heads spreading, hairless, pointed, with inrolled margins. Leaves 4 in. long or less, linear, sharp-tipped; the uppermost small and crowded. Stems smooth (in var. *pringlei*) or hairy (in var. *pilosum*). CT, MA, ME, NH, RI, VT

125

Symphyotrichum racemosum (Aster vimineus)
ASTERACEAE
Small white aster, small white American-aster
Summer and fall, 1–5 ft., perennial. Meadows, woodland edges, and river and pond shores.

Flower heads ¼–½ in. wide, with 15–30 white rays, arranged in a branching, densely flowered inflorescence; the whorled bracts beneath the flowers slender, green-tipped, scarcely spreading, with flat, hairless margins. Leaves 4 in. long or less, linear or narrowly lance-shaped, sessile; the upper leaves small and crowded. Stems smooth or sparsely hairy, often purple-tinged. CT, MA, ME, NH, RI, VT (rare)
  Symphyotrichum dumosum (bushy American-aster) is similar but usually with blue flowers.

Symphyotrichum tenuifolium (Aster tenuifolius)
ASTERACEAE
Perennial saltmarsh American-aster, perennial saltmarsh aster
Late summer to fall, 1–2 ft., perennial.
Salt and brackish marshes.

Flower heads ½–1 in. wide, with 10–25 light blue or white rays; the heads 3–20 on open, ascending branches; the whorled bracts beneath the heads flat, lance-shaped, with green tips and purple margins. Leaves 1½–6 in. long, few, linear, the uppermost small and bractlike. Stems smooth. CT, MA, NH, RI

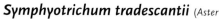

Symphyotrichum tradescantii (Aster tradescantii) ASTERACEAE
Tradescant's aster, Tradescant's American-aster
Summer and fall, 4–24 in., perennial. Rocky river shores.

Flower heads ½–¾ in. wide, long-stalked, with 15–30 white rays, arranged in a narrow, sparsely flowered inflorescence; the whorled bracts beneath the heads smooth, long-pointed, green or reddish at the tips. Leaves 1–4 in. long, linear or lance-shaped, entire or slightly toothed. Stems smooth, slender. MA (rare), ME, NH, RI, VT (rare)

Erigeron annuus ASTERACEAE
Annual fleabane, daisy fleabane
Spring to fall, 2–5 ft., annual or biennial. Fields, roadsides, and open, disturbed sites.

Flower heads ½–¾ in. wide, with 80–125 white or occasionally pink rays, arranged in a branching, flattish inflorescence; the central disks yellow. Leaves to 4 in. long, sharply toothed, petioled, oval or broadly lance-shaped. Stems with coarse, spreading hairs. CT, MA, ME, NH, RI, VT

Erigeron philadelphicus ASTERACEAE
Common fleabane, Philadelphia fleabane
Spring and summer, 6–30 in., biennial or short-lived perennial. Meadows, ledges, and open, disturbed habitats.

Flower heads ½–1 in. wide, with 150–400 white, pink, or magenta rays, arranged in a branching, flattish inflorescence. Leaves ¾–3½ in. long, clasping, oval or lance-shaped, entire or with a few scattered teeth. Stems densely hairy. CT, MA, ME, NH, RI, VT.

Erigeron strigosus ASTERACEAE
Rough fleabane, lesser daisy fleabane
Spring to fall, 1–3 ft., annual or biennial. Fields, roadsides, and open, disturbed sites.

Flower heads ½ in. wide, with 50–100 white (occasionally pink or violet) rays, arranged in a branching, many-flowered inflorescence; the central disks yellow. Leaves ½–4 in. long, linear or narrowly lance-shaped, sparsely toothed or entire. Stems with fine, pressed-in hairs. CT, MA, ME, NH, RI, VT

Eurybia divaricata (Aster divaricatus) ASTERACEAE
White wood-aster, common white heart-leaved aster
Late summer and fall, 6–36 in., perennial.
Deciduous and mixed forests and woodlands.

Flower heads ¾–1 in. wide, with 5–12 white rays, arranged in open, flattish panicles. Lower stem leaves 1–8 in. long and ¾–2½ in. wide, narrowly oval, sharply toothed, on long petioles; the upper leaves smaller; basal leaves usually withered by flowering time. Stems hairy or smooth. CT, MA, ME, NH, RI, VT

Eurybia schreberi (Aster schreberi) ASTERACEAE
Schreber's aster, Schreber's wood-aster
Summer and fall, 1–4 ft., perennial. Deciduous forests and forested floodplains.

Flower heads ¾–1 in. wide, with 6–12 white rays, arranged in a branching, flattish inflorescence; the stalks of the flower heads hairy, without glands. Basal leaves 4–12 in. long and 2–4 in. wide, present at flowering time, broadly oval, long-petioled, often with a rectangular notch at base; stem leaves smaller. Stems hairy or smooth. Frequently grows in colonies of basal leaves with few flowering stems. CT, MA, NH, RI, VT

Leucanthemum vulgare⁎ (Chrysanthemum leucanthemum) ASTERACEAE
Ox-eye daisy
Late spring to late summer, 1–3 ft., perennial.
Fields, roadsides, and open, disturbed sites.

Flower heads 1½–2½ in. wide, solitary, long-stalked, with 15–35 white rays and yellow disks. Lower leaves 1½–6 in. long, spoon-shaped or narrowly oval, toothed or lobed, on long petioles; the upper leaves smaller, sessile or short-petioled. Stems hairy or smooth. Native to Eurasia. CT, MA, ME, NH, RI, VT

Oclemena acuminata (*Aster acuminatus*)
ASTERACEAE
Whorled wood-aster, whorled aster, sharp-toothed nodding-aster
Summer and fall, 8–32 in., perennial. Forests and woodlands, in moist and dry soils.

Flower heads 1–1½ in. wide, with 10–20 white rays, arranged in open, flattish panicles; whorled bracts beneath the heads slender, sharp-pointed, light green. Leaves 2–7 in. long, broadly lance-shaped, sharply toothed, crowded on upper stem, appearing to be in whorls. Stems downy or hairy, zigzag in form. CT, MA, ME, NH, RI, VT

Lysimachia borealis (*Trientalis borealis*)
MYRSINACEAE
Starflower
Spring to early summer, 3–10 in., perennial. Forests.

Flowers white, ¼–½ in. wide, star-shaped, solitary or paired, stalked above leaf whorl; usually with 7 petals. Leaves 1½–4 in. long, lance-shaped, shining, in a single whorl at the top of the stem. Stems smooth. Fruit a rounded capsule, ⅛ in. long. CT, MA, ME, NH, RI, VT

Nymphaea odorata   NYMPHAEACEAE
Fragrant water-lily, white water-lily
Summer, slightly above water surface, perennial. Ponds, lakes, and slow-moving streams.

Flowers white or occasionally pink, 2–8 in. wide, floating, fragrant, with many bright petals and yellow centers. Leaves 4–12 in. long and wide, floating, round, purplish underneath, with a narrow sinus at the base. Stems submerged. Fruit a fleshy, globular berry ½–¾ in. long that matures underwater. CT, MA, ME, NH, RI, VT

7 or more radial petals; leaves simple, alternate, toothed or lobed

7 or more radial petals; leaves simple, whorled, entire

7 or more radial petals; leaves simple, basal, entire

Sanguinaria canadensis   PAPAVERACEAE
Bloodroot
Early spring, 2–12 in., perennial. Rich deciduous forests, woodlands, and clearings.

Flowers white, 1–2 in. wide, solitary, with 8–12 petals and yellow centers. Basal leaf 2–10 in. long, rounded, with broad teeth and undulating lobes, enfolds stem. Stems smooth, exuding an orange-red sap when broken. Fruit a narrow capsule, 1–2 in. long. CT, MA, ME, NH, RI, VT

Anthemis arvensis✳   ASTERACEAE
Field chamomile, corn chamomile
Summer and fall, 4–32 in., annual or biennial. Fields, roadsides, and open, disturbed sites.

Flower heads 1–1½ in. wide, with 5–20 white rays, solitary on long, branching stalk. Leaves 1–2¼ in. long, finely dissected into linear segments, odorless. Stems grayish hairy. Native to Europe. CT, MA, ME, NH, RI, VT

Anthemis cotula✳   ASTERACEAE
Stinking chamomile, mayweed, dogfennel
Summer and fall, 4–36 in., annual. Fields, roadsides, open, disturbed sites.

Flower heads ½–1 in. wide, with 10–16 white rays, solitary, on long, branching stalks. Leaves 1–2¼ in. long, finely dissected into linear segments, ill-scented. Stems reddish or green, hairy or smooth. Native to Eurasia. CT, MA, ME, NH, RI, VT

Matricaria chamomilla* (M. recutita)
ASTERACEAE
Wild chamomile
Spring to fall, 8–32 in., annual. Fields,
roadsides, open, disturbed sites.

Flower heads ¾–1 in. wide, with 10–20 white rays, solitary on long, branching stalks. Leaves ¾–2½ in. long,
finely dissected into threadlike segments, smelling of
pineapple. Stems smooth. Native to Eurasia. CT, MA, RI

Nabalus albus (Prenanthes alba) ASTERACEAE
White rattlesnake-root, white lettuce
Late summer and fall, 1–5 ft., perennial. Deciduous
forests and woodlands, often in rich soils.

Flower heads ½ in. wide, nodding, with 9–15 white or
pinkish rays; bracts beneath the rays 6–8, often purplish. Leaves variable, 1½–12 in. long, the lower on long
petioles, often deeply divided into 3 or more segments;
the upper smaller, on short petioles, shallowly lobed or
toothed. Stems with a whitish bloom. Fruit an achene
with a tuft of cinnamon-brown hairs. CT, MA, ME, NH, VT

Nabalus altissimus (Prenanthes altissima)
ASTERACEAE
Tall rattlesnake-root, tall white lettuce
Late summer and fall, 1–6 ½ ft.,
perennial. Deciduous forests.

Flower heads ¼–½ in. wide, with 5 or 6 creamy or greenish white rays; bracts below the rays 4–6, dark-tipped.
Lower leaves 1½–6 in. long, lance-shaped, oval or triangular, on long petioles, often lobed; the upper leaves
smaller on shorter petioles. Stems
mostly smooth, sometimes hairy at
base. Fruit an achene with a tuft of
creamy white hairs. CT, MA, ME, NH,
RI, VT

131

Nabalus boottii (*Prenanthes boottii*) ASTERACEAE
Boott's rattlesnake-root
Summer, 5–10 in., alpine perennial. Alpine
ridges and ledges at high elevations.

Flower heads white, ½ to ¾ in. wide, nodding or erect,
with 9–20 rays, bracts below the rays 8–11, dark green or
black. Leaves ¾–3 in. long, triangular or arrow-shaped,
the margins with a few blunt teeth or entire. Upper stems
hairy. Fruit an achene with a tuft of yellow or tan hairs.
Globally rare. ME, NH, VT (rare in all)

Nabalus serpentarius (*Prenanthes serpentaria*)
ASTERACEAE
Lion's foot, lion's-foot rattlesnake-root
Fall, 1½–5 ft., perennial. Sandplains, dry
woodlands, and rocky slopes.

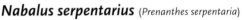

Flower heads ½ in. wide, nodding, with 8–14 creamy or
greenish white rays; bracts below the rays
8–10, green or purplish, sometimes speckled with black. Lower leaves 2–8 in. long,
often with winged petioles, usually deeply
divided; the upper leaves smaller. Stems
smooth or hairy. Fruit an achene with a tuft
of yellow or tan hairs. CT, MA (rare)

Nabalus trifoliolatus (*Prenanthes trifoliolata*)
ASTERACEAE
Three-leaved rattlesnake-root, gall-of-the-earth
Late summer and fall, 1–4 ft., perennial. Forests,
woodlands, clearings, ledges, and bald summits.

Flower heads ½ in. wide; nodding, with 8–13 creamy or
yellowish rays; bracts below the rays 7–14, smooth, green
or purplish, with waxy dots. Lower leaves 1¼–4 in. long,
on long petioles, deeply divided, arrow-shaped, or triangular. Stems smooth or slightly hairy. Fruit an achene
with a tuft of light brown or yellowish hairs. CT, MA, ME,
NH, RI, VT (rare)

*Tripleurospermum maritimum**

(*Matricaria maritima*) ASTERACEAE
Scentless chamomile
Summer and fall, 4–28 in., annual. Fields,
roadsides, open, disturbed sites.

Flower heads 1–1½ in. wide, solitary with 12–25 white
rays. Leaves 1–3¼ in. long, finely dissected into numerous linear segments, odorless. Stems reddish, smooth
or slightly hairy, with low, spreading, often prostrate
branches. Native to coastal habitats in Eurasia. CT, MA,
ME, NH

Podophyllum peltatum   BERBERIDACEAE

Mayapple, mandrake
Spring, 1–1½ ft., perennial. Rich deciduous forests
and woodlands, also along streambanks.

Flowers white, 1½–2 in. wide, with 6–9 petals, solitary,
nodding below leaves, stalked from junction of petioles. Leaves 12–16 in. long and wide, deeply and broadly
divided, with 3–7 lobes. Stems smooth. Fruit a lemonlike
yellow berry, 1–2 in. long. Immature plants with a single,
umbrella-like leaf. Native populations in northwest CT,
western MA, and western VT; introduced populations naturalized in CT, MA, ME, NH, RI, VT.

Thalictrum thalictroides (*Anemonella*

thalictroides) RANUNCULACEAE
Rue anemone
Early to late spring, 4–8 in., perennial. Moist or dry soils
in deciduous and mixed forests, woodlands, and thickets.

Flowers white or occasionally pink, ¾ in. wide, with 6–10
petal-like sepals, arranged in 1- to 6-flowered umbels.
Lower leaves subdivided into rounded leaflets, ½–1 in.
long, bluntly toothed or lobed at the tips; the upper leaves
divided into long-petioled leaflets that form the upper
whorl. Stems smooth, slender. Fruit an achene, ⅛–¼ in.
long. CT, MA, ME (rare), NH (rare), RI (rare), VT (rare)

7 or more radial petals; leaves deeply
divided, alternate, leaflets toothed or lobed

7 or more radial petals; leaves deeply
divided, opposite, leaflets toothed or lobed

7 or more radial petals; leaves deeply
divided, whorled, leaflets toothed or lobed

133

Petasites frigidus (*P. palmatus*) ASTERACEAE
Sweet coltsfoot, northern sweet coltsfoot
Early spring, 6–36 in., perennial. Northern white cedar swamps, rich seepages, and fens.

Flower heads white or creamy, ¼–½ in. wide, arranged in a rounded, dense, short-branching inflorescence on upper stem, appearing before emergence of leaves. Basal leaves 2–6 in. long, rounded, long-petioled, deeply cut, with 5–7 lobes, white-woolly beneath; stem leaves narrow and entire, ¾–2½ in. long, with sheathing bases. Stems hairy. CT (rare), MA (rare), ME, NH (rare), RI (rare), VT (rare)

Anaphalis margaritacea ASTERACEAE
Pearly everlasting
Summer and early fall, 8–36 in., perennial. Fields, woodland openings, and roadsides.

Flower heads bright white, ¼ in. wide, rounded, arranged in dense, flat-topped clusters; the "petals" are actually bracts that surround the yellow or brown disk. Leaves linear, 2–5 in. long, sessile, crowded, woolly or rusty underneath, the margins often inrolled. Stems woolly-hairy. CT, MA, ME, NH, RI, VT

Antennaria howellii (*A. neodioica*) ASTERACEAE
Small pussytoes
Early to late spring, 2–12 in., perennial. Fields, cliffs, ledges, woodlands, and roadsides.

Flower heads white, ¼ in. wide, arranged in small, dense clusters of 3–15. Basal leaves ¾–2 in. long, numerous, oval or spoon-shaped, overlapping and sharp-tipped, hairy underneath, smooth or hairy above, with one main nerve, forming a rosette. Stem leaves scaly, enfolding stem, their tips pointed and erect. Stems hairy. CT, MA, ME, NH, RI, VT

Antennaria neglecta ASTERACEAE
Field pussytoes
Early to late spring, 2–12 in., perennial. Fields,
cliffs, ledges, woodlands, and roadsides.

Almost identical to *Antennaria howellii* (small pussytoes),
but the basal leaves are hairy on both sides and the stem
leaves always have twisted, curling tips. CT, MA, ME, NH,
RI, VT

Antennaria plantaginifolia ASTERACEAE
Plantain-leaved pussytoes
Spring, 2–8 in., perennial. Fields, ledges,
woodlands, and roadsides.

Flower heads white, ¼–½ in. wide, arranged in a small,
dense cluster of 4–30; the whorl of bracts beneath the
flower heads ⅛–¼ in. long. Basal leaves 1½–3 in. long
and ½–1½ in. wide, broadly oval, with pointed tips, hairy
(sometimes sparsely) on the upper surface and densely
hairy underneath, with 3–5 primary veins, forming a
rosette. Stem leaves lance-shaped, hairy, ¼–1½ in. long.
Stems hairy. CT, MA, ME, NH, RI, VT
    Antennaria parlinii (smooth or Parlin's pussytoes) is
very similar, but upper surface of basal leaves smooth;
whorl of bracts beneath flower heads ¼–½ in. long.

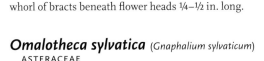

Omalotheca sylvatica (*Gnaphalium sylvaticum*)
ASTERACEAE
Woodland arctic-cudweed, woodland cudweed
Summer to early fall, 4–28 in., perennial. Fields,
clearings, and along logging roads.

Flower heads white, ⅛ in. wide, arranged in a leafy spike
of 10–90 heads. Leaves ¾–3 in. long, linear or narrowly
lance-shaped, woolly beneath and slightly hairy above.
Stems woolly. Northern and central ME, northern NH and
VT (rare)
    Omalotheca supina (alpine arctic-cudweed), a very rare
alpine species, is similar but smaller, ¾–4 in. tall, with
1–8 flower heads. Grows only in alpine zones of high
mountains. ME (rare), NH (rare)

Pseudognaphalium macounii (Gnaphalium macounii) ASTERACEAE
Clammy cudweed, clammy everlasting, Macoun's rabbit-tobacco
Summer and fall, 16–36 in., annual or biennial.
Woodland edges, fields, and open, disturbed sites.

Flower heads white, ¼ in. wide, woolly, arranged in small, dense, branching clusters. Leaves 1–4 in. long,

linear or lance-shaped, fragrant, woolly beneath and smooth or woolly above; the leaf bases with narrow wings that clasp the stem. Stems sticky with glandular hairs. CT, MA (rare), ME, NH, RI, VT (rare)

Pseudognaphalium obtusifolium (Gnaphalium obtusifolium) ASTERACEAE
Sweet everlasting, blunt-leaved rabbit-tobacco
Summer and fall, 8–36 in., annual or biennial.
Fields, roadsides, and open, disturbed sites.

Flower heads white, often yellow-tinged, ¼ in. wide, arranged in dense, flattish or rounded clusters. Leaves 1–4 in. long, linear or lance-shaped, sessile but not clasping, fragrant, woolly underneath and smooth or hairy above. Stems hairy but not glandular. CT, MA, ME, NH, RI, VT

Fallopia cilinodis (Polygonum cilinode) POLYGONACEAE
Fringed bindweed
Summer, to 6 ft. long, perennial vine. Forest clearings, woodlands, ledges, and roadsides.

Flowers white or greenish, ⅛ in. wide, arranged in branching axillary racemes. Leaves 2–5 in. long, broadly oval or triangular, with pointed tips and notched bases; sheaths at the base of the leaf petioles fringed. Stems twining, hairy, often reddish. Fruit a glossy black achene, ⅛–¼ in. long. CT, MA, ME, NH, RI, VT

*Fallopia convolvulus** *(Polygonum convolvulus)*
POLYGONACEAE
Black bindweed
Summer and fall, to 3 ft. long, annual vine. Thickets, fields, coastal beaches and headlands.

Flowers white or greenish, ⅛ in. wide, arranged in short, open, axillary racemes. Leaves 1–4 in. long, arrow-shaped, oval, or triangular, sheaths at the base of the leaf petioles without fringes. Stems trailing or twining. Fruit a black achene with finely ridged surface, ⅛–¼ in. long Native to Eurasia. CT, MA, ME, NH, RI, VT

*Fallopia japonica** *(Polygonum cuspidatum)*
POLYGONACEAE
Japanese knotweed
Late summer and early fall, 3–10 ft., perennial. Floodplains, river shores, swamp edges, ditches, thickets, fields, and roadsides. Invasive.

Flowers white or greenish white, ¼–⅜ in. wide, arranged in dense spreading or drooping racemes. Leaves 3–7 in. long, broadly oval or triangular, with pointed tips and flattened bases, smooth on lower surface. Stems smooth, thick, swollen at the nodes. Fruit an achene, ⅛ in. long, with broad, papery wings. Often in dense colonies. Native to Asia. CT, MA, ME, NH, RI, VT

*Fallopia sachalinensis** (giant knotweed) is similar, but the leaves are larger, 6–16 in. long and 2½–8 in. wide, rounded or heart-shaped at base, and hairy on lower surface. Native to Japan and Russian Far East. Grows in fields, river shores, and roadsides. It is much less common than *F. japonica*. CT, MA, ME, NH, RI

Fallopia scandens *(Polygonum scandens)*
POLYGONACEAE
Climbing false buckwheat, climbing bindweed
Late summer and fall, to 20 ft. long, perennial vine. Woodlands, floodplains, ridges, thickets, and roadsides.

Flowers white, yellowish, or greenish, ¼ in. wide, arranged in axillary racemes; the outer 3 petals with broadly winged margins. Leaves 2–5 in. long, oval, heart-shaped, or arrow-shaped, sheaths at bases of leaf petioles without fringes. Stems twining, reddish, roughened at the edges. Fruit a glossy black achene, ⅛–⅜ in. long, with winged margins. CT, MA, ME, NH, RI, VT

137

Persicaria arifolia (*Polygonum arifolium*)
POLYGONACEAE
Halberd-leaved tearthumb
Late summer to early fall, 2–6 ft., annual.
Swamps, marshes, and wet meadows.

Flowers white or pink, ⅛ in. wide, arranged in small heads, stalked from the leaf axils; the stalks bristly, with glandular hairs. Leaves 1–7 in. long, triangular with flaring basal lobes, sheaths at base of petiole prickly. Stems erect or scrambling, with hooked barbs. Fruit a broadly oval, brown achene, ⅛–¼ in. long. CT, MA, ME, NH, RI, VT

Persicaria hydropiperoides (*Polygonum hydropiperoides*) POLYGONACEAE
Mild water pepper, false water-pepper smartweed
Blooms in summer and fall, 6–36 in., perennial.
Pond and river shallows, marshes, and swamps.

Flowers white or pink, ⅛–¼ in. wide, arranged in long-stalked, often loosely flowered spikes; the spikes 1–3 in. long and ¼ in. wide. Leaves 2–10 in. long, linear or lance-shaped; the bristles on the sheaths about ¼ in. long. Stems erect or sprawling, hairy above, usually smooth below. Fruit a dark, shiny, oval achene, ¹⁄₁₆–⅛ in. long. CT, MA, ME, NH, RI, VT

Persicaria sagittata (*Polygonum sagittatum*)
POLYGONACEAE
Arrow-leaved tearthumb
Summer and early fall, 3–6 ft., annual.
Swamps, marshes, and wet meadows.

Flowers white or pink, ⅛–¼ in. wide, arranged in small heads, stalked from the leaf axils, the stalks smooth. Leaves 1–4 in. long, arrow-shaped, notched at the base, without flared lobes, midvein on the lower surface prickly. Stems erect or scrambling, with hooked barbs. Fruit a thick brown achene, ¹⁄₁₆–⅛ in. long. CT, MA, ME, NH, RI, VT

138

Persicaria virginiana (*Polygonum virginianum*, *Tovara virginiana*) POLYGONACEAE
Jumpseed, Virginia knotweed
Summer and fall, 1–3 ft., perennial. Forests, floodplains, woodlands, and thickets.

Flowers greenish white, ¼ in. wide, erect or slightly nodding, arranged in sparse, spikelike racemes, 4–16 in. long. Leaves 2–7 in. long, oval, with tapering tips and a thin, hairy sheath at base of petiole. Stems smooth or hairy. Fruit a single-seeded achene, ⅛ in. long; when touched, mature fruits can propel seed 12 ft. away. CT, MA, NH, RI, VT

Polygonum articulatum (*Polygonella articulata*) POLYGONACEAE
Sand jointweed, coastal jointed knotweed
Late summer and fall, 4–20 in., annual. Dunes, grasslands, fields, roadsides, and open, disturbed sites.

Flowers white or pink, ⅛ in. wide, spreading or nodding, arranged in racemes; the 5 petals (tepals) open or closed. Leaves ¼–¾ in. long, linear, with inrolled margins. Stems smooth, wiry. Fruit a shiny brown, narrow achene, ¹⁄₁₆–⅛ in. long. CT, MA, ME, NH, RI, VT

Polygonum aviculare⁕ POLYGONACEAE
Prostrate knotweed, dooryard knotweed, doorweed
Summer and fall, to 4 in., annual. Fields, roadsides, pavement cracks, and shorelines.

Flowers white, greenish, or pink-tinged, ⅛ in. wide, tucked in leaf axils. Leaves bluish green, ½–2½ in. long, lance-shaped or oval, with silvery sheaths. Stems smooth, sprawling or erect. Fruit a dark brown achene, ¹⁄₁₆–⅛ in. long. Native to Europe. CT, MA, ME, NH, RI, VT

Petals indistinguishable; leaves simple, alternate, entire

Polygonum douglasii   POLYGONACEAE
Douglas's knotweed
Summer and fall, 4–24 in., annual. Cliffs, bald summits, outcrops, and rocky woodlands.

Flowers white, greenish, or pink-tinged, ¼–⅛ in. long, nodding, arranged in sparsely flowered racemes. Leaves ½–2 in. long, linear or lance-shaped, sharply tipped, with a single vein; leaf margins sometimes inrolled. Stems smooth, angled. Fruit a shiny black achene, ⅛ in. long. ME, NH, VT (rare in all)

Polygonum glaucum   POLYGONACEAE
Seaside knotweed, seabeach knotweed
Summer and fall, 1–2 ft., annual. Sea beaches, reaching its northern range limit in New England.

Flowers white or pink, ⅛ in. long, tightly clustered in leaf axils. Leaves ½–1¼ in. long, whitish green, fleshy, lance-shaped or narrowly oval, with inrolled margins; the sheaths at base of petioles silvery. Stems smooth, sprawling. Fruit a black achene, ⅛ in. long. CT, MA, RI (rare in all)

Polygonum tenue   POLYGONACEAE
Slender knotweed
Summer and fall, 4–16 in., slender annual. Cliffs, ledges, open, rocky woodlands, and fields.

Flowers white, greenish, or pink, ⅛ in. wide, tucked singly or in pairs in leaf axils. Leaves ½–1¼ in. long, linear, sharp-tipped, with longitudinal furrows on each side of the midvein; the uppermost leaves small and bractlike. Stems smooth. Fruit a dark brown or black oval achene, 1⁄16–⅛ in. long. CT, MA (rare), NH (rare), RI, VT (rare)

Saururus cernuus SAURURACEAE
Lizard's-tail
Summer, 2–5 ft., perennial aquatic. Swamps,
marshes, and lake and river shores.

Flowers white, ⅛ in. wide, fragrant, with projecting stamens; densely clustered in a nodding or erect, tail-like
spike 4–12 in. long. Leaves 2–10 in. long, heart-shaped,
long-petioled and tapering to the tip. Stems creeping at
base. Fruits brown, wrinkled, capsulelike, ⅟₁₆–⅛ in. long.
CT (rare), RI (rare)

Sparganium americanum SPARGANIACEAE
American bur-reed, lesser bur-reed
Summer, 1–3 ft., perennial aquatic. Shallow
water and muddy shorelines.

Flowers white or green, tiny, aggregated in ball-like
heads; the female heads ½–1 in. wide, sessile, the male
heads smaller. The primary flower branch has 1–5 female
heads and 5–9 male heads; the side branches have fewer
heads of both. Leaves to 3 ft. long and ¼–½ in. wide,
erect, flat or weakly keeled. Fruit a dull brown, oval
achene, ⅛–¼ in. long, with a straight beak. CT, MA, ME,
NH, RI, VT

Sparganium androcladum SPARGANIACEAE
Branched bur-reed, branching bur-reed
Summer, 1½–4 ft., perennial aquatic.
Shallow water and muddy shorelines.

Flowers white or green, tiny, aggregated in ball-like
heads; the female heads 1–1½ wide, the male heads
smaller. The primary flower branch has 2–4 sessile
female heads and 4–10 male heads; side branches usually with only 3–10 male heads. Leaves to 32 in. long and
¼–½ in. wide, erect, strongly keeled. Fruit a light brown,
oval, shining achene, ¼ in. long, with a straight beak
about as long. CT, MA (rare), ME, RI, VT (rare)

Sparganium angustifolium SPARGANIACEAE
Narrow-leaved bur-reed
Summer, slightly above water surface,
perennial. Still or slow-moving water.

Flowers white or green, tiny, aggregated in ball-like heads
arranged on a single stalk just above water surface, with
1–3 female heads (⅜–¾ in. wide), the lowest stalked, and
1–6 smaller contiguous male heads. Leaves to 4 ft. long and
1/16–⅜ in. wide, floating. Fruit a brown achene, ⅛ in. long,
with a straight beak, 1/16 in. long. CT, MA (rare), ME, NH, VT

 Sparganium fluctuans (floating bur-reed) has separated
male heads, and the achene beaks are curved. CT (rare),
MA (rare), ME, NH, VT (rare)

 Sparganium natans (Arctic bur-reed, small bur-reed)
also has floating leaves but has only a single, terminal
head; the sparse female heads (¼–½ in. wide) are sessile,
and the achene beaks are tiny. CT (rare), MA (rare), ME,
NH(rare), VT (rare)

Sparganium emersum (S. chlorocarpum)
SPARGANIACEAE
Simple-stemmed bur-reed, green-fruited bur-reed
Summer, to 32 in., perennial aquatic. Shallow water and
shorelines, usually in high-pH conditions.

Flowers white or green, tiny, aggregated in
ball-like heads. The single inflorescence
has 1–3 female heads (⅜–¾ in. wide) and
4–9 distinctly smaller separated male
heads. Erect leaves to 32 in. long and ¼–½
in. wide, flat or keeled; floating leaves, if
present, are longer. Fruit an achene, ⅛ in.
long, with a green base; beak as long as
body. CT, MA, ME, NH, VT

Sparganium eurycarpum SPARGANIACEAE
Giant bur-reed, great bur-reed
Summer, 1½–7 ft., perennial. Lakes, ponds,
slow-moving streams, and shorelines.

Flowers white or green, tiny, aggregated in ball-like heads;
the female heads ¾–1¼ in. wide, the male heads distinctly
smaller. Inflorescence branches have 1–6 female heads,
mostly sessile, and several to 43 or more male heads.
Leaves 2–7 ft. long, ¼–¾ in. wide, keeled. Fruit a thick,
triangular achene widest at top, ¼–⅜ in. long, with a
straight beak. CT, MA, ME, NH, RI, VT

Erechtites hieraciifolius (E. hieraciifolia)
ASTERACEAE
Pilewort, American burnweed
Late summer and fall, 1–8 ft., annual. Fields, woodland clearings, recently burned areas, and disturbed sites.

Flower heads ¾ in. wide, greenish white, rayless, with swollen bases, arranged in a branching, many-flowered inflorescence; the disks produce long silken-haired fruit. Leaves 2–8 in. long, lance-shaped or oval, sharply toothed, upper leaves with clasping bases. Stems hairy or smooth. The common variety (var. *hieraciifolius*) grows in CT, MA, ME, NH, RI, VT. The uncommon variety (var. *megalocarpus*), with fleshy leaves and stems, grows on coastal beaches and salt marshes in CT, MA, RI.

Erigeron canadensis (Conyza canadensis)
ASTERACEAE
Horseweed
Summer and fall, 6–60 in., annual. Fields, roadsides, and open, disturbed sites.

Flower heads ⅛ in. long, white, rayless, arranged in a wide-branching, many-flowered inflorescence. Leaves ¾–4 in. long, linear or narrowly lance-shaped, the margins sparsely toothed or entire, fringed with small hairs. Upper stems hairy. CT, MA, ME, NH, RI, VT

Solidago bicolor ASTERACEAE
Silverrod, white goldenrod
Summer and fall, 4–40 in., perennial. Sandy or rocky woodlands, fields, and roadsides.

Flower heads ¼ in. wide, with 7–9 white rays, arranged in an erect, spikelike panicle; bracts beneath the flowers whitish with green tips. Lower stem leaves 1½–4 in. long, narrowly oval or broadly lance-shaped, with blunt teeth; the upper leaves smaller and entire. Stems hairy. The only white-flowered *Solidago* in New England. CT, MA, ME, NH, RI, VT

143

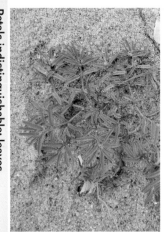

Euphorbia polygonifolia (Chamaesyce polygonifolia) EUPHORBIACEAE
Seaside spurge, seaside sandmat
Summer and fall, 4–12 in., annual. Sand
dunes and coastal beaches.

Flowers white or reddish, ⅛ in. wide, short-stalked, solitary or paired in the leaf axils; all flower parts smooth.
Leaves ½ in. long, light green, lance-shaped or narrowly
oval, entire, with a tiny, spinelike tip. Stems prostrate,
mat-forming, smooth, and reddish. Fruit a smooth capsule, ⅛ in. long. CT, MA, RI

Ageratina altissima (Eupatorium rugosum)
ASTERACEAE
White snakeroot
Late summer and fall, 1–5 ft., perennial.
Woodlands, forests, and thickets.

Individual flower heads white, ⅛–¼ in. wide, aggregated in flat or rounded, branching clusters usually
1–2 in. wide. Leaves 1½–4½ in. long, oval, tapering to
long-pointed tips, with 9–25 sharp teeth on each margin;
petioles of larger stem leaves ¾ in. long. CT, MA, ME, NH,
RI, VT

Ageratina aromatica (Eupatorium aromaticum)
ASTERACEAE
Lesser snakeroot
Late summer and fall, 1–2½ ft., perennial. Dry, rocky
woodland clearings and sand plain grasslands.

Individual flower heads white, ⅛–¼ in. wide, aggregated
into flat or rounded, branching clusters. Leaves 1½–3
in. long, thick, oval, with 7–12 rounded or blunt teeth on
each margin; petioles of larger stem leaves ½ in. long.
Stems smooth or finely hairy. A very rare species. CT
(rare), MA (rare)

Eupatorium novae-angliae (E. *leucolepis* var. *novae-angliae*) ASTERACEAE
New England boneset, New England thoroughwort
Late summer and fall, 1½–3 ft., perennial.
Coastal plain pond shores and occasionally
in moist sandy swales near coast.

Individual flower heads white, ⅛ in. wide, aggregated into flat-topped, narrowly branched clusters. Leaves 1–3 in. long, lance-shaped, sessile, hairy underneath; the leaf teeth sharp and narrow. Stems hairy. An extremely rare species occurring in southeastern MA and southern RI.

Eupatorium perfoliatum ASTERACEAE
Boneset, boneset thoroughwort
Midsummer to fall, 1–5 ft., perennial. Swamps, wet
meadows, swamps, ditches, and lake and pond shores.

Individual flower heads white, ¼ in. wide, densely aggregated in branching, flattish terminal and axillary clusters. Leaves 3–8 in. long, lance-shaped, conspicuously veined, finely toothed, tapering to a long-pointed tip; the paired leaf bases fused, pierced by the stem. Stems hairy.
CT, MA, ME, NH, RI, VT

Eupatorium pilosum ASTERACEAE
Rough boneset, ragged thoroughwort
Late summer and fall, 1–5 ft., perennial. Moist to
wet sandy fields, pond shores, and swales.

Individual flower heads white, ¼ in. wide, aggregated in short-branched, flattish clusters; the branches of the inflorescence clusters often alternate. Leaves 1¼–3½ in. long and ¾–1½ in. wide, oval, sessile or with very short petioles, each margin with 3–12 coarse or rounded teeth; the uppermost leaves often alternate. Stems hairy. CT, MA, RI

Eupatorium pubescens (hairy boneset, hairy thoroughwort; syn. *E. rotundifolium* var. *ovatum*) is similar, but the leaves have 12–25 teeth on each margin, and the uppermost leaves are all opposite. CT, MA, ME, NH (rare), RI

145

Eupatorium rotundifolium   ASTERACEAE
Upland boneset, upland thoroughwort
Late summer and fall, 1–5 ft., perennial. Forest edges, woodland clearings, fields, and pond shores.

Individual flower heads white, ¼ in. wide, aggregated in dense, branching, flat-topped clusters. Leaves ½–2¾ in. long and ½–2¼ in. wide (1–1½ times as long as wide), sessile, rounded or broadly triangular, with 8–20 teeth on each margin. Stems hairy. CT, MA

Eupatorium sessilifolium   ASTERACEAE
Upland boneset, upland thoroughwort
Late summer and fall, 2–5 ft., perennial.
Rocky woodlands and forest edges.

Individual flower heads white, ¼ in. wide, aggregated in open, narrowly branched, flat-topped clusters; the inflorescence branches with fine hairs. Leaves 3–6 in. long and ½–1¼ in. wide, lance-shaped, sessile, smooth, finely toothed, gland-dotted, tapering to a long point. Stems mostly smooth, sometimes finely hairy above. CT, MA, ME (rare), RI, VT (rare)

Mikania scandens   ASTERACEAE
Climbing hempweed, climbing hempvine
Summer and fall, to 16 ft. long, perennial vine.
Swamps, wet thickets, and floodplains.

Individual flowers white, pink, or lilac, ¼ in. wide, aggregated in long-stalked, dense, flattish or rounded clusters. Leaves 1–6 in. long, triangular, long-petioled, with long-pointed tips and notched bases; the margins coarsely toothed or wavy. Stems twining, climbing over other vegetation. MA, CT, NH (rare), RI

Euphorbia maculata (*Chamaesyce maculata*)
EUPHORBIACEAE
Spotted spurge, spotted sandmat
Summer and fall, 4–16 in., annual. Yards,
roadsides, vacant lots, and pavement cracks.

Flowers white or reddish, ¹⁄16–⅛ in. wide, solitary or in
small clusters in leaf axils; the ovary above the 4 tiny,
petal-like lobes hairy. Leaves ¼–¾ in. long, oval, slightly
toothed or entire, the blades often red-blotched. Stems
prostrate, mat-forming, hairy, exuding a milky sap when
broken. Fruit a hairy capsule, ¹⁄16 in. or less. CT, MA, ME,
NH, RI, VT

Euphorbia nutans (*Chamaesyce nutans*)
EUPHORBIACEAE
Eyebane, eyebane sandmat
Spring to fall, to 36 in., annual. Open, disturbed sites.

Flowers white or reddish, ¹⁄16–⅛ in. wide, arranged
in small, short-stalked terminal or axillary clusters.
Leaves ½–1½ in. long, narrowly oval, finely toothed,
blunt-tipped, usually green (occasionally marked with
red). Stems erect or ascending (not prostrate), reddish,
smooth or finely hairy, exuding a milky sap when broken.
Fruit a smooth, 3-parted capsule, ¹⁄16–⅛ in. long. CT, MA,
NH, RI (rare), VT (rare)

Euphorbia vermiculata (*Chamaesyce vermiculata*)
EUPHORBIACEAE
Hairy spurge, hairy sandmat
Summer and fall, to 16 in., annual. Roadsides,
vacant lots, and pavement cracks.

Flower white or reddish, less than ⅛ in. wide,
short-stalked, solitary or in small clusters in leaf axils;
the ovary above the 4 tiny petal-like lobes smooth. Leaves
¼–¾ in. long, with small, shallow teeth; the leaf blades
green or red-tinged but not blotched. Stems hairy, prostrate, mat-forming, exuding a milky sap when broken.
Fruit a smooth, 3-parted capsule, ¹⁄16 in. long or less. CT,
MA, ME, NH, RI, VT

Eupatorium hyssopifolium ASTERACEAE
Hyssop-leaved boneset
Late summer and fall, 1–4 ft., perennial. Dry sandy
fields, thickets, clearings, and roadsides.

Individual flower heads white, ¼ in. wide, aggregated
in branched, flat-topped clusters. Primary leaves 1–3 in.
long, linear, in whorls of 4, toothed on the upper margins
or entire; clusters of very small leaves grow from the axils
of the primary leaves. Stems hairy. CT, MA, RI

Polygala senega POLYGALACEAE
Seneca snakeroot, Seneca milkwort
Spring and early summer, 4–20 in., perennial. Rocky river
shores, clearings, and woodlands, in high-pH soils.

Flowers white, sometimes tinged with pink or green, ⅛
in. long, 5-parted, often closed, arranged in dense, spikelike racemes; the 2 lateral, winglike sepals larger than the
3 inner sepals. Leaves crowded, lance-shaped, the middle and upper 1¼–3 in. long, the lowermost very small.
Stems hairy. Fruit a rounded capsule, ⅛ in. wide. Plants
resemble knotweeds (*Polygonum spp.*), but stems lack
joints. CT, ME, VT (rare in all)

Polygala verticillata POLYGALACEAE
Whorled milkwort
Summer and fall, 4–16 in., annual. Fields,
clearings, ledges, roadsides, open woodlands.

Flowers white, pink, or green, ¼ in. long, arranged in a
pointed terminal raceme, ¼–2 in. long. Leaves ⅜–1¼ in.
long, linear, in whorls of 2–5. Stems smooth. Fruit a capsule. CT, MA (rare), ME, NH, RI (rare), VT (rare)

Eriocaulon aquaticum (*E. septangulare*)
ERIOCAULACEAE
Seven-angled pipewort
Midsummer to early fall, 3–8 in. (submerged
stems to 3 ft.), aquatic. Shorelines and shallows
of ponds, lakes, and slow-moving rivers.

Flowers grayish white, tiny, congested in solitary, buttonlike flower heads, ⅛–⅜ in. wide. Leaves ½–4 in. long,
grasslike, sharp-pointed, arranged in a rosette; each
rosette produces only 1 flower stem. Stems leafless, with
5–7 ribs. Fruit a tiny capsule. CT, MA, ME, NH, RI, VT

Eriocaulon parkeri   ERIOCAULACEAE
Parker's pipewort
Midsummer to early fall, 4–12 in., perennial.
Estuaries and mudflats, in both brackish and
freshwater conditions, coastal plain pond shores.

Flowers grayish white, tiny, congested
in solitary, buttonlike heads ⅛ in.
wide. Leaves ¾–2½ in. long, grasslike,
sharp-pointed, arranged in a rosette;
each rosette produces 1–4 flower
stems. Stems leafless, with 4 or 5 ribs.
Fruit a tiny capsule. Coastal counties
of CT, MA, ME (rare in all)

*Plantago aristata**   PLANTAGINACEAE
Bracted plantain
Summer and fall, 4–10 in., annual or
occasionally perennial. Dry fields, roadsides,
and open, disturbed habitats.

Flowers cream-colored, ⅛ in. wide, with 4 tiny lobes,
arranged in cylindrical spikes 1¼–2½ in. long; the
spikes dominated by thin, stiff bracts (¼–2 in. long)
which partially conceal the tiny flowers. Leaves to 7 in.
long, linear or narrowly lance-shaped. Stems hairy. Fruit
a dry, oval, 2-seeded capsule, ⅛ in. long. Native to midwestern United States, naturalized in New England. CT,
MA, ME, NH, RI, VT

149

*Plantago lanceolata** PLANTAGINACEAE
English plantain
Spring to fall, 6–24 in., perennial. Fields, roadsides, and open, disturbed habitats.

Flowers white, ⅛ in. wide, arranged in dense conical spikes ¾–3 in. long; the stamens projecting and prominent. Leaves 4–16 in. long, narrowly elliptical or lance-shaped, ascending, with 3–5 parallel veins running the length of the blade. Stems hairy. Fruit oval, capsulelike, ⅛ in. long. Native to Eurasia. CT, MA, ME, NH, RI, VT

*Plantago major** PLANTAGINACEAE
Common plantain
Late spring to fall, 2–20 in., annual or perennial. Fields, roadsides, and pavement cracks.

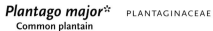

Flowers white, ¹⁄₁₆ in. wide; clustered in a narrow spike, 1–12 in. long. Leaves 1½–7 in. long, long-petioled, with 3–7 prominent parallel veins; base of petioles usually green or pale, occasionally red-tinged. Fruits oval, capsulelike, about ⅛ in. long. Native to Eurasia. CT, MA, ME, NH, RI, VT

Plantago maritima (P. juncoides)
PLANTAGINACEAE
Seaside plantain
Summer and early fall, 2–8 in., perennial. Salt marshes, beaches, and seaside rocks and cliffs.

Flowers yellowish white or brown, ¹⁄₁₆–⅛ in. wide, clustered in a narrow spike, ¾–4 in. long; the stamens prominent, ascending. Leaves 2–6 in. long, ascending, linear or narrowly lance-shaped, fleshy, with 1 primary vein. Upper stem often hairy. Fruit oval, capsulelike, ¹⁄₁₆ in. long. CT, MA, ME, NH, RI

Sanicula canadensis APIACEAE
Canada sanicle, short-styled snakeroot
Spring and early summer, 3–30 in., biennial.
Moist deciduous forests and woodlands.

Flowers greenish white, 1/16–1/8 in. long, clustered
in small, burlike heads; both fertile and male flowers short-stalked; the sharp-tipped green
sepals longer than the petals. Leaves 3/4–2½
in. long, sharply toothed, deeply divided,
with 3–5 lobes. Stems smooth. Fruits bristly, rounded, 1/8 in. long; the bristles longer than the persistent styles and the calyx
lobes. CT, MA (rare), VT

Sanicula marilandica APIACEAE
Black snakeroot, Maryland sanicle
Spring to midsummer, 1–4 ft., perennial.
Moist deciduous forests.

Flowers white or greenish white, 1/8 in. long, clustered in
small, burlike heads; both fertile and male flowers sessile
or very short-stalked; the sepals and petals about equal in
length. Lower leaves 2–6 in. long, long-petioled, sharply
toothed, deeply and broadly divided, with 5–7 lobes.
Stems smooth. Fruit bristly, oval, 1/8–1/4 in. long; the persistent, arching styles longer than the bristles. CT, MA,
ME, NH, RI, VT

Sanicula trifoliata APIACEAE
Large-fruited sanicle, long-fruited snakeroot
Summer, 1–2½ ft., biennial. Deciduous forests and
floodplains, usually in areas with high-pH soils.

Flowers white or greenish white, 1/8 in. long, clustered in
small, burlike heads; the male flowers stalked; the sepals
longer than the petals. Larger leaves 2½–4 in. long,
sharply toothed, deeply or shallowly divided, with 3 lobes.
Stems hairy or smooth. Fruits bristly, oval, 1/4 in. long; the
persistent calyx lobes fused, forming a beak just overtopping the bristles. CT, MA (rare), ME, NH (rare), VT (rare)

Petals indistinguishable; leaves deeply divided, alternate, leaflets toothed or lobed

Actaea pachypoda (*A. alba*) RANUNCULACEAE
White baneberry, doll's-eyes
Spring and early summer, 16–32 in.,
perennial. Rich deciduous forests.

Flowers white, ⅛ in. wide, with thin petals and bushy
stamens, arranged in a dense long-stalked, cylindrical raceme, 1½–3 in. long. Leaves pinnately divided
and subdivided into multiple, sharply toothed oval or
lance-shaped leaflets to 5 in. long, smooth on both surfaces. Stems smooth. Fruit a round or elliptical white
berry with a purple "eye," ¼–⅜ in. long, aggregated into
long, conspicuous clusters; the fruit stalks thick and red.
CT, MA, ME, NH, RI, VT

Actaea racemosa (*Cimicifuga racemosa*)
RANUNCULACEAE
Black cohosh, bugbane
Spring and early summer, 3–7 ft.,
perennial. Rich deciduous forests.

Flowers white, ½ in. wide, with prominent, bushy stamens, arranged in slender, erect, tapering, densely flowered racemes 1–3 ft. long. Leaves pinnately divided and
subdivided into 15–70 oval, sharply toothed leaflets to 5
in. long. Stems smooth. Fruit an oval follicle, ¼–½ in.
long. Native populations only in CT, MA (rare); introduced
populations naturalized in CT, MA, and ME.

Actaea rubra RANUNCULACEAE
Red baneberry
Spring and early summer, 16–32 in.,
perennial. Rich deciduous forests.

Flowers white, ¼ in. wide, with thin petals and bushy
stamens, arranged in a dense, long-stalked, rounded or
broadly pyramidal raceme, 1–3 in. long. Leaves pinnately
divided and subdivided into multiple, sharply toothed,
oval or lance-shaped leaflets to 5 in. long, hairy on the
undersurfaces. Stems hairy. Fruit a round or elliptical red
berry, ¼–⅜ in. long, aggregated into long, conspicuous
clusters; the fruit stalks slender, usually green. CT, MA,
ME, NH, RI (rare), VT

Hydrastis canadensis RANUNCULACEAE
Goldenseal
Early spring, 8–20 in., perennial. Rich deciduous forests.

Flower heads greenish white, ½ in. wide, solitary, composed of white stamens surrounding a cluster of green pistils; the head borne just above the uppermost leaf. Leaves usually 3 (1 basal and 2 on stem), 1¼–4 in. wide at flowering, sharply toothed and deeply divided, with 5–7 lobes. Fruit a crimson berry, densely aggregated into rounded heads ½ in. wide. MA, CT, VT (rare in all)

Thalictrum pubescens (*T. polygamum*)
RANUNCULACEAE
Tall meadow-rue
Summer, 3–8 ft., perennial. Swamps, marshes, wet meadows, river shorelines, and moist woodlands.

Flowers white, ⅛–¼ in. wide, erect, arranged in dense, feathery panicles; the flowers with 4 tiny sepals and bushy, prominent, starlike stamens. Leaves pinnately subdivided into many small, blunt, rounded or oval leaflets, ¼–1 in. long; the leaflets occasionally entire but more often with blunt lobes, smooth or finely hairy beneath. Stems smooth or finely hairy. Fruit an oval or elliptical achene, ⅛–¼ in. long. CT, MA, ME, NH, RI, VT

Thalictrum revolutum RANUNCULACEAE
Waxy meadow-rue, waxy-leaved meadow-rue, skunk meadow-rue
Summer, 3–6 ft., perennial. Rocky forests, woodlands, ridges, and fields.

Flowers white or green, ¼ in. wide, nodding, arranged in many-flowered panicles; the flowers with 4 or 5 tiny sepals and bushy, drooping stamens. Leaves dark green, pinnately subdivided into oval, bluntly lobed leaflets with inrolled margins, ¼–2 in. long, their undersurfaces dotted with short-stalked glands; crushed leaves exude a skunklike odor. Stems smooth. Fruit an oval, ribbed achene, ⅛–¼ in. long, covered with glandular hairs. CT, MA, NH (rare)

Sanguisorba canadensis ROSACEAE
Canada burnet, American burnet
Summer and early fall, 1–6 ft., perennial. Floodplains, swamps, wet meadows, and brackish marshes.

Flowers white, ¼ in. long, arranged in dense, long-stalked spikes, 1½–8 in. long; the flowers with 4 tiny sepals and bushy, prominent stamens. Leaves to 18 in. long, pinnately divided into 7–17 leaflets; the leaflets oblong or narrowly oval, 1–4 in. long. Stems smooth. Fruit a dry, rounded achene, ¼ in. long. CT, MA, ME (rare), NH, RI (rare), VT (rare)

Aralia nudicaulis APIACEAE
Wild sarsaparilla
Spring and early summer, 6–15 in., perennial. Deciduous and mixed forests.

Flowers greenish white, ⅛–¼ in. wide, clustered in 2–7 dense, ball-like umbels, borne on a stalk below the leaves. Leaves long-petioled, pinnately divided into 3 groups of 3–5 sharply toothed, oval or elliptical leaflets 3–5 in. long. Stems smooth, woody at base. Fruit blue-black, berrylike, ¼ in. long. CT, MA, ME, NH, RI, VT

Bartonia paniculata GENTIANACEAE
Twining screwstem
Late summer, 1½–18 in., perennial. Sandy or peaty swamps, wet meadows, and swales.

Flowers creamy white, ⅛ in. long, the 4 petals mostly closed; the flowers ascending or spreading, arranged on a sparse panicle. Stem leaves scaly, 1⁄16 in. long, mostly alternate. Stems smooth, erect or twining. Fruit a tiny, oval capsule. CT (rare), MA, ME (rare), NH (rare), RI (rare)

Platanthera blephariglottis (*Habenaria blephariglottis*) ORCHIDACEAE
White fringed orchid
Mid to late summer, 6–36 in., perennial. Bogs, fens, and acidic swamps, and peaty meadows.

Flowers white, ½–1 in. long, clustered in a dense, 20- to 45-flowered spike, 2–6 in. long; the flowers with a fringed lower lip projecting below the hood formed by the upper sepal and 2 small upper petals, and a conspicuous, slender spur, ½–1 in. long, that is much longer than the lip. Lower leaves 2–14 in. long, lance-shaped, the upper leaves linear and much smaller. Fruit an oval capsule. CT (rare), MA, ME, NH, RI (rare), VT (rare)

Platanthera dilatata (*Habenaria dilatata*) ORCHIDACEAE
Tall white bog orchid, white northern bog orchid, bog candles
Early to midsummer, 12–40 in., perennial. Bogs, fens, river shores, and moist, coniferous forest clearings.

Flowers white, fragrant, ½ in. long, clustered in a dense 20- to 100-flowered spike, 4–12 in. long; the flowers with a slender, nonfringed, tapering lower lip and spreading, winglike lateral sepals; the spur about as long as the lip. Lower leaves to 12 in. long, narrowly lance-shaped; the upper leaves much smaller. Fruit an elliptical capsule, ½ in. long. MA (rare), ME, NH, VT

Platanthera lacera (*Habenaria lacera*) ORCHIDACEAE
Ragged fringed orchid, green-fringed bog-orchid
Summer, 12–32 in., perennial. Moist to wet meadows, marshes, swamps, and thickets.

Flowers greenish white or greenish yellow, ¾ in. long, arranged in loose or dense spikes of 20–40 flowers; the flowers with a prominent lower lip dissected into many, threadlike lobes; the spur slender, elongate, ½–1 in. long. Lower leaves lance-shaped to oval, 2–6 in. long; the upper leaves linear and much smaller. Fruit an elliptical capsule, ¾ in. long. CT, MA, ME, NH, RI (rare), VT

Triphora trianthophora ORCHIDACEAE
Three-birds orchid, nodding pogonia
Late summer and early fall, 4–12 in., perennial.
Moist deciduous forests with deep leaf litter.

Flowers white or pinkish, ½–¾ in. long, nodding in clusters of 3–6 from upper leaf axils; the lower lip wavy-edged, pointed at tip, with a green center. Stem leaves ½–¾ in. long, oval, sessile or clasping. Fruit a capsule, ½ in. long. A seldom-encountered plant with a brief flowering period. CT, MA, ME, NH, VT (rare in all)

Viola canadensis VIOLACEAE
Canada violet, Canada white violet, tall white violet
Spring and summer, sometimes a second bloom in fall, 8–16 in., perennial. Rich, moist deciduous forests.

Flowers white, ¼–½ in. long, solitary, stalked above the leaves; the petals with yellow throats, purple-tinged on the back. Leaves heart-shaped, finely toothed, 2–4 in. long, the upper stem leaves often smaller and narrower. Stems smooth or hairy. Fruit an elliptical capsule. Primarily in western New England. CT (rare), MA, ME (rare), NH (rare), VT

Pycnanthemum tenuifolium LAMIACEAE
Narrow-leaved mountain-mint
Summer, 1–3 ft., perennial. Fields, thickets, and clearings.

Flowers white, ⅛–¼ in. long, arranged in dense, branching, flattish or rounded clusters; the lower lip 3-lobed and purple-spotted. Leaves ¾–2 in. long and usually ⅛ in. wide or less, linear, smooth. Stems smooth or sometimes with very sparse hairs on the ridge angles. Fruit 4-parted, capsulelike, less than 1/16 in. long. CT, MA, ME, NH, RI, VT

Pycnanthemum virginianum   LAMIACEAE
Virginia mountain-mint
Summer, 1–3 ft., aromatic, perennial.
Fields, clearings, and roadsides.

Flowers white, ¼ in. long, arranged in dense, branching, flattish or rounded clusters; the lower lip 3-lobed and purple-spotted. Leaves 1¼–2½ in. long and ⅛–⅜ in. wide, linear or narrowly lance-shaped, aromatic when crushed, mostly smooth but hairy on the midvein of lower surface. Stems hairy on the ridge angles. Fruit capsulelike, ⅛ in. long. CT, MA, ME, NH (rare), RI, VT

Galeopsis tetrahit⁎   LAMIACEAE
Hemp-nettle, brittle-stemmed hemp-nettle
Summer and early fall, 8–28 in., annual.
Meadows, thickets, and woodlands.

Flowers white or sometimes pink, ½–1 in. long, arranged in whorls in leaf axils and top of stem; the upper lip hairy, the lower lip purple-striped, flattened at tip, with 2 hornlike protuberances at the base; sepals long-tipped, spiny. Leaves 1¼–4 in. long, lance-shaped or oval, coarsely toothed. Stems densely hairy, swollen at the base of the leaf nodes. Fruit bristly, capsulelike. Native to Eurasia. CT, MA, ME, NH, RI, VT
   Galeopsis bifida (split-lipped hemp-nettle) is similar, but flowers are smaller (½ in.), usually pink, and lower lip is notched, not flattened. CT, MA, ME, NH, RI, VT

Lamium album⁎   LAMIACEAE
White henbit, white dead-nettle
Spring to fall, 8–20 in., annual. Fields,
roadsides, and gardens.

Flowers creamy white, ¾–1¼ in. long, arranged in dense whorls in upper leaf axils; the upper lip hairy and strongly arched; the lower lip deeply notched; the sepals spiny. Leaves 1¼–4 in. long, lance-shaped or oval, coarsely toothed. Stems hairy. Fruit triangular, capsulelike, ⅛ in. long. Native to Eurasia. MA, ME, RI

Flowers bilateral; leaves simple, opposite, entire

Flowers bilateral; leaves simple, opposite, toothed or lobed

Lycopus americanus LAMIACEAE
American water-horehound, cut-leaf water-horehound
Summer, 6–36 in., perennial. Marshes, wet meadows, and lake and river shores.

Flowers white, 1/8 in. long, arranged in tight clusters in the leaf axils; the 4-lobed petals about equal in length to the sharp-tipped sepals. Leaves 1¼–4 in. long, lance-shaped. deeply and irregularly toothed. Stems hairy or smooth. Fruit rounded, capsulelike, 1/16 in. long or less. CT, MA, ME, NH, RI, VT

Lycopus amplectens LAMIACEAE
Sessile-leaved water-horehound, clasping water-horehound
Late summer, 16–48 in., perennial. Sandy and peaty swamps; coastal plain pond shores.

Flowers white, 1/8 in. long, arranged in tight clusters in the leaf axils; the 5-lobed petals twice as long as the narrow sepals. Leaves 1–4 in. long, lance-shaped, sessile, with 4–6 blunt, shallow teeth on each margin, the leaf bases rounded. Stems hairy or smooth. Fruit capsulelike, 1/16 in. long or less. CT (rare), MA (rare)

Lycopus rubellus LAMIACEAE
Stalked water-horehound
Summer, 24–48 in., perennial. Swamps and coastal plain pond shores.

Flowers white, 1/8 in. long, arranged in tight clusters in the leaf axils; the 5-lobed petals flared, longer than the narrow, long-pointed sepals. Leaves 2–4 in. long, lance-shaped, tapering abruptly to a narrow base; the upper and middle margins sharply toothed, the narrowed lower margin entire. Stems hairy or smooth. Fruit capsulelike, 1/16 in. long or less. CT (rare), MA (rare)

Lycopus uniflorus   LAMIACEAE

Northern bugleweed, northern water-horehound
Summer, 8–36 in., perennial. Swamps,
marshes, and lake and river shores.

Flowers white, ⅛ in. long, arranged in tight clusters in
the leaf axils; the 5-lobed petals flared, longer than the
triangular sepals. Leaves ¾–2½ in. long, lance-shaped,
shallowly toothed, tapering gradually to the short-petioled
base. Stems smooth or sparsely and finely hairy. Fruit
capsulelike, ⅟16 in. long. CT, MA, ME, NH, RI, VT

Lycopus virginicus   LAMIACEAE

Virginia bugleweed, Virginia water-horehound
Summer, 8–36 in., perennial. Swamps,
marshes, and lake and river shores.

Flowers white, ⅛ in. long, arranged in tight clusters
in the leaf axils; the 4-lobed petals usually directed
forward, not flared, longer than the oval or triangular sepals. Leaves 2–5 in. long, lance-shaped or oval,
coarsely toothed, often purplish, tapering abruptly to the
short-petioled base; the lower margins without teeth.
Stems covered with fine, pressed-in hairs. Fruit capsulelike, ⅟16 in. long or less. CT, MA, ME, NH, RI, VT

Nepeta cataria✼   LAMIACEAE

Catnip
Summer, 1–4 ft., perennial. Fields,
roadsides, and open, disturbed sites.

Flowers white, purple-spotted, ¼–½ in. long, arranged
in densely flowered, spikelike clusters on upper stem
and leaf axils; the lower lip wavy-margined or lobed.
Leaves 1–3 in. long, oval or triangular, strongly aromatic,
coarsely toothed, long-petioled, with prominent veins.
Stems grayish downy. Fruit capsulelike, ⅟16 in. long.
Native to Eurasia. CT, MA, ME, NH, RI, VT

Flowers bilateral; leaves simple, opposite, toothed or lobed

Pycnanthemum incanum   LAMIACEAE
Hoary mountain-mint
Summer, 1–3 ft., perennial. Ridges, balds,
deciduous woodlands, and clearings.

Flowers white or lilac, purple-spotted, ¼–⅜ in. long,
arranged in flattish, terminal and axillary clusters ½–1¾
in. wide; the bracts beneath the flowers conspicuous,
white. Leaves 1–4 in. long, lance-shaped or oval, hairy on
the undersurface, usually more than 3 times as long as
broad, aromatic, with shallow teeth; the petioles ¼–½ in.
long. Stems densely hairy. Fruit capsulelike, 1⁄16 in. long
or less. CT, MA, NH (rare), RI, VT (rare)

Pycnanthemum muticum   LAMIACEAE
Broad-leaved mountain-mint, short-toothed mountain-mint
Summer, 1–3 ft., perennial. Ledges,
balds, woodlands, and fields.

Flowers white, purple-spotted, ¼ in. long, arranged in
small, dense terminal and axillary clusters about ½ in.
wide; the bracts beneath the flowers conspicuous, white.
Leaves 1½–3 in. long, oval, finely hairy on the undersurface, usually less than 3 times as long as wide, aromatic,
with shallow teeth; the petioles ⅛ in. long or less. Stems
hairy. Fruit capsulelike, less than 1⁄16 in. long. CT, MA,
NH, RI, VT (rare)

Chelone glabra   PLANTAGINACEAE
Turtlehead, white turtlehead
Midsummer to early fall, 1–3 ft., perennial. Swamps,
wet meadows, fens, and river and lake shores.

Flowers white, occasionally pink-tinged, 1–1½ in. long,
tubular, thick, clustered in a terminal spike, the lower lip
protruding, bearded with white or yellowish hairs. Leaves
sharply toothed, 4–6 in. long, lance-shaped, tapering to
a sharp tip. Stems smooth. Fruit an oval or rounded capsule, about ½ in. long. CT, MA, ME, NH, RI, VT

Gratiola neglecta PLANTAGINACEAE
Clammy hedge-hyssop
Late spring to fall, 4–16 in., annual. Swales,
pool margins, and muddy, disturbed soils.

Flowers yellowish white, ½ in. long, solitary on long
stalks branching from the leaf axils; the flower interiors
yellow and hairy. Leaves ½–2 in. long, lance-shaped, with
a few blunt teeth. Stems sticky-hairy. Fruit an oval or
rounded capsule, ⅛–¼ in. long. CT, MA, ME, NH, RI, VT

Penstemon digitalis PLANTAGINACEAE
Foxglove beardtongue, tall white beardtongue
Spring to midsummer, 2–4 ft., perennial.
Fields, roadsides, woodland clearings.

Flowers white, sometimes violet-tinged, ¾–1¼ in. long,
tubular, arranged in panicles; the floral tube narrow at
base, expanding abruptly at throat, the flower stalks often
sticky. Leaves 2–8 in. long, lance-shaped or oval, sessile,
smooth on both surfaces or with fine hairs on midvein of
lower surface. Stems smooth or finely downy. Fruit a capsule, about ½ in. wide. CT, MA, ME, NH, RI (rare), VT

Penstemon pallidus PLANTAGINACEAE
Eastern white beardtongue
Early spring to summer, 12–30 in., perennial.
Fields, clearings, woodlands, and roadsides,
usually in sandy or rocky soils.

Flowers white or violet, ½–¾ in. long, tubular, arranged
in panicles; the floral tube expanding gradually from
base to throat; the flower stalks often sticky. Leaves 1–3
in. long, lance-shaped, sessile, slightly toothed or entire,
hairy on both sides. Fruit a capsule, about ½ in. long. CT,
MA, ME, NH, RI, VT (rare)

Veronica peregrina   PLANTAGINACEAE
Purslane speedwell
Spring to fall, 2–10 in., annual. Fields and roadsides.

Flowers white, 1⁄16–1⁄8 in. wide, tucked in upper leaf axils. Leaves 1⁄4–1 in. long, linear or narrowly oval, sparsely toothed or entire; the lower opposite, sessile or short-petioled, the upper alternate, sessile. Fruit a broad capsule, 1⁄8 in. long. The native subspecies (subsp. *peregrina*) has smooth stems; the European subspecies (subsp. *xalapensis*) has glandular-hairy stems. Both subspecies in CT, MA, ME, NH, RI, VT.

Veronicastrum virginicum   PLANTAGINACEAE
Culver's-root
Summer, 2–7 ft., perennial. Rich deciduous forests, woodlands, and clearings.

Flowers white or pink, 1⁄4–3⁄8 in. long, tubular, with protruding stamens, arranged in long-stalked, densely flowered, tapering spikes 2–6 in. long. Leaves 1⁄2–6 in. long, lance-shaped, sharply toothed, in multiple whorls of 3–7. Fruit a narrow capsule, 1⁄8–1⁄4 in. long. Introduced in ME; native and introduced populations in CT, MA, VT (rare in all).

Calla palustris   ARACEAE
Wild calla
Late spring to summer, 6–12 in., perennial. Marshes, bogs, and pond and lake shallows.

Flowers greenish, tiny, clustered in a thick, dense spike, partially enfolded by a broad, petal-like white spathe 1–3 in. long. Leaves oval or rounded, 2–4 in. long, notched at base, on long petioles. Fruit a red berry, 1⁄4–1⁄2 in. long. CT, MA, ME, NH, RI, VT

Goodyera oblongifolia ORCHIDACEAE
Giant rattlesnake-plantain, green-leaved rattlesnake-plantain
Summer, 8–16 in., perennial. Coniferous forests.

Flowers white or greenish white, ½ in., arranged in a spiraling, spikelike raceme with 10–50 flowers; the lower lip ¼ in. long, with a concave base tapering to a boat-shaped tip. Leaves 1–4 in. long, lance-shaped or oval, dark green, whitened only along the midrib. Stems hairy. Fruit an oval capsule, about ⅜ in. long. Northern ME (rare)

Goodyera pubescens ORCHIDACEAE
Downy rattlesnake-plantain
Summer, 4–20 in., perennial. Moist and dry mixed forests.

Flowers white, ¼–⅜ in. long, arranged in a cylindrical terminal spike with 10–60 flowers; the lower lip ⅛ in. long, rounded at the tip. Leaves 1–2½ in. long, oval, dark green with a striking network of white, intricately interlaced veins. Stems woolly. Fruit an oval capsule, ¼ in. long. CT, MA, ME, NH, RI, VT

Goodyera repens ORCHIDACEAE
Dwarf rattlesnake-plantain
Summer, 1¼–7 in., perennial. Coniferous and mixed forests, often in moist, mossy soil.

Flowers white, ¼ in. long, arranged in a one-sided terminal spike with 7–35 flowers; the lower lip ⅛ in. long, with a deep pouch and hooked tip. Leaves ½–1¼ in. long, oval, bluish green, 5-nerved; the thickened lateral veins white, the longitudinal veins green with narrow white borders. Stems downy. Fruit a capsule, ¼ in. long. MA (rare), ME, NH, VT

Goodyera tesselata ORCHIDACEAE
Checkered rattlesnake-plantain
Summer, 6–14 in., perennial. Coniferous and mixed forests.

Flowers white, ½ in. long, arranged in a loose, spiraling spike with 5–70 flowers; the lower lip ⅛–¼ in. long, with

a shallow pouch and a spreading or slightly reflexed tip. Leaves ¾–2¼ in. long, oval, with 5–9 nerves; the thickened lateral veins white, the longitudinal veins green with narrow white borders. Stems hairy. Fruit an oval capsule, ¼ in. long. CT, MA, ME, NH, RI (rare), VT

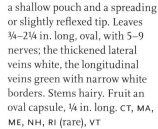

Malaxis monophyllos (*M. brachypoda*)
ORCHIDACEAE
White adder's-tongue, white adder's-mouth
Summer, 4–10 in., perennial. Coniferous fens and swamps on high-pH soils.

Flowers white, ⅛ in. long, arranged in a delicate, spike-like raceme with 5–80 flowers; the lower lip broadened at base and tapering to a point. Basal leaf single, sheathing, 1–2¼ in. long, oval, the base enveloping the stem. Stems smooth. Fruit an oval capsule, ⅛ in. long. CT, MA, ME, VT (rare in all)

Platanthera obtusata (*Habenaria obtusata*)
ORCHIDACEAE
Blunt-leaf bog-orchid, blunt-leaved orchis
Summer, 4–12 in., perennial. Rich coniferous swamps, fens, and wet meadows.

Flowers greenish white, ½ in. long, arranged in a sparse raceme of 2–20 flowers; the lip and spur both long and tapering. Leaves 1½–6 in. long and ⅜–2 in. wide, usually solitary, lance-shaped or oval, tapering to the base and rounded at the tip. Stems smooth. Fruit an oval capsule, ⅜ in. long. ME, NH, VT (rare)

Platanthera orbiculata (*Habenaria orbiculata*)
ORCHIDACEAE
Round-leaved orchid, round-leaved bog-orchid
Mid to late summer, 6–24 in., perennial.
Coniferous and mixed forests and swamps.

Flowers white, 1 in. long, arranged in an open raceme of 2–20 flowers; the lower lip narrow and elongate, ¼–½ in. long, and the slender, drooping spur ½–1 in. long. Leaves 2–8 in. long, broadly oval or rounded, shining, paired, smooth, flat, and padlike. Stems smooth. Fruit a stalked, cylindrical capsule, ¾ in. long. MA (rare), ME, NH, VT (rare)
  Platanthera macrophylla (large-leaved bog-orchid) has a longer spur, 1¼–1¾ in. long, and the leaves may reach 9–10 in. long. MA (rare), ME, NH, VT (rare)

Spiranthes cernua   ORCHIDACEAE
Nodding ladies'-tresses
Late summer and fall, 4–20 in., perennial. Moist meadows, thickets, open woodlands, and fens.

Flowers white, ½–¾ in. long, arranged in a dense, twisting spike of 10–40 spreading or nodding flowers; the lower lip broad, about ⅜ in. long, crisped or frayed at the tip and yellowish in the center. Leaves to 10 in. long, linear or lance-shaped. Stems smooth. Fruit an oval capsule. CT, MA, ME, NH, RI, VT
  Spiranthes ochroleuca (yellow ladies'-tresses) has creamy yellowish flowers, and the lower lip projects strongly downward. Meadows, woodland openings, and peaty wetlands. CT, MA, ME, NH, RI, VT (rare)

Spiranthes lacera (*S. gracilis*) ORCHIDACEAE
Slender ladies'-tresses
Mid to late summer, 4–16 in., perennial. Dry and moist meadows, thickets, and open woodlands.

Flowers white, ½ in. long, arranged in a short, spiraling, zipperlike spike of 9–35 flowers; the lower lip ¼ in. long, frayed or slightly toothed at the broadened tip, with a bright green spot in the center. Leaves oval, ¾–2 in. long, 1½–3½ times as long as wide, often withered by flowering time. Stems mostly smooth, sometimes sparsely hairy above. Fruit an oval capsule. CT, MA, ME, NH, RI, VT (rare)
  Spiranthes casei (Case's ladies'-tresses) leaves are longer, and linear or lance-shaped, present at flowering time. The lower lip is yellowish. Late summer and early fall. Meadows, ridges, and ledges. Northern ME, NH, VT (very rare in all)

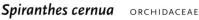

165

Spiranthes lucida   ORCHIDACEAE
Shining ladies'-tresses
Late spring to midsummer, 4–10 in., perennial. Open
seepages and river and lake shores in high-pH conditions.

Flowers white, ½ in. long, arranged in a short, twisted
spike of 5–20 flowers; the lower lip ¼ in. long, with a
crisped or frayed edge and a bright yellow center. Leaves
1–5 in. long, lance-shaped, shiny. Stems smooth or very
finely hairy. Fruit an oval capsule. CT, MA (rare), ME
(rare), NH (rare), VT (rare)

Spiranthes romanzoffiana   ORCHIDACEAE
Hooded ladies'-tresses
Midsummer to fall, 4–16 in., perennial.
Rich wet meadows and fens.

Flowers white, ½ in. long, fragrant, ascending, arranged
in a dense spike of 4–45 flowers; the lower lip ¼ in. long,
drooping, with green interior veins and a constriction
near the middle, projecting beneath an arching "hood"
formed of the sepals and upper petals. Leaves 4–8 in.
long, linear or lance-shaped. Stems smooth below, finely
hairy with glandular hairs above. Fruit an oval capsule,
¼–⅜ in. long. MA (rare), ME, NH, VT (rare)

Spiranthes tuberosa   ORCHIDACEAE
Little ladies'-tresses
Late summer and early fall, 6–12 in., perennial.
Dry fields, grasslands, and open woodlands.

Flowers white, ⅜–½ in. long, arranged in a slender, spiraling spike with 8–30 flowers; the lower lip ¼ in. long,
broad and crisped or frayed at the tip. Leaves 2–6 in. long,
oval, usually withered at flowering time. Stems smooth.
Fruit an oval capsule, ⅛–¼ in. long. CT, MA, RI (rare)

Spiranthes vernalis ORCHIDACEAE
Grass-leaved ladies'-tresses
Summer, 8–32 in., perennial. Fields, grasslands,
and open woodlands, usually in sandy soils.

Flowers white, fragrant, ½–¾ in. long, arranged in a
braided, spiraling, hairy spike with 12–50 flowers; the
lower lip ¼ in. long, with a frayed tip, white or pale yellow in the center. Leaves 2–10 in. long, linear or narrowly
lance-shaped. Stems hairy, especially above. Fruit an oval
capsule. CT, MA (rare), RI (rare)

Viola blanda VIOLACEAE
Sweet white violet
Spring, 1–10 in., perennial. Rich, mixed forests,
swamp edges, and river floodplains.

Flowers white, fragrant, ¼–½ in. long, solitary on a reddish stalk; the upper 2 petals twisted backwards, the lowermost petal marked with purple veins. Leaves 1½–3½
long and ¾–1½ in. wide, heart-shaped, narrowly notched
at base, with blunt teeth and broadly pointed tips. Stems
smooth, reddish. Fruit an oval capsule, red-spotted or
purple when ripe, ⅛–¼ in. long. CT, MA, ME, NH, RI, VT

Viola lanceolata VIOLACEAE
Lance-leaved violet
Spring and early summer, 2–6 in., perennial.
Sandy or peaty pond and river shores, wet
meadows, marshes, and ditches.

Flowers white, ¼–½ in. long, solitary, the lowermost
petal marked with purple veins. Leaves 1–4½ in. long
and ¼–1 in. wide, lance-shaped, tapering, more than 3
times as long as wide; the teeth tipped with tiny reddish
brown to black glands. Stems smooth. Fruit a green, narrowly oval capsule, ¼ in. long. CT, MA, ME, NH, RI, VT
(rare)

Flowers bilateral; leaves
simple, basal, entire

Flowers bilateral; leaves simple,
basal, toothed or lobed

Viola pallens *(V. macloskeyi)* VIOLACEAE
Northern white violet, smooth white violet
Early spring, 1–5 in., perennial. Seepages, swamps, streamsides, and cool, moist montane forests.

Flowers white, ¼–½ in. long, solitary on a greenish stalk; all 3 petals marked with purple veins, the upper 2 petals not twisted back. Leaves ½–2 in. long and ½–3 in. wide, heart-shaped or rounded, with blunt teeth, broadly notched at base. Stems smooth or hairy. Fruit an oval, green capsule, ⅛–¼ in. long. CT, MA, ME, NH, RI, VT

Viola primulifolia *(V. ×primulifolia)* VIOLACEAE
Primrose-leaved violet
Spring and early summer, 2–10 in., perennial. Pond and river shores, streambanks, wet meadows, and swamps.

Flowers white, ¼–½ in. long, solitary, the lowermost petal marked with purple veins. Leaves 1–5 in. long and ¾–3 in. wide, oval, 1½–2½ times as long as wide, widest at middle and tapering to base. Stems smooth. Fruit a green, narrowly oval capsule, ¼–⅜ in. long. CT, MA, ME, NH, RI

Viola renifolia VIOLACEAE
Kidney-leaf violet
Spring and early summer, 1–10 in., perennial. Coniferous and mixed forests and swamps

Flowers white, ¼–½ in. long, solitary, the lowermost petal marked with purple veins. Leaves ¾–2 in. wide at flowering time (later enlarging to 3 in. wide), broadly rounded or kidney-shaped, wider than long, bluntly toothed, with a broad basal notch. Stems, petioles, and lower leaf surfaces often hairy. Fruit a narrowly oval, reddish or purple capsule, ⅛–¼ in. long. CT (rare), MA (rare), ME, NH, VT

168

Lespedeza capitata   FABACEAE
Round-headed bush-clover
Summer and early fall, 2–5 ft., perennial. Sandy fields,
open woodlands and clearings, and roadsides.

Flowers creamy white, purple-spotted, ¼–½ in. long,
arranged in rounded, densely clustered, short-stalked
heads, crowded among the leaves in upper axils. Leaves
3-parted; the leaflets ¾–1½ in. long (2½–5 times longer
than wide), oval or elliptical, tipped with a small tooth.
Stems hairy. Fruit an oval pod, ¼ in. long. CT, MA, ME,
NH, RI, VT (rare)
    Lespedeza angustifolia (narrow-leaved bush-clover)
is similar, but the heads are more narrowly oval and
long-stalked from the axils, extending beyond the leaves.
The leaflets are narrowly lance-shaped, 4–8 times longer
than wide. Grows in sandy fields and pond shores mostly
near the coast. MA

Lespedeza hirta   FABACEAE
Hairy bush-clover
Summer and fall, 2–5 ft., perennial. Dry fields,
woodland clearings, and sandy roadsides.

Flowers creamy white, purple-spotted, ¼ in. long,
arranged in dense long-stalked, cylindrical heads; the
stalks of the flower heads ¾–2 in. long. Leaves 3-parted;
the leaflets ½–1½ in. long, broadly oval or rounded.
Stems hairy. Fruit a narrowly oval pod, ¼–⅜ in long. CT,
MA, ME (rare), NH, RI, VT (rare)

Melilotus albus*   FABACEAE
White sweet clover
Spring to fall, 1–8 ft., annual or biennial. Fields,
roadsides, and open, disturbed sites.

Flowers white, ⅛–¼ in. long, arranged in numerous,
tapering, long-stalked racemes, 3–8 in. long. Leaves
3-parted, long-petioled; the leaflets, ½–1 in. long,
lance-shaped or narrowly oval, toothed. Stems smooth or
hairy. Fruit a tiny pod, ⅛ in. long. Native to Eurasia. CT,
MA, ME, NH, RI, VT

Flowers bilateral; leaves deeply
divided, alternate, leaflets entire

Flowers bilateral; leaves deeply divided,
alternate, leaflets toothed or lobed

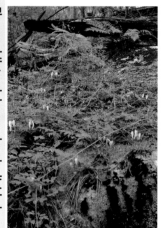

Adlumia fungosa   PAPAVERACEAE
Allegheny-vine, climbing fumitory
Summer and fall, to 12 ft. long, biennial vine. Rocky woodlands and talus slopes, usually in high-pH conditions.

Flowers white, pinkish, or pale purple, ½–¾ in. long, vase-shaped, arranged in small, drooping clusters from the leaf axils. Leaves pinnately divided and subdivided into many small leaflets, ½–¾ in. long, oval, with lobed margins. Stems scrambling or climbing, smooth. Fruit a narrowly oval capsule, ⅜ in. long. CT, MA (rare), ME (rare), NH (rare), RI (rare), VT

Trifolium repens*   FABACEAE
White clover
Spring to fall, 4–12 in., perennial. Fields, lawns, roadsides, and open, disturbed sites.

Flowers white or pinkish, ⅜ in. long, clustered in a solitary rounded head ½–1¼ in. wide, stalked above the leaves. Leaves 3-parted, the 3 leaflets ¼–¾ in. long and wide, rounded, finely toothed, with wavy white markings. Stems smooth or hairy, erect, but creeping at base and often colonial. Fruit a flattened pod, ⅛–¼ in. long. Native to Eurasia. CT, MA, ME, NH, RI, VT

Dicentra canadensis   PAPAVERACEAE
Squirrel-corn
Spring, 4–12 in., perennial. Rich deciduous forests.

Flowers white, ⅜–¾ in. long, with rounded spurlike lobes at the top and spreading petal tips at the bottom. Leaves 4–12 in. long, long-petioled, bluish green, finely dissected into many linear leaflet segments. Stems smooth. Fruit a green, narrowly oval, long-beaked capsule, ⅜–½ in. long. Underground bulblets yellow, resembling corn grains. CT (rare), MA, ME (rare), NH, VT

170

Dicentra cucullaria PAPAVERACEAE
Dutchman's-breeches
Early spring, 4–12 in., perennial. Rich, deciduous forests.

Flowers white, with yellow tips, ¾ in. long, nodding, stalked above the leaves, arranged in short, few- or many-flowered racemes; the flowers with divergent spur lobes at the top, and yellow, spreading petal lobes at the bottom. Leaves 4–14 in. long, long-petioled, sometimes yellowish green, finely dissected into many linear leaflet segments. Fruit a slender, tapering, long-beaked capsule, ⅜–½ in. long Underground bulblets scaly, white or pinkish. CT, MA, ME, NH, VT

Conopholis americana OROBANCHACEAE
American squaw-root, cancer root
Spring to midsummer, 2–8 in., perennial.
Deciduous forests, in rich soils.

Flowers creamy white or pale yellow, ¼–½ in. long, tubular, spreading, densely crowded on a thick, conical stalk that resembles a fungus. Stalks yellowish, covered with overlapping reddish brown scales; the scales ½ in. long, oval with pointed tips, turning dark brown by late summer. Fruit an oval capsule, ½ in. long. Roots parasitic on the roots of oak trees. CT, MA, ME, NH, RI (rare), VT (rare)

Flowers bilateral; leaves deeply divided, basal, leaflets toothed or lobed

Flowers bilateral; leaves absent, scaly, or needlelike

Lachnanthes caroliniana (*L. tinctoria*)
HAEMODORACEAE
Redroot, Carolina bloodroot
Mid to late summer, 8–32 in., perennial. Sandy
or peaty, coastal plain pond shores.

Flowers pale yellow, ⅜ in. long, densely clustered in compact, woolly heads 1–3 in. wide. Basal leaves 6–18 in. long,
erect, flattened, swordlike; the stem leaves smaller. Upper
stems woolly-hairy, lower stems smooth. Fruit a reddish,
rounded capsule, ⅛–¼ in. wide. CT, MA, RI (rare in all)

Xyris difformis   XYRIDACEAE
Bog yellow-eyed grass
Summer and fall, 6–30 in., perennial. Bogs
and sandy or peaty pond shorelines.

Flowers yellow, ¾ in. wide, on top of short, scaly spikes,
¼–⅝ in. long, pointed at tip; petals opening in the morning. Leaves 4–20 in. long and ¼ in. wide (or less), flat,
grasslike, reddish at base. Stems sometimes twisted, not
bulbous at base. Fruit a capsule. CT, MA, ME, NH, RI
Xyris smalliana (Small's yellow-eyed grass) is similar but generally taller (20–50 in.), and the scaly spike is
⅜–¾ in. long, blunt at the tip; petals opening in the afternoon. Leaves 8–24 in. long and up to ⅝ in. wide. Grows in
peaty and sandy shorelines and shallows near the coast.
CT (rare), MA, ME (rare), RI

Xyris montana   XYRIDACEAE
Northern yellow-eyed grass
Midsummer to early fall, 2–12 in., perennial.
Bogs and peaty openings and shorelines.

Flowers yellow, ¼ in. wide, on top of short, scaly, narrowly oval spikes, ⅜ in. long or less; petals opening in
the morning. Leaves 1½–6 in. long and 1/16–⅛ in. wide,
needle-thin, reddish at base. Stems wiry, less than 1/16
in. wide. Fruit a capsule. CT (rare), MA (rare), ME, NH, RI
(rare), VT (rare)

Xyris torta XYRIDACEAE
Slender yellow-eyed grass
Spring and summer, 6–30 in., perennial.
Bogs and sandy or peaty shorelines.

Flowers yellow, ¼ in. wide, on top of short, oval, scaly spikes, ¼–1 in. long; petals opening in the morning. Leaves 8–20 in. long and about ⅛ in. wide, linear and usually twisted. Stems bulbous at base and often sinuous or twisted. Fruit a capsule. CT, MA, NH, RI

Turritis glabra (Arabis glabra) BRASSICACEAE
Tower mustard
Spring and summer, 2–5 ft., biennial or perennial.
Fields, thickets, and open, disturbed sites.

Flowers pale yellow or white, ⅛–¼ in. long, arranged in narrow racemes. Stem leaves 2–5 in. long, lance-shaped, entire, clasping, the lower overlapping; basal leaves toothed or entire, often withered by flowering time. Lower stem hairy; the upper stem smooth with a whitish bloom. Fruit a linear, ascending silique, 2–3½ in. long. CT, MA, ME, NH, RI, VT

Ludwigia alternifolia ONAGRACEAE
Square-pod water-primrose, seedbox
Summer, 2–4 ft., perennial. Swamps, marshes, and wet meadows.

Flowers yellow, ½–¾ in. wide, short-stalked, solitary in leaf axils, the broad triangular sepals as long as the petals. Leaves 2–4 in. long, lance-shaped, tapering at both ends. Stems smooth, branching. Fruit a ridged, squarish capsule, ¼ in. long, with a rounded base and an open pore at top. CT, MA, RI

Oenothera fruticosa   ONAGRACEAE
Narrow-leaved evening-primrose, sundrops
Summer, 1–3 ft., perennial. Fields, roadsides, and occasionally shorelines of salt and brackish marshes.

Flowers bright yellow, 1–2 in. wide, in compact clusters, open during the day, with notched petals and 8 long stamens. Leaves 1–3 in. long, linear or lance-shaped, entire or sometimes with shallow teeth. Stems smooth or hairy. Fruit a ribbed, elliptical capsule, ¼–⅜ in. long. ME, MA, NH, RI (rare)

Oenothera perennis   ONAGRACEAE
Little evening primrose, small sundrops
Summer, 6–24 in., perennial. Fields and roadsides.

Flowers bright yellow, ½–¾ in. wide, arranged in leafy, loose racemes, open during the day; the petals with 4 long and 4 short stamens. Leaves 1–2 in. long, linear or lance-shaped. Stems smooth or hairy. Fruit a ribbed, elliptical capsule, ¼–⅜ in. long. CT, MA, ME, NH, RI, VT

Erysimum cheiranthoides⁎   BRASSICACEAE
Wormseed wallflower, wormseed mustard
Summer, 6–40 in., annual. Fields, roadsides, and open, disturbed sites.

Flowers bright yellow, ¼–⅜ in. wide, stalked, arranged in terminal and axillary racemes. Leaves 1–4 in. long, lance-shaped, crowded, usually slightly toothed, sometimes entire or wavy-margined. Stems hairy. Fruit a long-stalked, ascending or spreading linear silique, ½–1¼ in. long. Native to Eurasia and North Africa. CT, MA, ME, NH, RI, VT

Rhodiola rosea (*Sedum roseum*) CRASSULACEAE
Roseroot
Spring to midsummer, 4–16 in., perennial. Coastal
headlands in ME; cliffs on high-pH rock in VT.

Flowers yellow (female plants), or red (male plants), ¼
in. long, clustered in dense heads ½–2½ in. wide. Leaves
1–2½ in. long, oval, succulent, whitish green, slightly
toothed, sessile, crowded in a spiraling pattern. Stems
smooth. Fruit an erect, oval follicle, ¼–⅜ in. long. Native
in ME, VT (rare); introduced in CT.

Oenothera biennis ONAGRACEAE
Common evening-primrose
Summer to early fall, 1–5 ft., biennial. Fields,
roadsides, and dry, open sites.

Flowers bright yellow, 1–2 in. wide, with 8 long stamens, arranged in leafy spikes; the sepals hairy, reflexed,
as long as the petals; the flowers open in the evening.
Leaves 2–8 in. long, lance-shaped, crowded, shallowly
toothed. Stems branching, smooth or hairy. Fruit a narrow, ribbed, erect capsule, ¾–1½ in. long. CT, MA, ME,
NH, RI, VT

    Oenothera parviflora (small-flowered evening-primrose;
syn. *O. cruciata*) is similar, but the stems are
unbranched, the flowers on average are slightly smaller
(¾–1½ in. wide), and the reflexed sepals have a small
hornlike or hooklike appendage at the tips. Grows in
fields, roadsides, and open, disturbed sites. CT, MA, ME,
NH, RI, VT

*Galium verum** RUBIACEAE
Yellow bedstraw, Our Lady's bedstraw
Summer, 1–3 ft., perennial. Fields,
roadsides, and open, disturbed sites.

Flowers yellow, 1/16–⅛ in. wide, arranged in a dense, pyramidal panicle. Leaves ½–1½ in. long, needle-thin, hairy,
in whorls of 6–12. Stems finely hairy. Fruit oval, 1/16 in.
long. Native to Eurasia. CT, MA, ME, NH, RI, VT

Barbarea verna✻   BRASSICACEAE
Early yellow-rocket, early winter-cress
Spring, 4–32 in., biennial or perennial.
Fields and roadsides.

Flowers bright yellow, ½ in. wide, arranged in terminal and axillary racemes; the petals about ¼ in. long. Leaves ½–2½ in. long, of 2 distinct types; basal and lower leaves deeply divided into 8–20 rounded or triangular lateral lobes and a large terminal lobe; the upper leaves deeply divided into 6–16 linear lobes. Stems mostly smooth. Fruit a stalked, linear silique, 1½–3 in. long. Native to Eurasia. CT, MA, ME, RI

Barbarea vulgaris✻   BRASSICACEAE
Garden yellow-rocket, common winter-cress
Spring and early summer, 1–3 ft., biennial or perennial.
Fields, roadsides, and open, disturbed sites.

Flowers bright yellow, ½ in. wide, arranged in terminal and axillary racemes; the petals ¼ in. long, the sepals smooth. Basal and lower leaves 1–4 in. long, deeply divided into a broad terminal lobe and 2–8 smaller lateral lobes; the upper leaves smaller, often clasping, toothed or lobed, usually not deeply divided. Stems smooth. Fruit a linear silique, ⅝–1¼ in. long, ascending or spreading, angled at least slightly away from stem. Native to Eurasia. CT, MA, ME, NH, RI, VT

Barbarea stricta✻ (upright yellow rocket) is very similar, but the flowers are smaller (about ¼ in. wide), the sepal tips are hairy, and the fruiting pods are held erect along the stem. Grows in moist fields and river shores. Native to Europe. CT, MA, ME, NH, RI, VT

Brassica juncea✻   BRASSICACEAE
Chinese mustard, Indian mustard
Summer to fall, 1–3 ft., annual. Fields
and open, disturbed sites.

Flowers yellow, ½ in. wide, arranged in terminal and axillary racemes. Lower leaves to 8 in. long, sharply toothed, divided into a large, rounded terminal lobe and much smaller lateral lobes; the upper leaves smaller, bluntly toothed or entire, short-petioled or sessile. Stems smooth, often whitish. Fruit a linear, ascending silique, ½–1½ in. long, the beak ¼–⅜ in. long. Native to Eurasia. CT, MA, ME, NH, RI, VT

*Brassica nigra** BRASSICACEAE
Black mustard
Summer to fall, 1–6 ft., annual. Fields
and open, disturbed sites.

Flowers yellow, ½ in. wide, arranged in short, ascending racemes. Lower leaves to 12 in. long, sharply toothed,
divided into a large, broad terminal lobe and smaller lateral lobes; the upper leaves smaller, toothed or shallowly
lobed. Lower stems hairy. Fruit an erect silique, pressed
close to stem, ⅜–1 in. long, the beak about ¹⁄₁₆ in. long.
Native to Eurasia. CT, MA, ME, NH, RI, VT

*Brassica rapa** BRASSICACEAE
Rape, field mustard
Summer to fall, 1–4 ft., annual or biennial.
Fields and open, disturbed sites.

Flowers pale yellow, ½ in. wide, arranged in ascending racemes. Lower leaves to 16 in. long, sharply and
coarsely toothed, divided into a large terminal lobe and
smaller lateral lobes; the upper leaves smaller, clasping,
heart-shaped at base. Stems mostly smooth, sometimes
whitish. Fruit a linear, ascending silique, 1¼–2 in. long,
the beak about ½ in. long. Native to Eurasia. CT, MA, ME,
NH, RI, VT

*Raphanus raphanistrum** BRASSICACEAE
Wild radish
Spring to fall, 8–30 in., annual. Fields,
beaches, and disturbed, open sites.

Flowers pale yellow, fading to white, ½ in. wide, arranged
in loose, ascending racemes; the petals with distinct purplish veins. Lower leaves 4–8 in. long, sharply and irregularly toothed, divided into a large, broad terminal lobe
and 2–8 smaller lateral lobes; the upper leaves smaller,
variably toothed, short-petioled. Stems usually sparsely
hairy. Fruit a narrow, long-beaked silique, ⅜–1¼ in. long,
tightly constricted at seed joints. Native to Eurasia. CT,
MA, ME, NH, RI, VT

4 radial petals; leaves deeply divided,
alternate, leaflets toothed or lobed

Rorippa palustris (*R. islandica*) BRASSICACEAE
Common yellow-cress, marsh yellow-cress
Spring to fall, 1–4 ft., annual or biennial. Swamps, pond shores, marshes, and tidal marshes.

Flowers yellow, ⅛–¼ in. wide, arranged in terminal and axillary racemes, the petals equal to or shorter than the sepals. Lower leaves 2–8 in. long, lance-shaped, sharply toothed, irregularly divided into a large terminal lobe and smaller lateral lobes; the upper leaves variably toothed or lobed. Stems usually smooth, occasionally hairy. Fruit a spreading, oval silique, ⅛–⅜ in. long. CT, MA, ME, NH, RI, VT

Rorippa sylvestris⁕ BRASSICACEAE
Creeping yellow-cress
Spring to early fall, 6–30 in., perennial. Wet fields, lake and river shores, and ditches.

Flowers yellow, ¼ in. wide, arranged in terminal and axillary racemes, the petals about twice as long as the sepals. Lower leaves 1½–6 in. long, sharply toothed, deeply divided into a terminal lobe and many lance-shaped lateral lobes; the upper leaves smaller. Stems smooth or slightly hairy, often semierect or sprawling, Fruit a spreading, linear silique, ⅜–¾ in. long. Native to Eurasia. CT, MA, ME, NH, RI, VT

Sisymbrium altissimum⁕ BRASSICACEAE
Tumbling hedge-mustard, tumble mustard, Jim Hill mustard
Summer, 1–4 ft., annual. Fields and roadsides.

Flowers pale yellow or whitish, ¼–⅜ in. long, arranged in sparse racemes. Leaves 2–8 in. long, the lowermost divided into many toothed, lance-shaped segments; the upper leaves very finely divided into linear segments. Stems smooth above, hairy near base. Fruit an ascending, linear silique, 2–4 in. long. Native to Eurasia. CT, MA, ME, NH, RI, VT

Sisymbrium officinale* BRASSICACEAE
Common hedge-mustard, hedge mustard
Spring to fall, 1–3 ft., annual. Fields and roadsides.

Flowers yellow, ⅛–¼ in. wide, arranged in stiff, erect racemes. Leaves sharply toothed and divided; the lower leaves 1–6 in. long, the main lateral segments lance-shaped and horizontally spreading; the upper leaves smaller, roughly triangular, often with flared basal lobes. Stems hairy. Fruit an erect, linear silique, about ½ in. long, hugging stem. Native to Europe. CT, MA, ME, NH, RI, VT

Oenothera laciniata* ONAGRACEAE
Cut-leaved evening-primrose
Spring to fall, 6–30 in., annual. Fields and roadsides.

Flowers yellow, ½–1½ in. wide, sessile in upper leaf axils; the sepals reflexed, as long as the petals; the flowers open in the evening. Leaves 1–4 in. long, lance-shaped, deeply cut, with narrow, pointed lobes. Stems hairy, erect or reclining. Fruit a linear capsule, ⅝–1¼ in. long, erect or curving. Native to much of eastern and central United States, introduced in New England. CT, MA, ME, VT

Chelidonium majus* PAPAVERACEAE
Greater celandine
Spring to late summer, 12–30 in. tall, biennial.
Woodland edges, thickets, and roadsides. Invasive.

Flowers yellow, ¾ in. wide, arranged in sparse umbels on upper stem. Leaves deeply divided into 3–9 leaflets; the leaflets ½–3 in. long, oval, bluntly toothed or lobed. Stems hairy, branching, exuding orange or yellow sap when broken. Fruit a linear capsule, ¾–2 in. long. Native to Eurasia. CT, MA, ME, NH, RI, VT

4 radial petals; leaves deeply divided, alternate, leaflets toothed or lobed

4 radial petals; leaves deeply divided, alternate, leaflets toothed or lobed

Glaucium flavum* PAPAVERACEAE
Yellow horn-poppy, sea poppy
Summer, 1–3 ft., biennial or perennial. Sandy or rocky sea beaches, and disturbed sites near coast. Invasive.

Flowers yellow, 2–3 in. wide, solitary, long-stalked, with bushy stamens. Leaves 3–8 in. long, gray-green, hairy; the lower long-petioled and sharply cut into numerous segments; the upper more broadly lobed, clasping. Stems thick, with yellow sap. Fruit a narrow, curving capsule, 6–12 in. long. Native to Eurasia. CT, MA, RI

5 radial petals; leaves simple, alternate, entire

Onosmodium virginianum BORAGINACEAE
False gromwell
Early to midsummer, 1–2 ft., perennial. Riverbank terraces and dry woodland clearings on high-pH soils.

Flowers yellow or sometimes orange, ⅜ in. long, tubular, with protruding styles, arranged in a leafy, coiled, branching, one-sided inflorescence. Leaves 1¼–3½ in. long, lance-shaped or oval, hairy, crowded. Stems densely hairy. Fruit oval, capsulelike, 1/16–⅛ in. long. Northwestern CT (rare)

Crocanthemum bicknellii CISTACEAE
Hoary frostweed, Bicknell's rockrose
Early to midsummer, 8–20 in., perennial. Sandy fields, woodlands, and roadsides.

Flowers yellow, ¾–1¼ in. wide, arranged in flattish clusters of 2–20 on branch tips. Leaves ¾–1½ in. long, linear or lance-shaped, wedge-shaped at base, hairy on both surfaces. Stems clustered at base, unbranched or narrowly branched at flowering time. Fruit an oval capsule, ¼ in. long. In summer, stems produce more erect, lateral branches that are shorter than the main stem, and closed, petal-less flowers develop on the branch tips. CT, MA, ME, NH, RI, VT (rare)

Crocanthemum propinquum (low frostweed) is similar, with flattish clusters of 2–20 flowers, but stems are more thinly scattered, the leaves are more narrowed at base, and the lateral branches frequently overtop the main stem. Grows in sandy fields and woodlands. CT (rare), MA, RI (rare)

Crocanthemum canadense (*Helianthemum canadense*) CISTACEAE
Frostweed, Canada frostweed
Spring to early summer, 6–12 in., perennial.
Sandy fields, thickets, and woodlands.

Flowers yellow, ¾–1¼ in. wide; solitary or sometimes paired at branch tips. Leaves ¾–1½ in. long, narrowly oval, densely hairy on lower surface, less hairy on upper surface. Stems erect, leafy, unbranched or narrowly branched at flowering time; in summer, stems become bushier, elongating to 24 in., and developing closed, petal-less flowers on branch tips. Fruit an oval capsule, ⅜ in. long. CT, MA, ME, NH, RI, VT (rare)
   Crocanthemum dumosum (bushy frostweed; syn. *Helianthemum dumosum*), has shorter stems and both surfaces of main stem leaves are densely hairy. Grows in sandy fields and thickets near coast. CT, MA, RI (rare in all)

Sedum acre⁎ CRASSULACEAE
Mossy stonecrop, love-entangle
Late spring to midsummer, 2–6 in., perennial.
Rocks, ledges, and dry, open sites.

Flowers yellow, ⅜ in. wide, arranged in short-branched clusters, sharp-pointed, star-shaped, occasionally with 4 petals. Leaves ⅛–⅜ in. long, oval, mosslike, fleshy, overlapping. Stems creeping, mat-forming, evergreen. Fruit a white, 5-pointed, follicle, ¼ in. long. Native to Eurasia. CT, MA, ME, NH, RI, VT

Linum medium LINACEAE
Common yellow flax
Summer, 8–28 in., perennial. Open woodlands, fields, and roadsides.

Flowers bright yellow, ½ in. wide, short-stalked, loosely clustered in stiff, erect branches. Leaves ½–1 in. long, linear or narrowly lance-shaped, crowded (usually 20–70 on stem), the lowermost opposite, the middle and upper alternate. Stems smooth. Fruit a capsule with a rounded tip, 1⁄16 in. long. CT, MA (rare), RI
   Linum intercursum (sandplain flax) has more broadly lance-shaped leaves and longer capsules, with reddish, pointed tips. This rare species is known only in sandy fields and clearings in coastal regions. MA (rare)
   Linum sulcatum (grooved yellow flax), an annual, has a pair of small dark glands at the leaf bases. It occurs only in woodland clearings on dry, high-pH soils. CT (rare)

Linum virginianum   LINACEAE
Woodland yellow flax, wild yellow flax
Summer, 8–20 in., perennial. Dry
woodlands, fields, and clearings.

Flowers bright yellow, ⅜ in. wide, short-stalked, loosely
clustered on spreading branches that are rounded in
cross section. Leaves ½–1 in. long, lance-shaped or elliptic, usually 10–40 on stem, the lowermost opposite, the
middle and upper mostly alternate. Stems smooth. Fruit
a rounded capsule, ¹⁄₁₆–⅛ in. long. CT, MA, RI

Linum striatum (ridged yellow flax) is similar, but the
inflorescence is more erect, the upper stem and flower
branches are ridged, angular in cross section. Lower and
middle leaves are opposite; only the uppermost are alternate. Grows in wet meadows, bogs, and pond shores. CT,
MA (rare), RI

Portulaca oleracea⁎   PORTULACACEAE
Common purslane
Summer, to 20 in. long, annual. Fields
and open, disturbed sites.

Flowers yellow, ¼ in. wide, sessile in leaf axils, usually
with 5 petals (occasionally with 4 or 6); only open in the
morning. Leaves ⅜–1¼ in. long, paddle-shaped, fleshy,
sometimes opposite. Stems prostrate, mat-forming, succulent, reddish purple. Fruit an oval capsule, ¼ in. long.
Native distribution unclear, now cosmopolitan. CT, MA,
ME, NH, RI, VT

Ranunculus flammula (*R. reptans*)
RANUNCULACEAE
Creeping spearwort, creeping crowfoot
Summer, to 30 in. long, perennial. Marshes,
floodplains, and river and lake shores and shallows.

Flowers yellow, ¼–½ in. wide, solitary on ascending
stalks, sometimes with 6 petals, the petals about twice
as long as sepals. Leaves ¼–2½ in. long, entire, linear or
very narrowly lance-shaped, clustered at intervals along
the creeping stem. Stems smooth or sparsely hairy,
creeping. Fruit an achene, about ¹⁄₁₆ in. long. CT, MA, ME,
NH, RI, VT

Ranunculus ambigens (water plantain spearwort) is
similar, but the leaves are longer (3–6 in.), more broadly
lance-shaped, and slightly but distinctly toothed. Grows
in marshes and swamps. CT (rare)

Verbascum thapsus* SCROPHULARIACEAE
Common mullein
Summer to early fall, 2–6 ft., biennial. Fields, beaches,
ledges, roadsides, and disturbed, open sites.

Flowers yellow, ¾–1¼ in. wide, densely clustered on
thick, clublike spikes 8–20 in. long; the petals slightly
unequal. Leaves 2–12 in. long, broadly lance-shaped or
oval, crowded, woolly-velvety; the lower petioled, the
upper sessile. Stems woolly with grayish hairs. Fruit an
oval capsule, ⅜ in. long. Native to Eurasia. CT, MA, ME,
NH, RI, VT

Physalis grisea (P. pruinosa, P. pubescens var. grisea)
SOLANACEAE
Downy ground-cherry
Midsummer to fall, 1–2 ft., annual.
Fields and open, disturbed sites.

Flowers yellow with dark centers, ⅜ in. wide, solitary,
drooping from leaf axils. Leaves 1–3 in. long, broadly
oval or triangular, densely hairy, coarsely toothed. Stems
branching, grayish, with soft hairs. Fruit an orange berry,
¼–⅜ in. wide, covered by a veined, papery husk. CT, MA,
NH, RI, VT (rare)

Physalis heterophylla SOLANACEAE
Clammy ground-cherry
Summer, 1–3 ft., perennial. Fields and roadsides.

Flowers yellow with dark centers, ½–1 in. wide, solitary,
drooping from leaf axils. Leaves 1–3 in. long, oval or triangular, hairy, irregularly toothed, occasionally entire.
Stems branching, with sticky-glandular hairs mixed with
longer, nonglandular hairs. Fruit a yellow berry, ½ in.
wide, covered by a veined, papery husk. CT, MA, ME, NH,
RI, VT

185

Physalis virginiana   SOLANACEAE
Virginia ground-cherry
Spring to late summer, 1–3 ft., perennial. Woodland clearings, fields, and open, disturbed sites.

Flowers yellow with dark centers, ½–¾ in. wide, solitary, long-stalked, drooping from leaf axils. Leaves 1–2½ in. long, lance-shaped, with sparsely toothed, wavy, or entire margins. Stems branching, with downward-curving hairs. Fruit a red-orange berry, ½ in. wide, covered by a papery husk. CT, MA, ME, NH

Physalis longifolia (long-leaved ground-cherry) is similar, but the leaves are often longer (to 4 in.), the flowers are smaller (⅜–½ in. wide), the stems have erect, pressed-in hairs, and the berries are green. Grows in fields and roadsides. ME, NH, RI

Abutilon theophrasti✳   MALVACEAE
Velvet-leaf, Indian mallow
Midsummer to fall, 2–4 ft., annual.
Fields and disturbed, open sites.

Flowers yellow, ½–1 in. wide, stalked singly or in small clusters from the leaf axils. Leaves 2–8 in. long, broadly oval or rounded, long-petioled, velvety, with a heart-shaped base and a pointed tip. Stems branching, soft-hairy. Fruits round, capsulelike, ⅜–1 in. wide, divided into 10–15 segments. Native to Asia. CT, MA, ME, NH, RI, VT

Verbascum blattaria✳   SCROPHULARIACEAE
Moth-mullein
Summer, 1–4 ft., biennial. Fields, roadsides, and open, disturbed sites.

Flowers yellow or white, with purple centers, ¾–1¼ in. wide, arranged in a long, loosely flowered, spike-like raceme. Leaves 1–4 in. long, lance-shaped, smooth, coarsely toothed; the upper leaves sessile or clasping. Stems usually smooth below, glandular-hairy above. Fruit a rounded capsule, ¼ in. wide. Native to Eurasia. CT, MA, ME, NH, RI, VT

Hypericum ascyron (*H. pyramidatum*)
HYPERICACEAE
Great St. John's-wort
Summer, 2–6 ft., perennial. Wet meadows,
floodplains, and rocky river shores.

Flowers yellow, 1½–2½ in. wide, with numerous bushy
stamens, arranged in branching, compact clusters of
1–5. Leaves 1–4 in. long, lance-shaped or oval, sometimes
clasping. Stems smooth, ridged, slightly winged. Fruit a
cone-shaped capsule, ⅝–1¼ in. long. CT, MA, ME, NH, VT
(rare in all)

Hypericum canadense   HYPERICACEAE
Lesser Canada St. John's-wort, Canada St. John's-wort
Midsummer to early fall, 4–24 in., annual or perennial.
Wet meadows, swamps, and river and lake shores.

Flowers yellow, ⅛–¼ in. wide, arranged in narrow,
forking clusters. Leaves ⅜–1½ in. long and ⅛ in. wide,
linear or narrowly lance-shaped, sessile, with 1 or 3
veins on upper surface. Stems slender, smooth. Fruit a
red-purple, pointed, conical capsule, ¼ in. long. CT, MA,
ME, NH, RI, VT
  Hypericum majus (greater Canada St. John's-wort) is
similar, but the flowers are ¼–⅜ in. wide, the leaves are
¼ in. wide with 5 or 7 veins on the upper surface, and
the leaf bases clasp the stem. Grows in wet meadows,
swamps, and river and lake shores. CT, MA, ME, NH, RI, VT

Hypericum ellipticum   HYPERICACEAE
Pale St. John's-wort
Summer, 8–20 in., perennial. Wet meadows,
marshes, and pond and river shores.

Flowers bright yellow, ⅜–½ in. wide, with numerous
stamens, in a short-branched, sparsely flowered inflorescence at the top of the stem. Leaves ⅜–1¼ in. long, blunt,
oval or elliptic, tilted upward, rounded at base, with flat
margins; clusters of smaller leaves sometimes in axils of
the primary leaves. Stems smooth. Fruit a beaked, oval
capsule, about ¼ in. long. CT, MA, ME, NH, RI, VT
  Hypericum adpressum (creeping St. John's-wort) is
similar, but the leaves are 1¼–2½ in. long and narrowly
lance-shaped, with inrolled margins. Grows in sandy or
peaty, coastal plain pond shores. MA, RI (rare in both)

187

Hypericum mutilum   HYPERICACEAE
Dwarf St. John's-wort
Midsummer to early fall, 6–30 in., annual or
perennial. Wet meadows, swamp and marsh
edges, and lake and river shores.

Flowers yellow, ⅛–¼ in. wide, arranged in sparsely flowered, spreading, axillary branches; the petals smaller
than the sharp-tipped sepals; bracts at base of flower
stalks tiny and scalelike. Leaves ½–1½ in. long, oval or
elliptic, blunt, rounded at base. Stems slender, smooth.
Fruit an oval, green capsule, ¼ in. long, about equal to
the sepals. CT, MA, ME, NH, RI, VT
    Hypericum boreale (northern St. John's-wort) is simi-
lar, but the flowers are larger (¼ in. wide), the sepals are
blunt-tipped, the bracts at base of flower stalks are larger
and more leaflike, and the capsule is purple and longer
than the sepals. Grows in swamps, marshes, and pond
and river shorelines and shallows. CT, MA, ME, NH, RI, VT

Hypericum perforatum*   HYPERICACEAE
Common St. John's-wort
Summer to early fall, 1–3 ft., perennial. Fields,
thickets, roadsides, and open, disturbed sites.

Flowers bright yellow, with bushy stamens, ¾–1¼ in.
wide, numerous, arranged in many, spreading branches;
the petals black-dotted only on the edges. Leaves ¾–1½
in. long, crowded, narrowly oblong; smaller leaves often
clustered in the axils of primary leaves. Stems smooth,
slightly ridged. Fruit an oval capsule, ⅛–¼ in. long.
Native to Europe. CT, MA, ME, NH, RI, VT

Hypericum punctatum   HYPERICACEAE
Spotted St. John's-wort
Summer, 1–3 ft., perennial. Fields and woodland clearings.

Flowers bright yellow, with bushy stamens, ⅜–⅝ in.
wide, arranged in short, crowded branches; the petal surfaces streaked and spotted with black. Leaves 1½–2½ in.
long; oval or oblong, blunt, the undersurfaces conspicuously gland-spotted. Stems smooth. Fruit an oval capsule,
⅛–¼ in. long, spotted with tiny, amber glands. CT, MA,
ME, NH, RI, VT

Lysimachia ciliata MYRSINACEAE
Fringed yellow-loosestrife, fringed loosestrife
Summer, 1–3 ft., perennial. Moist forests and woodlands, floodplains, and thickets.

Flowers yellow, ½–1 in. wide, solitary, long-stalked and nodding from the leaf axils; the petals often red at base, with a sharp point at the tip. Leaves 1½–6 in. long and ¾–2 in. wide, broadly lance-shaped or oval, rounded at base; the petioles long, fringed their entire length. Stems smooth. Fruit an oval capsule, ¼ in. long. CT, MA, ME, NH, RI, VT

Lysimachia hybrida (*L. lanceolata* var. *hybrida*)
MYRSINACEAE
Lowland yellow loosestrife, lance-leaved loosestrife
Summer, 1–3 ft., perennial. Moist forests, floodplains, thickets, and river banks.

Flowers yellow, ½–1 in. wide, solitary, long-stalked and nodding from the leaf axils; the petals often red at base, with a sharp point at the tip. Leaves 1–4 in. long and ½–¾ in. wide, lance-shaped, tapered at base; the petioles fringed mostly near base. Stems smooth, often branching. Fruit a rounded capsule, ¼ in. long. CT, MA, ME, NH, RI, VT (rare)

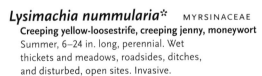

Lysimachia nummularia⁕ MYRSINACEAE
Creeping yellow-loosestrife, creeping jenny, moneywort
Summer, 6–24 in. long, perennial. Wet thickets and meadows, roadsides, ditches, and disturbed, open sites. Invasive.

Flowers yellow, ¾–1¼ in. wide, long-stalked, paired in the leaf axils. Leaves ½–1½ in. long, rounded, short-petioled, crowded. Stems creeping and mat-forming. Fruit an oval capsule, ¼ in. long. Native to Eurasia. CT, MA, ME, NH, RI, VT

Lysimachia terrestris MYRSINACEAE
Swamp yellow-loosestrife, yellow loosestrife, swamp candles
Summer, 1–3 ft., perennial. Swamps, marshes, wet meadows, river and lake shores.

Flowers yellow, ½–¾ in. wide, with red centers and dark-ish dots and streaks, long-stalked, crowded in erect, terminal racemes 2–12 in. long. Leaves 1½–4 in. long, lance-shaped, smooth; cone-shaped red bulblets develop in leaf axils in late summer. Stems smooth, often branching. Fruit an oval capsule, ¼ in. long. CT, MA, ME, NH, RI, VT

Lysimachia thyrsiflora MYRSINACEAE
Tufted yellow-loosestrife, tufted loosestrife
Summer, 12–30 in., perennial. Swamps, fens, and lake shores.

Flowers yellow, ¼ in. wide, with 5–7 narrow petals and protruding stamens, arranged in dense, long-stalked, rounded or cylindrical heads in middle leaf axils. Leaves 2–5 in. long, lance-shaped, sessile, hairy underneath. Stems hairy. Fruit a rounded capsule, ⅛ in. long. CT, MA, ME, NH (rare), RI, VT

Lysimachia quadrifolia MYRSINACEAE
Whorled yellow-loosestrife, whorled loosestrife
Late spring to summer, 1–3 ft., perennial. Woodlands, dry fields, and roadsides.

Flowers yellow with red centers and darkish dots and streaks, ½–¾ in. wide, solitary, arranged in long-stalked whorls in the upper and middle leaf axils. Leaves 1½–4 in. long, lance-shaped or oval, short-petioled or sessile, hairy underneath, in whorls of 4 or 5. Stems smooth or finely hairy. Fruit an oval capsule, ¼ in. long. CT, MA, ME, NH, RI, VT

Lysimachia vulgaris MYRSINACEAE
Garden yellow-loosestrife, garden loosestrife
Summer, 1–4 ft., perennial. Fields, roadsides,
and disturbed, open sites. Invasive.

Flowers bright yellow, ½ in. wide, arranged in branching, compact clusters at the top of the stem and upper leaf
axils. Leaves 2½–5 in. long, lance-shaped, short-petioled
or sessile, hairy underneath, in whorls of 3 or 4. Stems
hairy. Fruit a rounded capsule, ¼ in. long. Native to Eurasia. CT, MA, ME, NH, RI, VT

Nymphoides peltata MENYANTHACEAE
Yellow floating-heart
Summer, 3–6 in. above water surface, perennial.
Ponds, lakes, and slow-moving streams. Invasive.

Flowers bright yellow, 1–1¼ in. wide, usually solitary,
long-stalked above the floating leaves; the 5 petals fringed
on the margins. Leaves 2–6 in. long and wide, padlike,
rounded, heart-shaped at base, purplish underneath.
Stems thick, rooted in substrate below water surface.
Fruit an oval capsule, ½–1 in. long. Often forms massive
colonies. Native to Eurasia. CT, MA, NH, RI, VT

Ranunculus cymbalaria RANUNCULACEAE
Seaside crowfoot
Late spring to fall, 2–6 in., perennial. Salt and brackish
marshes, and very occasionally in freshwater wetlands.

Flowers yellow, ¼–⅜ in. wide, slightly overtopping
the leaves, the narrow petals slightly longer than the
sepals. Leaves ⅜–1½ in. long, oval or rounded, shallowly
toothed, often forming massive colonies. Stems smooth.
Fruit a tiny achene, aggregated into oval heads ⅛–½ in.
long. CT (rare), MA, ME, NH

5 radial petals; leaves
simple, whorled, entire

5 radial petals; leaves
simple, basal, entire

5 radial petals; leaves simple,
basal, toothed or lobed

Taenidia integerrima   APIACEAE
Yellow pimpernel
Spring to early summer, 16–32 in., perennial. Rocky woodlands and clearings near large rivers and lakes.

Flowers yellow, ⅛ in. wide, arranged in spreading umbels with 7–16 slender, spokelike branches. Leaves pinnately compound; the larger leaves divided 2 or 3 times into 9 or more oval or lance-shaped leaflets, ⅜–1¼ in. long, with entire margins. Stems smooth. Fruit elliptical, ribbed, ¼–⅛ in. long. CT (rare), VT (rare)

Oxalis stricta (*O. europea*) OXALIDACEAE
Common wood sorrel
Spring to fall, 4–16 in., perennial. Fields, roadsides, and open, disturbed sites.

Flowers yellow, ⅜ in. wide, arranged in clusters of 5–7 on erect or ascending stalks. Leaves 3-parted; the 3 leaflets heart-shaped at the tip, ⅜–¾ in. wide. Stems usually erect, branching, with dense, spreading hairs. Fruit a ribbed, cylindrical capsule, ¼–½ in. long. CT, MA, ME, NH, RI, VT

Oxalis dillenii (slender yellow wood sorrel) is very similar, but the stem hairs are erect and pressed in, not spreading outward. CT, MA, ME, NH, RI, VT

Oxalis corniculata* (creeping yellow wood sorrel) is also similar, with spreading hairs on the stem, but the flower clusters have 1–3 flowers, and the stems and leaves are creeping and colonial. Region of origin uncertain; now globally distributed. CT, MA, ME, NH, RI, VT

*Pastinaca sativa**   APIACEAE
Wild parsnip
Summer, 2–5 ft., biennial. Fields and roadsides.

Flowers yellow, ⅛ in. wide, arranged in spreading umbels, 4–8 in. wide, with 15–25 spokelike branches. Leaves 6–12 in. long, pinnately compound, with 5–15 oval, sharply toothed, sometimes lobed leaflets, 2–3 in. long. Stems thick, hairy, grooved. Fruit flattened, elliptical, ¼ in. long. The foliage can cause irritation if it contacts skin in the presence of sunlight. Native to Eurasia. CT, MA, ME, NH, RI, VT

Sanicula odorata (*S. gregaria*) APIACEAE
Clustered sanicle, clustered snakeroot
Summer, 1–2½ ft., perennial. Rich forests and floodplains.

Flowers greenish yellow, tiny, with protruding stamens, arranged in rounded umbels ¼–½ in. wide. Lower leaves to 5 in. long, deeply 5-parted, long-petioled, sharply toothed; the upper leaves smaller, short-petioled or sessile. Fruits short-stalked, bristly, rounded, ⅛ in. long; the persistent styles longer than the bristles. CT, MA (rare), ME, NH (rare), VT

Zizia aurea APIACEAE
Common golden-alexanders, golden-alexanders
Spring, 1–3 ft., perennial. Floodplains, moist woodlands, and swamp edges.

Flowers golden yellow, ⅛ in. wide, arranged in umbels 1–2 in. wide, with 10–18 ascending or spreading branches. Leaves pinnately compound, sharply toothed; the 3 primary leaflets divided 2 or 3 times into 9 or more lance-shaped leaflet segments, ¾–3 in. long. Stems smooth. Fruit oval, ⅛ in. long. CT, MA, ME, NH, RI, VT

Hibiscus trionum* MALVACEAE
Flower-of-an-hour, Venice rose-mallow
Summer to early fall, 1–2 ft., annual.
Fields and disturbed, open sites.

Flowers yellow or white, dark-centered, 1–2 in. wide, stalked from leaf axils, blooming only for a few hours. Leaves ¾–2½ in. long, deeply divided into 3 lobed or coarsely toothed leaflets, the middle leaflet longest. Stems hairy. Fruit a hairy capsule, ½–1 in. long, enclosed within the veined, papery calyx. Native to Europe. CT, MA, ME, NH, RI, VT

5 radial petals; leaves deeply divided, alternate, leaflets toothed or lobed

Ranunculus abortivus RANUNCULACEAE

Kidney-leaved crowfoot, kidney-leaved buttercup

Spring to early summer, 4–16 in., annual, biennial, or perennial. Moist forests and woodlands and rocky slopes.

Flowers yellow, 1/4 in. wide, solitary, on long, branching stalks; petals smaller than the smooth, hairless sepals. Basal leaves 1/2–2 1/2 in. long, long-petioled, rounded, sometimes lobed; the stem leaves divided into 3–5 narrow segments. Stems smooth. Fruit an achene, 1/16 in. long, with a miniscule beak; the fruiting heads 1/8–1/4 in. long. A common species. CT, MA, ME, NH, RI, VT

Ranunculus allegheniensis (Allegheny crowfoot), a much less common species, is similar, also with smooth stems. It has sepals that are hairy underneath, and a larger, strongly hooked beak on the achene. Grows in rich forests and woodlands. CT, MA (rare), RI (rare), VT (rare)

Ranunculus micranthus (small-flowered crowfoot) is also similar, but the stems, especially the lower stems, are densely hairy. The sepals also are hairy, and the fruit is an achene with a tiny beak. Grows in rich, rocky forests and woodlands. CT, MA, RI (rare in all)

*Ranunculus acris** RANUNCULACEAE

Tall buttercup, tall crowfoot, blister-weed

Spring to fall, 1–3 ft., perennial. Moist fields, clearings, and roadsides.

Flowers bright yellow, 3/4–1 1/4 in. wide, solitary on long, branching stalks; the sepals spreading outward. Leaves divided; the larger leaves 3/4–2 in. long and 1 1/2–4 in. wide, deeply cut into 3–7 sharply lobed, stalkless leaflets. Stems hairy. Fruit a beaked achene, 1/16 in. long, aggregated into heads 1/4–3/8 in. wide. Native to Europe. CT, MA, ME, NH, RI, VT

*Ranunculus bulbosus** RANUNCULACEAE

Bulbous crowfoot, bulbous buttercup, St. Anthony's turnip

Spring to early summer, 8–24 in., perennial. Fields, clearings, and roadsides.

Flowers bright yellow, 1–1 1/4 in. wide, solitary on long stalks; the sepals strongly reflexed. Leaves 1–2 in. long and wide, deeply divided into 3 sharply toothed leaflets, the terminal one often long-stalked. Stems hairy, bulbous at base. Fruit a beaked achene, 1/8 in. long, aggregated into heads 3/8 in. wide. Native to Europe. CT, MA, ME, NH, RI, VT

Ranunculus fascicularis RANUNCULACEAE
Early crowfoot, early buttercup
Early spring, 4–12 in., perennial. Rich,
rocky forests and woodlands.

Flowers bright yellow, ¾–1 in. wide, solitary on long
stalks, the 5–7 narrow petals slightly longer than the
sepals. Basal leaves 1–2 in. long, long-petioled, divided
into 3 stalkless leaflets, thin lobes lance-shaped or oval;
the stem leaves smaller, short-petioled or sessile. Stems
hairy. Fruit a beaked achene, ⅛ in. long, aggregated into
heads ¼ in. long. CT, MA (rare), ME (rare), NH (rare)

Ranunculus flabellaris RANUNCULACEAE
Yellow water buttercup, greater yellow water crowfoot
Spring to early summer, to 30 in. long, perennial.
Swamps, ponds, and slow streams.

Flowers yellow, ½–1 in. wide, long-stalked, arranged in
racemes of 1–7 flowers. Submerged leaves finely dissected
into linear filaments; above-surface leaves (when present) divided into 3 broad leaflets with incised, often lobed
margins. Stems hollow, floating or occasionally rooted in
mud. Fruit a beaked achene, 1⁄16 in. long, aggregated into
heads ¼–½ in. long. CT, MA, ME, NH, RI (rare), VT (rare)

Ranunculus hispidus RANUNCULACEAE
Hispid crowfoot, hispid buttercup
Spring, 1–2 ft., perennial. Forests, woodlands,
ledges, and fields, often in high-pH conditions.

Flowers yellow, 1–1½ in. wide, solitary, long-stalked; the
petals much longer than the sepals. Leaves 1–5 in. long,
broadly divided into 3 leaflets, at least the terminal one
stalked; the leaflet margins with irregular, sharp-pointed
lobes. Stems hairy, erect or semierect. Fruit a beaked
achene, ⅛ in. long, aggregated into heads ¼–⅜ in. long.
CT, MA, ME, RI (rare), VT (rare)
Ranunculus caricetorum (swamp buttercup; syn. *R.
septentrionalis*) is very similar, but the hairy stems are up
to 3 ft. long, usually sprawling, and rooting at the nodes.
Grows in swamps, marshes, and floodplains. CT, MA, ME,
NH, VT

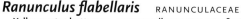

5 radial petals; leaves deeply divided,
alternate, leaflets toothed or lobed

Ranunculus pensylvanicus   RANUNCULACEAE
Bristly crowfoot
Summer, 1–2 ft., annual or perennial. Swamps,
marshes, and river and lake shores.

Flowers pale yellow, ⅛–¼ in. wide, stalked from upper
leaf axils; the petals shorter than the hairy, reflexed
sepals. Leaves 1–3 in. long, deeply cut into 3 sharply
toothed, incised leaflets, the terminal one stalked. Stems
hairy. Fruit an achene, ¹⁄₁₆–⅛ in. long, aggregated into
oval heads ½ in. long. MA (rare), ME, NH, RI, VT (rare)

Ranunculus recurvatus   RANUNCULACEAE
Hooked crowfoot, hooked buttercup
Spring to early summer, 1–2 ft., perennial. Rich,
moist forests, shaded swamps, and streambanks.

Flowers yellow, ¼ in. wide, stalked from the upper leaf
axils; the petals usually shorter than the hairy, reflexed
sepals. Leaves 1–3 in. long, broadly divided into 3 coarsely
toothed, unstalked lobes attached at the base. Stems
hairy. Fruit an achene with a hooked beak, ¹⁄₁₆–⅛ in.
long, aggregated into fruiting heads ¼–⅜ in. long. CT,
MA, ME, NH, RI, VT

Ranunculus repens✳   RANUNCULACEAE
Creeping buttercup
Spring and summer, 6–24 in., perennial. Swamps,
wet meadows, and ditches. Invasive.

Flowers ¾–1¼ in. wide, long-stalked, the petals much
longer than the sepals. Leaves long-petioled, often
white-mottled, divided into 3 deeply cut, coarsely toothed
leaflets, ¾–1½ in. long, the terminal and often the laterals stalked. Stems creeping, hairy, often forming massive
colonies. Fruit an achene, ¹⁄₁₆–⅛ in. long, aggregated into
rounded heads ¼ in. long. Native to Europe. CT, MA, ME,
NH, RI, VT

Ranunculus sceleratus RANUNCULACEAE
Cursed crowfoot
Spring to summer, 6–24 in., annual or perennial. Swamps, freshwater and brackish marshes, and ditches.

Flowers yellow, ¼–⅜ in. wide, long-stalked, petals shorter than the sepals. Leaves ½–2 in. long, long-petioled, divided into 3 deeply cut, bluntly toothed, unstalked leaflets. Stems smooth, hollow. Fruit an achene, ¹⁄₁₆ in. long, aggregated into heads ⅛–⅜ in. long. CT (rare), MA, ME, NH, RI (rare), VT

Agrimonia gryposepala ROSACEAE
Common agrimony
Summer, 1–5 ft., perennial. Forests, clearings, and roadsides.

Flowers yellow, ⅛–¼ in. wide, clustered on long, thin, hairy, gland-dotted spikes. Leaves pinnately divided into 5–9 large, lance-shaped leaflets, intermixed with much smaller ones; the primary leaflets 1–3½ in. long, their lower surfaces gland-dotted, hairy on the veins. Stems hairy. Fruit an oval achene with spreading bristles, ¼ in. long. The most common agrimony species. CT, MA, ME, NH, RI, VT

Agrimonia rostellata (beaked agrimony) is very similar, but much less common. The flower spike is gland-dotted, but without (or with very few) hairs. Grows in rocky woodlands and talus slopes. CT, MA (rare)

Agrimonia parviflora ROSACEAE
Small-flowered agrimony, southern agrimony
Late summer and early fall, 2–6 ft., perennial. Marshes and wet meadows.

Flowers yellow, ⅛ in. wide, clustered on long, thin, arching, hairy, gland-dotted spikes. Leaves pinnately divided into 11–23 narrowly lance-shaped leaflets, intermixed with much smaller ones; the primary leaflets 2–3 in. long, their lower surfaces finely hairy and gland-dotted. Stems hairy. Fruit an oval achene with spreading bristles, ¼ in. long. CT, MA (rare)

Agrimonia pubescens   ROSACEAE
Downy agrimony
Summer, 1–4 ft., perennial. Rocky
woodlands in high-pH soils.

Flowers yellow, ⅛ in. wide, clustered on long, thin, hairy, nonglandular spikes. Leaves pinnately divided into 5–13 large, lance-shaped leaflets intermixed with smaller ones; the primary leaflets 2–3 in. long, their lower surfaces hairy, without glandular dots. Stems hairy. Fruit an oval achene with erect or ascending bristles, ⅛–¼ in. long. CT, MA (rare)

Agrimonia striata   ROSACEAE
Roadside agrimony, woodland agrimony
Midsummer to early fall, 1–4 ft., perennial.
Forests, clearings, and roadsides.

Flowers yellow, ¼ in. wide, clustered on long, thin, hairy, nonglandular spikes. Leaves pinnately divided into 7–11 large, lance-shaped leaflets intermixed with smaller ones, the primary leaflets 1–3 in. long, their lower surfaces gland-dotted, sparsely hairy on the veins. Stems hairy. Fruit an oval achene with erect or ascending bristles, ¼ in. long. CT, MA, ME, NH, RI, VT

Argentina egedii (Potentilla anserina var. groenlandica)
ROSACEAE
Pacific silver-weed
Spring to summer, to 15 in. long, perennial. Salt marshes.

Flowers yellow, ⅝–1 in. wide, solitary on long, often reddish stalks. Leaves shiny green, pinnately divided into 7–25 lance-shaped, sharply toothed leaflets, ½–1½ in. long, the undersurfaces primarily covered with short white hairs, with longer, silky hairs on the veins. Stems creeping. Fruit an achene, 1/16 in. long. A maritime species only on coast. CT, MA, ME, NH, RI

Argentina anserina (common silverweed; syn. Potentilla anserina) is similar but occurs in inland habitats. The leaf undersurfaces are completely covered with long, silvery, silky hairs. Grows in river and lake shores and low swales. CT, MA, ME, NH (rare), RI, VT

198

Geum aleppicum   ROSACEAE
Yellow avens
Summer, 1–3 ft., perennial. Forests, woodlands, and fields.

Flowers bright yellow, ½ in. wide, solitary or in
few-flowered clusters, stalked from upper leaf axils;
petals slightly longer than the sepals. Leaves sharply
toothed; the lower irregularly divided into 5–9 primary leaflets interspersed with numerous small ones;
the terminal leaflet largest, 2–4 in. long, often lobed,
wedge-shaped at base. Stems hairy. Fruit a tiny achene
aggregated into rounded, bristly heads ½–1 in. wide. CT,
MA, ME, NH, RI, VT

Geum laciniatum   ROSACEAE
Rough avens, floodplain avens
Late spring and summer, 1–3 ft., perennial. Floodplains,
forests, woodland edges, and meadows.

Flowers pale yellow or creamy white, ¼–¾ in. wide, solitary or in few-flowered clusters on upper stem, with
densely hairy stalks; sepals much longer than the petals.
Leaves variable; the basal leaves long-petioled, with 5 or
more sharply toothed, deeply cut leaflets; the stem leaves
3-parted, with sharply toothed, lance-shaped, oval, or triangular leaflets. Stems densely hairy. Fruit an achene, ⅛
in. long, aggregated into bristly heads ¾ in. wide. CT, MA,
ME, NH, VT (rare)

Geum macrophyllum   ROSACEAE
Large-leaved avens
Late spring to midsummer, 1–3 ft., perennial.
Forests, fields, and swamp edges.

Flowers yellow, ¼–½ in. wide, solitary or in few-flowered
clusters, stalked from upper leaf axils; petals longer than the sepals. Leaves sharply toothed, the lower
long-petioled, deeply divided into a broad, often lobed terminal leaflet 2–4½ in. long and wide, and much smaller
lateral leaves. Stems bristly-hairy. Fruit a tiny achene
aggregated into rounded, bristly heads ½–¾ in. wide. ME,
NH, VT

Geum peckii   ROSACEAE
White Mountain avens
Summer, 6–16 in., perennial. Alpine
meadows at high elevations.

Flowers bright yellow, ½–1 in. wide, long-stalked, solitary or in small clusters of 2–5; petals longer than the sepals. Basal leaves 2–4½ in. long, divided into a broad, sharply toothed terminal leaflet and tiny lateral leaflets; stem leaves few and very small. Stems hairy. Fruit a tiny achene aggregated into rounded fruiting heads ½ in. wide. Only in White Mountains. NH (rare)

Geum virginianum   ROSACEAE
Cream-colored avens
Summer, 1–3 ft., perennial. Floodplains, forests, and fields.

Flowers pale yellow or creamy white, ¼–¾ in. wide, solitary or in few-flowered clusters on upper stem, with thin, sparsely hairy stalks; sepals much longer than the petals. Leaves variable; the basal leaves long-petioled, divided into 3–7 leaflets, the terminal leaflet broadly oval or rounded, much larger than lateral leaflets; the stem leaves usually 3-parted, broadly triangular. Stems hairy. Fruit an achene, ⅛ in. long, aggregated into bristly heads ½–¾ in. wide. CT, MA (rare), RI

Potentilla argentea⁕   ROSACEAE
Silver-leaved cinquefoil, silvery cinquefoil
Summer, 4–16 in., perennial. Dry fields,
lawns, and disturbed, open sites.

Flowers yellow, ¼–⅜ in. wide, arranged in stalked, branching, axillary clusters of one to several flowers; petals equal to or slightly longer than the sepals. Leaves palmately divided into 5 narrow leaflets, ½–1¼ in. long, silvery-woolly underneath, with deeply toothed and slightly inrolled margins. Stems downy with whitish hairs. Fruit a tiny, dry achene. Native to Eurasia. CT, MA, ME, NH, RI, VT

Potentilla canadensis   ROSACEAE
Dwarf cinquefoil
Spring to early summer, 2–6 in., perennial. Spring to
early summer. Dry fields, lawns, and roadsides.

Flowers yellow, about ½ in. wide, solitary on long, axillary stalks, usually produced from the axil of the first
well-developed stem leaf. Leaves palmately divided
into 5 oval leaflets, ¼–1½ in. long, rounded at tip,
wedge-shaped at base, the margins sharply toothed for
about ⅔ of their length; terminal leaflet less than twice
as long as wide. Stems hairy, initially erect, later trailing.
Fruit an achene, ¹⁄₁₆ in. long. CT, MA, ME, NH, RI, VT
    Potentilla simplex (common cinquefoil) is similar,
with the flower produced usually from the axil of the 2nd
well-developed stem leaf, and with the terminal leaflet of
leaves usually more than 2 times as long as wide.

Potentilla norvegica   ROSACEAE
Norwegian cinquefoil, rough cinquefoil
Summer to fall, 1–3 ft., annual or perennial.
Thickets, fields, and roadsides.

Flowers bright yellow, ⅜ in. wide, numerous, arranged
in wide-branching clusters; the petals shorter than
the sepals. Leaves divided into 3 lance-shaped or oval,
coarsely toothed leaflets, ½–2½ in. long, the lower
long-petioled. Stems hairy. Fruit an achene, about ¹⁄₁₆ in.
long. CT, MA, ME, NH, RI, VT

Potentilla recta✲   ROSACEAE
Sulphur cinquefoil, rough-fruited cinquefoil
Late spring to late summer, 1–2 ft., perennial.
Fields, roadsides, and disturbed, open sites.

Flowers pale yellow, ½–1 in. wide, numerous, arranged
in a wide-branching, flattish, terminal inflorescence; the
petals longer than the sepals. Leaves divided into 5–7
lance-shaped, coarsely toothed leaflets, 1–6 in. long; the
lower leaves long-petioled. Stems finely hairy. Fruit an
achene, about ¹⁄₁₆ in. long. Native to Europe. CT, MA, ME,
NH, RI, VT

5 radial petals; leaves deeply divided,
alternate, leaflets toothed or lobed

Potentilla robbinsiana ROSACEAE
Robbins' cinquefoil
Midspring to early summer, ½–1½ in., perennial.
Rocky alpine zones at very high elevations.

Flowers yellow, ¼ in. wide, solitary on long stalks; the petals slightly longer than the sepals. Leaves clumped, mostly basal, divided into 3 oval leaflets, ¼–½ in. long, with 2–4 teeth on each side. Stems creeping, woody. Fruit an achene, about 1/16 in. long. Formerly listed as a federally endangered species. Only in White Mountains. NH (rare)

Potentilla simplex ROSACEAE
Common cinquefoil, old-field cinquefoil
Spring to early summer, 4–16 in., perennial.
Thickets, fields, lawns, and roadsides.

Flowers yellow, ½ in. wide, solitary on long stalks from upper leaf axils, usually produced from the axil of the second well-developed stem leaf; the petals longer than the sepals. Leaves divided into 5 lance-shaped leaflets, ¾–3 in. long, the margins sharply toothed about ¾ of their length; terminal leaflet more than twice as long as wide. Stems hairy, initially erect, later arching or trailing. Fruit an achene, 1/16 in. long. CT, MA, ME, NH, RI, VT

Potentilla canadensis (dwarf cinquefoil) is similar, with the flower produced usually from the axil of the 1st well-developed stem leaf, and with the terminal leaflet of the leaves usually less than 2 times as long as wide.

Geum fragarioides (*Waldsteinia fragarioides*)
ROSACEAE
Appalachian barren-strawberry, barren strawberry
Spring, 3–6 in., perennial. Forests, thickets, fields, and seepages, in high-pH soils.

Flowers yellow, ⅜–⅝ in. wide, solitary or few-flowered on stalks separate from leaves; petals longer than the sepals. Leaves 3-parted, long-petioled; the 3 leaflets 1–2 in. long, broad at tip, wedge-shaped at base, coarsely and irregularly toothed. Stems creeping. Fruit a dry achene (not a strawberry), 1/16 in. long. CT (rare), MA (rare), ME (rare), NH (rare), VT

Potentilla indica ✴ (*Duchesnea indica*)
ROSACEAE
Indian-strawberry, mock-strawberry
Spring to early summer, 1–4 in., perennial.
Fields, lawns, and disturbed, open sites.

Flowers yellow, ½–¾ in. wide, solitary, stalked from
leaf nodes, with a whorl of toothed bracts just below the
sepals. Leaves long-petioled, 3-parted;
the 3 leaflets ¾–1½ in. long, oval,
narrowed at tip. Stems creeping. Fruit
a tiny achene, aggregated into a red,
strawberry-like head, ⅜ in. wide, dry
and insipid to taste. Native to Asia. CT

Hudsonia ericoides CISTACEAE
Pine-barren false-heather, golden-heather
Spring to early summer, 4–8 in., perennial. Sandy
fields and woodlands and open, rocky summits.

Flowers bright yellow, ¼–⅜ in. wide, numerous, stalked
from leaf axils; the flower stalks ¼–½ in. long. Leaves
⅛–¼ in. long, needlelike, green, sparsely hairy, erect or
ascending. Stems low, spreading, downy, mat-forming.
Fruit an oval capsule. CT (rare), MA, ME, NH (rare), RI
(rare), VT

Hudsonia tomentosa CISTACEAE
Woolly beach-heather, false heather, hudsonia
Spring to early summer, 4–8 in., perennial. Dunes
and dry, sandy openings, primarily along coast.

Flowers bright yellow, ¼–⅜ in. wide, numerous, stalked
from leaf axils; the flower stalks ⅛ in. long (or less).
Leaves ⅛ in. long, scaly, grayish, densely woolly, hugging
stem. Stems low, spreading, grayish downy, mat-forming.
Fruit an oval capsule. CT (rare), MA, ME, NH (rare), RI, VT
(rare)

203

Hypopitys monotropa (Monotropa hypopithys)
ERICACEAE
Yellow pine-sap, pine-sap
Early to mid or late summer, 4–12 in., perennial. Forests.

Flowers tan or yellow, ¼–½ in. long, arranged in clusters of 3–10, nodding when young, later becoming erect. Leaves ¼ in. long, lacking chlorophyll, scaly, linear, same color as stem. Stems fleshy, yellow or tan. Fruit an erect, oval, ridged capsule, ⅜ in. long. Saprophytic on roots of oak and pine. CT, MA, ME, NH, RI, VT

Hypopitys lanuginosa (hairy pine-sap) is similar but is entirely pink or red and blooms from mid or late summer to early fall. Grows in oak and pine forests. CT, MA, RI (rare)

Hypericum gentianoides   HYPERICACEAE
Orange grass, orange-grass St. John's-wort
Midsummer to fall, 4–20 in., annual. Dry, sandy fields, grasslands, and open ledges.

Flowers yellow, ⅛–¼ in. wide, loosely clustered on stiff, ascending branches. Leaves ⅛ in. long scaly, sharp-pointed, pressed to stem. Stems wiry, branching, turning red in fall. Fruit a narrowly oval capsule, ¼ in. long. CT, MA, ME, NH, RI, VT (rare)

Uvularia grandiflora   COLCHICACEAE
Large-flowered bellwort
Early to late spring, 8–24 in., perennial. Rich, moist forests and woodlands.

Flowers bright yellow, 1–2 in. long, nodding, solitary or in small clusters; the petals smooth on the inside, twisted at the tips. Leaves pierced by stem, 2½–5 in. long, lance-shaped or oval, whitish underneath; 1 or 2 leaves below the fork in the stem. Stems smooth. Fruit a triangular capsule, ½ in. long. CT (rare), MA (rare), NH (rare), VT

Uvularia perfoliata   COLCHICACEAE
Perfoliate bellwort
Spring to early summer, 8–16 in.,
perennial. Woodlands and thickets.

Flowers pale yellow; ¾–1½ in. long, nodding, solitary or
in small clusters; the petals roughened with yellow or
orange grains on the inside, upturned at the tips. Leaves
pierced by stem, 1½–4 in. long, lance-shaped or oval; 1–4
leaves below the fork in the stem. Stems smooth. Fruit a
triangular capsule, ⅜ in. long. CT, MA, ME, NH (rare), VT
(rare)

Uvularia sessilifolia   COLCHICACEAE
Sessile-leaved bellwort
Spring to early summer, 4–12 in., perennial.
Forests, woodlands, and clearings.

Flowers pale yellow or creamy, ½–1 in. long, nodding,
solitary, the petals smooth on the inside, upturned at the
tips. Leaves sessile, 1½–3 in. long, oval, pale underneath;
0–2 leaves below the fork in the stem. Stems smooth.
Fruit a winged, oval capsule, ¾–1¼ in. long. CT, MA, ME,
NH, RI, VT

Iris pseudacorus⁕   IRIDACEAE
Yellow iris
Late spring to summer, 1–3 ft., perennial. Marshes, wet
meadows, river and pond shores and shallows. Invasive.

Flowers bright yellow, 4 in. wide, solitary to several
at the stem tips; the 3 long, broad, drooping sepals
brown-veined at base. Leaves to 3 ft. long, erect, swordlike, sharply pointed, usually taller than flowering stems.
Stems thick, smooth. Fruit an elliptical, 6-angled capsule, 1½–2½ in. long. Native to Europe. CT, MA, ME, NH,
RI, VT

Polygonatum pubescens RUSCACEAE
Hairy Solomon's-seal
Midspring to early summer, 1–3 ft.,
perennial. Moist forests.

Flowers greenish yellow, ⅜–½ in. long, tubular, solitary
or paired, dangling from the leaf axils. Leaves 1½–4½
in. long, lance-shaped or oval, the undersurfaces with
3–9 prominent, finely hairy veins. Stem usually arching.
Fruit a blue berry, ¼ in. long. CT, MA, ME, NH, RI, VT
  Polygonatum biflorum (King Solomon's-seal, smooth
Solomon's-seal) is similar, but the flowers are longer
(½–1 in. long), dangling in clusters of 1–10 from leaf
axils. The leaf undersurfaces are entirely smooth, with
7–19 prominent veins. Grows in forests, floodplains, and
fields. CT, MA, ME, NH, RI, VT (rare)

Lilium canadense LILIACEAE
Canada lily, yellow wild-lily
Summer, 2–6 ft., perennial. Floodplains,
swamp edges, and wet meadows.

Flowers yellow, sometimes orange or red, dark-spotted
on the inside, 2–3 in. wide, bell-shaped, nodding on
long, arching stalks, the petals upturned at the tips.
Leaves 3–7 in. long, in multiple whorls of 4–12, the edges
and lower surfaces roughened. Stems smooth. Fruit an
erect, cylindrical capsule, 1¼–2 in. long. CT, MA, ME, NH,
RI (rare), VT

Medeola virginiana LILIACEAE
Indian cucumber root
Midspring to early summer, 12–28
in., perennial. Moist forests.

Flowers 3–9, greenish yellow, ½ in. wide, dangling below
the upper leaf whorl; the petals strongly reflexed and
the 3 reddish styles wide-spreading. Leaves 2½–5 in.
long, oval, clustered in an upper whorl of 3–5 leaves and
a lower whorl of 5–9 leaves. Stems woolly-hairy when
young. Fruit a dark, fleshy berry, ⅜ in. wide. CT, MA, ME,
NH, RI, VT

Hypoxis hirsuta HYPOXIDACEAE
Common star-grass, yellow star-grass
Spring to midsummer, 2–10 in., perennial.
Sandy fields, thickets, and woodlands.

Flowers bright yellow, ¼–¾ in. wide, star-shaped,
arranged in branching clusters of 2–7. Leaves 4–16 in.
long, grasslike, hairy, overtopping the flowers. Stems
hairy. Fruit an oval capsule, ⅛–¼ in. long. CT, MA, NH
(rare), RI

Clintonia borealis LILIACEAE
Yellow blue-bead lily, blue-bead lily, corn-lily
Spring and summer, 6–16 in.,
perennial. Cool, moist forests.

Flowers greenish yellow, ½–¾ in. wide, nodding, with
protruding stamens, arranged in long-stalked, spreading
clusters of 2–8. Leaves 5–12 in. long, basal, dark green,
oval, shining, with pointed tips. Stems usually hairy.
Fruit a dark blue berry, ⅜ in. long. CT, MA, ME, NH, RI
(rare), VT

Erythronium americanum LILIACEAE
American trout-lily, trout-lily, dog-tooth violet
Early spring, 4–10 in., perennial. Rich, moist forests.

Flowers yellow, ¾–2 in. wide, nodding, solitary, with
reflexed petals and protruding stamens. Leaves 3–8 in.
long, lance-shaped or oval, shiny, mottled with dark,
troutlike markings. Stems smooth. Fruit a rounded capsule, ½ in. long. CT, MA, ME, NH, RI, VT

Hemerocallis lilioasphodelus (*H. flava*)
LILIACEAE
Yellow day-lily
Late spring to midsummer, 2–4 ft., perennial.
Fields, thickets, and roadsides.

Flowers yellow, 2–3 in. wide, in clusters of 3–9 at the
top of the stem, ascending or upright, lemon-scented,
remaining open at night. Leaves 1–3 ft. long, in a basal
cluster, linear or narrowly lance-shaped. Stems smooth.
Fruit an oval, 3-angled capsule, 1–2 in. long. Native to
East Asia. CT, MA, ME, RI, VT

Nuphar variegata   NYMPHAEACEAE
Bullhead pond-lily, yellow pond-lily, spatterdock
Summer, to 6 in. above water surface, perennial.
Ponds and slow-moving streams.

Flowers yellow, 1–2 in. wide, stalked above the floating leaves, the 6 petal-like sepals partially enclosing the
small petals, stamens, and yellowish green stigmatic
disk. Leaves 2–12 in. long, floating, padlike, broadly oval,
rounded at tip, with a narrow sinus at base. Stems mostly
submerged. Fruit a purplish, ridged, cylindrical berry,
¾–1½ in. long. CT, MA, ME, NH, RI, VT
  Nuphar microphylla (small-leaved pond-lily), a much
less common species, is similar but has only 5 petal-like
sepals. The flowers (⅜–¾ in. wide) and leaves (1½–4 in.
long) are smaller, and the flower's stigmatic disk is red.
Grows in ponds and slow-moving streams with a high
pH. CT (rare), MA (rare), ME, VT

Asparagus officinalis   ASPARAGACEAE
Asparagus
Spring, 2–6 ft., perennial. Fields, roadsides,
and disturbed, open sites.

Flowers greenish yellow, ¼ in. long, bell-shaped, axillary, solitary or paired, drooping. True leaves are tiny,
sharp-pointed scales at bases of the linear, forking, feathery branches. Stems smooth. Fruit a red berry, ¼–⅜ in.
long. Native to Eurasia and North Africa. CT, MA, ME, NH,
RI, VT

208

Pityopsis falcata (*Chrysopsis falcata*) ASTERACEAE
Sickle-leaved golden-aster, sickle-leaved silk-grass
Midsummer to early fall, 4–12 in., perennial. Near coast in sandy fields and woodland clearings.

Flower heads ½–¾ in. wide, with 9–15 golden yellow rays, solitary or in small clusters on tips of wide-branching stalks. Leaves ½–3½ in. long, linear, crowded, stiff, often arching. Stems with woolly hairs. CT (rare), MA, RI (rare)

Chrysopsis mariana (Maryland golden-aster) is similar, but the leaves are lance-shaped or oval and the flower heads are on average wider, ¾–1 in., and more densely clustered at the top of the stem. An extremely rare species that occurs in sandy fields in coastal RI.

*Tragopogon pratensis** ASTERACEAE
Meadow goat's-beard, jack go-to-bed-at-noon
Midspring to late summer, 1–2½ ft., biennial. Fields and roadsides.

Flower heads 2 in. wide, solitary, with 16–25 yellow rays; the pointed green bracts beneath the heads about same length as the rays; the flowers open only in the morning. Leaves to 12 in. long, linear, clasping, ascending, keeled, broader at base. Stems smooth, with milky sap. Fruiting head a silky dome, 3–4 in. wide. Native to Europe. CT, MA, ME, NH, RI, VT

*Tragopogon dubius** (fistulous goat's-beard) is similar, but the pointed green bracts are distinctly longer than the rays, and the flower stalks are thickened near the base of the heads. Native to Europe. CT, MA, NH, VT

*Nelumbo lutea** NELUMBONACEAE
American lotus
Summer, 1–3 ft. above water surface, perennial. Ponds and slow-moving streams.

Flowers 5–10 in. wide, solitary, with 14–30 petals, stalked higher than the leaves well above the water surface. Leaves rounded, 12–28 in. wide, cupped in the center, stalked 1–2 ft. above water. Fruit a rounded nut, ½ in. long. Sometimes forms massive populations. Native to much of eastern and central United States, possibly native in CT, but most New England populations are introduced. CT, MA, ME, RI

Cirsium horridulum   ASTERACEAE
Yellow thistle
Spring to late summer, 1–5 ft., biennial or perennial.
Sandy meadows and edges of tidal marshes.

Flower heads yellow, occasionally purplish, 1½–3 in.
wide, solitary or in short-branched clusters on upper
stem; the heads surrounded by a whorl of erect, spiny,
linear bracts. Leaves 4–16 in. long, lance-shaped, with
saw-toothed, spine-tipped margins. Stems thick, hairy.
Coastal regions of CT, MA, RI (rare in all)

Grindelia squarrosa⁎   ASTERACEAE
Curly-top gum-weed, tar-weed
Midsummer to fall, 6–36 in., biennial or perennial.
Dry fields, roadsides, and disturbed, open sites.

Flower heads ⅜–¾ in. wide, numerous, with 25–40 short
yellow rays and a broad central disk; the heads arranged
in branching, flattish clusters; whorled bracts beneath
the rays resinous, with reflexed tips. Leaves ½–3 in.
long, lance-shaped or oval, clasping, gland-dotted, finely
toothed. Stems smooth. Native to western United States.
CT, MA, ME, NH, RI, VT

Helenium autumnale   ASTERACEAE
Fall sneezeweed, common sneezeweed
Late summer to fall, 2–5 ft., perennial.
Fields, wet meadows, and clearings.

Flower heads 1–2 in. wide, with 13–21 downturned
yellow rays and a prominent yellow knoblike disk; the
heads arranged in branching clusters. Leaves 2–6 in.
long, lance-shaped, sessile, usually finely toothed. Stems
smooth or hairy, prominently winged. CT, MA (rare), ME,
RI, VT (rare)

Helenium flexuosum (H. nudiflorum) ASTERACEAE
Purple-headed sneezeweed
Early summer to fall, 1–3 ft., perennial.
Fields, wet meadows, and clearings.

Flower heads yellow, 1–2 in. wide, with 8–13 downturned
yellow rays and a prominent brown or purple knoblike
disk; the heads arranged in branching clusters. Leaves
1–4½ in. long, linear or lance-shaped, sessile, slightly
toothed or sometimes entire. Stems smooth or hairy,
prominently winged. CT, MA, ME, NH, RI, VT

Helianthus annuus* ASTERACEAE
Common sunflower
Midsummer to fall, 3–10 ft., annual. Fields,
roadsides, and disturbed, open sites.

Flower heads 3–6 in. wide, with 20–40 orange-yellow
rays, solitary, on long, branching stalks; the central disk
reddish brown or purple, 1½–3 in. wide. Leaves 4–16 in.
long, oval or triangular, long-petioled, rough on both surfaces; the lowermost leaves often opposite. Stems hairy.
Native to central and western United States. CT, MA, ME,
NH, RI, VT

Helianthus tuberosus ASTERACEAE
Tuberous sunflower, Jerusalem artichoke
Midsummer to fall, 2–7 ft., perennial. Fields,
floodplains, and disturbed, open sites.

Flower heads 2–4 in. wide, with 10–20 yellow rays,
numerous, long-stalked; the central disk yellow, ½–1 in.
wide. Leaves 4–9 in. long, lance-shaped or oval, rough on
upper surface; the lower and middle leaves sometimes
opposite. Stems hairy. CT, MA, ME, NH, RI, VT

Hieracium kalmii (*H. canadense*) ASTERACEAE
Canada hawkweed
Midsummer to fall, 1–5 ft., perennial. Fields, woodland edges, and roadsides.

Flower heads yellow, 1 in. wide, numerous, on long, branching stalks. Leaves 1–6 in. long, lance-shaped or oval, sessile or clasping, the margins with sharp-tipped, irregular teeth. Stems leafy, hairy at base. CT, MA, ME, NH, RI, VT

Hieracium lachenalii⁕ (*H. vulgatum*) ASTERACEAE
Common hawkweed
Summer to fall, 1–3 ft., perennial. Fields, roadsides, and disturbed, open sites.

Flower heads yellow, 1–1½ in. wide, arranged in a narrow, flattish, open inflorescence; the stalk and whorled bracts just below the heads covered with black, gland-tipped hairs. Basal leaves 2–4 in. long, in a rosette, oval or lance-shaped; stem leaves few, smaller, sessile. Stems with long, scattered hairs. Native to Europe. CT, MA, ME

Hieracium paniculatum ASTERACEAE
Panicled hawkweed
Midsummer to early fall, 1–3 ft., perennial. Forests and woodlands, usually in dry soils.

Flower heads yellow, ¼–½ in. wide, numerous, with 10–20 rays, spreading widely on open, slender, horizontal branches. Leaves 1½–4½ in. long, lance-shaped, sessile, slightly toothed. Stems hairy at base, smooth and slender above, with milky sap. CT, MA, ME, NH, RI, VT

Hieracium scabrum ASTERACEAE
Rough hawkweed
Midsummer to early fall, 1–5 ft.,
perennial. Fields and woodlands.

Flower heads yellow, ½–1 in. wide, clustered on ascending branches, the flower stalks and the bracts just below the heads covered with gland-tipped hairs. Lower and middle leaves 1–5 in. long, lance-shaped or oval, slightly toothed or entire; the uppermost leaves very small. Stems thick, densely hairy, with milky sap. CT, MA, ME, NH, RI, VT

Inula helenium✳ ASTERACEAE
Horse yellowhead, elecampane
Spring to late summer, 2–6 ft., perennial.
Fields, wet meadows, and roadsides.

Flower heads 2–4 in. wide, with 50–100 or more thin, yellow straplike rays; the central disk yellow, 1¼–2 in. wide. Leaves 4–16 in. long, oval, finely toothed, woolly underneath; the upper leaves clasping. Stem finely hairy. Native to Europe. CT, MA, ME, NH, RI, VT

Lapsana communis✳ ASTERACEAE
Common nipplewort, nipplewort
Summer, 1–4 ft., annual. Woodland edges,
thickets, fields, and roadsides.

Flower heads yellow, ¼–½ in. wide, with 8–15 yellow rays, arranged in sparse, ascending panicles. Leaves 4–12 in. long, oval, coarsely toothed, tapering to a long-pointed tip; the lower leaves often lobed at the base. Stems slender, smooth or slightly hairy, with milky sap. Native to Europe. CT, MA, ME, RI, VT

213

Rudbeckia hirta (R. serotina) ASTERACEAE
Black-eyed Susan, black-eyed coneflower
Summer to fall, 1–3 ft., perennial.
Fields, clearings, and roadsides.

Flower heads 2–3 in. wide, solitary, with 8–21 yellow or orange-yellow rays; the disks ½–¾ in. wide, dark purple or brown. Leaves 2–8 in. long, lance-shaped or oval; the margins toothed or occasionally entire. Stems hairy. Native to much of North America, but most New England populations are introduced. CT, MA, ME, NH, RI, VT

Sonchus asper⁎ ASTERACEAE
Spiny-leaved sow-thistle
Midsummer to fall, 1–5 ft., annual. Fields, roadsides, and open, disturbed sites.

Flower heads yellow, ⅝–1 in. wide, arranged in a long-stalked, branching, open inflorescence; the flower stalks with gland-tipped hairs. Leaves 3–12 in. long, lance-shaped or oval, spiny, usually with tough, spiny margins; the rounded leaf bases almost enfolding stem. Stems hairy or smooth. Native to Europe. CT, MA, ME, NH, RI, VT
Sonchus oleraceus (common sow-thistle) is similar, but with divided leaves.

Caltha palustris RANUNCULACEAE
Marsh-marigold
Early to late spring, 6–24 in., perennial.
Swamps and floodplains.

Flowers bright yellow, ½–1½ in. wide, arranged in compact clusters, stalked above leaves; the flowers with 5–9 petal-like sepals (plant lacks true petals). Leaves 1–5 in. long and wide, broadly rounded, notched at base; the margins finely toothed. Stems thick, fleshy, smooth. Fruit an elliptical, beaked follicle, ⅜–½ in. long. CT, MA, ME, NH, RI, VT

Ficaria verna✳ *(Ranunculus ficaria)* RANUNCULACEAE
Lesser celandine, fig crowfoot, fig buttercup
Early spring, 4–12 in., perennial. Lawns, low fields,
and moist thickets and woodlands. Invasive.

Flowers bright yellow, ¾–1 in. wide, stalked above
leaves, with 8–12 petals; the 3 sepals shorter than the
petals. Leaves ½–2 in. long, shiny, oval or triangular,
wavy-toothed on the margins. Stems smooth, creeping,
often forming extensive leafy colonies. Fruit an achene,
¹⁄₁₆–⅛ in. long, aggregated into heads ¼ in. wide. Native
to Europe. CT, MA, NH, RI

Arnica lanceolata *(A. mollis)* ASTERACEAE
Lance-leaved arnica, hairy arnica, New England arnica
Summer, 8–30 in., perennial. Alpine and subalpine
seepages and ravines; rocky, ice-scoured river shores.

Flower heads 1½–2½ in. wide, arranged in long-stalked,
few-flowered clusters; the heads with 10–15 spreading
or drooping yellow rays and a yellow central disk, ¾ in.
wide. Leaves 2–8 in. long, lance-shaped, finely toothed,
the uppermost sessile. Stems hairy. Only in high mountains and northernmost regions. ME, NH (rare in both)

Bidens beckii *(Megalodonta beckii)* ASTERACEAE
Beck's water-marigold, Beck's beggar-ticks, water-marigold
Midsummer to fall, 1–6 in. above water surface,
perennial. Ponds and slow streams, aquatic.

Flower heads 1–1½ in. wide, solitary, with 6–10 yellow
rays. Above-surface leaves ¾–1 in. long, lance-shaped or
oval, usually toothed; submerged leaves finely dissected,
appearing whorled. Stems floating, smooth, fleshy. Fruit
an achene with 3–6 barbed awns, the achene body ½ in.
long. CT (rare), MA (rare), ME, NH (rare), RI, VT

Bidens cernua   ASTERACEAE
Nodding beggar-ticks, nodding bur-marigold
Midsummer to fall, 1–3 ft., annual.
Marshes and river and lake shores.

Flower heads ½–1 in. wide, long-stalked, with 6–8 yellow rays ⅛–½ in. long (occasionally rayless); the heads nodding in late bloom and fruit. Leaves 1½–8 in. long lance-shaped, sessile or clasping, usually coarsely toothed. Stems smooth or hairy. Fruit an achene with 2–4 barbed awns, the achene body ¼ in. long. CT, MA, ME, NH, RI, VT

Bidens hyperborea   ASTERACEAE
Northern beggar-ticks, estuary beggar-ticks
Midsummer to fall, 6–24 in., annual.
Brackish and freshwater estuaries.

Flower heads ½–1 in. wide, long-stalked, with 6–8 yellow rays ¼–½ in. long (sometimes rayless); the heads erect in bloom and fruit. Leaves 2–5 in. long, lance-shaped, sessile or very short-petioled, with sparsely toothed or entire margins. Stems smooth or hairy. Fruit a hairy achene with 2–4 barbed awns, the achene body ¼ in. long. A very rare species confined to estuary habitats. MA, ME
   Bidens eatonii (Eaton's beggar-ticks), also only found in estuaries, is similar, but the leaves are coarsely toothed, and have distinct, winged petioles ½–1¼ in. long. The flower heads frequently lack rays. CT, MA, ME (rare in all)

Bidens laevis   ASTERACEAE
Smooth beggar-ticks, larger bur-marigold
Midsummer to fall, 1–3 ft., annual or perennial.
Marshes and river and lake shores.

Flower heads 1½–2½ in. wide, long-stalked, with 7 or 8 yellow rays, ⅝–1¼ in. long; the heads usually erect, occasionally nodding in fruit. Leaves 2–6 in. long, lance-shaped or oval, sessile. Stems smooth. Fruit an achene with 2–4 barbed awns, the achene body ¼–⅜ in. long. CT, MA, NH (rare), RI

Helianthus decapetalus   ASTERACEAE
Thin-leaved sunflower
Midsummer to fall, 2–5 ft., perennial.
Woodlands, forest edges, and streambanks.

Flower heads 2–3½ in. wide, long-stalked, narrowly branched, with 8–15 yellow rays; the central disk yellow. Bracts at base of flower heads spreading, longer than the central disk. Leaves 3–8 in. long, lance-shaped or oval, thin-textured, rough on upper surface, green on lower, sharply toothed, the uppermost sometimes alternate; petioles narrowly winged, ¼–2 in. long. Stems smooth below inflorescence. CT, MA, ME, NH, VT, RI

Helianthus divaricatus   ASTERACEAE
Woodland sunflower
Midsummer to fall, 2–6 ft., perennial. Woodlands, clearings, thickets, and dry fields.

Flower heads 1½–3 in. wide, long-stalked, stiffly branched, with 8–15 yellow rays; the central disk yellow. Leaves 2½–6 in. long, lance-shaped, all opposite, rough on both surfaces, finely toothed, sessile or nearly so. Stems smooth or slightly hairy. CT, MA, ME, NH, RI (rare), VT

Helianthus strumosus   ASTERACEAE
Pale-leaved sunflower, rough-leaved sunflower
Midsummer to fall, 2–6 ft., perennial.
Woodlands, clearings, and fields.

Flower heads 1½–4 in. wide, long-stalked, with 8–15 yellow rays; the central disk yellow. Bracts at base of flower heads ascending, equal to or shorter than the central disk. Leaves 3–7 in. long, lance-shaped or oval, rough on upper surface and often whitish downy on lower surface, very finely toothed, the uppermost sometimes alternate; petioles ¼–1 in. long. Stems smooth or slightly hairy below inflorescence. CT, MA, ME, NH, RI, VT (rare)

Heliopsis helianthoides⁕ ASTERACEAE
Sunflower-everlasting, ox-eye, false sunflower
Midsummer to fall, 2–5 ft., perennial.
Thickets, fields, and roadsides.

Flower heads 1½–3½ in. wide, long-stalked, with 8–16 persistent yellow rays; the central disk yellow, cone-shaped. Leaves 2–6 in. long, oval, tapering to sharp-pointed tips, often rough on upper surface, sharply toothed; petioles of larger leaves to 1 in. long. Stems mostly smooth. Native to most of eastern and central United States, introduced in New England. CT, MA, ME, NH, VT

Silphium perfoliatum⁕ ASTERACEAE
Cup-plant rosinweed; cup-plant
Midsummer to early fall, 4–8 ft., perennial. Thickets, ditches, and disturbed, open sites. Invasive.

Flower heads 2–3 in. wide, long-stalked, with 16–35 yellow rays; the central disk yellow. Leaves 6–14 in. long, oval or triangular, rough, finely or coarsely toothed, the bases fused around the stem, forming a cup. Stem smooth and 4-angled. Native to most of eastern and central United States, introduced in New England. CT, MA, ME, NH, VT

Hieracium caespitosum⁕ (H. pretense)
ASTERACEAE
Yellow hawkweed, king devil, field hawkweed
Late spring to late summer, 1–3 ft., perennial. Fields and roadsides.

Flower heads yellow, ½–¾ in. wide, in compact clusters of 5–30; bracts beneath the flower heads covered with black, gland-tipped hairs. Leaves 1½–7 in. long, in a basal cluster, lance-shaped, green, hairy on both sides; leaf margins occasionally with very small teeth. Stems densely hairy, the upper with dark, glandular hairs. Native to Europe. CT, MA, ME, NH, RI, VT

218

Hieracium flagellare ASTERACEAE
Whip hawkweed, large mouse-ear hawkweed
Spring to early summer, 6–18 in.,
perennial. Fields and roadsides.

Flower heads yellow, 1 in. wide, usually in clusters of
2–4; bracts beneath the flower heads covered with black,
gland-tipped hairs. Leaves 1–5 in. long, in a basal cluster, lance-shaped or oval, with scattered, spreading hairs,
green on both surfaces. Stems hairy. Native to Europe.
CT, MA, ME, NH, VT

Hieracium pilosella ASTERACEAE
Mouse-ear hawkweed
Spring to early fall, 4–16 in., perennial.
Fields and roadsides.

Flower heads yellow, 1 in. wide, usually solitary, with
many rays; the bracts beneath the flower heads covered
with black, gland-tipped hairs. Leaves in a basal cluster, lance-shaped or oval, ½–3 in. long, covered with
long, spreading hairs; the lower surfaces whitish. Stems
densely hairy. Native to Europe. CT, MA, ME, NH, RI, VT

Hieracium piloselloides (*H. florentinum*)
ASTERACEAE
Glaucous hawkweed, smooth hawkweed
Summer to early fall, 1–3 ft., perennial.
Fields and roadsides.

Flower heads yellow, ½–¾ in. wide, in clusters of 5–30;
bracts beneath the flower heads covered with black,
gland-tipped hairs. Leaves 1½–6 in. long, in a basal cluster, lance-shaped, whitish green, mostly smooth on upper
surface, hairy on margins and along veins of lower surface. Stems with scattered hairs. Native to Europe. CT,
MA, ME, NH, RI, VT

Hieracium venosum   ASTERACEAE
Rattlesnake hawkweed, rattlesnake-weed
Spring to midsummer, 8–30 in., perennial.
Dry woodlands and clearings.

Flower heads yellow, ½–¾ in. wide, loosely clustered on long, slender, forking branches. Basal leaves 1½–5 in. long, oval or lance-shaped, dark green with conspicuous purple veins, hairy, occasionally slightly toothed. Stems hairy. CT, MA, ME (rare), NH, RI, VT (rare)

Arnoseris minima⁎   ASTERACEAE
Lamb-succory
Late spring to summer, 4–12 in., annual. Fields, roadsides, and sandy, disturbed sites.

Flower heads yellow, ½–¾ in. wide, on long, sparsely branching, erect or ascending stalks conspicuously inflated below the heads. Leaves ½–3 in. long, in a basal cluster, lance-shaped, coarsely toothed. Stems smooth or slightly hairy. Native to Europe. ME, NH

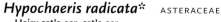

Hypochaeris radicata⁎   ASTERACEAE
Hairy cat's-ear, cat's-ear
Late spring to late summer, 6–24 in., perennial.
Fields, roadsides, and disturbed, open sites.

Flower heads yellow, 1–1½ in. wide, few, solitary on the ends of sparse, ascending branches. Leaves 2–12 in. long,

in a basal cluster, lance-shaped, very hairy on both sides, coarsely toothed or lobed. Stems mostly smooth, sometimes hairy just below the inflorescence, often with several tiny, scaly bracts. Native to Eurasia. CT, MA, ME, NH, RI, VT

Crepis capillaris* ASTERACEAE
Smooth hawk's-beard
Midsummer to fall, 12–30 in., annual or biennial.
Fields, roadsides, and disturbed, open sites.

Flower heads yellow, ½–¾ in. wide, often numerous, on
ascending, narrowly forking branches. Basal leaves 2–12
in. long, lance-shaped, deeply and irregularly divided into
sharp, narrow segments; stem leaves
smaller, toothed or lobed, the upper
clasping. Stems hairy, at least towards
base. Native to Europe. CT, MA, ME,
NH, RI, VT

Jacobaea vulgaris* (Senecio jacobaea) ASTERACEAE
Tansy ragwort, stinking Willie
Midsummer to fall, 1–3 ft., biennial or
perennial. Fields, roadsides, and disturbed,
open sites, mostly near coast. Invasive.

Flower heads ½–¾ in. wide, numerous in a
wide-branching, flattish inflorescence; the heads with
10–15 yellow rays and a yellow central disk. Leaves 3–8
in. long, deeply and irregularly divided into many toothed
or lobed segments. Stems with woolly hairs. Native to
Europe. MA, ME

Lactuca canadensis ASTERACEAE
Tall lettuce, wild lettuce
Midsummer to fall, 4–10 ft., annual or biennial.
Forest edges and clearings, fields, and roadsides.

Flower heads yellow, ¼ in. wide, with 13–22 rays; the
heads numerous in a long, open, branching inflorescence. Leaves 4–12 in. long, lance-shaped, variable but
not prickly, the lower often deeply divided into long,
narrow segments; the upper variably lobed, toothed, or
entire. Stems usually smooth, with milky sap. CT, MA,
ME, NH, RI, VT

Lactuca hirsuta (tall hairy lettuce),
a much less common species, is similar, but with hairy leaf surfaces, reddish stems that are very hairy near
the base, and reddish inflorescence
branches. Grows in dry woodlands.
MA (rare), ME, NH, RI, VT (rare)

Lactuca serriola✻ (*L. scariola*) ASTERACEAE
Prickly lettuce
Midsummer to fall, 1–5 ft., annual or biennial.
Fields, roadsides, and disturbed, open sites.

Flower heads yellow, ¼ in. wide, with 12–20 rays; the heads numerous in a long, open, branching inflorescence. Leaves 2–6 in. long, lance-shaped, prickly on the

margins and lower midvein; the lower deeply cut, with broad, variable lobes; the upper toothed or entire. Stems mostly smooth, often with prickles near base, with milky sap. Native to Europe. CT, MA, ME, NH, RI, VT

Mycelis muralis✻ (*Lactuca muralis*) ASTERACEAE
Wall-lettuce
Summer, 1–3 ft., annual or biennial. Moist forests and woodlands, seepages, and fields. Invasive.

Flower heads yellow, ¼ in. wide, with 5 rays; the heads numerous in a wide-branching inflorescence. Leaves lance-shaped; the lower 2½–7 in. long, deeply and sharply divided, with a broad, arrow-shaped terminal segment,

smaller lateral segments, and a clasping base. Stems smooth, often with a whitish bloom. Native to Europe. MA, ME, NH, VT

Packera aurea (*Senecio aureus*) ASTERACEAE
Golden groundsel, golden ragwort
Spring to early summer, 10–30 in., perennial.
Swamps, wet meadows, and streambanks.

Flower heads ½–¾ in. wide, with 8–13 golden yellow, spreading or drooping rays; arranged in a branching, flattish inflorescence. Basal leaves 1–2½ in. long, heart-shaped, rounded at tip, coarsely toothed,

long-petioled; stem leaves smaller, variably divided into sharply toothed segments. Stems hairy when young, later smooth.
CT, MA, ME, NH, RI, VT

Packera obovata (*Senecio obovatus*) ASTERACEAE
Running groundsel, round-leaf ragwort
Spring to early summer, 8–28 in., perennial.
Rich, rocky forests and woodlands.

Flower heads ½–1 in. wide, with 8–13 yellow rays, arranged in a long-stalked, branching inflorescence. Basal leaves 1½–4 in., broadly oval or spoon-shaped, rounded at tip, with long, winged petioles; stem leaves variably divided into numerous segments. Stems hairy when young, later smooth. Often forming large colonies.
CT, MA, NH (rare), RI (rare), VT

Packera paupercula (*Senecio pauperculus*)
ASTERACEAE
Balsam groundsel, balsam ragwort
Spring to early summer, 4–20 in., perennial. Rocky woodlands, ledges, and river shore outcrops.

Flower heads ½–1 in. wide, with 8–13 yellow rays, arranged in a flattish, branching inflorescence. Basal leaves 1¼–2½ in. long, lance-shaped or narrowly oval, the long petioles not winged; stem leaves variably divided into irregular segments. Stems hairy when young, later smooth. Does not form large colonies. CT, MA, ME, NH (rare), VT

Packera schweinitziana (*Senecio robbinsii*)
ASTERACEAE
New England groundsel, Robbins' ragwort
Late spring to midsummer, 1–3 ft., perennial.
Swamps and wet meadows.

Flower heads ½–¾ in. wide, with 8–13 yellow rays, arranged in a flattish, branching inflorescence. Basal leaves 1–3 in. long, lance-shaped or narrowly oval, often long-pointed at tip, sharply toothed, long-petioled, the broad leaf bases abruptly contracted to the petiole; stem leaves smaller, variably divided into irregular segments. Stems hairy when young, later smooth. ME, NH, VT

Rudbeckia laciniata ASTERACEAE
Green-headed coneflower, cut-leaf coneflower
Midsummer to early fall, 3–10 ft., perennial.
Swamps, river floodplains, wet meadows.

Flower heads 2–3 in. wide, with 8–12 drooping yellow
rays and a greenish yellow, thimble-shaped central disk;
the heads numerous, on long, ascending stalks. Leaves
6–20 in. long, lance-shaped, deeply cut into 3–7 sharply
toothed and sometimes lobed leaflets; the upper leaves
smaller, often undivided. Stems smooth. CT, MA, ME, NH,
RI (rare), VT

Sonchus arvensis✳ ASTERACEAE
Field sow-thistle
Midsummer to fall, 2–6 ft., perennial. Fields,
roadsides, and disturbed, open sites.

Flower heads yellow, 1–2 in. wide, in an open, flattish
inflorescence; the stalks and bracts beneath the heads
gland-tipped or smooth. Leaves 3–16 in. long, green,
lance-shaped, prickly, the bases with broad lobes that
clasp stem; the lower leaves sharply and
irregularly divided, with a narrow terminal lobe. Stems smooth, grooved, with
milky sap. Native to Europe. CT, MA, ME,
NH, RI, VT

Sonchus oleraceus✳ ASTERACEAE
Common sow-thistle
Midsummer to fall, 2–6 ft., annual. Fields,
roadsides, and disturbed, open sites.

Flower heads pale yellow, ⅝–1 in. wide, arranged in
an open, flattish inflorescence; the stalks and bracts
beneath the heads smooth. Leaves 3–14 in. long, bluish green, lance-shaped, prickly, the bases with narrow,
sharp-pointed lobes that clasp stem; the lower leaves
divided into a broadly triangular
terminal lobe and irregular lateral lobes. Stems smooth, with
milky sap. Native to Europe. CT,
MA, ME, NH, RI, VT

Krigia virginica ASTERACEAE
Virginia dwarf-dandelion, dwarf dandelion
Spring to midsummer, 3–12 in., annual. Woodland clearings, sandy fields, and open ledges.

Flower heads yellow, ¼–½ in. wide, solitary on an unbranched, erect stalk. Leaves ¾–5 in. long, in a basal cluster, lance-shaped, slightly hairy, bluntly toothed or divided into a large terminal segment and several pairs of smaller lateral segments. Stems mostly smooth, sometimes with glandular hairs just below flower head. CT, MA, ME (rare), NH, VT

Scorzoneroides autumnalis✳ (*Leontodon autumnalis*) ASTERACEAE
Fall dandelion
Early summer to fall, 6–30 in., perennial. Fields, roadsides, and disturbed, open sites.

Flower heads yellow, 1 in. wide, sparsely clustered on long, erect or ascending branches; bracts beneath the flower heads hairy, tapering to a narrow base. Leaves 4–14 in. long, in a basal cluster, linear or narrowly lance-shaped, mostly smooth, coarsely toothed or deeply cut into multiple narrow segments. Stems slender, hairy below flower heads, with several tiny, scaly bracts. Native to Eurasia. CT, MA, ME, NH, RI, VT

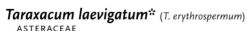

Taraxacum laevigatum✳ (*T. erythrospermum*) ASTERACEAE
Red-seeded dandelion
Early spring to fall, 2–12 in., perennial. Fields, lawns, roadsides.

Flower heads yellow, ½–¾ in. wide, long-stalked, solitary; outer bracts at base of heads usually spreading, inner bracts with tiny, slightly thickened knobs at the tips. Leaves 2–10 in. long, in a basal cluster, narrowly lance-shaped, deeply divided into many narrow, sharp-pointed segments. Stems smooth, hollow, with milky sap. Fruit a red or reddish achene, ⅛ in. long, attached to a silken plume. Native to Eurasia. CT, MA, ME, NH, RI, VT

225

7 or more radial petals; leaves deeply divided, basal, leaflets toothed or lobed

7 or more radial petals; leaves absent, scaly, or needlelike

Taraxacum officinale✳ ASTERACEAE
Common dandelion
All year, 2–10 in., perennial. Fields, lawns,
and roadsides, widespread.

Flower heads yellow, 1–2 in. wide, long-stalked, solitary;
outer bracts at base of heads fully reflexed, inner bracts
without knobs at the tips. Leaves 2–15 in. long, in a basal
cluster, lance-shaped, deeply divided into many, variable,
sharp segments, the terminal often largest. Stems mostly
smooth, hollow, with milky sap. Fruit a grayish brown
achene, ⅛ in. long, attached to a silken plume. Native to
Eurasia. CT, MA, ME, NH, RI, VT

Tussilago farfara✳ ASTERACEAE
Coltsfoot
Early spring, 3–12 in., perennial. Fens, roadsides, stony
rubble, and disturbed, open or shaded sites. Invasive.

Flower heads bright yellow, 1–1¼ in. wide, solitary,
with many narrow rays; central disk yellow. Basal leaves
develop after flowering time; the leaves are broadly
rounded, 2–8 in. long and wide, with shallow teeth and
a notched base. Stems hairy, with many scaly, clasping,
lance-shaped bracts. Fruiting head fluffy, dandelion-like.
Native to Eurasia. CT, MA, ME, NH, RI, VT

Opuntia humifusa CACTACEAE
Eastern prickly-pear
Early to midsummer, to 20 in. long, perennial.
Dry fields, dunes, and ledges.

Flowers 1½–3 in. wide, solitary, pale or bright yellow,
with 8–12 petals. Stems sprawling, mat-forming, with
fleshy, rounded, padlike joints, 2–6 in. long; small grayish bumps on pads bear a tiny barbed spine and sometimes 1 (rarely 2) longer, thin spines. Fruit an edible red
berry 1–2 in. long. Only native cactus in region. CT, MA,
RI (rare in all)

Euthamia caroliniana (*Solidago tenuifolia*)
ASTERACEAE
Coastal plain grass-leaved goldenrod, slender-leaved goldenrod
Late summer to fall, 1–3 ft., perennial. Coastal plain pond shores, sandy or peaty meadows near coast.

Flower heads yellow, ⅛ in. wide, with 7–17 tiny rays; the heads clustered in a branching, flat-topped inflorescence. Leaves 1–3 in. long and ⅛ in. (or less) wide, fragrant, linear, conspicuously resin-dotted, without distinct veins flanking the middle vein; clusters of very small leaves often in axils of primary leaves. Stems smooth or slightly hairy. CT, MA, ME (rare), NH (rare), RI

Euthamia graminifolia (*Solidago graminifolia*)
ASTERACEAE
Common grass-leaved goldenrod, lance-leaved goldenrod, flat-top goldenrod
Midsummer to fall, 1–4 ft., perennial. Fields, thickets, swamp edges, and roadside.

Flower heads yellow, ⅛ in. wide, with 15–25 tiny rays; the heads clustered in a branched, flat-topped inflorescence. Leaves 1½–5 in. long and ⅛–½ in. wide, fragrant, narrowly lance-shaped, sparsely resin-dotted, with a pair of distinct veins flanking the middle vein; clusters of smaller leaves seldom present. Stems usually finely hairy. CT, MA, ME, NH, RI, VT

Solidago odora   ASTERACEAE
Licorice goldenrod, sweet goldenrod
Midsummer to fall, 2–5 ft., perennial.
Dry woodlands and fields.

Flower heads yellow, ¼ in. wide, with 3–6 tiny rays; the heads arranged in one-sided arrays on spreading, slightly curved branches. Leaves 1–4½ in. long lance-shaped, sessile, anise-scented, dotted with translucent glands. Stems finely hairy below inflorescence. CT, MA, NH (rare), RI, VT (rare)

227

Solidago sempervirens ASTERACEAE
Seaside goldenrod
Midsummer to late fall, 2–6 ft., perennial.
Sea beaches, dunes, and salt marshes;
occasionally inland along salted roadways.

Flower heads yellow, ⅜ in. wide, with 8–17 tiny rays;
the heads arranged in dense, leafy, one-sided arrays on
spreading or ascending, slightly curved branches. Leaves
4–16 in. long, fleshy, lance-shaped, clasping. Stems thick,
smooth below the inflorescence. CT, MA, ME, NH, RI

Solidago speciosa ASTERACEAE
Showy goldenrod
Late summer to fall, 2–6 ft., perennial.
Woodlands, thickets, and fields.

Flower heads yellow, ¼ in. wide, with 3–9 tiny rays; the
heads densely clustered on narrow, ascending branches,
forming a pyramidal inflorescence 4–12 in. long. Leaves
3–12 in. long, lance-shaped or oval, the lower ones
long-petioled and sometimes slightly toothed. Stem
thick, mostly smooth below the inflorescence. CT, MA
(rare), ME (rare), NH (rare), RI, VT

Euphorbia cyparissias⁎ EUPHORBIACEAE
Cypress spurge
Spring to late summer, 6–12 in., perennial. Sandy
fields, open ledges, and roadsides. Invasive.

Flowers tiny, yellowish green, borne above 2 yellow, oval,
saucerlike bracts; the flowers arranged in flat-topped
umbels with 7–17 spokelike branches. Leaves 3–12 in.
long and 1/16–⅛ in. wide, needle-thin, crowded, pale
green; the uppermost sometimes opposite or whorled.
Stems smooth, with milky sap. Fruit a rounded capsule,
⅛ in. long. Native to Eurasia. CT, MA, ME, NH, RI, VT

Euphorbia esula✳ EUPHORBIACEAE
Leafy spurge, wolf's-milk
Late spring to early fall, 12–30 in., perennial.
Thickets, fields, and roadsides. Invasive.

Flowers tiny, yellowish green, borne above 2 yellow, oval, saucerlike bracts; the flowers arranged in flat-topped umbels with 8–20 spokelike branches. Leaves 1¼–3 in. long and ¼–⅜ in. wide, linear or narrowly lance-shaped, crowded. Stems smooth, with milky sap. Fruit a rounded capsule, ¼ in. long. Native to Eurasia. CT, MA, ME, NH, RI, VT

Oligoneuron rigidum (Solidago rigida)
ASTERACEAE
Stiff flat-topped goldenrod, stiff goldenrod, hard-leaved goldenrod
Late summer to fall, 1–4 ft., perennial. Dry, sandy or rocky woodlands and thickets.

Flower heads yellow, ¼–½ in. wide, with 7–14 very short rays; the heads densely clustered in a stiffly branched, flattish inflorescence. Lower leaves 2½–10 in. long and 1–4 in. wide, long-petioled, thick, rough, broadly lance-shaped, finely toothed or entire; the upper leaves smaller, sessile. Stems thick, hairy. CT (rare)

Solidago altissima ASTERACEAE
Tall goldenrod
Late summer to fall, 2–6 ft., perennial.
Fields, thickets, and roadsides.

Flower heads yellow, ⅛–¼ in. long, with 8–13 tiny rays; the heads densely clustered on spreading or ascending, curving branches, forming a pyramidal inflorescence. Leaves 1–6 in. long, lance-shaped, sparsely toothed or entire, with 2 prominent veins parallel to the middle vein; the undersurfaces hairy and the upper surfaces rough. Stems covered with short, grayish hairs. CT, MA, ME, NH, RI, VT

Solidago arguta ASTERACEAE
Forest goldenrod, sharp-leaved goldenrod
Late summer to fall, 2–5 ft., perennial.
Forests, woodlands, and forest edges.

Flower heads yellow, ⅛ in. long, with 2–8 tiny rays; the heads densely clustered on spreading or ascending, curving branches, forming a pyramidal inflorescence. Lower leaves 4–12 in. long, oval or lance-shaped, smooth or slightly rough on upper surface, tapering to a long, winged petiole, the margins sharply and irregularly toothed; the upper leaves smaller. Stems mostly smooth below inflorescence. CT, MA, ME, NH, RI, VT

Solidago caesia ASTERACEAE
Axillary goldenrod, blue-stemmed goldenrod
Late summer fall, 1–3 ft., perennial. Rich, moist forests, woodlands, and forest edges.

Flower heads yellow, ⅛ in. wide, with 3–5 tiny rays; the heads arranged in small, compact, axillary clusters extending from the middle to the top of the stem. Leaves 1–4 in. long, lance-shaped, dark green, sharply toothed. Stems smooth, arching, often bluish, with a white bloom. CT, MA, ME, NH, RI, VT

Solidago canadensis ASTERACEAE
Canada goldenrod
Midsummer to fall, 2–5 ft., perennial.
Fields, thickets, and roadsides.

Flower heads yellow, less than ⅛ in. long, with 8–14 tiny rays; the heads densely clustered on spreading or ascending, curving branches, forming a pyramidal inflorescence. Leaves 1–6 in. long, lance-shaped, crowded, sharply toothed, with 2 prominent veins parallel to the middle vein; the undersurfaces hairy along the veins, the upper surfaces usually smooth. Upper stems hairy, lower smooth. CT, MA, ME, NH, RI, VT

Solidago flexicaulis   ASTERACEAE
Zig-zag goldenrod
Midsummer to fall, 1–3 ft., perennial.
Rich, moist forests and woodlands.

Flower heads yellow, ⅛–¼ in. wide, with 3 or 4 tiny
rays; the heads arranged in compact, separated clusters on upper stem. Leaves 2½–6 in. long, oval, very
sharply toothed and taper-tipped, narrowing at base to
the winged petiole; undersurfaces usually hairy along
the veins. Stems angled, zigzagging between leaf nodes,
smooth or slightly hairy below inflorescence. CT, MA, ME,
NH, RI (rare), VT

Solidago gigantea   ASTERACEAE
Smooth goldenrod, late goldenrod
Late summer to fall, 2–7 ft., perennial. Moist
to wet fields, thickets, and roadsides.

Flower heads yellow, ¼ in. long, with 9–15 tiny rays; the
heads densely clustered on spreading or ascending, curving branches, forming a pyramidal inflorescence. Leaves
2–7 in. long, lance-shaped, sharply toothed, with 2 prominent veins parallel to the middle vein; undersurfaces
smooth or with fine hairs on veins. Stems smooth below
inflorescence, sometimes with a whitish bloom. CT, MA,
ME, NH, RI, VT

Solidago hispida (*S. bicolor* var. *concolor*)
ASTERACEAE
Hairy goldenrod
Late summer to fall, 1–3 ft., perennial. Open
ledges, river outcrops, and dry woodlands,
usually in high-pH conditions.

Flower heads yellow, ¼ in. long, with 7–14 tiny rays; the
heads densely clustered in narrow, stiffly erect or ascending branches. Leaves 1–8 in. long, oval or lance-shaped,
hairy on both sides, crowded on the lower stem, sparser
on upper stem. Stems densely hairy. CT, ME, NH, RI, VT

231

Solidago juncea   ASTERACEAE
Early goldenrod
Midsummer to early fall, 1–4 ft., perennial. Fields, thickets, open woodlands, and roadsides.

Flower heads yellow, ⅛–¼ in. long, with 7–12 tiny rays; the heads densely clustered on wide-spreading, curving branches, the inflorescence about as broad as high. Lower leaves 4–16 in. long, lance-shaped or oval, smooth, tapering to a winged petiole; the upper leaves smaller, sparser, often with tiny, bractlike leaves in the axils. Stems smooth below inflorescence. CT, MA, ME, NH, RI, VT

Solidago latissimifolia (*S. elliottii*) ASTERACEAE
Elliott's goldenrod, coastal swamp goldenrod
Late summer to fall, 2–6 ft., perennial. Freshwater and brackish swamps and wet meadows; coastal.

Flower heads yellow, ¼ in. long, with 6–10 tiny rays; the heads densely clustered on spreading or ascending, curving branches, forming a pyramidal inflorescence. Leaves 1–6 in. long, lance-shaped or oval, crowded, mostly smooth, sessile or very short-petioled; the upper surfaces with many distinct veins extending from the middle vein to the margins. Stems smooth below inflorescence. CT, MA, RI (rare)

Solidago leiocarpa (*S. cutleri, S. multiradiata*)
ASTERACEAE
Cutler's goldenrod
Mid to late summer, 2–14 in., perennial. Alpine summits and ravines at high elevations.

Flower heads yellow, ¼ in. long, with 6–15 tiny rays; the heads clustered in a small, compact inflorescence at the top of the stem. Leaves 1–6 in. long, lance-shaped or spoon-shaped, tapering to a winged petiole. Stems finely hairy below inflorescence. ME, NH, VT (rare in all)

Solidago macrophylla   ASTERACEAE
Large-leaved goldenrod
Midsummer to early fall, 1–3 ft., perennial. Cool coniferous forests; alpine and subalpine zones in mountains.

Flower heads yellow, large for a goldenrod, ¼–½ in. long, with 7–12 small rays; the heads arranged in compact clusters in upper axils and top of stem, forming a long, erect, interrupted inflorescence. Lower and middle leaves 1–6 in. long, oval, sharply toothed, tapering to a long, winged petiole; the upper leaves short-petioled or sessile. Leaf undersurfaces hairy along veins. Stems smooth or finely hairy below inflorescence. MA (rare), ME, NH, VT

Solidago nemoralis   ASTERACEAE
Gray goldenrod
Late summer to fall, 1–3 ft., perennial.
Dry fields, thickets, and roadsides.

Flower heads yellow, ¼ in. long, with 5–9 tiny rays; the heads densely clustered on upper stem, forming a plume-like inflorescence, nodding or arching at the tip. Leaves ½–4 in. long, lance-shaped, grayish, densely covered with fine hairs. Lowest leaves bluntly toothed; middle and upper often entire, with tiny, bractlike leaves in the axils. Stems covered with grayish hairs. CT, MA, ME, NH, RI, VT

Solidago patula   ASTERACEAE
Rough-leaved goldenrod, swamp goldenrod
Late summer to fall, 3–6 ft., perennial.
Swamps, fens, and wet thickets.

Flower heads yellow, ⅛ in. long, with 5–12 tiny rays; the heads densely clustered on spreading or ascending, curving branches, forming a broadly pyramidal inflorescence. Lower leaves 3–16 in. long, oval, sharply toothed, tapering to a long, winged petiole, the upper surfaces very rough; middle and upper leaves smaller, narrow, short-petioled or sessile. Stems angular, thick, smooth below inflorescence. CT, MA, VT (rare)

Solidago puberula ASTERACEAE
Downy goldenrod
Late summer to fall, 1–3 ft., perennial. Sandy
fields, open ledges, and roadsides.

Flower heads yellow, ¼ in. long, with 9–16 tiny rays; the
heads densely clustered on short, ascending branches,
forming a narrow, erect inflorescence. Lower leaves 2–6
in. long, oval or lance-shaped, toothed, tapering to a
winged petiole; the upper leaves smaller, often entire,
sometimes with tiny, bractlike leaves in the axils. Leaves
covered with fine, downy hairs. Stems often purplish,
with very fine hairs. CT, MA, ME, NH, RI, VT

Solidago rugosa ASTERACEAE
Wrinkle-leaved goldenrod, rough-stemmed goldenrod
Late summer to fall, 3–6 ft., perennial. Fields,
thickets, roadsides, and wetland edges.

Flower heads yellow, ¼ in. long, with 6–9 tiny rays; the
heads densely clustered on spreading or ascending,
curving branches, forming a pyramidal inflorescence.
Leaves 1½–5 in. long, lance-shaped or oval, very crowded,
sharply toothed, with a prominent middle vein and
numerous veins extending to the margins; the lower surfaces hairy. Stems densely hairy. CT, MA, ME, NH, RI, VT
  Solidago aestivalis (swamp wrinkle-leaved goldenrod; syn. *S. rugosa* var. *sphagnophila*) is similar, but the
stems and leaves are smooth. Its blooming period (mid to
late summer) begins 3–5 weeks earlier. Grows primarily in wet, acidic forests and woodlands, including cedar
swamps. Limited to coastal areas. CT, MA, ME, NH, RI

Solidago simplex (S. simplex subsp. randii var.
monticola, S. glutinosa, S. randii) ASTERACEAE
Rand's goldenrod
Late summer to fall, 1–2 ft., perennial.
Cliffs, ledges, and bald summits.

Flower heads yellow, ⅛–¼ in. long, with 7–16 tiny
rays; the heads densely clustered on short, ascending
branches, forming a narrow, erect inflorescence. Whorled
bracts at base of flower heads shiny, sticky to touch.
Lower leaves 2–12 in. long, lance-shaped or oval, smooth,
finely toothed, often resinous; the upper leaves smaller.
Stems smooth or slightly hairy below inflorescence. MA
(rare), ME, NH, VT (rare)

Solidago squarrosa   ASTERACEAE
Squarrose goldenrod, stout goldenrod
Late summer to fall, 1–5 ft., perennial. Forest
clearings and edges, fields, and roadsides.

Flower heads yellow, ¼–⅜ in. long, larger than most
goldenrods, with 10–16 rays; the heads densely clustered
on short, ascending branches, forming a narrow, erect
inflorescence; whorled bracts below the heads with conspicuously reflexed tips. Lower leaves 2–8 in. long, oval,
mostly smooth, tapering to winged petiole; the upper
leaves smaller. Stems stout, smooth below the inflorescence. CT, MA, ME, NH, VT (rare)

Solidago uliginosa (*S. purshii*) ASTERACEAE
Bog goldenrod
Late summer to fall, 2–5 ft., perennial.
Bogs, fens, and wet, peaty meadows.

Flower heads yellow, ¼ in. long, with 1–8 tiny rays; the
heads densely clustered on short, ascending branches,
forming a narrowly erect on slightly spreading inflorescence. Lower leaves 4–12 in., lance-shaped, smooth, finely
toothed, the long, winged petiole sheathing the stem; the
upper leaves smaller. Stems smooth below inflorescence.
CT, MA, ME, NH, RI, VT

Solidago ulmifolia   ASTERACEAE
Elm-leaved goldenrod
Late summer to fall, 2–4 ft., perennial.
Woodlands and thickets.

Flower heads yellow, ⅛–¼ in. long, with 3–6 tiny rays;
the heads clustered on divergent branches, forming an
open, wide-spreading inflorescence. Lower leaves 2–4 in.
long, lance-shaped or oval, sharply toothed, tapering to
a winged petiole, the undersurfaces hairy on the veins;
the upper leaves smaller, short-petioled or sessile. Stems
smooth or slightly hairy below inflorescence. CT, MA, ME,
RI, VT (rare)

Petals indistinguishable; leaves
simple, alternate, toothed or lobed

Acorus americanus   ACORACEAE
Several-vined sweetflag, sweetflag
Spring to midsummer, 2–6 ft., perennial.
Marshes, wet meadows, and stream sides.

Flowers tiny, greenish yellow, densely clustered in a stiff spike, 1½–3 in. long and ¼–¾ in. wide, ascending at an angle from point of attachment near middle of long, leaf-like stem. Leaves 2–6 ft. long and ⅛–⅜ in. wide, sword-like, aromatic, with 2–6 prominent, parallel veins and numerous fainter veins. Fruit a fleshy berry ¼ in. wide. CT, MA, ME, NH, RI, VT

*Acorus calamus** (single-veined sweetflag), a sterile introduction from Europe, is very similar, but the leaves have only a single prominent, central vein; on average are wider (⅜–½ in. wide); and the leaf margins are often curled or crisped. CT, MA, ME, NH, RI, VT

Orontium aquaticum   ARACEAE
Golden-club
Spring, 1–2 ft., perennial. Marshes, swamps, estuaries, and pond shallows.

Flowers tiny, golden yellow, arranged in a narrow, densely flowered terminal spike, 1–4 in. long. Leaves 2½–8 in. long, oval, long-petioled, blue-green, floating or stalked above the water surface. Stem white, erect or spreading. Fruit a fleshy berry, ¼ in. wide. CT, MA, RI (rare in all)

Symplocarpus foetidus   ARACEAE
Skunk cabbage
Late winter to early spring, 1–2 ft. (leaves), perennial. Swamps and floodplain forests.

Flowers tiny, clustered in a thick, yellowish or reddish spike (spadix) enclosed within a purple-mottled, cowl-like spathe, 3–6 in. long, that resembles a sorcerer's hood. Leaves 6–24 in. long, broadly oval, emerging after the flowers and reeking of skunk when bruised. Fruit a fleshy berry, ⅜–½ in. wide. The spathe-sheltered flowers produce heat, melting the surrounding snow. CT, MA, ME, NH, RI, VT

Artemisia stelleriana* ASTERACEAE
Beach wormwood, dusty miller
Late spring to late summer, 1–2 ft., perennial. Sea beaches and dunes, occasionally inland on sandy lake shores.

Flower heads pale yellow, ¼ in. wide, rayless, borne in erect, stiffly branched, spikelike clusters. Leaves 1–4 in. long, grayish green, woolly, deeply divided with blunt lobes that resemble small oak leaves. Stems woolly, forming leafy mats. Native to Northeast Asia. CT, MA, ME, NH, RI, VT

Matricaria discoidea* (*M. matricarioides*)
ASTERACEAE
Rayless chamomile, pineapple-weed
Late spring to fall, 2–16 in., annual. Disturbed, open sites, bare ground, pavement cracks.

Flower heads greenish yellow, ¼–⅜ in. wide, rayless, conical, often numerous on wide-branching stems. Leaves ½–2 in. long, deeply and finely divided into many short, linear segments; the foliage pineapple-scented when crushed. Stems smooth, often bushy and sprawling. Native to northwestern United States. CT, MA, ME, NH, RI, VT

Senecio vulgaris* ASTERACEAE
Common ragwort, common groundsel
Early spring to fall, 4–16 in., annual. Fields, bare ground, pavement cracks.

Flower heads yellow, ¼–⅜ in. wide, rayless, cylindrical, numerous on wide-branching stems; the whorled bracts surrounding the flower disk tipped with black. Leaves 1–4 in. long, lance-shaped, divided into jagged, irregular segments; the lower tapering to a petiole, the upper sessile or clasping. Stems cobwebby early in season, later smooth. Native to Eurasia. CT, MA, ME, NH, RI, VT

Petals indistinguishable; leaves deeply divided, alternate, leaflets toothed or lobed

Tanacetum vulgare:∗ ASTERACEAE
Common tansy
Midsummer to fall, 1–4 ft., perennial. Fields,
roadsides, open, disturbed sites.

Flower heads yellow, ¼–⅜ in. wide, rayless, buttonlike,
crowded in branching, flat-topped clusters. Leaves 2–8
in. long, lance-shaped, aromatic when bruised, deeply
divided into many fine, sharp-toothed, fernlike leaflets. Stems smooth. Native to Eurasia, first introduced to
North America in 1631. CT, MA, ME, NH, RI, VT

Bidens connata ASTERACEAE
Purple-stemmed beggar-ticks
Late summer to fall, 1–5 ft., annual. Marshes,
swamps, and lake and river shores.

Flower heads orange-yellow, ⅜–¾ in. wide, rayless or
with several tiny rays; base of flower head with 4–9 leaflike bracts. Leaves 1½–6 in. long, lance-shaped, sharply
toothed; the lower leaves with long, winged petioles and
often with spreading lobes near the base. Stems purplish,
smooth. Fruit an achene, ⅛–¼ in. long, with ridged surfaces and 4 barbed awns, the 2 central awns shorter than
the 2 laterals. CT, MA, ME, NH, RI (rare), VT
   Bidens tripartita (three-lobed beggar-ticks) is very similar, but the flower heads are pale yellow and on average
slightly larger (⅝–1 in. wide). Fruit an achene, ¼–⅜ in.
long, with flattened surfaces and 3 barbed awns, the central awn shorter than the 2 laterals. CT, MA, ME, NH, RI, VT

Bidens discoidea ASTERACEAE
Small beggar-ticks, few-bracted beggar-ticks
Late summer to fall, 1–3 ft., annual.
Swamps and river and lake shores.

Flower heads orange-yellow, ⅛–⅜ in. wide, rayless,
with 3–5 leaflike bracts at base. Leaves lance-shaped,
long-petioled, the lower and middle 3-parted; the
long-tapering, sharply toothed leaflets ¾–2 in. long.
Stems smooth, slender, often red. Fruit a hairy achene,
⅛–¼ in. long, with 2 very short barbed awns (sometimes
awnless). CT, MA, ME, NH, RI, VT (rare)

Bidens frondosa   ASTERACEAE
Devil's beggar-ticks, sticktight
Summer to fall, 1–4 ft., annual. Moist thickets
and fields, swamp and marsh edges, ditches.

Flower heads orange-yellow, ½ in. wide, rounded or
cylindrical, rayless, long-stalked, with 5–10 (often 8)
leafy, ascending bracts at the base of the heads. Leaves
long-petioled, pinnately divided into 3–5 lance-shaped,
long-pointed, sharply toothed leaflets, 1–4 in. long. Stems
smooth or slightly hairy, often greenish red or purple.
Fruit a flat, dark brown or black achene, ¼–⅜ in. long,
with 2 sharp barbs. CT, MA, ME, NH, RI, VT
   Bidens vulgata (tall beggar-ticks) is very similar, but
with 10–20 (often 13) leafy bracts at the base of the flower
head. Grows in fields, roadsides, and ditches. CT, MA, ME,
NH, RI, VT

Bartonia virginica   GENTIANACEAE
Virginia screwstem, yellow screwstem
Late summer, 2–16 in., perennial. Wet, sandy or peaty
meadows and occasionally in drier, sandy fields.

Flowers ⅛ in. long, yellow or straw-colored, closed, tip-
ping the ends of short, slender, opposite, ascending or
erect branches, the branches ¼–1¾ in. long. Leaves tiny,
scaly, opposite. Stems smooth. Fruit an oval capsule,
⅛–¼ in. long. CT, MA, ME, NH, RI, VT (rare)

Crotalaria sagittalis   FABACEAE
Arrowhead rattlebox, rattlebox
Summer, 4–16 in., annual. Sandy fields,
roadsides, and open, disturbed sites.

Flowers yellow, ¼–½ in. long, the fused upper petals
larger than lower petals; the flowers arranged in stalked
axillary clusters of 1–4; a winged, double-tipped stipule is
at the base of the stalk. Leaves 1–3 in. long, lance-shaped,
hairy, short-petioled. Stems hairy, erect or ascending.
Fruit a bloated pod, ¾–1½ in. long, with a tiny, pointed
tip; when shaken, seeds rattle inside the pod. CT, MA, RI
(rare), VT (rare)

Cypripedium parviflorum (*C. calceolus*)
ORCHIDACEAE
Yellow lady's-slipper
Late spring to early summer, 10–30 in., perennial.
Rich, moist forests, fens, and high-pH swamps.

Flowers 1 or 2, bright yellow; the broad, pouchlike lip ¾–2 in. long, and the narrow, twisted, purplish bronze lateral petals 1–3 in. long; the upper sepal broad, bronze-purple, with a tapering tip, arching above the lip. Leaves 2½–8 in. long, oval, deeply veined, sheathing at base. Stems hairy. Fruit a capsule, 1–1½ in. long. CT, MA, ME, NH, RI, VT

Impatiens pallida BALSAMINACEAE
Pale jewelweed, pale touch-me-not
Summer, 3–6 ft., annual. Rich, moist forests and woodlands, wetland edges, and streambanks.

Flowers pale yellow, 1–1½ in. long, stalked from upper axils, with a short hood, a broad lip, a tubular throat, and a hooked or angled spur ⅛–¼ in. long. Leaves 2–4 in. long, pale green, long-petioled, with blunt marginal teeth. Stems smooth, succulent, exuding a watery sap when broken. Fruit a lance-shaped capsule, ¾–1 in. long; ripe capsules explosively propel seeds when touched. CT, MA, ME (rare), NH, RI, VT

Viola pubescens (now includes *V. pensylvanica*)
VIOLACEAE
Forest yellow violet, downy yellow violet
Spring, 4–12 in., perennial. Forests,
usually deciduous and moist.

Flowers yellow, ¾ in. wide, with a broad, brown-veined lower petal, bearded lateral petals, and reflexed upper petals. Leaves 2–4 on upper stem, heart-shaped, 2–3 in. long and about as wide; stipules at base of petioles lance-shaped, slightly toothed. Basal leaves one to several, long-petioled. Stems downy (in var. *pubescens*) or smooth (in var. *scabriuscula*). Fruit an oval capsule, ⅜–½ in. long. CT, MA, ME, NH, RI (rare), VT

Melampyrum lineare OROBANCHACEAE
Cow-wheat
Summer, 2–16 in., hemiparasitic, annual. Dry woodlands, thickets, ridges, fields, and sometimes in bogs.

Flowers yellowish or creamy, ¼–½ in. long, paired in upper leaf axils, the lower lip yellow, projecting, 3-lobed. Leaves ¾–2½ in. long, linear or narrowly lance-shaped; the lower and middle leaves entire, the upper leaves often serrated at the base. Stems smooth. Fruit an oval capsule, ⅜ in. long. CT, MA, ME, NH, RI, VT

Linaria vulgaris* PLANTAGINACEAE
Butter and eggs toadflax, butter n' eggs
Summer, 1–3 ft., perennial. Fields, roadsides, and open, disturbed sites.

Flowers yellow, ¾–1¼ in. long, long-spurred, 2-lipped, with a bright orange palate in the center; the flowers arranged in a dense, terminal raceme. Leaves 1–2½ in. long and ⅛ in. wide, linear, crowded; the upper alternate, the lower appearing whorled. Stems smooth. Fruit an oval capsule, ⅜–½ in. long. Native to Eurasia. CT, MA, ME, NH, RI, VT

Linaria dalmatica (Dalmatian toadflax) is similar, but the leaves are oval, ⅜–1 in. wide, bluish green, and strongly clasp the stem. Native to Eurasia, very invasive in western United States, occasionally naturalized in open, disturbed sites in New England. CT, MA, ME, NH, RI, VT

Agastache nepetoides LAMIACEAE
Catnip giant-hyssop, yellow giant-hyssop
Midsummer to early fall, 2–5 ft., perennial. Forest edges and clearings and rocky slopes with a high pH.

Flowers pale yellow, ⅜ in. long, tubular, with 4 long-protruding stamens and a slightly fringed lower lip narrowed at base; the flowers crowded in narrow spikes, 4–8 in. long. Leaves 1–5 in. long, oval or lance-shaped, coarsely toothed, the lower and middle long-petioled. Stems 4-angled, smooth or slightly hairy. Fruit capsule-like, 1/16–⅛ in. long. CT, VT (rare in both)

Collinsonia canadensis   LAMIACEAE
Northern horse-balm
Midsummer to early fall, 2–4 ft.,
perennial. Rich, moist forests.

Flowers yellow, ½ in. long, tubular, lemon-scented, with
2 long-protruding stamens and a prominent, deeply
fringed lower lip; the flowers numerous, stalked in pairs
in a wide-branching panicle. Leaves 2–8 in. long, oval,
coarsely toothed, the lower long-petioled, the upper
short-petioled or sessile. Stems square, mostly smooth.
Fruit capsulelike. CT, MA, RI, VT (rare)

Lamium galeobdolon✣ (*Lamiastrum galeobdolon*)
LAMIACEAE
Yellow henbit, yellow archangel
Spring to early summer, 1–2 ft., perennial.
Woodland edges, thickets, and fields.

Flowers yellow, ¾ in. long, arranged in terminal and axillary whorls; the hooded upper lip arching over the 3-lobed
lower lip. Leaves 1–3 in. long, oval or lance-shaped,
coarsely toothed, hairy, often with silver streaks. Stems
square, hairy. Fruit capsulelike. Native to Eurasia, invasive in western United States, naturalized as a weedy
groundcover in New England. MA, ME

Monarda punctata   LAMIACEAE
Spotted bee-balm, horsemint
Late summer to fall, 1–3 ft., perennial.
Dry, sandy fields and roadsides.

Flowers creamy yellow and purple-spotted, ¾–1 in.
long, the upper lip narrow, hairy, arching well above
the broader lower lip; the flowers whorled in upper
leaf axils, the whorls underlain by conspicuous, white
or lilac-colored, leaflike bracts. Leaves 1–3½ in. long,
lance-shaped, slightly toothed; the uppermost sometimes
entire. Stems hairy, angular. Fruit capsulelike, ¹⁄₁₆ in.
long. Native in CT, VT (rare); introduced in MA.

Pedicularis lanceolata OROBANCHACEAE
Swamp lousewort
Late summer to fall, 12–30 in., perennial. Marshes, wet
meadows, and streambanks, often in calcareous soils.

Flowers pale yellow, ¾–1 in. long, tubular, smooth,
crowded in spikes about 4 in. long; the curving,
short-beaked upper lip and the lower lip about equally
long, appearing fused for most of their length. Leaves
2–4 in. long, lance-shaped, the margins with sharply
toothed lobes. Stems mostly smooth. Fruit an oval capsule, ⅜ in. long. CT, MA (rare in both)

Rhinanthus minor (*R. crista-galli*)
OROBANCHACEAE
Little yellow-rattle, yellow-rattle
Spring to late summer, 4–24 in., annual. Fields and thickets
(subsp. *minor**) and alpine zones (subsp. *groenlandicum*).

Flowers yellow, ⅜–⅝ in. long, sessile in the upper
leaf axils; the 2-lipped petals protruding from a green,
conspicuously inflated calyx. Leaves 1–2½ in. long,
lance-shaped or oval, sessile, sharply toothed. Fruit a capsule contained within the papery calyx (tan-colored and
further enlarged in fruit). The native subspecies (subsp.
groenlandicum) has oval leaves and is a rare plant growing
only in alpine zones in White Mountains, NH; the introduced subspecies (subsp. *minor**) has lance-shaped leaves
and occurs in CT, MA, ME, NH, VT.

Mimulus moschatus PHRYMACEAE
Musky monkey-flower, musk-flower
Summer, 8–16 in., perennial. Springs,
seepages, and streamsides.

Flowers yellow, ½–1 in. long, tubular, stalked singly in
leaf axils, with broad, slightly asymmetrical petals. Leaves 1–2½ in. long,
oval or lance-shaped, slightly toothed,
short-petioled. Stems densely hairy,
sticky, creeping at base. Fruit an oval
capsule, ¼–⅜ in. long. Native and rare
in MA, NH, VT; introduced in CT, ME.

243

Isotria medeoloides ORCHIDACEAE
Small whorled pogonia
Late spring to early summer, 3–10 in., perennial.
Upland, deciduous woodlands on acidic soils.

Flowers 1 or 2, yellowish green, ¾ in. long, tubular, stalked above the leaf whorl the lower lip slightly protruding; the 3 sepals arching, green, ½–1 in. long. Leaves 1–2½ in. long, oval or broadly lance-shaped, in a single whorl of 4–6. Stems smooth, slightly fleshy. Fruit an erect, oval capsule, ½–1 in. long. An extremely rare species. CT, MA, ME, NH (rare in all)

Isotria verticillata ORCHIDACEAE
Large whorled pogonia
Late spring to early summer, 8–16 in., perennial.
Deciduous forests and woodlands, usually on acidic soils.

Flowers solitary, yellowish green, ¾–1 in. long, stalked above the leaf whorl; the lower lip drooping; the 3 sepals elongate, needle-thin, mostly purple, wide-spreading, 1½–2½ in. long. Leaves 1–2 in. long, oval or lance-shaped, in a single whorl of 5 or 6. Stems smooth, slightly fleshy. Fruit an oval, long-stalked capsule, erect or ascending, ¾–1½ in. long. CT (rare), MA, NH (rare), RI (rare), VT (rare)

Liparis loeselii ORCHIDACEAE
Loesel's wide-lipped orchid, Loesel's twayblade, bog twayblade
Early to midsummer, 4–10 in., perennial. Fens, wet meadows, and river and lake shorelines.

Flowers greenish or whitish yellow, ¼–⅜ in. long, with spreading, threadlike, lateral petals and an oval lower lip; the inflorescence a narrow raceme with 2–15 flowers. Leaves 2–6 in. long, lance-shaped or oval, keeled, paired at the base. Stems smooth, angled, sometimes slightly winged. Fruit an oval capsule, ⅜–½ in. long. CT, MA, ME, NH (rare), RI (rare), VT (rare)

Viola rotundifolia VIOLACEAE
Round-leaved violet, round-leaved yellow violet
Early to midspring, 2–5 in., perennial.
Rich deciduous and mixed forests.

Flowers yellow, ⅝–¾ in. long, solitary; the lower petal
brown-veined, the 2 lateral petals bearded. Leaves at
flowering time ¾–1½ in. long, broadly oval, bluntly
toothed, notched at base; in summer enlarging to 2–4 in.
long. Stems smooth, with a pair of tiny, pointed stipules.
Fruit an oval capsule, ¼–⅜ in. long. CT, MA, ME, NH, RI
(rare), VT

Baptisia tinctoria FABACEAE
Yellow wild indigo, wild indigo
Summer, 1–3 ft., perennial. Dry, sandy
woodlands, fields, and roadsides.

Flowers yellow, ½ in. long, with a winglike upper
petal and blunt, partially fused lower petals; the flowers loosely arranged in open racemes. Leaves 3-parted,
short-petioled, often bluish green; the 3 leaflets ⅜–1 in.
long, oval, broader at the tip and narrowing to the base.
Stems smooth, bushy, blue when young. Fruit an oval
pod, ¼–½ in. long. CT, MA, ME (rare), NH, RI

Chamaecrista fasciculata (*Cassia fasciculata*)
FABACEAE
Partridge sensitive-pea, partridge-pea
Summer, 6–30 in., annual. Dry, sandy fields and roadsides.

Flowers yellow, 1–1½ in. wide, with 10 stamens, arranged
in axillary clusters of 1–6; the petals broad, slightly
unequal in size, often red-streaked at base. Leaves pinnately divided into 10–36 narrow, oblong, spine-tipped
leaflets, ½–¾ in. long, often folding up when touched;
the petiole has a small, unstalked gland. Stems erect or
spreading, slightly hairy. Fruit a narrow pod, 1–2½ in.
long. CT, MA, ME, NH, RI

Chamaecrista nictitans (*Cassia nictitans*)
FABACEAE
Wild sensitive-pea, wild sensitive plant
Summer, 4–20 in., annual. Dry, sandy fields and roadsides.

Flowers yellow, ¼–½ in. wide, with 5 stamens, in axillary clusters of 1–3; the lower petal largest. Leaves pinnately divided into 14–40 linear, spine-tipped leaflets, ¼–½ in. long, recoiling when touched; the petiole has a small stalked gland. Stems erect, smooth or hairy. Fruit a narrow pod, ¾–1½ in. long. CT, MA, RI, VT (rare)

Lotus corniculatus✵ FABACEAE
Bird's-foot trefoil
Summer to early fall, 6–24 in., perennial.
Fields and roadsides.

Flowers yellow, ½ in. long, turning orange in late bloom, with a fanlike upper petal and folded lower petals; the flowers arranged in branching, headlike clusters of 4–8. Leaves divided into 5 oval leaflets, ¼–½ in. long, the upper 3 cloverlike, the lower 2 at the base of the petiole. Stems smooth, erect or sprawling, often colonial. Fruit a linear pod, ½–1¼ in. long, in spreading clusters of 3, resembling a bird's foot. Native to Eurasia. CT, MA, ME, NH, RI, VT

Senna hebecarpa FABACEAE
Northern wild senna
Summer, 2–6 ft., perennial. Forest
edges, fields, and floodplains.

Flowers yellow, ½–¾ in. wide, stalked, with 10 stamens of varying lengths and slightly asymmetrical petals; the flowers densely clustered in stalked, terminal and axillary heads. Leaves pinnately divided into 12–20 oval or lance-shaped leaflets 1–1½ in. long; a stalked, club-shaped gland is near base of the leaf petiole. Stems thick, slightly hairy. Fruit a hairy, linear pod, 2¾–5 in. long. CT, MA, NH, VT (rare in all)

Tephrosia virginiana   FABACEAE
Wild goat's-rue, goat's-rue
Summer, 1–2 ft., perennial. Sandy woodlands and fields.

Flowers ½–¾ in. long, the fanlike upper petal yellow,
the partially fused lower petals pink or reddish purple;
the flowers arranged in terminal racemes, 1½–3 in. long.
Leaves pinnately divided into 10–30 leaflets; the leaflets
⅜–1 in. long, linear or oblong, with a tiny spine at the tip.
Stems hairy. Fruit a narrow, densely hairy pod, 1½–2¼
in. long. CT, MA, NH (rare), RI (rare)

Medicago lupulina⁕   FABACEAE
Black medick, nonesuch
Spring to fall, 2–24 in. long, annual or biennial.
Fields, roadsides, and disturbed, open sites.

Flowers yellow, ⅛ in. long, arranged in rounded,
long-stalked heads about ¼ in. long. Leaves 3-parted; the
3 leaflets ½–¾ in. long, oval, finely toothed, with a single, tiny spine at tip. Uppermost leaflet distinctly stalked,
the laterals sessile or very short-stalked. Stems trailing
or prostrate, finely hairy, often colonial. Fruit a coiled,
kidney-shaped pod, ⅛ in. long, black when ripe, aggregated into cylindrical heads. Native to Eurasia. CT, MA,
ME, NH, RI, VT

Melilotus officinalis⁕   FABACEAE
Yellow sweet-clover
Summer, 2–7 ft., biennial. Fields, roadsides,
and disturbed, open sites.

Flowers yellow, ¼ in. long, tilted downward, arranged in
dense, spikelike racemes, 2–6 in. long. Leaves 3-parted;
the 3 leaflets ½–1 in. long, lance-shaped or oval, sharply
toothed. Stems smooth. Fruit an oval pod with ridged
surfaces, ⅛–¼ in. long. Native to Eurasia. CT, MA, ME,
NH, RI, VT

Flowers bilateral; leaves deeply
divided, alternate, leaflets entire

Flowers bilateral; leaves deeply divided,
alternate, leaflets toothed or lobed

Trifolium aureum (*T. agrarium*) FABACEAE
Palmate hop clover, hop clover
Late spring to fall, 6–16 in., annual or biennial.
Fields, roadsides, and disturbed, open sites.

Flowers yellow, ¼ in. long, densely clustered in long-stalked, cylindrical heads ½–¾ in. long. Leaves 3-parted; the 3 leaflets ⅜–¾ in. long, oval, finely toothed, sessile or very short-stalked. Stems erect, finely hairy. Fruit a brown, papery, oval pod, ⅛–¼ in. long, aggregated into rounded, hopslike heads. Native to Eurasia. CT, MA, ME, NH, RI, VT

Trifolium campestre (*T. procumbens*) FABACEAE
Pinnate hop clover, low hop clover
Late spring to fall, 4–16 in., annual. Fields, roadsides, and disturbed, open sites.

Flowers yellow, ⅛–¼ in. long, densely clustered in stalked, cylindrical heads of 20–30 flowers; the heads ⅜–½ in. long. Leaves 3-parted; the 3 leaflets oval, ⅜–⅝ in. long, finely toothed, the uppermost distinctly stalked, the laterals sessile or very short-stalked. Stems prostrate, finely hairy, branching, often colonial. Fruit a brown, papery, oval pod, 1/16 in. long, aggregated into rounded, hopslike heads. Native to Eurasia and North Africa. CT, MA, ME, NH, RI, VT

Trifolium dubium FABACEAE
Lesser hop clover, least hop clover
Summer, 4–16 in., annual. Fields, roadsides, and disturbed, open sites.

Flowers yellow, ⅛ in. long, densely clustered in stalked, rounded heads of 3–15 flowers; the heads ¼–⅜ in. long. Leaves 3-parted; the 3 leaflets oval, ¼–½ in. long, finely toothed, slightly notched at tip; the uppermost leaflet short-stalked, the laterals sessile. Stems prostrate, smooth or finely hairy, branching, often colonial. Fruit a tiny pod, 1/16 in. long, aggregated into brown, rounded, hopslike heads. Native to Europe. CT, MA, ME, RI, VT

Pedicularis canadensis OROBANCHACEAE
Forest lousewort, wood-betony, chickens'-heads
Early to late spring, 6–16 in., perennial.
Woodlands, forest edges and clearings.

Flowers bicolored yellow and red-purple (occasionally all yellow), ¾–1 in. long; the slender, hooded, upper lip arching over the short, broad lower lip. Flowers arranged in dense spikes, 1½–2 in. long, elongating in fruit. Lower leaves 2–6 in. long, lance-shaped, long-petioled, divided into numerous toothed, fernlike segments. Stems hairy. Fruit a lance-shaped capsule, ½–⅜ in. long. CT, MA, ME, NH, RI, VT

Pedicularis furbishiae (Furbish lousewort), an extremely rare species found only along the banks of the St. John River, is similar in form, but taller (16–24 in.); the flowers are entirely yellow; and the leaves are more finely divided into deeply toothed segments, sharp-pointed at tip. Northern ME

Aureolaria flava (*Gerardia flava*) OROBANCHACEAE
Smooth false foxglove
Mid to late summer, 2–5 ft., perennial.
Dry woodlands and ridges.

Flowers yellow, 1¼–1¾ in. long, paired in upper leaf axils, tubular, smooth on the outside, with 5 spreading lobes. Leaves 2–6 in. long, lance-shaped, smooth or finely hairy, the lower deeply and irregularly divided, the upper smaller, shallowly lobed or entire. Stems entirely smooth and often purplish. Fruit a smooth, oval capsule, ⅜–½ in. long. CT, MA, ME, NH, RI, VT (rare)

Aureolaria pedicularia (*Gerardia pedicularia*)
OROBANCHACEAE
Fern-leaved false foxglove
Late summer to early fall, 1–4 ft., annual. Dry woodlands, ridges, and rocky slopes.

Flowers yellow, 1¼–1½ in. long, paired in upper leaf axils, tubular, finely hairy on the outside, with 5 spreading lobes. Leaves 1–3 in. long, lance-shaped, finely hairy, intricately cut into many toothed or lobed, fernlike segments. Stems bushy, branching, at least the lower with sticky, glandular hairs. Fruit a hairy, oval capsule, ⅜–⅝ in. long. CT, MA, ME (rare), NH, RI, VT (rare)

Flowers bilateral; leaves deeply divided, alternate, leaflets toothed or lobed

Flowers bilateral; leaves deeply divided, opposite, leaflets toothed or lobed

Aureolaria virginica (*Gerardia virginica*)
OROBANCHACEAE
Downy false foxglove
Mid to late summer, 2–5 ft., perennial.
Dry woodlands and ridges.

Flowers yellow, 1¼–1¾ in. long, paired in upper leaf axils, tubular, smooth on the outside, with 5 spreading lobes. Leaves 2–6 in. long, lance-shaped, finely hairy, the lower usually with 2 blunt basal lobes and rounded lateral lobes; the upper leaves often entire. Stems finely and entirely hairy. Fruit a densely hairy, oval capsule, ⅜–½ in. long. CT, MA, NH (rare), RI, VT (rare)

Utricularia cornuta LENTIBULARIACEAE
Horned bladderwort
Midsummer to early fall, 3–14 in., annual or perennial.
Bogs, fens, and sandy, muddy, or peaty pond shores.

Flowers yellow, ½–1 in. long, with an erect, fan-shaped upper lip, a broad, hump-backed lower lip, and a conspicuous, downward-projecting spur, ¼–½ in. long; the inflorescence an open raceme with 1–6 flowers. Stems smooth, wiry, rooted in substrate, with several scaly bracts; the finely dissected leaves are subterranean. Fruit an oval capsule, ⅛–¼ in. long. CT, MA, ME, NH, RI, VT
    Utricularia subulata (slender bladderwort), the only other terrestrial (nonfloating) bladderwort in the region, is similar, but the flower has a small, rounded upper lip, a spreading lower lip, and a very short spur (about ⅛ in. long) pressed to and concealed by the lower lip. Distribution limited to sandy or peaty pond shores near coast. CT, RI (rare in both)

Utricularia gibba LENTIBULARIACEAE
Creeping bladderwort, humped bladderwort
Summer, 2–4 in., perennial. Lakes and ponds.

Flowers yellow, ¼–½ in. long; the lower lip humped at throat, fan-shaped at tip, covering the short, thick spur; the inflorescence an open raceme with 1–4 flowers. Leaves floating below surface, or creeping and mat-forming when stranded in mud; the leaf branches dissected into short, filamentous segments with tiny, scattered, bladderlike traps. Stems floating, erect or slightly bent. Fruit an oval capsule, ¹⁄₁₆–⅛ in. long. CT, MA, ME, NH, RI (rare), VT (rare)

Utricularia intermedia LENTIBULARIACEAE
Flat-leaved bladderwort, northern bladderwort
Summer, 2–6 in., perennial aquatic. Lake
and pond shallows, pools in bogs.

Flowers yellow, ½ in. long; the broad lower lip much
larger than upper lip, humped at throat; the spur nearly
as long as the lower lip; the inflorescence a raceme, with
2–5 flowers. Leaves finely dissected, lying below surface;
the bladderlike traps short-stalked, borne on whitish,
nonforking branches separate from the leaf branches.
Stems floating or creeping in mud. Fruit a capsule, ⅛ in.
long. CT, MA, ME, NH, RI (rare), VT
   Utricularia minor (lesser bladderwort) has shorter flowers and the bladderlike traps are borne on finely dissected
leaves. CT, MA (rare), ME, RI, VT (rare)

Utricularia radiata (*U. inflata* var. *minor*)
LENTIBULARIACEAE
Floating bladderwort
Summer to early fall, 1–4 in., annual or
perennial aquatic. Lake and ponds.

Flowers yellow, ½–⅝ in. long, the lower lip broad, shallowly
3-lobed, with a narrow hump at throat; spur shorter than
and pressed to lower lip; the inflorescence with 1–5 flowers.
Leaves at water surface 4–7, white, radiating, conspicuously
inflated, ½–1½ in. long, with short, threadlike branches at
the tips. Subsurface leaves green, finely dissected, bearing
many pale, bladderlike traps. Stems floating. Fruit a capsule. CT, MA, ME, NH, RI, VT (rare)
   *Utricularia inflata** (swollen bladderwort) has longer
flowers and longer floating, inflated leaves. Introduced in
New England and potentially invasive. MA, RI

Utricularia vulgaris LENTIBULARIACEAE
Common bladderwort, greater bladderwort
Summer, 3–8 in., perennial aquatic. Lakes,
ponds, and slow-moving streams.

Flowers yellow, ½–1 in. long, with a forward-projecting
spur; the lips about equal in length, the lower with a
hump; the inflorescence an open raceme of 6–20 stalked
flowers. Leaves floating just below surface, finely dissected,
with many green or black bladderlike traps. Stems floating, with one to several scaly bracts beneath lowest flower.
Fruits capsulelike, ⅛ in. long. CT, MA, ME, NH, RI, VT
   Utricularia geminiscapa (mixed bladderwort) is smaller,
with smaller and fewer flowers. Stems lack scaly bracts.
CT, MA, ME, NH, RI (rare), VT (rare)

Corallorhiza trifida ORCHIDACEAE
Early coral-root
Spring to early summer, 4–12 in., perennial.
Swamps and wet forests.

Flowers yellow, ⅜ in. long, arranged in a raceme of 5–15; the sepals and lateral petals greenish yellow, sometimes purple-streaked at the tips; the lip white. Leaves tiny, bractlike, pressed against stem. Stems smooth, greenish yellow, with several scaly sheaths near base. Fruit a drooping, oval capsule, ¼–½ in. long. CT (rare), MA, ME, NH, RI (rare), VT

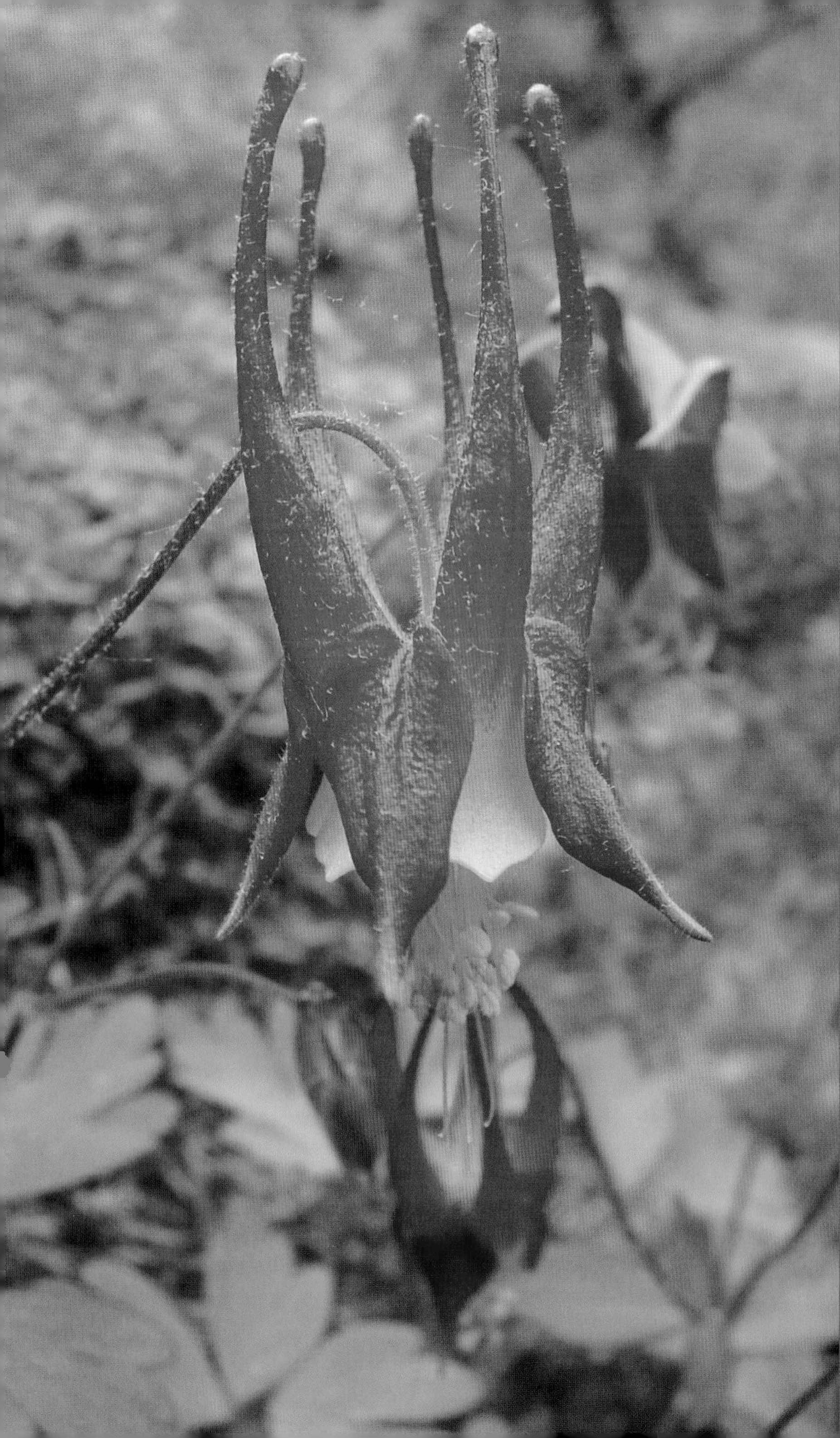

Trillium erectum   MELANTHIACEAE
Red trillium, wake-robin, stinking Benjamin
Spring, 8–24 in., perennial. Moist
deciduous and mixed forests.

Flowers maroon, 1–3 in. wide, carrion-scented, solitary,
often nodding; the petals and sepals sharp-pointed and of
equal length. Leaves 2–8 in. long and wide, broadly oval
or diamond-shaped, tapering abruptly to a pointed tip.
Stems smooth. Fruit a broadly oval, dark red berry, ½ in.
long. CT, MA, ME, NH, RI (rare), VT

Asarum canadense   ARISTOLOCHIACEAE
Wild ginger, Canada wild ginger
Early spring, 2–8 in., perennial. Rich
deciduous and mixed forests.

Flowers reddish brown, ¾–1¼ in. wide, solitary
with a tubular base and tapering, reflexed petal tips,
short-stalked along the ground from the base of fuzzy,
paired leaf petioles. Leaves 2, about 3 in. long and 4 in.
wide at flowering time, expanding later, heart-shaped, the
bases deeply notched. Fruit a capsule. CT, MA, ME (rare),
NH, RI (rare), VT

Boechera stricta (*Arabis drummondii*)
BRASSICACEAE
Canada rockcress, Drummond's rockcress
Spring and summer, 1–3 ft., biennial or
perennial. Ledges, talus slopes, and rocky
woodlands, usually in high-pH conditions.

Flowers pink, white, or bluish, ⅜–½ in. long, clustered in
narrow racemes. Leaves ¾–3 in. long, lance-shaped, sessile or clasping. Stems leafy, mostly smooth. Fruit a narrow, erect silique, pressed against stem, 1½–3½ in. long.
CT, MA (rare), ME, NH, RI (rare), VT (rare)

Vaccinium macrocarpon   ERICACEAE
Large cranberry
Summer, 1½–6 in., trailing shrub.
Bogs, fens, and marshes.

Flowers pink or white, ½ in. long, with reflexed petals, in stalked clusters of 1–6; the flower stalks with 2 small, green, leaflike bracts above the middle of stalk. Leaves evergreen, ½ in. long, oval or elliptic, with flat or slightly inrolled margins and blunt tips. Stems trailing, often forming dense colonies. Fruit a red, juicy berry, ½ in. thick. CT, MA, ME, NH, RI, VT

Vaccinium oxycoccos   ERICACEAE
Small cranberry
Late spring and summer, ½–2 in., trailing shrub. Bogs, fens, and marshes.

Flowers pink, ½ in. long, with reflexed petals, in stalked clusters of 1–4; the flower stalks with 2 tiny, reddish, scalelike bracts at or below the middle of stalk. Leaves evergreen, ⅛–⅜ in. long, oval or triangular, with strongly inrolled margins and pointed tips, whitened underneath. Stems trailing, colonial. Fruit a red berry, ¼–½ in. thick. CT, MA, ME, NH, RI, VT

Vaccinium uliginosum   ERICACEAE
Alpine blueberry, alpine bilberry
Summer, 2–24 in., shrub. Alpine meadows and ridges and subalpine thickets.

Flowers pink or sometimes white, ⅛–¼ in. long, nodding, broadly urn-shaped, in clusters of 1–4 at the ends of branches. Leaves ⅜–⅝ in. long, bluish green, broadly ovate or elliptic, finely veined. Stems creeping, branching, often forming dense patches. Fruit a sweet, blue or black berry with a whitish bloom, ¼ in. thick. ME, NH, VT (rare)

Vaccinium vitis-idaea   ERICACEAE
Mountain cranberry, lingonberry
Summer, 3–8 in., shrub. Alpine and subalpine ridges and ledges; also in bogs and river and lake shores.

Flowers pink, ⅛–¼ in. long, nodding, bell-shaped, in small clusters at branch tips. Leaves evergreen, ¼–¾ in. long, oval or elliptic, shining, dotted with black glands on the lower surface. Stems creeping, often mat-forming. Fruit a red berry, ⅜–½ in. thick. MA (rare), ME, NH, VT

Epilobium strictum   ONAGRACEAE
Downy willow-herb
Summer and early fall, 12–24 in., perennial. Marshes, wet meadows, bogs, and fens.

Flowers pink or sometimes white, ½ in. wide, stalked in upper leaf axils, the petals notched. Leaves ¾–1½ in. long, linear or narrowly lance-shaped, occasionally opposite, the margins inrolled. Stems and leaves with straight or spreading, grayish downy hairs. Fruit a hairy, linear capsule, 3 in. long, the seed hairs light brown. CT, MA, ME, NH, RI, VT

Cardamine douglassii   BRASSICACEAE
Purple cress, pink bitter-cress
Early spring, 3–12 in., perennial. Wet meadows, floodplains, and shaded seeps and springs with a high pH.

Flowers pink or purple, ½–1 in. wide, long-stalked, arranged in a compact terminal raceme. Leaves ½–2 in. long; the basal leaves rounded, long-petioled, the stem leaves oval, short-petioled or sessile, broadly toothed. Stems hairy. Fruit a slender silique, ½–1½ in. long. CT (rare), MA (rare)

*Hesperis matronalis** BRASSICACEAE
Dame's-rocket
Spring and early summer, 1–3 ft., biennial or perennial.
Old fields, floodplains, ditches, and roadsides. Invasive.

Flowers pink, purple, or white, ¾–1 in. wide, fragrant,
arranged in terminal and axillary racemes. Leaves 3–8
in. long, lance-shaped or narrowly oval, the margins with
small, sharp-tipped teeth. Stems hairy. Fruit a linear,
needlelike silique, 2–4½ in. long. Native to Europe. CT,
MA, ME, NH, RI, VT

*Lunaria annua** BRASSICACEAE
Annual honesty, honesty, money-plant
Late spring and summer, 1–3 ft., annual. Fields,
thickets, and open, disturbed sites.

Flowers pink, purple, or occasionally white, ¾ in. wide,
fragrant, arranged in racemes 2–6 in. long. Leaves 1–7
in. long, broadly oval or heart-shaped, coarsely toothed,
notched at base. Stems hairy or sometimes smooth. Fruit
a flat, round, coinlike silicle, 1¼–2 in. long and ¾–1½ in.
wide. Native to Eurasia. CT, MA, ME, RI, VT

Chamerion angustifolium (*Epilobium*
angustifolium) ONAGRACEAE
Narrow-leaved fireweed, fireweed
Summer and early fall, 2–8 ft., perennial. Old fields,
thickets, roadsides, and recently burned clearings.

Flowers magenta, ¾–1 in. wide, with prominent stamens, crowded in narrow, spirelike racemes. Leaves
2–8 in. long, lance-shaped, the margins slightly toothed,
wavy, or entire. Stems mostly smooth below infflores-
cence. Fruit a linear capsule, 1–3½ in. long, the seed
hairs white. CT, MA, ME, NH, RI, VT

4 radial petals; leaves simple, alternate, toothed or lobed

Epilobium ciliatum (*E. adenocaulon, E. glandulosum*)
ONAGRACEAE
Fringed willow-herb, American willow-herb
Summer and early fall, 12–40 in., perennial. Wet
meadows, forest seeps, swamps, and streambanks.

Flowers pink or occasionally white, ¼–½ in. wide,
long-stalked from upper leaf axils, the petals notched.
Leaves 1–4 in. long, oval, shallowly toothed, with
gland-tipped teeth; the upper usually alternate, the lower
opposite. Stems downy, widely branching. Fruit a linear
capsule, 1½–4 in. long, the seed hairs white. CT, MA, ME,
NH, RI, VT

4 radial petals; leaves simple, opposite, entire

Rotala ramosior   LYTHRACEAE
Toothcup
Late summer, ½–1½ in., annual. Pond
shores with late summer drawdowns.

Flowers red, ⅛–¼ in. long, tubular, tucked in leaf
axils; the petals minute, pink or whitish, attached to
the tips of floral tubes. Leaves ½–1¼ in. long, linear
or spoon-shaped, occasionally whorled. Stems erect or
reclining, square, turning red in late summer. Fruit a
capsule, ⅛–¼ in. long, tipped with 4 teeth. CT, MA, RI
(rare in all)

Epilobium leptophyllum   ONAGRACEAE
Bog willow-herb, narrow-leaved willow-herb
Summer to fall, 8–40 in., perennial. Wet
meadows, marshes, swamps, bogs, and fens.

Flowers pink or white, ¼–½ in. wide, stalked in upper
leaf axils, the petals notched. Leaves ¾–3 in. long and
1/16–⅛ in. wide, linear, sometimes alternate, hairy on
upper surface, with inrolled margins; clusters of smaller
leaves often tucked in axils of primary leaves. Stems
branching, with flattened, pressed-in hairs. Fruit a hairy,
linear capsule, 1½–3 in. long, the seed hairs white. CT,
MA, ME, NH, RI, VT

Epilobium palustre ONAGRACEAE
Marsh willow-herb
Summer, 4–32 in., perennial. Coniferous and mixed
swamps, fens, and bogs, also in mossy subalpine habitats.

Flowers pink or white, ½ in. wide, stalked in upper leaf
axils, the petals notched. Leaves 1–3 in. long and ⅛–½ in.
wide, linear to narrowly lance-shaped, smooth on upper
surface, with inrolled margins; clusters of smaller leaves
often tucked in axils of primary leaves. Fruit a hairy, linear capsule, 1¼–3½ in. long, the seed hairs white. ME,
MA, NH, RI (rare), VT (rare)

Linnaea borealis CAPRIFOLIACEAE
American twinflower, twinflower
Summer, 1½–4 in., perennial. Coniferous and mixed
forests and bogs, extending into subalpine zones.

Flowers pink, ⅜–½ in. long, nodding in pairs at the tips
of slender, forking stalks. Leaves ¼–¾ in. long, paired
on lower stem, oval or rounded, with blunt teeth. Stems
hairy, creeping at base. Fruit a dry achene, ⅛ in. long. CT
(rare), MA (rare), ME, NH, VT

Rhexia virginica MELASTOMATACEAE
Virginia meadow-beauty
Summer, 8–40 in., perennial. Wet sandy
or peaty fields and pond shores.

Flowers magenta or pink-purple, 1–1½ in. wide, arranged
in terminal racemes, with bright yellow, projecting stamens. Leaves 1–3 in. long, oval, 3-veined, finely toothed,
⅓–½ as wide as long. Stems sparsely hairy (but bristly at
leaf nodes), angular, finely winged. Fruit an urn-shaped
capsule, ⅜ in. long. CT, MA, ME, NH, RI, VT (rare)
   Rhexia mariana (Maryland meadow-beauty) is similar, but the petals are pale pink or sometimes white, the
leaves are narrower (⅓ or less as wide as long), and the
stems are very hairy and not winged. Only found in sandy
pond shores in coastal regions. MA (rare)

4 radial petals; leaves simple, opposite, entire

4 radial petals; leaves simple, opposite, toothed or lobed

Epilobium coloratum   ONAGRACEAE
Purple-leaved willow-herb, eastern willow-herb
Summer and fall, 6–36 in., perennial. Marshes, swamps, river and lake shores, and ditches.

Flowers pink or white, ¼ in. wide, stalked in upper leaf axils, often numerous, forming a bushy inflorescence; the petals notched. Leaves to 4 in. long and ¾ in. wide, lance-shaped, grayish green, veiny on both surfaces, sharply toothed. Stems hairy, green or purple. Fruit a linear capsule, 1–2 in. long, the seed hairs reddish brown.
CT, MA, ME, NH, RI, VT

Epilobium hirsutum*   ONAGRACEAE
Hairy willow-herb
Summer and early fall, 2–6 ft., perennial. Wet fields and thickets, ditches, and roadsides. Invasive.

Flowers magenta, 1 in. wide, long-stalked from upper leaf axils, the petals shallowly notched. Leaves 2–5 in. long, lance-shaped, sharply toothed, sessile or clasping the stem. Stems thick, hairy, branching. Fruit a linear capsule, 2–3 in. long, the seed hairs white. Native to Eurasia.
CT, MA, ME, NH, RI, VT

Diodia teres   RUBIACEAE
Buttonweed
Summer to early fall, 6–30 in., annual. Sandy coastal beaches, fields, and dry, open, disturbed sites.

Flowers pink, white, or lilac, ¼ in. wide, funnel shaped, sessile, arranged in pairs at the top of the stem and in leaf axils. Leaves ¾–1½ in. long, narrowly lance-shaped, stiff, sessile; the leaf nodes with long bristles. Stems hairy, erect or sometimes prostrate. Fruit hairy, capsulelike, ⅛–¼ in. long. Native in CT, RI; introduced in MA.

Galium lanceolatum   RUBIACEAE
Lance-leaved licorice bedstraw, lance-leaved wild licorice
Summer, 12–28 in., perennial. Dry
deciduous forests and woodlands.

Flowers purple or yellowish, ⅛ in. wide, sparsely clustered in spreading, forking branches; the petals smooth,
pointed at the tips. Leaves 1–3 in. long, lance-shaped,
3-veined, widest below middle, taper-
ing to pointed tips, in whorls of 4.
Stems smooth. Fruits rounded, bristly,
⅛–¼ in. long. CT, MA, ME, NH, RI, VT
   Galium circaezans (forest licorice
bedstraw) is similar, but with greenish
flowers.

Galium pilosum   RUBIACEAE
Hairy bedstraw
Summer, 8–40 in., perennial. Dry woodlands and ridges.

Flowers red-purple or greenish white, ⅛ in. wide,
arranged in wide-branching, axillary clusters. Leaves
½–1½ in. long, oval, hairy, with a prominent midvein on
upper surface and tiny glandular dots on lower surface,
in whorls of 4. Stems hairy, erect. Fruits round, bristly,
1⁄16–⅛ in. long. CT, MA, NH (rare),
RI, VT

Calluna vulgaris*   ERICACEAE
Heather
Summer and fall, 6–36 in., shrub.
Sandy fields and roadsides.

Flowers pink, ⅛ in. long, arranged in crowded spikes;
the sepals longer than the petals. Leaves 1⁄16–⅛ in. long,
needlelike, densely packed on twigs. Stems low, branching, often mat-forming. Fruit a dry, hairy capsule, 1⁄16 in.
long. Native to Europe. CT, MA, ME, NH, RI, VT

Cynoglossum officinale✷ BORAGINACEAE
Hound's-tongue, common hound's-tongue
Spring and summer, 1–4 ft., biennial.
Fields, pastures, and roadsides.

Flowers red-purple, ¼ in. wide, arranged in coiled clusters on spreading, terminal and axillary branches. Leaves 3–8 in. long, lance-shaped or oval, crowded, the lower long-petioled, the upper progressively smaller. Stems leafy, hairy. Fruit bristly, ¼ in. long. Native to Eurasia. CT, MA, NH, RI, VT

Symphytum officinale✷ BORAGINACEAE
Common comfrey
Late spring and summer, 1–4 ft., perennial.
Ditches, meadows, gardens, roadsides.

Flowers pink or purplish, sometimes blue or yellowish, ½ in. long, drooping, tubular. Leaves 6–12 in. long, oval or lance-shaped, with finely hairy margins and prominent veins. Stems hairy. Fruit black, shining, ¼ in. long. Native to Europe. CT, MA, ME, NH, RI, VT

Calystegia sepium (*Convolvulus sepium*)
CONVOLVULACEAE
Hedge bindweed, hedge false-bindweed
Summer and fall, to 10 ft. long, perennial vine. Old fields, thickets, wetland and salt marsh edges.

Flowers either pink to red or white, 1½–3 in. wide, funnel-shaped; 2 leafy bracts at flower base cover the

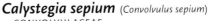

sepals. Leaves 2–4 in. long, triangular, long-petioled, pointed at tip, with arrow-shaped basal lobes. Stem twining or climbing, hairy or smooth. Fruit a dark, rounded capsule, ¼–½ in. wide. CT, MA, ME, NH, RI, VT

Andromeda polifolia (*A. glaucophylla*) ERICACEAE
Bog rosemary
Spring to early summer, 4–30 in., shrub. Bogs and fens.

Flowers pink, bell-shaped, ¼ in. long, stalked, arranged in nodding clusters. Leaves ¾–2 in. long, linear or narrowly lance-shaped, with inrolled margins, whitened underneath. Stems smooth. Fruit a rounded capsule, ¼–⅜ in. long. CT (rare), MA, ME, NH, VT

Gaylussacia baccata ERICACEAE
Black huckleberry
Midspring to midsummer, 1–3 ft., shrub. Forests, woodlands, clearings, and rocky ridges.

Flowers red, ¼ in. long, conical, covered with minute yellow resin dots, arranged in dangling clusters. Leaves yellowish green, oval, 1–2 in. long, spotted with reflective yellow resin dots on both surfaces, especially the lower. Stems smooth, densely branching. Fruit a sweet, round, black berry ¼ in. thick. CT, MA, ME, NH, RI, VT

Rhododendron lapponicum ERICACEAE
Lapland rosebay
Early summer, to 1 ft., shrub. Alpine thickets on high mountains.

Flowers red-purple, ½–¾ in. wide, borne in sparse clusters above the leaves. Leaves oval or elliptic, ½ in. long, evergreen, leathery, speckled on both sides with tiny, brownish scales. Stems hairy, mat-forming. Fruit a long-stalked, oval capsule, ¼ in. long. ME, NH (rare in all)

Hylotelephium telephium✲ (Sedum purpureum, S. telephium) CRASSULACEAE
Purple orpine, live-forever, sedum, frog's-belly
Summer and early fall, 8–32 in., perennial. Moist woodlands, thickets, fields, and roadsides.

Flowers pink or red, ¼–½ in. long, 5-pointed, clustered in dense, rounded or flattish heads ½–8 in. wide. Leaves 1½–4 in. long, fleshy, sometimes whitish, coarsely toothed, oblong. Stems smooth, succulent. Fruit a follicle, ⅛–¼ in. long. Native to Europe. CT, MA, ME, NH, RI, VT

Hibiscus moscheutos (H. palustris) MALVACEAE
Swamp rose-mallow
Late summer and early fall, 3–7 ft., perennial. Salt, brackish, and freshwater marshes.

Flowers pink, red, or white, 4–8 in. wide, stalked from upper axils; the flowers with a column of bushy stamens, the interior often ringed with crimson. Leaves 4–6 in. long, lance-shaped or oval, sometimes lobed, downy on the undersurface. Stems downy. Fruit an oval capsule, ½–1 in. long. Primarily coastal. CT, MA, NH (rare), RI

Malva neglecta✲ MALVACEAE
Common mallow, cheeses
Spring to fall, 6–24 in., annual or biennial. Fields, roadsides, and gardens.

Flowers pale pink or white, ½–¾ in. wide, stalked from the leaf axils; the petal tips slightly notched. Leaves ¾–2½ in. long and wide, long-petioled, heart-shaped or rounded, sharply toothed, with 5–9 broad, shallow lobes. Stems trailing, hairy. Fruit a flattened disk, ¼ in. wide, divided into 12–15 sections. Native to Eurasia and North Africa. CT, MA, ME, NH, RI, VT

*Malva sylvestris** MALVACEAE
High mallow
Summer, 1–3 ft., biennial. Fields, roadsides,
and open, disturbed sites.

Flowers rose-purple, 1–2 in. wide, long-stalked from
upper leaf axils; the petals purple-veined and notched at
the tips. Leaves 1½–6 in. long and wide, with 5–7 broad
lobes, the margins crinkled and toothed. Stems hairy,
erect. Fruit a disk, ¼–⅜ in. wide, divided into 10–12 sections. Native to Eurasia and North Africa. CT, MA, ME,
NH, RI, VT

Spiraea tomentosa ROSACEAE
Steeplebush, rosy meadowsweet
Summer and early fall, 1–4 ft., shrub. Wet
meadows, bogs, swamps, and old fields.

Flowers pink, ⅛–¼ in. wide, densely clustered in a spirelike terminal panicle, 2–6 in. long. Leaves 1–2 in. long,
lance-shaped or oval, crowded, the lower surfaces covered with fuzzy white or reddish brown hairs. Stems
woolly-hairy. Fruit an oval follicle, ⅛ in. long. CT, MA, ME,
NH, RI, VT

Apocynum androsaemifolium
APOCYNACEAE
Spreading dogbane
Summer, 8–32 in., perennial. Open woodlands,
thickets, meadows, and roadsides.

Flowers pink-striped, ¼–⅜ in. wide, fragrant, nodding from the leaf axils in small clusters; the petal tips
reflexed. Leaves 1–3½ in. long, lance-shaped or oval,
often drooping, with sharp-pointed tips. Stems branched,
erect or arching, green or red, with milky sap. Fruit a follicle, needlelike, drooping, paired, 2–6 in. long. CT, MA,
ME, NH, RI, VT

265

Asclepias amplexicaulis   APOCYNACEAE
Blunt-leaved milkweed
Summer, 1–3 ft., perennial. Sandy fields and woodlands.

Flowers pink-purple, ⅜ in. wide, clustered in a stalked, erect, solitary umbel 3–4 in. wide; the reflexed petals greenish purple and the erect corona lobes pink. Leaves 2½–6 in. long, blunt, sessile, wavy-margined, rounded at both ends. Stems smooth, with milky sap. Fruit an erect, smooth or slightly downy follicle, 4–5 in. long. CT, MA, NH (rare), RI (rare), VT (rare)

Asclepias incarnata   APOCYNACEAE
Swamp milkweed
Summer, 2–5 ft., perennial. Wet meadows, marshes, swamps, and ditches.

Flowers pink to magenta, ⅜ in. wide, clustered in several to many, flattish umbels, 1–3 in. wide; the reflexed petals magenta and the erect corona lobes light pink. Leaves 2½–6 in. long, lance-shaped, tapering, the lateral veins projecting upwards, forming an acute angle with the midvein. Stems usually hairy, with milky sap. Fruit an erect follicle, 2½–4 in. long. CT, MA, ME, NH, RI, VT

Asclepias purpurascens   APOCYNACEAE
Purple milkweed
Summer, 1–3 ft., perennial. Dry fields, woodland clearings, and roadsides.

Flowers bright purple, ¼ in. wide, clustered in one to several umbels 1–3½ in. wide; the reflexed petals and the erect corona lobes purple or magenta. Leaves 4–6 in. long, oval or oblong, downy underneath, the lateral veins approximately perpendicular to the midvein. Stems smooth or finely hairy, with milky sap. Fruit an erect, smooth or finely downy follicle, 4–6 in. long. CT (rare), MA (rare)

Asclepias syriaca   APOCYNACEAE
Common milkweed
Summer, 3–5 ft., perennial. Fields,
clearings, and roadsides.

Flowers bright pink or pale purple, ¼ in. wide, fragrant,
clustered in several to many erect or drooping umbels,
2–4 in. wide; the reflexed petals greenish purple and the
erect corona lobes light pink. Leaves 6–9 in. long, oval or
oblong, hairy underneath, the lateral veins approximately
perpendicular to the midvein. Fruit an erect, hairy follicle, covered with warts, 3–4½ in. long. CT, MA, ME, NH,
RI, VT

*Cynanchum louiseae** (*C. nigrum, Vincetoxicum*
nigrum) APOCYNACEAE
Black swallowwort
Late spring and summer, 3–6 ft. long, perennial vine.
Woodlands, thickets, fields, and roadsides. Invasive.

Flowers dark maroon, ⅛–¼ in. wide, arranged in small
axillary clusters; the petals finely hairy and broadly
triangular. Leaves 2–3 in. long, dark green, oval or
heart-shaped, tapering to the tip. Stems twining, climbing, finely hairy. Fruit a linear, elongate follicle, 1½–3 in.
long. Native to Europe. CT, MA, ME, NH, RI, VT

*Cynanchum rossicum** (*Vincetoxicum rossicum*)
APOCYNACEAE
Pale swallowwort
Late spring to summer, 3–6 ft. long, perennial vine.
Woodland edges, fields, and roadsides. Invasive.

Almost identical to *Cynanchum louiseae*, but the flowers
are pale pink, ¼ in. wide, with smooth, narrow, finger-
like petals. Leaves 2–3 in. long, oval or heart-shaped, dark
green, tapering to tip. Stems twining, climbing, finely
hairy. Fruit a linear, elongate follicle, 1½–3 in. long.
Native to Europe. CT, MA, ME, NH

5 radial petals; leaves simple,
opposite, entire

Triosteum aurantiacum CAPRIFOLIACEAE
Orange-fruited horse-gentian
Late spring to midsummer, 2–4 ft., perennial.
Deciduous woodlands and thickets.

Flowers red-purple, ½ in. long, tubular, solitary or in few-flowered clusters, tucked in the leaf axils. Leaves 4–12 in. long, broadly oval, sessile, tapering to the base. Stems hairy. Fruits red-orange, oval, berrylike, ½ in. thick. CT, MA, ME (rare), NH (rare), RI (rare), VT (rare)

Triosteum perfoliatum CAPRIFOLIACEAE
Perfoliate-leaved horse-gentian, wild coffee
Late spring to midsummer, 2–4 ft., perennial.
Sandy woodlands and shrub thickets.

Similar to *Triosteum aurantiacum* (orange-fruited horse-gentian), but bases of the primary leaves are fused, pierced by the stem. Flowers reddish brown, ⅜–½ in. long, tubular, solitary or in few-flowered clusters, tucked in the leaf axils. Leaves 4–12 in. long, broadly oval, gradually tapering to the united bases. Stems hairy. Fruit orange-yellow, round, berrylike, ⅜ in. thick. CT, MA (rare), RI (rare)

Dianthus armeria⁕ CARYOPHYLLACEAE
Deptford pink
Late spring to midsummer, 6–24 in., annual or biennial. Fields, thickets, and roadsides.

Flowers pink, ½ in. wide, arranged in narrow, terminal and upper axillary clusters, underlain by needle-like bracts; the petals narrowly oval, white-spotted, and toothed on the upper margins. Leaves 1–3 in. long, linear or narrowly lance-shaped. Stems hairy. Fruit a narrow capsule, ½ in. long. Native to Europe. CT, MA, ME, NH, RI, VT

Dianthus deltoides ∗ CARYOPHYLLACEAE
Maiden pink
Summer, 4–16 in., perennial. Fields,
roadsides, and open, disturbed sites.

Flowers pink, ½–¾ in. wide, long-stalked, terminal, solitary or in few-flowered clusters; the petals broad and
toothed at the tips, with a dark streak at the base. Leaves
1–2 in. long, linear. Stems finely hairy. Fruit a narrow
capsule, ½ in. long. Native to Eurasia. CT, MA, ME, NH,
RI, VT

Lychnis flos-cuculi ∗ CARYOPHYLLACEAE
Ragged-robin
Late spring to midsummer, 12–32 in., perennial. Fields,
floodplains, roadsides, and open, disturbed sites. Invasive.

Flowers pink or occasionally white, ¾–1 in. wide,
arranged in open panicles; the petals deeply and irregularly cleft, divided into forking, linear lobes. Leaves 2–4
in. long, lance-shaped. Stems finely hairy, sticky above.
Fruit an oval capsule, ¼–⅜ in. long. Native to Europe. CT,
MA, ME, NH, RI, VT

Silene acaulis CARYOPHYLLACEAE
Moss campion
Summer, 1–2½ in., perennial. Alpine summits and ridges.

Flowers pink or purple, ½ in. wide, solitary, stalked
just above the matted leaves; the petal tips rounded and
often notched; the sepals smooth, fused into a veined,
slightly inflated tube. Leaves ⅛–½ in. long, linear or
lance-shaped, clumped in mosslike cushions. Fruit an
oval capsule, about ½ in. long. NH (rare)

Silene caroliniana CARYOPHYLLACEAE
Wild pink, wild campion
Spring, 3–12 in., perennial. Rocky or sandy
deciduous woodlands, clearings, and roadsides.

Flowers pink or occasionally white, 1 in. wide, arranged
in compact clusters; the petal tips broad, sometimes
toothed or notched. Basal leaves to 5 in. long, crowded,
oval or spoon-shaped; stem leaves ½–2 in. long sessile,
lance-shaped. Stems hairy and sticky. Fruit an oval capsule, ½ in. long. CT, MA (rare), RI

Silene dioica✻ (Lychnis dioica) CARYOPHYLLACEAE
Red campion
Spring to early fall, 1–4 ft., perennial. Fields,
roadsides, and open, disturbed sites.

Flowers red, 1 in. wide, scentless, arranged in open, forking panicles, the petals with broad, notched tips; the calyx
sac reddish and hairy. Stem leaves oval, 1–4 in. long, the
upper leaves often sessile; the basal leaves long-stalked.
Stems downy. Fruit a broadly oval or rounded capsule, ½
in. long. Native to Europe. CT, MA, ME, NH, RI, VT
  Hybrids with *Silene latifolia* (white campion) produce
pink flowers.

Spergularia marina (S. salina) CARYOPHYLLACEAE
Salt-marsh sand-spurry
Summer, 3–12 in., annual. Salt and brackish marshes.

Flowers pink or white, ¼ in. wide, stalked from the
leaf axils; the oval sepals longer than the petals. Leaves
¼–1½ in. long, fleshy, linear, with a short, pointed
tip. Stems branching, often mat-forming, smooth or
glandular-hairy. Fruit an oval capsule, ¼ in. long. CT, MA,
ME, NH, RI, VT
  Spergularia canadensis (Canada sand-spurry) is very
similar, but the leaves are blunt, lacking a sharp-pointed
tip. Grows in salt marshes and beaches. CT (rare), MA, ME,
NH, RI (rare)

*Spergularia rubra** CARYOPHYLLACEAE
Sand spurry, red sand-spurry
Late spring to early fall, 2–12 in., annual or perennial.
Sandy fields, roadsides, and open, disturbed sites.

Flowers pink, ⅛–¼ in. long, stalked from the leaf axils;
the lance-shaped, glandular sepals slightly longer than
the petals. Leaves ¼–⅜ in. long, linear, needlelike; clusters of tiny leaves bunched within the paired primary
leaves, appearing whorled. Stems branching, often
mat-forming, glandular-hairy. Fruit a glandular-hairy,
oval capsule, ⅛–¼ in. long. Native to Europe. CT, MA, ME,
NH, RI, VT

Triadenum virginicum (*Hypericum virginicum*)
CLUSIACEAE
Virginia marsh-St. John's-wort
Summer, 1–2 ft., perennial. Bogs,
marshes, and pond shores.

Flowers pink, ½–¾ in. wide, arranged in small terminal
and axillary clusters; the petals ⅜ in. long, and the purple, sharp-tipped sepals ¼–⅜ in. long. Leaves 1¼–2½ in.
long, oblong or oval, sessile, purplish green above, purplish beneath, spotted with translucent glands. Stems
smooth. Fruit a gradually tapering, cylindrical capsule,
⅜–½ in. long. CT, MA, ME, NH, RI, VT
  Triadenum fraseri (Fraser's marsh-St. John's-wort) is
similar, but the petals are shorter (¼–⅜ in. long), the
sepals are blunt-tipped and smaller (⅛–¼ in. long), and
the fruiting capsule tapers abruptly. Grows in marshes,
bogs, and pond shores. More common in northern New
England. CT, MA, ME, NH, VT

Geocaulon lividum COMANDRACEAE
False toadflax, northern comandra
Summer, 3–12 in., perennial. Heathlands and
coniferous woodland openings in alpine and subalpine
zones; also cold coastal bogs of northern ME.

Flowers greenish purple, ⅛ in. wide, arranged in
short-stalked clusters of 2–4 in the upper and middle
leaf axils. Leaves ½–1½ in. long, oval or elliptic, veiny,
blunt-tipped, turning purple by midsummer. Stems
smooth, often red at flowering time. Fruits orange or red,
berrylike, ¼–⅜ in. wide. ME (rare), NH (rare)

Kalmia polifolia ERICACEAE
Bog laurel, swamp laurel, bog American-laurel
Spring to early summer, 1–3 ft., shrub.
Bogs and moist alpine slopes.

Flowers deep pink or red, ½–¾ in. wide, clustered at the top of the stem; the 10 stamens tipped with dark anthers. Leaves ½–1½ in. long, linear or lance-shaped, strongly whitened underneath, the margins usually inrolled. Stems narrowly branched, with 2-edged twigs. Fruit an oval capsule, ¼ in. long. CT, MA, ME, NH, VT

Kalmia procumbens (*Loiseleuria procumbens*)
ERICACEAE
Alpine-azalea
Summer, to 4 in., shrub. Alpine ridges at high elevations.

Flowers pink, crown-shaped, ⅛–¼ in. wide, stalked just above the leaves; the petal tips pointed. Leaves ¼ in. long, oval, evergreen, densely crowded, forming cushions. Stems matted, densely branched, smooth or slightly hairy. Fruit an oval capsule, about ⅛ in. long. ME (rare), NH (rare)

Centaurium pulchellum* GENTIANACEAE
Branched centaury
Summer, 1–12 in., annual. Fields, roadsides, and open, disturbed sites.

Flowers pink, starlike, ½ in. wide, stalked at the base, arranged in dense terminal and axillary clusters; the fused calyx about ⅜ in. long. Leaves ¼–1 in. long, sessile, lance-shaped to broadly oval; basal leaves absent. Stems smooth, slightly ridged. Fruit an oval capsule, ⅜ in. long. Native to Eurasia and North Africa. CT, MA, ME, VT

*Centaurium erythraea** (European centaury), also native to Eurasia and North Africa, is similar, but the flowers are not stalked at the base, the calyx is ⅛–¼ in. long, and basal leaves are present. Grows in fields and roadsides. CT, MA

Sabatia stellaris   GENTIANACEAE
Sea pink, annual rose-gentian
Midsummer to early fall, 8–24 in., annual.
Salt and brackish marshes.

Flowers pink or occasionally white, ½–1 in. wide, solitary on terminal and axillary stalks; the centers yellow, ringed with red; the petals oval, usually longer than the narrow sepals. Leaves ¾–1½ in. long, oval or lance-shaped, widest at or above middle, tapering to the base. Stems smooth. Fruit a capsule, ¼–½ in. long. CT, MA, RI (rare in all)

The extremely rare, perennial *Sabatia campanulata* (marsh pink) is similar, but the sepals are equal to or slightly longer than the petals, the leaves are usually widest below middle and rounded at the base, and it only grows in freshwater, coastal plain pond shores with a peaty substrate. MA (rare)

Lysimachia maritima (*Glaux maritima*)
MYRSINACEAE
Sea-milkwort
Summer, 2–16 in., perennial. Salt marshes and shorelines.

Flowers pink, purple, or occasionally white, ⅛–¼ in. wide; tucked in the axils of the fleshy leaves. Leaves ¼–1 in., lance-shaped or oval and densely crowded; the uppermost sometimes alternate. Stems smooth, erect or spreading. Fruit an oval capsule, ¼ in. long. MA, ME, NH

Phlox maculata∗   POLEMONIACEAE
Spotted phlox, wild sweet-William
Summer, 1–3 ft., perennial. Fields, roadsides, and lawns, usually in moist soils.

Flowers red-purple, ½–1 in. wide, with a long corolla tube; the inflorescence dense, short-branched, 2–16 in. long. Leaves 2–5 in. long, lance-shaped or oval, broadest near base, with faint veins; the margins without fine hairs. Stems smooth, purple-spotted. Fruit an oval capsule, ¼–½ in. long. Native in much of eastern and central United States, introduced in New England. CT, MA, ME, VT

Phlox paniculata⁕   POLEMONIACEAE
Garden phlox, summer phlox
Summer to fall, 1–6 ft., perennial.
Fields, roadsides, and gardens.

Flowers red-purple, sometimes white, ½–1 in. wide,
with a long corolla tube; the inflorescence pyramidal or
dome-shaped, hairy, 3–4 in. wide. Leaves 3–6 in. long,
lance-shaped or oval, broadest near middle, with conspicuous veins; the margins with fine hairs. Stems smooth,
without spots. Fruit an oval capsule, ¼ in. long. Native to
much of eastern and central United States, introduced in
New England. CT, MA, ME, NH, RI, VT

Phlox subulata⁕   POLEMONIACEAE
Moss phlox
Spring, 5–8 in., perennial. Sandy or rocky,
disturbed ground, roadsides, gardens.

Flowers pink, purple, or white, ½–1 in. wide, stalked
just above the matted leaves; the petal tips rounded and
indented; the sepals linear, sharp-tipped and hairy.
Leaves ¼–¾ in. long, needlelike, crowded, with clusters of tiny leaves often in the axils of the paired, primary
leaves. Stems densely branched, mat-forming. Fruit an
oval capsule, ⅛–¼ in. long. Native to much of eastern
United States, introduced in New England. CT, MA, ME,
NH, RI, VT

Claytonia caroliniana   PORTULACACEAE
Carolina spring-beauty
Early spring, 2–10 in., perennial. Rich deciduous forests.

Flowers pink or white, ½ in. wide, with rose-colored
veins, erect or nodding, arranged in small, open racemes;
the bract beneath the lowest flower thin and weak. Leaves
1–3 in. long, oval or spoon-shaped, 3–8 times as long
as wide, tapering into a distinct petiole. Stems smooth.
Fruit an oval capsule, ⅛–¼ in. wide. CT, MA, ME, NH, VT

Claytonia virginica PORTULACACEAE
Virginia spring-beauty
Early spring, 2–10 in., perennial. Rich deciduous forests.

Flowers pink or white, ½ in. wide, with rose-colored veins, erect or nodding, arranged in small, open racemes; the bract beneath the lowest flower firm. Leaves 1½–6 in. long, linear or narrowly lance-shaped, 8 or more times as long as wide, the petiole scarcely distinguishable from the blade. Stems smooth. Fruit an oval capsule, ⅛–¼ in. wide. CT, MA (rare), VT (rare)

Kalmia angustifolia ERICACEAE
Sheep laurel
Late spring to late summer, 1–3 ft., shrub. Fields, thickets, woodlands, bogs, and mountain ridges.

Flowers pink or red, ¼–½ in. wide, bowl-shaped, in spreading clusters below the uppermost leaves; the 10 white, spokelike stamens tipped with dark red anthers. Leaves 1–3 in. long, evergreen, lance-shaped or oval, in whorls of 3, pale green underneath; many leaves tilted downwards. Stems wide-branching. Fruit a rounded, drooping capsule, ⅛–¼ in. long. CT, MA, ME, NH, RI, VT

Drosera filiformis DROSERACEAE
Thread-leaved sundew
Midsummer to early fall, 3–12 in., perennial. Sandy, coastal plain pond shores.

Flowers purple, ¼–½ in. wide, arranged in coiled racemes with 4–16 flowers, uncoiling in fruit. Leaves erect, threadlike, green or purplish, about as long as flower stalk, covered with dew-tipped, insect-trapping glandular hairs; the young, unfurled leaves have fiddle-head tips. Stems smooth. Fruit an oval capsule, ¼ in. long. A carnivorous species. Limited to coastal plain. MA

Pyrola asarifolia ERICACEAE
Pink pyrola, pink shinleaf
Summer, 4–16 in., perennial. Rich, moist
mixed forests and coniferous swamps.

Flowers pink, ¼–½ in. wide, arranged in slender, nodding racemes of 4–30; the stamens protruding. Basal
leaves 1–3 in. long, leathery, broadly oval or rounded,
long-petioled. Stems smooth. Fruit a
rounded capsule, ¼ in. wide. MA (rare),
ME, NH (rare), VT (rare)

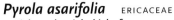

Primula laurentiana PRIMULACEAE
Bird's-eye primrose, Laurentide primrose
Late spring to early summer, 4–16 in.,
perennial. Coastal headlands and cliffs.

Flowers pink, lavender, or purple, ½ in. wide, arranged in
a terminal cluster; the flowers with a yellow eye and distinctly notched petals; the sepals ¼–⅜ in. long. Leaves
1½–3 in. long, lance-shaped or spoon-shaped, the margins finely toothed, forming a rosette. Stems smooth.
Fruit an oval capsule, ½ in. long. Mostly along the coast
in northeastern ME (rare).

Primula mistassinica PRIMULACEAE
Lake Mistassini primrose, Mistassini primrose
Spring, 1–8 in., perennial. Rocky river and
lake shorelines on high-pH rock.

Flowers pink or rose, ½ in. wide, arranged in a terminal cluster; the flowers with a yellow eye and shallowly
notched petals; the sepals ⅛–¼ in. long. Leaves ¾–2¼ in.
long, lance-shaped or spoon-shaped, the margins finely
toothed, forming a rosette. Stems smooth, with a whitish
powder. Fruit an oval capsule, ¼ in. long. Northern interior ME (rare), northern VT (rare)

Sarracenia purpurea   SARRACENIACEAE
Pitcher-plant, purple pitcher-plant
Spring and summer, 10–30 in., perennial. Bogs and fens.

Flowers red or purplish, 2 in. wide, solitary, nodding; the
sepals and petals folded over the yellow, disk-shaped style.
Leaves 4–8 in. long, hooded, pitcherlike, purple-veined,
partially filled with water, the interior with reflexed, bristly hairs that entrap insects. Stems green or red, smooth.
Fruit a rounded capsule, ½–¾ in. wide. Carnivorous. CT,
MA, ME, NH, RI, VT

Geranium bicknellii   GERANIACEAE
Bicknell's crane's-bill, northern crane's-bill
Summer, 6–24 in., annual or biennial.
Woodlands, clearings, and rocky slopes.

Flowers magenta, ¼–½ in. wide, loosely clustered on
long (½–2½ in.), glandular-hairy stalks; the petals
notched. Leaves ¾–2½ in. long and wide, deeply divided
into 5-lobed segments. Stems branching, hairy. Fruit linear, capsulelike, ¾–1 in. long; the beak ⅛–¼ in. long. ME,
MA (rare), NH, RI (rare), VT (rare)

Geranium carolinianum   GERANIACEAE
Carolina crane's-bill
Summer, 4–24 in., perennial. Woodlands,
ledges, and dry fields.

Flowers pink or whitish, ½ in. wide, densely clustered
on short (less than ½ in. long) glandular-hairy stalks; the
petals notched. Leaves 1–2½ in. long and at least as wide,
deeply divided into 5- to 9-lobed segments. Stems branching, hairy. Fruit linear, capsulelike, 1 in. long; the beak
1/16 in. long. CT, MA, ME, NH (rare), RI

*Malva moschata** MALVACEAE
Musk mallow
Summer, 1–3 ft., perennial. Fields, roadsides, and gardens.

Flowers pink or white, 2–3 in. wide, long-stalked, with notched petals, arranged in crowded terminal panicles. Leaves 1–2½ in. long, divided into linear segments; the upper leaves very finely dissected. Stems hairy. Fruit a flattened disk, ⅜ in. wide, divided into 9–15 sections. Native of Eurasia. CT, MA, ME, NH, RI, VT

Aquilegia canadensis RANUNCULACEAE
Wild columbine, red columbine
Spring, 6–36 in., perennial. Ledges, talus slopes, and rocky woodlands.

Flowers red, 1–2 in. long, nodding, on long, arching stalks; the upturned base of the flowers with 5 long

spurs, the flower center and protruding stamens yellow. Leaves divided into 3 oval, long-stalked, lobed leaflets, wedge-shaped at base, ½–2 in. long. Stems smooth or hairy. Fruit a narrow, ascending follicle, ½–1½ in. long, with an awnlike beak. CT, MA, ME, NH, RI, VT

Geranium maculatum GERANIACEAE
Wild geranium, spotted crane's-bill
Spring and early summer, 12–28 in., perennial. Forests, woodlands, thickets, and fields.

Flowers pink or rose, occasionally white, 1–1½ in. wide, loosely clustered on long, hairy, nonglandular stalks. Basal leaves long-petioled and deeply cleft; the single pair of stem leaves 1–5 in. long and wide, deeply divided into 5- to 7-lobed segments. Stems hairy. Fruit linear, capsule-like, 1–1½ in. long; the beak ¼–⅜ in. long. CT, MA, ME, NH, RI, VT

The introduced *Geranium pratense** (meadow crane's-bill) is similar, but the flowers are bluish or violet, and the flower stalks are glandular as well as hairy. Native to Europe. Grows in fields and roadsides. CT, MA, ME, VT

Geranium robertianum GERANIACEAE
Herb-Robert, mountain crane's-bill
Spring to fall, 4–20 in., annual or biennial. Rocky
woodlands, talus slopes, ledges, and beaches.

Flowers pink, ½ in. wide, numerous, clustered on long,
branching stalks. Leaves 1–1½ in. long and wide, fernlike, musk-scented, divided into 3 or 5 finely incised leaflets, the terminal leaflet stalked. Stems branching, very
hairy. Fruit beaked, capsulelike, with a swollen base, ¾–1
in. long. CT, MA, ME, NH, RI, VT

Oxalis violacea OXALIDACEAE
Violet wood sorrel
Spring to early summer, 4–8 in., perennial.
Rich, rocky, deciduous woodlands.

Flowers violet, ½ in. wide, erect or nodding, arranged
in stalked umbels of 2–12 flowers. Leaves 1 in. long and
wide, 3-parted, long-stalked, green
or purple-tinged; the 3 leaflets
heart-shaped at tip. Stems smooth.
Fruit a rounded capsule, ⅛–¼ in.
long. CT, MA, RI (rare in all)

Phyllodoce caerulea ERICACEAE
Mountain heath, purple mountain heath
Summer, 2–6 in., shrub. Alpine ravines and summits.

Flowers pink or purple ½ in. long, bell-shaped, nodding
in stalked clusters from branch tips. Leaves ¼–⅜ in.
long, needlelike, crowded, the margins finely serrated.
Stems creeping, mat-forming. Fruit a rounded capsule, ⅛
in. long. ME (rare), NH (rare)

5 radial petals; leaves deeply divided, opposite, leaflets toothed or lobed

5 radial petals; leaves deeply divided, basal, leaflets entire

5 radial petals; leaves absent, scaly, or needlelike

Pterospora andromeda   ERICACEAE
Pine drops, giant bird's-nest
Summer, 1–3 ft., perennial. Forests.

Flowers white or reddish, ¼ in. long, bell-shaped, drooping, clustered on a long raceme. Leaves scalelike. Stems reddish brown, densely glandular-hairy. Fruit a rounded capsule, ¼ in. long. A very rare parasitic plant that obtains nutrients through a root association with a fungal host. NH (rare), VT (rare)

Streptopus lanceolatus (*S. roseus*) LILIACEAE
Rose twisted-stalk, lance-leaved twisted-stalk
Spring to midsummer, 12–32 in., perennial. Mixed and coniferous forests, subalpine zones.

Flowers rose-pink, ⅜ in. long, with reflexed tips, dangling singly from leaf axils on short, hairy stalks. Leaves 2–4 in. long, oval or lance-shaped, sessile, with a corrugated surface. Stems branching, hairy, with a zigzag pattern. Fruit a red, elliptical berry, ¼–⅜ in. long. CT, MA, ME, NH, VT

Lythrum alatum   LYTHRACEAE
Winged loosestrife
Summer, 1–3 ft., perennial. Marshes, wet meadows, and river banks.

Flowers purple, ½ in. long, with a long calyx tube, clustered singly in upper leaf axils. Leaves to 2 in. long, sessile, lance-shaped; the lowermost opposite, the upper alternate, crowded. Stems smooth, branching, 4-angled. Fruit a capsule. CT (rare), MA (rare), ME, NH, RI (rare)

Lythrum hyssopifolia   LYTHRACEAE
Hyssop loosestrife
Summer, 4–24 in., annual. Salt and brackish marshes;
moist depressions on the lee side of dunes.

Flowers pink or pale purple, ¼ in. long, clustered singly
or in pairs in leaf axils. Leaves ½ in. long, linear or narrowly oblong, sessile, crowded, the lowermost sometimes
opposite. Stems smooth, pale green, 4-angled. Fruit an
oval capsule, ¼ in. long. MA, ME, NH, RI

Lythrum salicaria*   LYTHRACEAE
Purple loosestrife
Summer, 1½–5 ft., perennial. Marshes, wet
meadows, lake and river shores. Invasive.

Flowers red-purple, ½–1 in. long, arranged in long, dense
spikes, with sharp-pointed bracts beneath the flowers.
Leaves 1–4 in. long, sessile, lance-shaped, sometimes in
whorls of 3. Stems square, often hairy. Fruit an oval capsule, ⅛–¼ in. long. Native to Eurasia. CT, MA, ME, NH,
RI, VT

Allium canadense   ALLIACEAE
Meadow garlic
Spring to early summer, 8–24 in., perennial. Forested
floodplains and moist deciduous woodlands.

Flowers pink, sometimes white, ⅜–½ in. wide, arranged
in a long-stalked, often sparse umbel; the flower stalks
extend above dense clusters of sessile bulblets. Leaves
8–20 in. long, solid, linear, flattish, sheathing. Stems
smooth. Fruit an oval capsule. CT, MA, ME (rare), NH
(rare), RI, VT (rare)

6 radial petals; leaves simple, alternate, entire

6 radial petals; leaves simple, opposite, entire

6 radial petals; leaves simple, basal, entire

Allium schoenoprasum   ALLIACEAE
Wild chives
Summer, 6–20 in., perennial. Native strains grow
in riverbanks, meadows, and shorelines; nonnative
strains grow in roadsides and open, disturbed sites.

Flowers pink ⅜–½ in. wide, arranged in a dense, compact umbel ½–1½ in. wide; the inflorescence lacks bulblets. Leaves 8–12 in. long, hollow, linear, round in cross
section. Fruit a 3-ribbed oval capsule, ¼ in. long. Native
in ME, NH (rare), VT (rare); introduced in CT, MA, RI.

Butomus umbellatus⁕   BUTOMACEAE
Flowering rush
Summer, to 3½ ft., perennial. Lakes, ponds,
and river shorelines and shallows. Invasive.

Flowers pink, sometimes white, ¾–1 in. long, arranged
in long-stalked, ascending umbels. Leaves to 3 ft. or more
long and ¼–½ in. wide, linear; erect or floating. Stems
rounded, smooth. Fruit an oval, beaked follicle, ⅜–½ in.
long. Native to Eurasia. CT, MA, ME, VT

Brasenia schreberi   NYMPHAEACEAE
Water shield
Summer, to 6 ft. long, perennial. Ponds,
lakes, and slow-moving streams.

Flowers reddish purple, 1 in. wide, with bushy stamens,
stalked above the leaves. Leaves 1½–5 in. long and wide,
floating, oval or rounded, reddish and gelatinous underneath; the submerged petioles attach to center of leaf.
Stems submerged, slimy. Fruit an oval, beaked achene,
¼–⅜ in. long. CT, MA, ME, NH, RI, VT

Coreopsis rosea ASTERACEAE
Rose coreopsis, pink tickseed
Midsummer to early fall, 8–24 in., perennial. Sandy or
peaty coastal pond shores, swales, and boggy depressions.

Flower heads pink or white, 1 in. wide, long-stalked, with
6–10 pink or white rays and yellow centers; the ray tips
with 3 small teeth. Leaves 1–2½ in. long, threadlike, linear. Stems smooth. MA, RI (rare)

Sabatia kennedyana GENTIANACEAE
Plymouth gentian, Plymouth rose-gentian
Midsummer to early fall, 12–28 in., perennial.
Sandy or peaty freshwater pond shores.

Flowers pink, occasionally white, 1½–2½ in. long, with
7–13 petals, solitary at the ends of long branching stalks;
the petal interiors with a bright yellow ring; the sepals
linear, less than ⅟16 in. wide, with 1–3 obscure veins.
Leaves ¾–2 in. long, linear or lance-shaped, sessile.
Stems smooth. Fruit an oval capsule, ⅜–½ in. long. MA,
RI (rare)
   Large *Sabatia dodecandra* (marsh pink, perennial
rose-gentian) is similar, but the sepals are lance-shaped
or spoon-shaped, ⅟16–⅛ in. wide, with 3–5 distinct veins.
Grows only in salt and brackish marshes on the coast of
CT (extremely rare).

Arctium lappa∗ ASTERACEAE
Great burdock
Midsummer to fall, 3–9 ft., biennial. Fields,
roadsides, and open, disturbed sites.

Flower heads pink or purple, 1–1½ in. wide, bristly,
long-stalked, arranged in flattish clusters; the flower
stalks with gland-tipped hairs. Leaves 10–32 in. long, oval
or rounded; petioles of lower leaves usually solid. Stems
hairy. Fruiting head a bristly, clinging bur, ½ in. wide.
Native to Eurasia. CT, MA, ME, NH, RI, VT

Arctium minus ASTERACEAE
Common burdock
Blooms from midsummer to fall, 2–4 ft., biennial.
Fields, roadsides, and open, disturbed sites.

Flower heads pink or purple, ½–1 in. wide, bristly, short-stalked or sessile, arranged in ascending, raceme-like clusters. Leaves 6–20 in. long, oval; petioles of lower leaves long and usually hollow. Stems hairy. Fruiting head a bristly, clinging bur, ½ in. wide. Native to Eurasia. CT, MA, ME, NH, RI, VT

Liatris novae-angliae (L. borealis, L. scariosa var. *novae-angliae*) ASTERACEAE
Northern blazing-star
Late summer and early fall, 1–3 ft., perennial.
Sandy grasslands, woodlands, calcareous
ledges, beaches, and dry, open sites.

Flower heads pink-purple, ¾–1 in. wide, short-stalked, arranged in spikelike racemes; the bracts below the heads blunt and darkened at the tip. Leaves 4–12 in. long, crowded, linear or narrowly lance-shaped. Stems hairy or smooth. CT, MA, ME (rare), NH (rare), RI (rare)

Polygala nuttallii POLYGALACEAE
Nuttall's milkwort
Summer, 2–12 in., annual. Sandy fields and
thickets and dry, open woodlands.

Flowers pink, purple, or greenish white, ⅛ in. long, clustered in short, blunt heads about ½ in. long and ¼ in. (or less) wide; tiny, hooked bracts often just below the inflorescence. Leaves ¼–¾ in. long, linear. Stems smooth. Fruit a capsule, 1/16–⅛ in. long. CT (rare), MA, RI

Polygala polygama   POLYGALACEAE
Racemed milkwort
Summer, 4–10 in., biennial. Sandy
fields and woodland clearings.

Flowers pink, occasionally white, ¼–⅜ in. long, with
oval, winglike sepals; the inflorescence a slender, tapering raceme, 1–4 in. long. Leaves ½–1½ in. long, linear
or lance-shaped, numerous, ascending, sessile. Stems
smooth. Fruit a capsule, ⅛ in. long. CT, MA, ME, NH, RI,
VT (rare)

Polygala sanguinea   POLYGALACEAE
Blood milkwort, purple milkwort
Summer and fall, 4–16 in., annual. Fields,
clearings, woodland edges, and roadsides.

Flowers red, pink, white, or greenish, ⅛ in. long, aggregated in dense cylindrical heads about 1 in. long and ½
in. wide; the heads often underlain by a "screwstem"
whorl of tiny, hooklike bracts. Leaves ½–1½ in. long, narrowly lance-shaped. Stems smooth. Fruit a rounded capsule, ¹⁄₁₆ in. long. CT, MA, ME, NH, RI, VT

Persicaria amphibia (*Polygonum amphibium*)
POLYGONACEAE
Water smartweed
Summer, 8–36 in., perennial. Pond and river
shallows, marshes, swamps, and ditches.

Flowers pink or red, ⅛–¼ in. wide, densely clustered
in 1 or 2 thick, usually erect spikes ¾–1¼ in. long and
½ in. wide. Leaves 2–6 in. long and about 1 in. wide,
lance-shaped, with pointed tips; the sheaths in terrestrial
forms spreading and often coarsely hairy. Stems smooth
or hairy; terrestrial plants erect, aquatic plants floating.
Fruit a dark, shiny achene, ⅛ in. long. CT, MA, ME, NH,
RI, VT

Persicaria careyi (*Polygonum careyi*)
POLYGONACEAE
Carey's smartweed
Midsummer to fall, 1–4 ft., annual. Wet meadows, swamps, fields, and roadsides.

Flowers pink or white, ⅛ in. wide, arranged in slender, drooping spikes, ½–4 in. long and ¼ in. wide, with glandular-hairy stalks. Leaves 2–7 in. long, narrowly lance-shaped; the sheaths fringed and hairy. Stems with bristly hairs. Fruit a black, shiny achene, 1/16–⅛ in. long. CT, MA, ME, NH, RI, VT (rare)

Persicaria coccinea (*Polygonum coccineum*)
POLYGONACEAE
Swamp smartweed, scarlet smartweed
Summer, 8–36 in., perennial. Pond and river shallows, marshes, swamps, and ditches.

Flowers pink or red, ⅛–¼ in. wide, clustered in spikes 1¼–3½ in. long and ½–¾ in. wide. Larger leaves 4–8 in. long and 1¼–2½ in. wide, lance-shaped; the sheaths in terrestrial forms smooth or finely hairy, not spreading outward. Stems smooth or hairy; terrestrial plants erect or sprawling, aquatic plants floating. Fruit a dark, shiny achene, ⅛ in. long. CT, MA, ME, NH, RI, VT

Persicaria lapathifolia (*Polygonum lapathifolium*)
POLYGONACEAE
Pale smartweed, nodding smartweed, dock-leaved smartweed
Midsummer to early fall, 1–3 ft., annual. Wet meadows, swamps, shorelines, and ditches.

Flowers pink or whitish, ⅛ in. wide, arranged in numerous, nodding, slender spikes 1¼–3 in. long and about ¼ in. wide. Leaves 1½–5 in. long, lance-shaped, long-pointed, sometimes with a dark, triangular blotch; sheath margins entire or torn, lacking bristles. Stems smooth or hairy. Fruit a dark, flat achene, 1/16–⅛ in. long. CT, MA, ME, NH, RI, VT

Persicaria longiseta* (Polygonum caespitosum,
P. cespitosum) POLYGONACEAE
Cespitose knotweed, oriental lady's-thumb smartweed
Summer and fall, 1–2½ ft., annual. Woodlands,
floodplains, trail edges, and roadsides. Invasive.

Flowers pink or white, ⅛–¼ in. wide, arranged in one to
several narrow spikes ½–1½ in. long and ⅛–¼ in. wide.
Leaves ¾–3 in. long, lance-shaped; the sheath bristles
¼–½ in. long. Stems smooth. Fruit an oval achene, ⅛ in.
long. Native to East Asia. CT, MA, ME, NH, RI, VT

Persicaria maculosa* (Polygonum persicaria)
POLYGONACEAE
Lady's thumb, lady's-thumb smartweed
Summer and fall, 6–36 in., annual. Fields,
roadsides, ditches, and open, disturbed sites.

Flowers pink, ⅛–¼ in. wide, arranged in spikes
½–1½ in. long and ⅜ in. wide. Leaves 2–4 in. long,
lance-shaped, usually marked with a black, triangular
blotch; the sheath bristles 1/16–⅛ in. long. Stems erect,
smooth or hairy. Fruit a dark, shining achene, ⅛ in. long.
Native to Europe. CT, MA, ME, NH, RI, VT
  Persicaria puritanorum (Puritan smartweed) is very
similar, but the leaves do not have dark blotches, the
flower spikes are narrower (¼ in. wide), and the achenes
are 1/16 in. long. Stems usually sprawling. A native species
found only in sandy, coastal plain pond shores. MA, ME
(rare in both)

Persicaria orientalis* (Polygonum orientale)
POLYGONACEAE
Prince's feather, kiss-me-over-the-garden-gate
Summer to fall, 2–8 ft., annual. Fields,
roadsides, and open, disturbed sites.

Flowers bright red, ¼ in. wide, arranged in numerous,
dense, drooping spikes ½–6 in. long. Leaves 2½–12 in.
long, oval, long-petioled; the sheaths hairy, spreading and
short-fringed at the top. Stems branching, hairy. Fruit a
dull, flat achene, ⅛ in. long. Native to South Asia. CT, MA,
ME, NH, RI, VT

Persicaria pensylvanica (*Polygonum pensylvanicum*) POLYGONACEAE
Pennsylvania smartweed
Summer and early fall, 1–6 ft., annual. Wet meadows, marshes, swamps, and ditches.

Flowers rose-pink or occasionally whitish, ⅛–¼ in. wide, arranged in erect spikes ½–2½ in. long and about ½ in. wide. Leaves 1½–9 in. long, lance-shaped; the sheaths usually torn, without fringes. Upper stems and flower stalks covered with sticky, glandular hairs. Fruit a dark, broad achene, ⅛–¼ in. long. CT, MA, ME, NH, RI, VT

Rumex acetosella ✳ POLYGONACEAE
Sheep sorrel, sheep dock
Spring and summer, 4–16 in., perennial. Fields, rocky ridges, roadsides, freshwater shorelines, and open, disturbed sites. Invasive.

Flowers red or greenish, 1/16–⅛ in. long, loosely clustered in narrow, ascending, spikelike racemes. Leaves ¾–2½ in. long, lance-shaped, often with flaring lobes at base. Stems smooth, branching. Fruit a triangular achene, 1/16 in. long. Native to Eurasia. CT, MA, ME, NH, RI, VT

Chenopodium capitatum AMARANTHACEAE
Strawberry-blite
Summer, 1–3 ft., annual. Woodland clearings, often after fire, roadsides, and open, disturbed sites.

Flowers reddish green, tiny, aggregated into fleshy, round heads ¼–⅜ in. diameter; the heads sessile, arranged in upper leaf axils and often a terminal spike. Leaves 1–4 in. long, lance-shaped or triangular, often coarsely toothed, occasionally with basal lobes, the lower on long petioles. Stems smooth. Fruit a bright red, fleshy achene. CT, MA, ME, NH, VT

Chenopodium rubrum AMARANTHACEAE
Coast blite, red goosefoot
Summer and fall, 4–32 in., annual. Salt and brackish
marshes, occasionally in inland ditches.

Flowers greenish pink, tiny, aggregated into crowded
globular heads ⅛–¼ in. wide, in the upper axils. Leaves
½–3 in. long, triangular or diamond-shaped, coarsely
toothed, the lowermost teeth or lobes prominent. Stems
smooth, branching, green or red. Fruit a tiny, oval, flattened achene, ¹⁄₁₆ in. long or less. Native populations in
MA, ME (rare), NH (rare), primarily in salt marshes. Introduced populations in MA, ME, in ditches and disturbed
ground.

Centaurea jacea* ASTERACEAE
Brown knapweed
Summer, 8–32 in., perennial. Fields,
roadsides, and open, disturbed sites.

Flower heads pink-purple, ¾–1¼ in. wide, the spreading, marginal rays distinctly larger than the erect central flowers; the whorled bracts beneath the flower heads
oval, brown, short-fringed. Larger leaves 4–6 in. long,
lance-shaped, the margins toothed, lobed, or entire; the
upper leaves small and narrow. Stems hairy. Native to
Europe. Hybridizes with *Centaurea nigra*. CT, MA, ME,
NH, RI, VT

Centaurea nigra* ASTERACEAE
Black knapweed
Summer and early fall, 8–32 in., perennial.
Fields, roadsides, and open, disturbed sites.

Flower heads pink-purple, ¾–1¼ in. wide, the marginal
rays about equal to the central flowers; the whorled bracts
beneath the flower heads narrow, dark, with 7–15 long,
comblike fringes on each margin. Leaves 2–10 in. long,
lance-shaped, the margins toothed, lobed, or entire.
Stems hairy. Native to Europe. Hybridizes with *Centaurea
jacea*. CT, MA, ME, NH, RI, VT
  Centaurea nigrescens (short-fringed knapweed) is very
similar, but the whorled bracts have only 5–8 comblike
fringes on each margin. Grows in fields and roadsides.
CT, MA, ME, NH, RI, VT

Petals indistinguishable; leaves
simple, alternate, toothed or lobed

Pluchea odorata (*P. purpurascens*) ASTERACEAE
Salt-marsh fleabane, sweet-scented camphorweed
Late summer to early fall, 1–3 ft., annual.
Salt and brackish marshes.

Flower heads pink-purple, ¼–⅜ in. wide, rayless, stalked, arranged in dense, flattish panicle. Leaves 1½–6 in. long, oval, finely toothed; bruised foliage has a camphorlike fragrance. Stems sticky with glandular hairs. CT, MA, NH (rare), RI

Gentianella quinquefolia (*Gentiana quinquefolia*)
GENTIANACEAE
Stiff dwarf-gentian, stiff gentian, agueweed
Late summer and fall, 8–32 in., annual or biennial.
Fields and thickets on high-pH soils.

Flowers pink-purple or lilac, ½–1 in. long, funnel-shaped, closed, arranged in dense, erect panicles at the top of the stem and in upper axils; the closed petal lobes with pointed, sometimes whitened tips. Leaves ½–2½ in. long, light green or oval, with 3–7 prominent veins. Stems smooth. Fruit a 2-parted, elliptical capsule, ½–1 in. long. CT, MA, NH, VT (rare in all)

Chrysosplenium americanum
SAXIFRAGACEAE
Golden saxifrage
Spring, 2–12 in., perennial. Swamps, streamsides, and forested seepages.

Flowers greenish yellow, ¼ in. wide, solitary, tipped with a jewel-like ring of 4 or 8 conspicuous red anthers; the flowers borne just above the uppermost leaves of the creeping branches. Leaves ¼–½ in. long, round or broadly oval, obscurely toothed; the lower opposite, the upper often alternate. Stems creeping, mat-forming. Fruit a tiny capsule, ¹⁄₁₆ in. long. CT, MA, ME, NH, RI, VT

Sclerolepis uniflora ASTERACEAE
Pink bog-button, sclerolepis
Midsummer to fall, 4–12 in., perennial.
Sandy and gravelly lake shores.

Flower heads pink or white, ¼–½
in. wide, rayless, solitary, buttonlike.
Leaves ¼–1 in. long, linear, in whorls
of 4–6. Stems rooted in water or wet
shoreline substrate; aquatic forms
mostly submerged, terrestrial forms
erect. At northern edge of range in New
England. MA, NH, RI (rare in all)

Eutrochium dubium (*Eupatorium dubium*)
ASTERACEAE
**Coastal plain Joe-Pye weed, eastern Joe-Pye weed, three-
nerved Joe-Pye weed**
Midsummer to fall, 2–5 ft., perennial. Swamps, wet
meadows, and pond and river shores, mostly near coast.

Individual flower heads red-purple, ¼–⅜
in. long, clustered, each head with 5–9 disk
flowers; the clusters aggregated into broad,
domelike, terminal and upper axillary panicles. Leaves 2–6 in. long, lance-shaped or
oval, in whorls of 3 or 4, sharply toothed,
with 2 prominent lateral veins spreading outward from the middle vein. Stems purple-spotted, hairy
near top. CT, MA, ME, NH, RI

Eutrochium fistulosum (*Eupatorium fistulosum*)
ASTERACEAE
Hollow Joe-Pye weed, trumpetweed
Midsummer to fall, 2–7 ft., perennial. Swamps,
wet meadows, and floodplain forests.

Individual flower heads
red-purple or whitish, ¼ in.
long, clustered, each head with
5–8 disk flowers; the clusters
aggregated into broad, domelike, terminal and upper axillary
panicles. Leaves 3–11 in. long,
lance-shaped, in whorls of 4–7,

with blunt teeth and a single main central vein. Stems
hollow, usually purple, mostly smooth. CT, MA, ME (rare),
NH (rare), RI

Eutrochium maculatum (*Eupatorium maculatum*)
ASTERACEAE
Spotted Joe-Pye weed
Midsummer to fall, 2–7 ft., perennial. Swamps, marshes, and wet meadows, from low to high elevations.

Individual flower heads red-purple, ¼–⅜ in. long, clustered, each head with 9–22 disk flowers; the clusters aggregated into broad, flattish, terminal and upper axillary panicles. Leaves 2–8 in. long, lance-shaped, mostly in whorls of 4 or 5, sharply toothed, with a single main central vein. Stems purple-spotted or -streaked, hairy at top. CT, MA, ME, NH, RI, VT

Eutrochium purpureum (*Eupatorium purpureum*)
ASTERACEAE
Purple Joe-Pye weed, sweet-scented Joe-Pye weed, purple-node Joe-Pye weed
Midsummer to fall, 2–7 ft., perennial. Upland deciduous forests and woodlands.

Individual flower heads light purple or whitish, ¼–⅜ in. long, clustered, each head with 4–7 disk flowers; the clusters aggregated into broad, domelike, terminal and upper axillary panicles. Leaves 3–12 in. long, lance-shaped or oval, mostly in whorls of 3 or 4, with a single main central vein, vanilla-scented when bruised. Stems dark purple at the leaf nodes, otherwise green or purple-tinged, often with a whitish bloom, smooth below the inflorescence. CT, MA, NH, RI, VT (rare)

*Petasites hybridus** ASTERACEAE
Butterbur, butterbur sweet-coltsfoot
Early spring, 4–16 in. (leaves to 3 ft. after flowering), perennial. Wet meadows and stream corridors, sometimes invasive.

Flower heads purple, ¼–½ in. long, rayless, arranged in a dense, leafless, cone-shaped raceme. Basal leaves 12–36 in. long and wide, heart-shaped, long-petioled, coarsely toothed, emerging later than the flowers; stem leaves much smaller, lance-shaped, scalelike, alternate, entire, purple-tinged. Stems with woolly hairs. Native to Eurasia. CT, MA, VT

*Petasites japonicus** (Japanese butterbur, Japanese sweet-coltsfoot) has white or yellowish flowers. Native to East Asia. An occasional garden escape in ME.

Centaurea stoebe✻ (C. bieberteinii, C. maculosa)

ASTERACEAE

Spotted knapweed

Summer, 1–4 ft., biennial or perennial. Dry fields,
pastures, roadsides, and open, disturbed sites. Invasive.

Flower heads pink-purple ½–1 in. wide, numerous, on
wide-branching stalks; the whorled bracts beneath the
flower heads with fringed, black tips. Larger stem leaves
3–6 in. long, lance-shaped, deeply divided into linear segments; the upper leaves smaller. Stems wiry, branching,
hairy. Native to Europe. CT, MA, ME, NH, RI, VT

Cirsium arvense✻ ASTERACEAE

Canada thistle, creeping thistle

Summer, 1–6 ft., perennial. Fields,
pastures, and roadsides. Invasive.

Flower heads pink, numerous, wide-branching, ½–¾ in.
wide; the whorled bracts beneath the flowers tipped with
short, weak spines. Leaves 1–10 in. long, lance-shaped,
toothed or lobed, with wrinkled, spine-tipped margins.
Stems usually hairy, lacking spines. Native to Europe. CT,
MA, ME, NH, RI, VT

Cirsium discolor ASTERACEAE

Field thistle

Summer, 2–6 ft., biennial or perennial. Fields, roadsides,
and open, disturbed sites, often in moist soil.

Flower heads pink-purple, 1½–2 in. wide, on long,
branching stalks; the whorled bracts beneath the flowers
with long, pale spines. Leaves 4–10 in. long, lance-shaped
or oval, spiny, deeply cut into sharp, variable segments,
densely white-woolly underneath; the uppermost leaves
sessile at the base of the flower heads. Stems hairy, lacking spines. CT, MA, ME, NH, RI, VT (rare)

Petals indistinguishable; leaves deeply
divided, alternate, leaflets toothed or lobed

Cirsium muticum ASTERACEAE
Swamp thistle
Summer, 2–7 ft., biennial. Swamps, marshes, lake shorelines, and salt marsh edges.

Flower heads rose-purple, 1½–2½ in. wide on long, branching stalks, cobwebby at base; the whorled bracts beneath the flowers hairy, spineless or with very short spines. Leaves 6–20 in. long, lance-shaped, spiny, deeply cut into narrow segments, smooth or hairy beneath. Stems branching, hollow, hairy or smooth, lacking spines. CT, MA, ME, NH, RI, VT

Cirsium pumilum ASTERACEAE
Pasture thistle
Summer, 1–3 ft., biennial or perennial. Fields, pastures, and roadsides.

Flower heads red-purple, 2–3 in. wide, arranged on few-flowered stalks, fragrant; the whorled bracts beneath the flower heads with short, slender, erect or spreading spines. Leaves 2–12 in. long, lance-shaped, deeply cut into short segments, hairy underneath, the margins very spiny with both short and longer spines. Stems densely hairy, lacking spines. CT, MA, ME, NH, RI, VT

Cirsium vulgare✻ ASTERACEAE
Bull thistle, common thistle
Summer and early fall, 2–6 ft., biennial. Fields, pastures, and roadsides.

Flower heads red-purple, 1–2 in. wide on branching stalks with one to several flowers; the ball of whorled bracts beneath the flower heads with rigid, yellow-tipped spines. Leaves 6–15 in. long, lance-shaped, spiny, deeply cut, hairy underneath, the terminal segment often narrow and elongate. Stems winged with spines. Native to Eurasia. CT, MA, ME, NH, RI, VT

Onopordum acanthium* ASTERACEAE
Scotch thistle, Scotch cotton-thistle
Summer and fall, 3–6 ft., biennial. Fields,
roadsides, and open, disturbed sites. Invasive.

Flower heads red-purple, 1–2 in. wide, often numerous
in a branching inflorescence; the whorled bracts beneath
the flower heads cobwebby, with long, slender spines.
Leaves 4–12 in. long, lance-shaped or oval, spiny, toothed
or broadly lobed, usually white-hairy underneath. Stems
whitish, hairy, winged with jagged saw-tooth ridges.
Native to Eurasia. CT, MA, RI, VT

    Carduus acanthoides (plumeless thistle) has ridged,
spiny stems, but the foliage is green, not whitened, and
the leaves are deeply cut, with bristly-spiny lobes. Grows
in fields and roadsides. CT, MA, ME, RI, VT

Corema conradii ERICACEAE
Broom crowberry
Early spring, 6–20 in., shrub. Sandy or rocky coastal
meadows, heathlands, and pitch pine woodlands.

Flowers reddish purple, ⅛–¼ in. wide, clustered on
branch tips; the stamens of male plants purple, projecting above the petal-like lobes. Leaves ⅛–¼ in. long,
needlelike, densely crowded. Stems erect or creeping,
wide-branching, colonial. Fruit red, berrylike, dry, not
fleshy, ⅟₁₆ in. thick. MA (rare), ME

Empetrum nigrum ERICACEAE
Black crowberry
Midspring to early summer, to 16 in., shrub. Cliffs,
balds, alpine ridges, and rocky coastal headlands.

Flowers purple, ⅛ in. wide, tucked in leaf axils; the stamens projecting from the petals. Leaves ⅛–⅜ in. long,
needlelike, crowded. Stems creeping, mat-forming; the
young twigs with glandular hairs. Fruit berrylike, black
when ripe, fleshy, ¼ in. thick. ME, NH, VT (rare)

    Empetrum atropurpureum (purple crowberry, red
crowberry) is very similar, but the young twigs are
white-woolly, not glandular, and the mature fruits are red
or purple, not black. Grows only in alpine and subalpine
zones of the highest mountains. ME, NH

Rhododendron canadense ERICACEAE
Rhodora
Early spring, 1–3 ft., shrub. Bogs, peaty
shorelines, and mountain summits.

Flowers magenta, 1 in. long, clustered on stem tips, with
10 protruding stamens and 2 lips; the upper lip with 3
shallow lobes, the lower lip with 2 deeply divided, divergent lobes. Leaves ¾–2 in. long, appearing after flowers, lance-shaped or elliptic, grayish green, with inrolled
edges. Stems hairy, with many ascending branches. Fruit
a hairy, elliptical capsule, ½ in. long. CT (rare), MA, ME,
NH, RI, VT

Cypripedium arietinum ORCHIDACEAE
Ram's-head lady's-slipper
Mid to late spring, 4–15 in., perennial. Moist,
mixed forests and coniferous fens.

Flowers ½–1 in. long, usually solitary; the pouchlike
flower with bold red-purple veins and a jutting chinlike
base; the uppermost sepal purple-bronze, arching over
the lip. Leaves 2–4 in. long, lance-shaped or oval, sessile.
Stems hairy. Fruit a ridged, elliptical capsule, ¾ in. long.
MA, ME, NH, VT (rare in all)

Cypripedium reginae ORCHIDACEAE
Showy lady's-slipper
Early summer, 1–3 ft., perennial.
Calcareous fens and swamps.

Flowers 1–2 in. long, the pouchlike lip prominent,
rounded, blushed with pink or crimson, occasionally
pure white; the uppermost sepal white, rounded, ascending above the lip. Leaves 4–10 in. long, broadly oval,
ribbed, clasping. Stems hairy. Fruit a ridged, elliptical
capsule about 1½ in. long. CT (rare), MA (rare), ME (rare),
NH (rare), VT

Platanthera grandiflora (*Habenaria fimbriata,*
H. psycodes var. *grandiflora*) ORCHIDACEAE
Larger purple-fringed orchid, greater purple-fringed bog-orchid
Early to midsummer, 2–4 ft., perennial. Wet forests, swamp edges, wet meadows, and streambanks.

Flowers purple, magenta, pink, or occasionally white, ¾–1 in. long, spurred and deeply fringed; the 3-lobed lower lip ½–1 in. wide, the lobes fringed ⅓ or more of their lengths; the inflorescence a dense raceme, 3–10 in. long and 2–3½ in. wide. Leaves 3–10 in. long, lance-shaped or oval, the uppermost smaller. Stems smooth, somewhat fleshy. Fruit a capsule. CT, MA, ME, NH, RI, VT

Platanthera psycodes (*Habenaria psycodes,*
H. psycodes var. *psycodes*) ORCHIDACEAE
Smaller purple-fringed orchid, lesser purple-fringed bog-orchid
Mid to late summer, 1–3 ft., perennial. Wet forests, swamp edges, wet meadows, and streambanks.

Flowers purple, magenta, or occasionally white, ½–¾ in. long; the 3-lobed lower lip ¼–½ in. wide, the lobes fringed less than ⅓ of their length; the inflorescence a dense raceme, 2–8 in. long and 1¼–1½ in. wide. Leaves 2–9 in. long, lance-shaped or oval. Stems smooth, somewhat fleshy. Fruit a capsule. CT, MA, ME, NH, RI (rare), VT

Pogonia ophioglossoides ORCHIDACEAE
Rose pogonia, snakemouth
Late spring and early summer, 4–16 in., perennial. Bogs and wet, acidic, peaty meadows.

Flowers pink, ¾ in. long; the lip protruding, fringed, bearded in the center with white or yellow hairs; the 3 sepals and 2 upper petals spreading above the lip. Single stem leaf 1–3½ in. long, lance-shaped or oval. Stems smooth. Fruit an elliptical capsule, ½–1¼ in. long. CT, MA, ME, NH, RI, VT

Polygala paucifolia   POLYGALACEAE
Fringed milkwort, fringed polygala, gaywings
Spring to early summer, 3–6 in., perennial.
Deciduous and mixed forests and woodlands.

Flowers ½–¾ in. long, bright pink, occasionally purple or white, single or paired, crested with a conspicuous pink or white fringe; the lateral sepals broad, winglike, flanking the fringed floral tube. Primary leaves ¾–1½ in. long, oval, clustered at the top of the stem. Stems smooth, often colonial. Fruit a rounded, notched capsule, ¼ in. long. CT, MA, ME, NH, RI, VT

Lobelia cardinalis   CAMPANULACEAE
Cardinal flower, red lobelia
Midsummer to early fall, 2–5 ft., perennial. Wet meadows, marshes, streambanks, and pond shores.

Flowers blazing scarlet, 1½ in. long, arranged in a long terminal raceme; the flowers with a 3-parted lower lip, a 2-parted upper lip, and projecting, white-tipped stamens. Leaves 2–6 in. long, lance-shaped or narrowly oval. Stems hairy or smooth. Fruit an oval, long-beaked capsule, ⅜ in. long. CT, MA, ME, NH, RI, VT

Clinopodium vulgare✲ (*Satureja vulgaris*)
LAMIACEAE
Wild basil
Summer and early fall, 8–20 in., perennial.
Woodlands, fields, and roadsides.

Flowers pink, sometimes purple or white, ½ in. long, clustered in dense, sessile, bristly whorls; the lower lip broad, protruding, the upper lip small, arched forward. Leaves ¾–1½ in. long, lance-shaped or oval, the margins occasionally toothed. Stems hairy. Fruit capsulelike, less than 1/16 in. long. Native to Eurasia. CT, MA, ME, NH, RI, VT

Origanum vulgare✳ LAMIACEAE
Wild marjoram, oregano
Summer and early fall, 10–24 in.,
perennial. Fields and roadsides.

Flowers pink or purple, ¼–⅜ in. long, arranged in
stalked, rounded, terminal and upper axillary clusters;
the lower lip deeply 3-parted, the stamens protruding.
Leaves ½–1½ in. long, oval, aromatic, occasionally with
blunt teeth. Stems hairy. Fruit capsulelike, about ⅛ in.
long. Native to Eurasia. CT, MA, VT

Stachys hyssopifolia LAMIACEAE
Hyssop hedge-nettle, hyssop-leaved hedge-nettle
Summer, 12–20 in., perennial. Coastal plain pond shores.

Flowers pink, sometimes white, ½ in. long, arranged
in one to several sessile whorls on upper stem; the
lower lip broad, notched, mottled with purple, upper lip
spoon-shaped, narrowed at base. Leaves ¾–3 in. long,
linear or narrowly oblong, smooth. Stems smooth. Fruit
dark, capsulelike, about ¹⁄₁₆ in. long. Native in CT, MA, RI
(rare in all); introduced in ME.

Thymus pulegioides✳ (*T. serpyllum*) LAMIACEAE
Wild thyme
Summer, 2–12 in., perennial. Fields and roadsides.

Flowers pink or purple, ¼ in. long, densely clustered at
the stem tips; the lower lip broadly 3-lobed, the sepals
hairy, sharp-pointed, the stamens protruding. Leaves
¼–½ in. long, lance-shaped or oval, strongly aromatic.
Stems hairy, mat-forming. Fruit capsulelike, less than ¹⁄₁₆
in. long. Native to Europe. CT, MA, ME, NH, RI, VT

Agalinis acuta *(Gerardia acuta)* OROBANCHACEAE
Sandplain gerardia, sandplain agalinis
Late summer, 4–16 in., annual. Sandy
grasslands, scrub barrens, and roadsides.

Flowers pink, ⅜–½ in. wide, long-stalked, in branching
racemes; the petals square-tipped or slightly notched; the
sepals pointed, finely and distinctly veined. Leaves ½–1
in. long, threadlike, yellowish green. Stems smooth. Fruit
a rounded capsule, ⅛ in. long. A federally endangered
species mostly near coast. CT, MA, RI (rare in all)

Agalinis maritima *(Gerardia maritima)*
OROBANCHACEAE
Seaside gerardia, salt-marsh agalinis
Midsummer to early fall, 4–16 in., annual.
Salt marshes and meadows.

Flowers pink or purple, ½–¾ in. wide, short-stalked,
arranged in short racemes; the petals round-tipped; the
sepals blunt and obscurely veined. Leaves ¾–1¼ in. long,
linear, fleshy dark green. Stems smooth. Fruit a rounded
capsule, ⅛–¼ in. long. CT, MA, ME (rare), NH (rare), RI

Agalinis paupercula *(Gerardia paupercula)*
OROBANCHACEAE
Small-flowered gerardia, small-flowered agalinis
Late summer and early fall, 8–30 in., annual. Fields,
clearings, marsh edges, river and lake shores.

Similar to *Agalinis purpurea* (purple gerardia) but with
smaller flowers and a shorter style, ¼–⅜ in. long. Flowers pink or purple, ⅜–⅝ in. wide, short-stalked, arranged
in racemes; the petals round-tipped, the sepals pointed,
obscurely veined. Leaves ¾–1¾ in. long, linear. Stems
smooth. Fruit a rounded capsule, ⅛–¼ in. long. CT, MA,
ME, NH, RI, VT

Agalinis purpurea (*Gerardia purpurea*)
OROBANCHACEAE
Purple gerardia, purple agalinis
Late summer and early fall, 8–36 in., annual. Moist,
peaty or sandy meadows and salt marsh borders.

Similar to *Agalinis paupercula* (small-flowered gerardia) but with larger flowers and a longer style, ⅝–¾ in.
long. Flowers pink or purple, ¾–1½ in. wide, arranged
in racemes, very short stalked, almost sessile; the petals
round-tipped, the sepals sharp-pointed, obscurely veined.
Leaves ½–1½ in. long, linear. Stems smooth. Fruit a
rounded capsule, ¼ in. long. CT, MA, ME (rare), RI

Agalinis tenuifolia (*Gerardia tenuifolia*)
OROBANCHACEAE
Slender gerardia, slender agalinis
Late summer and fall, 4–24 in., annual. Fields,
woodlands, clearings, and trail and road edges.

Flowers pink or purple, ⅜–⅝ in. wide, on long, delicate
stalks, arranged in racemes; the petals round-tipped,
hairless on the inside, the upper 2 arching forward;
sepals broadly triangular, toothed at the tips. Leaves ¾–2
in. long, linear. Stems smooth. Fruit a rounded capsule,
⅛–¼ in. long. CT, MA, ME, NH, RI (rare), VT

*Lamium amplexicaule** LAMIACEAE
Henbit, henbit deadnettle
Spring to fall, 4–16 in., annual. Fields
and open, disturbed sites.

Flowers red or purple, ½–¾ in. long, clustered in upper
axillary whorls, underlain by clasping leaves; the flowers long-tubed, often purple-spotted, with a hairy upper
lip and a notched lower lip, the sepals pointed forward.
Lower leaves to ¾ in. long, oval, long-petioled, with scalloped edges; the upper leaves smaller, sessile or clasping.
Stems smooth or hairy, weak. Fruit oval, capsulelike, 1/16
in. long. Native to Eurasia and North Africa. CT, MA, ME,
NH, RI, VT

Lamium purpureum⁎ LAMIACEAE
Red dead-nettle, purple deadnettle
Spring to fall, 4–16 in., annual. Fields
and open, disturbed sites.

Flowers red or purple, ⅜–¾ in. long, clustered in
upper stem whorls among crowded, short-petioled,
purple-tinged leaves; the flowers long-tubed, often
purple-spotted, with a hairy upper lip and a notched
lower lip, the sepals spreading outward. Lower leaves
½–1¼ in. long, rounded, long-petioled, shallowly toothed;
the upper leaves smaller, short-petioled. Stems hairy,
weak. Fruit capsulelike, ¹⁄₁₆ in. long. Native to Eurasia. CT,
MA, ME, NH, RI, VT

Mentha spicata⁎ LAMIACEAE
Spearmint
Summer and early fall, 12–36 in., perennial.
Wet fields, ditches, and roadsides.

Flowers pink or pale violet, ⅛ in. long, arranged in
dense, branching spikes 1½–4 in. long; the stamens
long-protruding. Leaves 1–3½ in. long, lance-shaped or
oval, sessile, sharply toothed, strongly aromatic. Stems
smooth. Fruit capsulelike, ¹⁄₁₆ in. long. Native to Europe.
CT, MA, ME, NH, RI, VT

Monarda didyma⁎ LAMIACEAE
Bee-balm, scarlet bee-balm, Oswego tea
Summer, 2–5 ft., perennial. Thickets,
roadsides, and open, disturbed sites.

Flowers bright scarlet, 1¼–1¾ in. long, slender, 2-lipped,
clustered on bristly heads; the whorled, leafy bracts
beneath the flower heads red. Leaves 3–6 in. long,
lance-shaped or oval, dark green, on petioles ½–1½ in.
long. Stems hairy. Fruit capsulelike, ¹⁄₁₆–⅛ in. long.
Native to much of eastern United States, introduced in
New England. CT, MA, ME, NH, VT

Monarda fistulosa LAMIACEAE
Wild bergamot, wild bee-balm
Summer, 2–4 ft., perennial. Dry fields,
thickets, and woodland clearings.

Flowers pale pink or lilac, ⅜–1¼ in. long, slender,
2-lipped, hairy, densely clustered on bristly heads; the
whorled, leafy bracts beneath the flower heads tinged
with pink. Leaves 1½–4½ in. long, lance-shaped,
gray-green, on petioles about ½ in. long, strongly aromatic when bruised. Fruit capsulelike, ¹/₁₆ in. long. CT,
MA, ME, NH, VT

Physostegia virginiana LAMIACEAE
False dragonhead, obedience-plant
Summer, 1–5 ft., perennial. Floodplains, freshwater
shorelines, and bottomland thickets.

Flowers pink or rose-purple, ¾–1½ in. long, arranged
in spikelike racemes 2–8 in. long; the flowers broadly
2-lipped, the lower lip purple-spotted. Leaves 1–7 in. long,
lance-shaped, sharply toothed, mostly sessile. Fruit capsulelike, ⅛ in. long. Flowers "obediently" stay in place if
rotated on the raceme. Native in ME, VT; introduced in CT,
MA, NH, RI.

Stachys hispida (S. tenuifolia var. hispida) LAMIACEAE
Hispid hedge-nettle
Summer, 1½–3 ft., perennial. Swamps,
floodplains, and lake and river shores.

Flowers lavender or white, ½–¾ in. long, arranged in
whorled terminal and axillary clusters; the lower lip
broad, purple-spotted, the upper hoodlike; the calyx hairs
all nonglandular. Leaves 1½–5 in. long, lance-shaped or
narrowly oval, sessile or short-petioled. Stems square,
with hairs only on the angles. Fruit capsulelike, ¹/₁₆ in.
long. CT, MA, ME, NH, RI (rare), VT

Stachys palustris ⁘   LAMIACEAE
Marsh hedge-nettle, woundwort
Summer, 1–3 ft., perennial. Fields, river and lake shores, and roadsides.

Flowers rose-pink or purple, ½–¾ in. long, arranged in whorled clusters in leaf axils and top of stem; the lower lip broad, purple-spotted, the upper hoodlike; the calyx hairs glandular and nonglandular, both types of equal length. Leaves 1½–3½ in. long, triangular or lance-shaped, sessile or short-petioled. Stems square, entirely hairy. Fruit capsulelike, ¹⁄₁₆ in. long. Native to Europe. CT, MA, ME, NH, RI, VT

Stachys pilosa (hairy hedge-nettle) is very similar, but the flowers are usually light pink or light purple, and the nonglandular calyx hairs are much longer than the glandular hairs. Grows in fields, thickets, and wetland edges. CT, MA, ME, NH, RI, VT

Teucrium canadense   LAMIACEAE
American germander
Summer, 1–3 ft., perennial. Fresh and tidal marshes, beach fronts, and lake and river shores.

Flowers pink or purple, ½–¾ in. long, clustered in narrow racemes; the lower lip broad, protuberant, scoop-shaped; the stamens erect. Leaves 2–5 in. long, lance-shaped or oval, downy. Stems hairy. Fruit capsulelike, ¹⁄₁₆ in. long. CT, MA, ME, NH, RI, VT

Chelone lyonii ⁘ (*C. lyoni*) PLANTAGINACEAE
Pink turtlehead
Summer and early fall, 12–28 in., perennial. Wet thickets.

Flowers rose-pink, 1–1½ in. long, clustered in a short, compact spike; the upper lip broad, arching, the lower lip tonguelike, cleft at the tip and yellow-bearded in the center. Leaves 2½–5 in. long, oval, sharply toothed, long-petioled. Fruit a capsule. Native to southeastern United States, a garden escape in New England. CT, MA, ME

Phryma leptostachya   PHRYMACEAE
Lopseed
Midsummer to early fall, 1–3 ft., perennial.
Rich deciduous forests and woodlands.

Flowers pink or whitish, ¼ in. long, arranged in spreading pairs on long, leafless spikes; the flowers tubular,
with a notched upper lip and a lobed lower lip. Leaves 2–6
in. long, the larger broadly oval, long-petioled, coarsely
toothed. Fruit an elliptical achene, ⅛–¼ in. long; the
fruits paired, drooping along upper stem. CT, MA, NH,
RI, VT

Polygala cruciata   POLYGALACEAE
Whorled milkwort, drum-heads milkwort
Summer, 4–12 in., annual. Damp, sandy or peaty soils
of pond shores, swamps, and bogs near coast.

Flowers pink, rose, or greenish, ⅛–¼ in. wide, clustered in dense, cylindrical heads ½–2½ in. long and
½ in. thick; the individual flowers with triangular,
sharp-pointed wings. Leaves ½–1½ in. long, linear or
narrowly lance-shaped, in whorls of 3 or 4. Fruit a capsule, ⅛ in. long. CT (rare), MA, RI (rare)

*Impatiens glandulifera**   BALSAMINACEAE
**Ornamental jewelweed, Himalayan balsam, Himalaya
touch-me-not**
Summer, 2–6 ft., annual. Floodplains, wet
meadows, and ditches. Invasive.

Flowers magenta, pink, or occasionally white, 1½ in.
long, suspended on long, slender stalks; the lower lip
broadly lobed and spreading; the upper lip upright; the
body tubular, with a short, hooked spur. Leaves 2½–6 in.
long, lance-shaped, whorled or opposite, long-petioled;
dark glands present on leaf nodes, petioles, and teeth
tips. Stems hollow, succulent. Fruit a ridged, elliptical
capsule, ½–1 in. long. Native to Himalayan region. CT,
MA, ME, NH, VT

Amerorchis rotundifolia (*Orchis rotundifolia*)
ORCHIDACEAE
Round-leaved orchid, one-leaf orchis
Late spring and early summer, 4–10 in., perennial. Rich
swamps and fens, usually shaded by northern white cedar.

Flowers pink, white, or mauve, ½–¾ in. long, arranged
in a short, loosely flowered spike; the purple-spotted lip
with 2 spreading lateral lobes and a long terminal lobe
widened at the tip. Single basal leaf 1½–4½ in. long, oval
or rounded. Stems slender, smooth. Fruit an elliptical
capsule, ⅝ in. long. Northern ME (rare)

Calopogon tuberosus (*C. pulchellus*)
ORCHIDACEAE
Grass pink, tuberous grass-pink
Early summer, 5–30 in., perennial.
Bogs, fens, and wet meadows.

Flowers magenta, occasionally white, 1–1½ in. wide,
arranged in a loosely flowered raceme; the lip erect,
crested with white or yellow-tipped hairs; the sepals
spreading, winglike. Basal leaf 2–18 in. long, linear or
narrowly lance-shaped. Stems smooth. Fruit an elliptical
capsule, ½–1¼ in. long. CT, MA, ME, NH, RI, VT

Calypso bulbosa   ORCHIDACEAE
Calypso
Spring, 4–8 in., perennial. Cold, coniferous
swamps, often with northern white cedar.

Flowers pink or pale purple, ¾–1½ in. long, usually solitary, occasionally 2; the lip with a slipperlike, purple-lined
pouch and a white, yellow-bearded apron; the sepals and
upper petals spreading above the lip. Single basal leaf
broadly oval or rounded, ½–2½ in. long and wide. Stems
smooth. Fruit an elliptical capsule, 1 in. long. ME, VT
(rare)

Cypripedium acaule ORCHIDACEAE
Pink lady's-slipper, moccasin flower
Midspring to early summer, 6–20 in., perennial. Deciduous
and mixed forests, occasionally in bogs and swamp edges.

Flowers pink or red, occasionally white, 2½–4 in. long,
solitary, rarely 2; the slipperlike pouch inflated, veined,
fissured in the center; sepals and upper petals green or
purple-bronze, slender, spreading. Basal leaves 4–12 in.
long, paired, oval, strongly ribbed. Stems hairy. Fruit an
elliptical capsule, 1¼–1¾ in. long. CT, MA, ME, NH, RI, VT

Galearis spectabilis (Orchis spectabilis)
ORCHIDACEAE
Showy orchid, showy orchis
Spring, 4–8 in., perennial. Rich deciduous forests.

Flowers bicolored pink and white, 1 in. long, arranged in
a leafy, loosely flowered raceme; the sepals and lateral petals fused into a pink or mauve hood above the apronlike,
white lip. Basal leaves 3–8 in. long, paired, oval, shining, with sheathing bases. Stems smooth, fleshy. Fruit an
elliptical capsule, ¾–1 in. long. CT (rare), MA (rare), ME
(rare), NH (rare), VT

Apios americana FABACEAE
Ground-nut
Midsummer to early fall, 1–4 ft. long, perennial vine.
Damp thickets, shorelines, and wetland edges.

Flowers maroon or chocolate-colored, ½ in. long,
arranged in compact racemes; the upper petals forming a
cowl over the coiled central petal and winglike lower petals. Leaves long-petioled, pinnately divided into 5–7 oval,
pointed leaflets 1½–2½ in. long. Stems hairy or smooth,
twining, trailing or climbing. Fruit a narrow pod, 2–4 in.
long. CT, MA, ME, NH, RI, VT

Desmodium canadense   FABACEAE
Showy tick-trefoil, Canada tick-trefoil
Mid to late summer, 2–6 ft., perennial. Fields,
thickets, woodlands, and roadsides.

Flowers rose-purple, ½ in. long, arranged in long
racemes. Leaves short-petioled, 3-parted; the 3 leaflets
lance-shaped or narrowly oval, 2–3½ in. long, with flattened hairs underneath; stipules at base of leaf petioles
linear, ¼ in. long. Stems hairy, often striated with purplish lines. Fruit a sticky-hairy pod with 3–5 joints. CT,
MA, ME, NH, RI, VT

Desmodium canescens   FABACEAE
Hoary tick-trefoil
Mid to late summer, 2–5 ft., perennial. Dry
woodlands, fields, and roadsides.

Flowers pink, greenish in late bloom, ¼–½ in. long,
arranged in racemes. Leaves long-petioled, 3-parted; the 3
leaflets lance-shaped or oval, 2–4½ in. long, with hooked
hairs underneath; stipules at base of leaf petioles oval,
persistent, ¼–½ in. long. Stems much branching, with
spreading hairs. Fruit a sticky-hairy pod with 4–6 joints.
CT, MA (rare), RI

Desmodium ciliare   FABACEAE
Hairy small-leaved tick-trefoil, small-leaved tick-trefoil
Mid to late summer, 1–3 ft., perennial.
Dry woodlands and forest edges.

Flowers rose-purple, ¼ in. long, long-stalked; loosely
arranged on long, spreading branches. Leaves
short-petioled, 3-parted; the 3 leaflets blunt, hairy on
both surfaces, oval, ⅜–1¼ in. long; the stipules at base
leaf petioles linear, not persistent, ⅛–¼ in. long. Stems
with spreading hairs. Fruit a hairy pod with 1–3 joints.
CT, MA, RI (rare)
   Desmodium obtusum (stiff tick-trefoil) is similar, but
the terminal leaflets are larger (1½–2½ in. long), distinctly longer than the lateral leaflets, and the stems have
hooked rather than spreading hairs. Grows in dry woodlands and forest edges. CT, MA, RI

308

Desmodium cuspidatum   FABACEAE
Large-bracted tick-trefoil
Midsummer to early fall, 1–4 ft., perennial. Rocky
woodlands, thickets, and overgrown fields.

Flowers pink, ¼–½ in. long, arranged in sparse racemes.
Leaves long-petioled, 3-parted; the 3
leaflets oval, pointed at tip, pale underneath, 2–5 in. long; stipules at base of
leaf petioles lance-shaped, persistent,
⅜–¾ in. long. Stems smooth or slightly
hairy. Fruit a pod, hairy on edges, with
3–7 narrow joints. CT, MA, RI, VT (rare
in all)

Desmodium marilandicum   FABACEAE
Smooth small-leaved tick-trefoil
Mid to late summer, 2–4 ft., perennial.
Dry woodlands and forest edges.

Flowers pink or rose, ¼ in. long, long-stalked, arranged
in loosely flowered racemes. Leaves long-petioled,
3-parted; the 3 leaflets oval, blunt at tip, mostly or entirely
smooth, dark green, ½–1½ in. long; stipules at base of
leaf petioles linear, not persistent, ⅛–¼ in. long. Stems
smooth. Fruit a downy pod with 1–3 joints. CT, MA, NH
(rare), RI

Desmodium paniculatum   FABACEAE
Panicled tick-trefoil
Mid to late summer, 2–4 ft., perennial. Dry,
deciduous and mixed forests and woodlands.

Flowers pink or rose, ¼ in. long, arranged in loosely flowered, spreading branches. Leaves 3-parted, long-petioled
(½–2 in. long); the 3 leaflets narrowly lance-shaped, ¾–4
in. long and ¼–½ in. wide; the stipules at base of leaf
petioles linear, not persistent, ¼ in. long or less. Stems
smooth. Fruit a downy pod with 3–6 joints. CT, MA, ME,
NH, RI, VT (rare)
   Desmodium sessilifolium (sessile-leaved tick-trefoil),
a very rare species in dry, sandy fields and roadsides, is
similar, but the leaves are sessile or very short-petioled
(¼ in. or less), the stems are hairy, and the pods have 1–3
joints. RI (rare)

Desmodium perplexum (*D. dillenii*) FABACEAE
Perplexed tick-trefoil
Mid to late summer, 1½–4 ft., perennial.
Deciduous and mixed forests and woodlands.

Flowers pink, ¼ in. long, arranged in many-flowered,
divergent racemes. Leaves long-petioled, 3-parted; the
3 leaflets oval, 1–4½ in. long and ½–1¼ in. wide; stip-

ules at base of leaf petioles linear, not
persistent, ⅛–¼ in. long. Stems with
spreading hairs. Fruit a downy pod
with 2–4 segments. CT, MA, ME, NH,
RI, VT (rare)

Desmodium glabellum (smooth
tick-trefoil), a very rare species that
grows in woodlands, is very similar, but has hooked hairs
on the stems and petioles (*D. perplexum* has straight,
spreading hairs on the stems and petioles). CT (rare)

Desmodium rotundifolium FABACEAE
Prostrate tick-trefoil, dollar-leaf
Midsummer to early fall, to 3 ft. long, perennial. Rocky
deciduous and mixed forests and woodlands.

Flowers pink or rose, ⅜ in. long, arranged in sparse
racemes. Leaves long-petioled, 3-parted; the 3 leaflets
rounded, 1–2½ in. long; the stipules at the base of the leaf
petioles oval, ⅜ in. long. Stems prostrate, creeping, hairy.
Fruit a hairy, jointed pod with 3–6 segments. CT, MA, NH
(rare), RI, VT (rare)

Kummerowia striata✼ (*Lespedeza striata*)
FABACEAE
Japanese-clover
Summer, 2–16 in., annual. Fields,
roadsides, and sandy pond shores.

Flowers bicolored pink and white, ¼ in. long, arranged
in axillary clusters of 1–3 flowers. Leaves short-petioled,
3-parted; the 3 leaflets oval, with pointed tips and distinct parallel veins, ¼–1 in. long; the stipules at the base
of the leaf petioles lance-shaped, striated, ⅛ in. long.
Stem hairs point downwards. Fruit a tiny pod, ⅛ in. long.
Native to East Asia. CT, MA

310

Lathyrus japonicus (*L. maritimus*) FABACEAE
Beach pea, beach vetchling
Summer and early fall, 1–4 ft. long, perennial.
Coastal beaches, dunes, and tidal marshes;
also on shores of Lake Champlain.

Flowers rose-purple, violet, or blue, ½–1 in. long,
arranged in stalked clusters of 3–10 flowers. Leaves pinnately divided into 4–16 leaflets; the leaflets fleshy, oval or
elliptic, ½–2 in. long; the stipules at the base of the leaf
petioles broadly oval or triangular, with a broad, clasping base. Stems smooth or hairy, semierect or sprawling,
twining. Fruit a pod, 1–2½ in. long and ¼–½ in. wide.
CT, MA, ME, NH, RI, VT (rare)

Lathyrus latifolius⁕ FABACEAE
Everlasting pea, everlasting vetchling
Summer and fall, 2–6 ft. long, perennial
vine. Fields, thickets, and roadsides.

Flowers rose-pink, occasionally white, ¾–1¼ in. long,
arranged in dense clusters of 4–10 flowers. Leaves
2-parted; the leaflets thick, lance-shaped or oval, 1½–3½
in. long; stipules at base of leaf
petioles lance-shaped, 1–1½ in.
long. Stems smooth, sprawling
or climbing, broadly winged,
twining. Fruit a narrow pod, 2–4
in. long. Native to Europe. CT,
MA, ME, NH, RI, VT

Lathyrus palustris FABACEAE
Marsh vetchling, marsh pea
Summer and early fall, 1–4 ft. long, perennial vine.
Wet meadows, river shores, and tidal marshes.

Flowers red-purple, ½–¾ in. long, arranged in short
racemes of 3–6 flowers. Leaves pinnately divided into
4–10 leaflets; the leaflets linear or elliptic, not fleshy, 1–3
in. long; the stipules at the base of the leaf petioles narrowly lance-shaped, much smaller than the leaflets, the
bases split into 2 narrow, clasping divisions. Stems hairy,
climbing or reclining, twining, sometimes narrowly
winged. Fruit a pod, 1½–2½ in. long and ⅜–½ in. wide.
CT, MA, ME, NH, RI, VT (rare)

311

Lespedeza frutescens (*L. violacea*)
FABACEAE
Violet bush-clover
Midsummer to early fall, 1–3 ft., perennial.
Dry, rocky woodlands and ledges.

Flowers pink, red, or purple, ¼–⅜ in. long, arranged in branching, sparsely flowered racemes longer than the leaves. Leaves long-petioled, 3-parted; the 3 leaflets oval, ½–1½ in. long and about ½ as wide, finely hairy on the undersurface; the terminal leaflet long-stalked. Stems smooth or sparsely hairy. Fruit a finely hairy, broadly oval pod, ⅛–¼ in. long. CT, MA (rare), NH, RI, VT (rare)

Lespedeza procumbens FABACEAE
Trailing bush-clover
Late summer and early fall, 1–4 ft. long, perennial.
Dry woodlands, ledges, and roadsides.

Flowers pink or violet, ¼–⅜ in. long, arranged in erect racemes with 8–12 flowers, the racemes 1–3½ in. long. Leaves 3-parted; the 3 leaflets rounded or oval, hairy, ⅜–1 in. long. Stems prostrate, trailing; the stem hairs spreading. Fruit a broadly oval pod, ⅛–¼ in. long. CT, MA, NH (rare), RI, VT (rare)

Lespedeza repens (creeping bush clover) is very similar, but the stem hairs are flattened, not spreading, and the racemes have 4–8 flowers. Grows in dry, rocky woodlands. CT (rare)

Lespedeza stuevei FABACEAE
Velvety bush-clover, tall bush-clover
Late summer and early fall, 2–4 ft., perennial.
Sandy woodlands, clearings, and roadsides.

Flowers pink, red, or purple, ¼ in. long, arranged in short, dense, axillary racemes of 4–14 flowers. Leaves 3-parted; the 3 leaflets oval or elliptic, ½–1½ in. long, the upper surface hairy and the lower woolly-velvety. Stems densely downy. Fruit a hairy, broadly oval pod, ¼ in. long. CT, MA (rare), RI

Lespedeza violacea (*L. intermedia*) FABACEAE
Wand bush-clover
Midsummer to early fall, 1–3 ft., perennial. Old
fields, dry woodlands, and open ledges.

Flowers pink or purple, ¼ in. long, arranged in short,
axillary racemes of 4–14 flowers. Leaves 3-parted; the 3
leaflets oval, ½–1½ in. long, the
upper surface smooth and the lower
surface hairy. Stems with flattened
hairs. Fruit a hairy, broadly oval
pod, ¼ in. long. CT, MA (rare), ME,
NH, RI, VT

Lespedeza virginica FABACEAE
Slender bush-clover
Late summer and early fall, 1–4 ft., perennial.
Dry woodlands and clearings.

Flowers pink, red, or purple, ¼ in. long, arranged in
short, dense, axillary racemes of 4–14 flowers. Leaves
erect or ascending, 3-parted; the 3 leaflets narrowly
lance-shaped, ½–1½ in. long and ⅛–¼ in. wide. Stems
upright, finely hairy. Fruit a broad, finely hairy pod, ⅛–¼
in. long. CT, MA, NH (rare), RI

Securigera varia✳ (*Coronilla varia*) FABACEAE
Crown vetch, purple crown-vetch
Spring and summer, 1–3 ft., perennial. Fields,
roadsides, and open, disturbed sites.

Flowers bicolored pink and white, ⅜ in. long, densely
clustered in cloverlike heads 1–1½ in. wide. Leaves pinnately divided, with 11–25 leaflets; the leaflets ½–¾ in.
long, oval or oblong, with tiny spires at the tips. Stems
smooth or hairy, creeping, densely colonial. Fruit a linear
pod, 1–3 in. long, with 3–7 joints. Native to Eurasia and
North Africa. Often planted on roadsides for erosion control. CT, MA, ME, NH, RI, VT

Strophostyles helvola (S. helvula) FABACEAE
Trailing wild bean, annual woolly bean
Summer and fall, to 6 ft. long, annual vine. Sea beaches and sandy thickets near coast.

Flowers pink or greenish purple, ½ in. long, arranged in stalked, axillary, few-flowered clusters; a hornlike projection on lower petal curls back into flaring upper petal. Leaves long-petioled, 3-parted; the 3 leaflets oval, ¾–2¼ in. long, often with 1 or 2 bulging lobes; the terminal leaflet longer-stalked than the lateral leaflets. Stems smooth or hairy, twining, trailing or climbing. Fruit a linear, finely hairy pod, 1½–3 in. long. CT, MA, ME, RI

Trifolium arvense✻ FABACEAE
Rabbit-foot clover
Spring to fall, 4–16 in., annual or biennial. Dry fields, roadsides, and disturbed, sparsely vegetated sites.

Flowers grayish pink, ¼ in. long, densely aggregated into fuzzy, cylindrical, stalked heads ½–1½ in. long and ½ in. wide. Leaves 3-parted; the 3 leaflets narrowly oval, silky-hairy, ½–1 in. long. Stems hairy, branching. Fruit a tiny, oval pod, 1/16 in. long or less. Native to Eurasia. CT, MA, ME, NH, RI, VT

Vicia sativa✻ (V. angustifolia) FABACEAE
Common vetch, narrow-leaved vetch
Summer, 1–3 ft. long, annual vine. Fields, river and lake shores, and roadsides.

Flowers red-purple, ¾–1¼ in. long, single or paired in the leaf axils. Leaves pinnately divided into 8–16 leaflets; the leaflets linear or narrowly oblong, ¾–1¼ in. long, with a tiny spine at the tip. Stems hairy or smooth, climbing or scrambling. Fruit a flattish pod, 1–3 in. long. Native to Europe. CT, MA, ME, NH, RI, VT

Trifolium hybridum* FABACEAE
Alsike clover
Spring to fall, 6–24 in., perennial. Fields,
roadsides, and open, disturbed sites.

Flowers pink and creamy white, fragrant, ¼ in. long,
densely aggregated into long-stalked, rounded heads
½–1 in. long and about as wide. Leaves 3-parted; the 3
leaflets oval, ½–1¼ in. long, narrowing to tip, without
white markings; the broad stipules at the base of petioles spreading, with long-tapering tips. Stems smooth or
hairy. Fruit a pod, ⅛ in. long. Native to Eurasia. CT, MA,
ME, NH, RI, VT

Trifolium incarnatum* FABACEAE
Crimson clover
Spring and summer, 6–30 in., annual. Fields,
roadsides, and open, disturbed sites.

Flowers bright crimson, ⅜ in. long, densely aggregated
into long-stalked, cylindrical heads 1½–2½ in. long.
Leaves 3-parted; the 3 leaflets broadly wedge-shaped,
⅜–1¼ in. long, hairy, rounded at the tip, narrowing to the
base; the stipules at base of petioles mostly attached to
the stem, sheathing, with blunt tips. Stems hairy. Fruit a
pod, ⅛ in. long. Native to Europe. CT, MA, ME, NH, RI, VT

Trifolium pratense* FABACEAE
Red clover
Spring to fall, 10–30 in., perennial. Fields,
roadsides, and open, disturbed sites.

Flowers red, ½–¾ in. long, aggregated into short-stalked,
oval or rounded heads 1–1½ in. long and about 1 in. wide.
Leaves 3-parted; the 3 leaflets oval, marked with white
chevron stripes, ⅜–1¼ in., very finely toothed; the stipules at base of petioles sheathing, free only at the sharp,
narrow tips. Stems hairy. Fruit a pod, 1/16–⅛ in. long.
Native to Europe. CT, MA, ME, NH, RI, VT

Castilleja coccinea OROBANCHACEAE
Indian paintbrush, painted cup, scarlet painted cup
Early spring to summer, 8–24 in., annual or biennial. Fields and wet meadows in high-pH soils.

Actual flowers yellowish green, tubular, ¾–1 in. long, clustered in short, dense spikes, mostly surrounded and concealed by the broad, scarlet, flowerlike bracts. Stem leaves to 3 in. long, divided into 3–5 deeply cut, narrow lobes; basal leaves entire. Stems hairy. Fruit an oval capsule, ¼–⅜ in. long. CT (rare)

Capnoides sempervirens (*Corydalis sempervirens*)
PAPAVERACEAE
Pink corydalis, pale corydalis
Spring to early fall, 12–32 in., biennial. Rocky woodlands, bald summits, and open ledges.

Flowers pink, ½–¾ in. long, with upturned yellow lips and a short spur, arranged in branched, nodding clusters of 1–8. Leaves finely and deeply divided, pale green; the leaflets ¼–¾ in. long. Stems smooth. Fruit an erect, linear capsule, 1¼–2 in. long. CT, MA, ME, NH, RI, VT

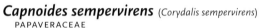

Fumaria officinalis ✳ PAPAVERACEAE
Common fumitory, earth-smoke
Spring and summer, 8–32 in., annual. Fields and roadsides.

Flowers pink-purple, ¼–½ in. long, with maroon tips and a short spur, arranged in many-flowered racemes. Leaves finely and deeply divided, grayish green; the leaflets ⅛–½ in. long. Stems smooth, erect or reclining. Fruit a rounded capsule, ⅛ in. long. Native to Eurasia. CT, MA, ME, NH, RI, VT

Leonurus cardiaca* LAMIACEAE
Motherwort
Summer, 2–5 ft., perennial. Fields,
thickets, and woodland edges.

Flowers pink or whitish, ¼–½ in. long, arranged in interrupted, axillary whorls from the middle to upper stem;
the upper lip prominent, densely hairy, hoodlike. Lower
leaves 2–4 in. long, sharply toothed, broadly divided into
3–5 sharp-pointed lobes; the upper leaves smaller, with
narrowed bases and trident-shaped tips. Stems hairy or
smooth. Fruit capsulelike, ⅟16 in. long. Native to Europe.
CT, MA, ME, NH, RI, VT

Hylodesmum glutinosum (*Desmodium*
glutinosum) FABACEAE
Pointed-leaved tick-trefoil
Summer, 1–4 ft., perennial. Rocky
deciduous and mixed forests.

Flowers pink or rose, ¼–⅜ in. long;
arranged in a solitary, long-stalked,
erect raceme, 12–32 in. long, extending from the axil of the leaves. Leaves
3-parted, long-petioled, whorled
below the long flower stalk; the terminal leaflet oval, 2½–7 in. long, the
lateral leaflets shorter and narrower.

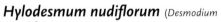

Stems hairy. Fruit a pod with 1–4 joints. CT, MA, ME, NH,
RI, VT

Hylodesmum nudiflorum (*Desmodium*
nudiflorum) FABACEAE
Naked-flowered tick-trefoil, cluster-leaved tick-trefoil
Summer, 1–3 ft., perennial. Rocky
deciduous and mixed forests.

Flowers pink or rose, ¼–⅜ in. long, arranged in a solitary, loose, leafless raceme, 16–40 in. long, rising from
the ground separate from the leaves. Leaves long-petioled,
3-parted, whorled at top of leaf stalk; the terminal leaflet broadly oval, 2–4 in. long, the lateral leaflets slightly
smaller. Stems hairy or smooth. Fruit a pod with 1–4
joints. CT, MA, ME, NH, RI, VT

Flowers bilateral; leaves deeply divided,
opposite, leaflets toothed or lobed

Flowers bilateral; leaves deeply
divided, whorled, leaflets entire

Flowers bilateral; leaves deeply
divided, basal, leaflets entire

Arethusa bulbosa   ORCHIDACEAE
Dragon's-mouth, arethusa
Mid to late spring, 4–12 in., perennial. Bogs, wet meadows, and conifer swamps.

Flowers pink or magenta, 1½–3 in. long, solitary, rarely 2; the lip white, purple-streaked, bearded with white or yellow hairs; the sepals erect and the upper petals arching. Leaf grasslike, 2–8 in. long; develops after the blooming period. Stems smooth, with several scaly bracts. Fruit an oval capsule, ¾–1 in. long. MA (rare), ME, NH (rare), RI (rare), VT (rare)

Corallorhiza maculata   ORCHIDACEAE
Spotted coral-root
Summer, 8–20 in., perennial. Deciduous, mixed, and coniferous forests, usually with dry soils.

Flowers pink-purple and white, ½ in. long, arranged in a long, narrow raceme; the lip purple-spotted, ¼ in. long, the sepals and upper petals spreading. Stems smooth, purplish, with a few scaly bracts pressed close to the stem. Fruit a drooping, narrowly oval capsule, ⅜–1 in. long. Roots saprophytic on decaying organic matter. CT, MA, ME, NH, RI (rare), VT

Corallorhiza odontorhiza   ORCHIDACEAE
Fall coral-root; autumn coral-root
Late summer to fall, 4–8 in., perennial. Deciduous and mixed forests, often with high-pH soil.

Flowers purplish, white, or yellowish, ¼ in. long, arranged in a narrow raceme; the lip purple-margined and spotted, 1⁄16–⅛ in. long, the sepals and upper petals spreading forward over the lip. Stems smooth, usually brownish or purplish, with a few scaly bracts pressed close to the stem. Fruit a drooping, oval capsule, ¼–⅜ in. long. Roots saprophytic on decaying organic matter. CT, MA (rare), ME (rare), RI (rare), NH (rare), VT (rare)

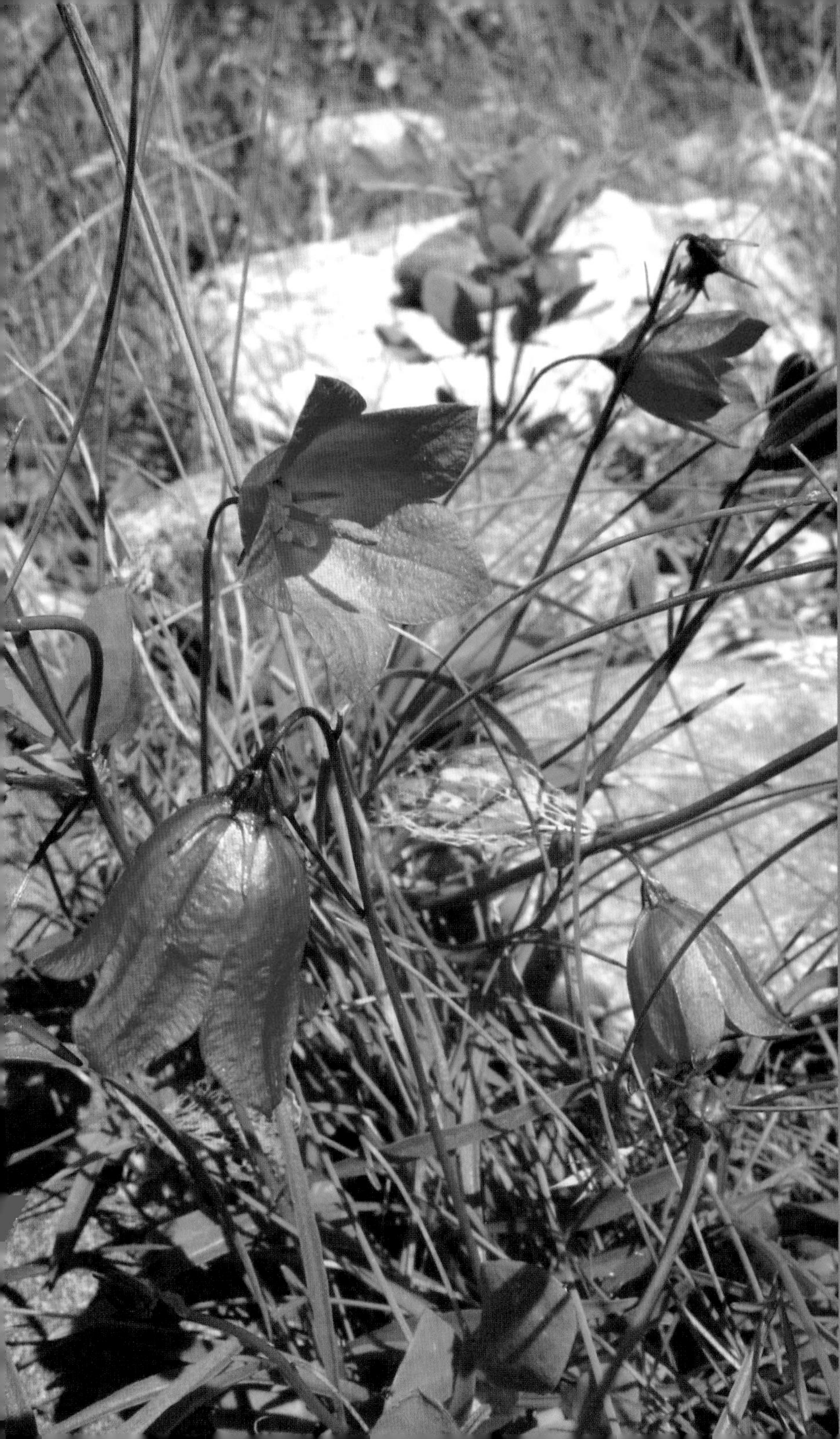

Tradescantia ohiensis COMMELINACEAE
Smooth spiderwort, widow's-tears
Spring, 1–3 ft., perennial. Fields, clearings, and roadsides.

Flowers blue or rose-purple, 1–1½ in. wide, with smooth stalks and sepals; the flowers arranged in terminal clusters, underlain by leafy, sharp-pointed bracts. Leaves 2–18 in. long, linear or lance-shaped, light green, sheathing the stem. Stems smooth, with a whitish bloom. Fruit an oval capsule, ¼ in. long. Native populations in CT, MA; introduced in ME, NH, RI, VT

Tradescantia virginiana COMMELINACEAE
Virginia spiderwort, cow-slobber
Spring, 4–16 in., perennial. Fields, clearings, and roadsides.

Flowers blue or rose-purple, 1 in. wide, with hairy stalks and sepals; the flowers arranged in terminal clusters, underlain by leafy, sharp-pointed bracts. Leaves 5–15 in. long, linear or lance-shaped, sheathing the stem. Stems smooth or sparsely hairy, without a whitish bloom. Fruit an oval capsule, ¼ in. long. Native to much of eastern and central United States, introduced in New England. CT, MA, ME, NH, RI, VT

Iris prismatica IRIDACEAE
Slender blue flag, slender blue iris
Spring and early summer, 1–3 ft., perennial. Tidal marshes and meadows, and freshwater marshes near coast.

Flowers blue-purple, 2½–3 in. wide, solitary or in few-flowered clusters; the 3 sepals spreading, white-blotched, purple-veined, the 3 petals smaller, erect, 1½–2 in. long. Leaves 12–28 in. long and ¼ in. wide, flat, linear. Stems smooth. Fruit a sharply 3-ridged oval capsule, 1¼–2 in. long. CT, MA, ME (rare), NH (rare), RI

Iris versicolor   IRIDACEAE
Northern blue flag, northern blue iris
Spring and early summer, 4–32 in., perennial.
Marshes, wet meadows, river and lake shores.

Flowers blue-purple, 4 in. wide, solitary or in few-flowered clusters; the 3 sepals spreading, white-blotched and purple-veined, the 3 petals smaller, erect, 1–2 in. long. Leaves 1–3 ft. long and ⅜–1¼ in. wide, flat, linear or lance-shaped. Stems smooth. Fruit a bluntly ridged, oval capsule, ¾–2½ in. long. CT, MA, ME, NH, RI, VT

Iris hookeri (beach-head iris, Arctic blue flag), limited to beaches in northern ME, has bristle-tipped petals only ½ in. long, much smaller than the sepals, and the petal bases are folded in.

Cakile edentula   BRASSICACEAE
Sea rocket
Summer and early fall, 4–32 in., annual. Sea beaches.

Flowers blue, pale purple, or white, ¼ in. wide, arranged in racemes in upper leaf axils. Leaves fleshy, 2½–5 in. long, coarsely and irregularly toothed. Stems smooth, succulent, bushy, often sprawling. Fruit an oval pod, ½–1 in. long, constricted in the middle, the basal portion narrowed. CT, MA, ME, NH, RI

Gentianopsis crinita (*Gentiana crinita*)
GENTIANACEAE
Greater fringed gentian, fringed gentian
Late summer to fall, 12–32 in., annual or biennial. Wet meadows, fens, and thickets.

Flowers violet-blue, 1½–2¼ in. long, funnel-shaped, with conspicuously fringed petals, arranged singly on long, erect stalks. Leaves 1¼–2½ in. long, oval or lance-shaped, sessile. Stems smooth, often branching. Fruit an elliptical capsule, about 1½ in. long. CT, MA, ME, NH (rare), RI (rare), VT (rare)

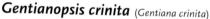

3 radial petals; leaves simple, alternate, entire

4 radial petals; leaves simple, alternate, toothed or lobed

4 radial petals; leaves simple, opposite, entire

Halenia deflexa   GENTIANACEAE
American spurred gentian, spurred gentian
Summer, 8–30 in., annual. Moist forests and thickets.

Flowers greenish purple, ½ in. long, mostly closed, the petals with pointed tips, arranged in compact clusters on upper stem; 4 conspicuous spurs spread downwards from the base of the flowers. Leaves 1–2 in. long, lance-shaped or oval, sessile or very short petioled. Stems smooth. Fruit a narrowly oval capsule, ¼ in. long. MA, ME, NH, VT (rare in all)

Houstonia caerulea (*Hedyotis caerulea*)
RUBIACEAE
Little bluet, bluets, Quaker-ladies
Spring to fall, 2–7 in., perennial. Forests, woodlands, ledges, and fields.

Flowers pale blue or whitish, yellow in center, ⅜–½ in. wide, with spreading petals, arranged singly on slender stalks. Leaves ¼–½ in. long, mostly at base, long-petioled, narrowly oval or spoon-shaped. Stems smooth or slightly hairy. Fruit a 2-parted capsule, ¹⁄₁₆–⅛ in. long. CT, MA, ME, NH, RI, VT

Houstonia longifolia (*Hedyotis longifolia*)
RUBIACEAE
Long-leaved bluets
Summer, 2–8 in., perennial. Dry fields, ledges, gravel banks, quarries, and roadsides.

Flowers lavender or white, without a yellow center, ¼–⅜ in. wide, the petals recurved at the tips; the flowers arranged in small, stalked clusters on upper stems. Leaves ⅜–1¼ in. long, linear or lance-shaped, all along stem, sessile. Stems smooth or slightly hairy. Fruit a 2-parted capsule, ¹⁄₁₆–⅛ in. long. CT, MA, ME, NH, VT (rare in all)

4 radial petals; leaves deeply divided, opposite, leaflets toothed or lobed

5 radial petals; leaves simple, alternate, entire

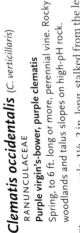

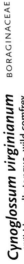

Clematis occidentalis (*C. verticillaris*)
RANUNCULACEAE
Purple virgin's-bower, purple clematis

Spring, to 6 ft. long or more, perennial vine. Rocky woodlands and talus slopes on high-pH rock.

Flowers purple, 1½–2 in. long, stalked from the leaf axils; the petal-like sepals often drooping. Leaves 3-parted, long-petioled; the 3 leaflets oval, pointed, 1½–3 in. long, bluntly toothed or lobed, sometimes entire. Stems climbing or scrambling, woody, hairy. Fruit a tiny achene, densely aggregated into long-silken heads 1½–2 in. wide. CT, MA (rare), ME (rare), NH (rare), RI (rare), VT

Cynoglossum virginianum BORAGINACEAE
Wild hound's-tongue, wild comfrey

Spring and early summer, 16–32 in., perennial. Rich deciduous and mixed forests and woodlands.

Flowers pale blue or whitish, ⅜–½ in. wide, arranged in spreading or nodding, sparse racemes. Basal and lower leaves, 4–8 in. long, oval, long-petioled; the upper leaves progressively smaller, clasping. Stems hairy. Fruit bristly, capsulelike, ¼ in. long. MA, ME, NH, VT (rare in all)

Mertensia maritima BORAGINACEAE
Seaside bluebells, oysterleaf, sea lungwort

Summer, to 3 ft. long, perennial. Stony, gravelly, and sandy sea beaches.

Flowers pink when young, turning blue, bell-shaped, ¼–⅜ in. long, arranged in leafy, compact racemes. Leaves 1–2½ in. long, fleshy, gray-green, broadly oval, with broad petioles and pointed tips. Stems sprawling, often mat-forming. Fruit angular, capsulelike, ⅛–¼ in. long. MA (rare), ME

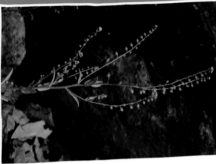

Mertensia virginica ✣ BORAGINACEAE
Eastern bluebells, Virginia bluebells, mertensia

Spring, 12–28 in., perennial. Moist forests and woodlands. Flowers pink when young, turning blue, ¾–1 in. long, tubular, nodding; arranged in coiled racemes. Leaves succulent, oval or spoon-shaped, ¾–2½ in. long, the lower long-petioled. Stems smooth. Fruit bluntly angled, capsulelike, ⅛ in. long. Native to much of eastern and central United States, occasionally naturalized as a garden escape in New England. MA, ME, VT

Myosotis arvensis ✣ BORAGINACEAE
Field forget-me-not

Summer, 4–16 in., annual or biennial. Fields, roadsides, and open, disturbed sites.

Flowers light blue, occasionally white, with yellow centers, ⅛ in. wide, arranged in branching clusters; the petals tilted slightly upwards. Leaves ½–2 in. long, lance-shaped, sessile. Stems densely hairy. Fruit capsulelike, ⅛ in. long. Native to Eurasia. CT, MA, ME, NH, RI, VT

Myosotis laxa BORAGINACEAE
Smaller forget-me-not

Spring and summer, 4–16 in., annual or perennial. Streambanks, seepages, and pond shores.

Flowers light blue with yellow centers, ⅛–¼ in. wide; the long clusters tightly coiled in bud, elongating in full bloom. Leaves ½–3 in. long, lance-shaped or oval. Stems rounded, finely hairy. Fruit capsulelike, ⅟16 in. long. CT, MA, ME, NH, RI, VT (rare)

Myosotis scorpioides* BORAGINACEAE
Water forget-me-not, true forget-me-not
Spring to early fall, 8–24 in., perennial. Streambanks,
shallows, pond shores, and ditches. Invasive.

Flowers light blue with yellow centers, ¼–½ in. wide;
the long clusters tightly coiled in bud, elongating in full
bloom. Leaves 1–3 in. long, lance-shaped or oval. Stems
angular, hairy, with creeping bases, often densely colonial. Fruit capsulelike, ¹⁄₁₆ in. long. Native to Eurasia. CT,
MA, ME, NH, RI, VT

Myosotis stricta* (*M. micrantha*) BORAGINACEAE
Blue forget-me-not, blue scorpion-grass
Early spring to midsummer, 2–8 in., annual.
Fields, roadsides, and open, disturbed sites.

Flowers light blue, without yellow centers, ¹⁄₁₆–⅛ in.
wide; the long racemes tightly coiled in bud, elongating over most of stem in bloom. Leaves hairy, narrowly
oval or spoon-shaped, the largest about 1 in. long. Stems
densely hairy. Fruit capsulelike, ¹⁄₁₆ in. or less. Native to
Eurasia. CT, MA, ME, NH, VT

Myosotis sylvatica* BORAGINACEAE
Garden forget-me-not, woodland forget-me-not
Spring and summer, 8–20 in., perennial. Fields,
woodland edges, and open, disturbed sites.

Flowers light blue, occasionally white, with yellow centers, ¼–⅜ in wide, arranged in crowded racemes; the
petals spreading horizontally. Leaves 1–3 in. long, oval or
lance-shaped, sessile or very short petioled. Stems hairy.
Fruit capsulelike, ¹⁄₁₆ in. long or less. Native to Eurasia.
MA, ME, NH, RI, VT

Campanula rotundifolia CAMPANULACEAE
Scotch bellflower harebell
Summer and early fall, 4–32 in., perennial.
Ledges, dry fields, and rocky summits.

Flowers blue, ¾–1 in. long, bell-shaped, nodding or erect; solitary or in small clusters. Stem leaves linear, sessile, ¾–3 in. long; basal leaves rounded, toothed, usually withered by flowering time. Stems slender, smooth or slightly hairy. Fruit a ridged, nodding capsule, ¼–½ in. long. CT, MA, ME, NH, VT

Ipomoea purpurea⁎ CONVOLVULACEAE
Common morning-glory
Summer and early fall, to 10 ft. long, annual vine.
Fields, roadsides, and open, disturbed sites.

Flowers blue or purple, sometimes red or white, 1½–2½ in. wide, funnel-shaped; sepals hairy, lance-shaped, about ½ in. long. Leaves 2–6 in. long and almost as broad, heart-shaped, notched but not lobed at base; the petioles 1–5 in. long. Stems climbing, hairy. Fruit a rounded capsule, ⅜ in. wide. Native to tropical America. CT, MA, ME, NH, RI, VT

Ipomoea hederacea⁎ (ivy-leaved morning-glory) is similar, but the leaves are deeply cut, with 3 tridentlike lobes, and the sepals are ⅝–1 in. long. Native to tropical America. CT, MA, ME, NH, VT

Linum usitatissimum⁎ LINACEAE
Common flax, cultivated flax
Summer, 1–4 ft., annual. Fields, roadsides, and open, disturbed sites.

Flowers blue, ¾ in. wide, long-stalked, with broad, slightly overlapping petals; arranged in branching, open, leafy racemes. Leaves ¾–1¼ in. long, linear or narrowly lance-shaped, sessile. Stems smooth, grayish green, branching. Fruit a rounded capsule, ¼–¾ in. long. Native to Europe. CT, MA, ME, NH, RI, VT

Campanula aparinoides CAMPANULACEAE
Marsh bellflower
Summer, 8–24 in., perennial. Marshes,
wet meadows, and streambanks.

Flowers pale blue or whitish, ¼–½ in. wide, bell-shaped,
solitary on long, slender, loosely branching stalks. Leaves
⅜–1¼ in. long, linear or lance-shaped, finely toothed.
Stems weak, reclining, with small, rasping prickles. Fruit
an oval capsule, about ⅛ in. long. CT, MA, ME, NH, RI, VT

Campanula rapunculoides*
CAMPANULACEAE
Creeping bellflower, roving bellflower
Summer, 1–3 ft., perennial. Fields, thickets, and roadsides.

Flowers blue or purple, 1–1½ in. long, bell-shaped,
nodding, arranged in long, one-sided racemes. Lower
leaves 2–4 in. long, oval or triangular, coarsely toothed,
long-petioled; the upper smaller, short-petioled or sessile. Stems smooth or slightly hairy. Fruit an oval capsule,
¼–½ in. long. Native to Eurasia. CT, MA, ME, NH, RI, VT

Triodanis perfoliata (*Specularia perfoliata*)
CAMPANULACEAE
Venus' looking-glass, clasping-leaved Venus' looking-glass
Spring and summer, 4–36 in., perennial. Ledges,
talus slopes, dry fields, and disturbed, open sites.

Flowers blue-purple, ⅜–⅝ in. wide, tucked in leaf axils
along much of the stem. Leaves ¼–1¼ in. long, clasping,
broadly oval or heart-shaped. Stems angled, hairy. Fruit
an oval capsule, ¼–⅜ in. long. CT, MA, ME, NH, RI, VT

Datura stramonium[☆] SOLANACEAE
Jimson-weed, thorn-apple
Summer, 2–5 ft., annual. Fields, beach
fronts, and open, dry sites. Invasive.

Flowers violet or white, 2–4 in. long, tubular, the ridged
green calyx 1–2 in. long. Leaves 2–8 in. long, oval or triangular, coarsely toothed, with large, irregular teeth. Stems
smooth or hairy. Fruit a sharp-spined, oval capsule, 1–2½
in. long. A poisonous plant, with hallucinogenic proper-
ties. Native to Mexico. CT, MA, ME, NH, RI, VT

Vinca minor[☆] APOCYNACEAE
Lesser periwinkle, creeping myrtle
Early to midspring, to 3 ft. long and 4–8 in. high,
creeping perennial. Woodlands, fields, and roadsides.

Flowers blue or violet, occasionally white, 1–1¼ in.
wide, solitary, tubular below the broad, square-tipped,
pinwheel-like petals. Leaves 1–2 in. long, oval, glossy,
evergreen, with a white midvein. Stems trailing or
scrambling, smooth, densely colonial. Fruit a cylindrical follicle, ⅜–1¼ in. long. Native to Eurasia. CT, MA, ME,
NH, RI, VT

Mirabilis nyctaginea[☆] NYCTAGINACEAE
Heart-leaved umbrella-wort, four-o'clocks
Late spring to early fall, 1–5 ft., perennial. Fields,
roadsides, and open, disturbed sites.

Flowers purple or pink, ⅜–½ in. long, notched at tip, in
stalked clusters of 3–5, borne above a large, star-shaped
whorl of hairy bracts. Leaves 1¼–4 in. long, broadly oval or
triangular, the margins sometimes wavy or finely toothed.
Stems smooth. Fruit a hairy achene, ⅛–¼ in. long. Native
to central United States. CT, MA, ME, NH, RI, VT

Verbena hastata   VERBENACEAE
Blue vervain
Summer and early fall, 1½–5 ft., perennial. Wet
meadows, marshes, swamps, and pond shores.

Flowers blue or violet, ⅛ in. wide, arranged in thin,
candelabra-like spikes; the crowded flowers blooming
sequentially from the base to the top. Leaves 1½–7 in.
long, lance-shaped or oval, sharply toothed, occasionally
with basal lobes. Stems hairy, branching, grooved. Fruit
capsulelike, 1/16 in. long. CT, MA, ME, NH, RI, VT

Verbena simplex   VERBENACEAE
Narrow-leaved vervain
Spring and summer, 4–28 in., perennial. Open ledges
and open, sandy or stony ground in high-pH conditions.

Flowers lavender or light purple, ¼ in. wide, crowded on
narrow spikes, 2–8 in. long. Leaves 1–4 in. long, linear or
narrowly lance-shaped, shallowly toothed, narrowed at
base. Stems slender, finely hairy, sparsely branched. Fruit
capsulelike, ⅛ in. long. MA (rare)

Verbena stricta*   VERBENACEAE
Hoary vervain
Summer, 8– 40 in., perennial. Fields, roadsides,
and dry, disturbed, open sites.

Flowers deep blue or purple, ¼–⅜ in. wide, densely
crowded on thick spikes, 8–16 in. long. Leaves 1–4 in.
long, broadly oval, coarsely toothed, hairy on both sides.
Stems thick, densely hairy. Fruit capsulelike, ⅛ in.
long. Native to central United States, introduced in New
England. CT, MA, VT

5 radial petals; leaves simple, basal, entire

5 radial petals; leaves deeply divided, alternate, leaflets entire

Limonium carolinianum (*L. nashii*)
PLUMBAGINACEAE
Carolina sea-lavender
Midsummer to early fall, 8–28 in., perennial.
Salt marshes, tidal flats, and beaches.

Flowers lavender, ¼ in. wide; arranged in delicate, one-sided panicles on stiffly forking branches. Leaves 2–12 in. long, long-petioled, broadly oval or spoon-shaped, with a prominent midvein. Stems smooth, wide-branching. Fruit a brown achene, ⅛–¼ in. long. CT, MA, ME, NH, RI

Polemonium reptans⁕   POLEMONIACEAE
Spreading Jacob's-ladder, Greek valerian
Spring and early summer, 8–20 in.,
perennial. Woodlands and thickets.

Flowers blue or violet, ½–¾ in. wide, arranged in open panicles, the stamens not protruding beyond the forward-tilted petals. Leaves pinnately divided into 7–17 leaflets; the leaflets ¾–1½ in. long, oval, blunt-tipped. Stems smooth, often reclining. Fruit an oval capsule, ¼ in. long. Native to much of eastern and central United States, naturalized in New England. CT, MA, NH, RI, VT

Polemonium vanbruntiae   POLEMONIACEAE
Bog Jacob's-ladder, Appalachian Jacob's-ladder
Early to midsummer, 1½–3 ft., perennial. Wet
meadows, woodland seepages, and roadside ditches.

Flowers blue or violet, ½–¾ in. wide, bell-shaped, arranged in compact, nodding clusters, the stamens protruding beyond the petals. Leaves pinnately divided into 15–21 leaflets; the leaflets ¾–1½ in. long, narrowly lance-shaped, pointed. Stems hairy, erect. Fruit an oval capsule, ¼ in. long. ME (rare), VT (rare)

Solanum dulcamara* SOLANACEAE
Bittersweet nightshade, climbing nightshade
Spring to fall, 1–6 ft. long, perennial vine.
Woodlands, clearings, fields, swamp edges,
streambanks, and roadsides. Invasive.

Flowers purple or violet, ¼–⅜ in. long, with reflexed
petals and conical yellow centers, arranged in branching, long-stalked, drooping clusters. Leaves 1¼–3½ in.
long, oval, often with 2 spreading basal lobes, sometimes
divided into 3–5 leaflets. Stems twining, scrambling, or
climbing. Fruit a red, oval berry, ⅜–½ in. long. Native to
Eurasia. CT, MA, ME, NH, RI, VT

Comarum palustre (*Potentilla palustris*) ROSACEAE
Marsh cinquefoil, purple marsh-locks
Summer, 8–24 in., perennial. Fens,
marshes, and wet meadows.

Flowers purple or red, ¾–1 in. wide; the broad sepals
twice as long as the small, narrow petals; the flowers
arranged in compact, upper stem clusters. Leaves pinnately divided into 5–7 leaflets; the leaflets 1–2½ in. long,
lance-shaped or oval, sharply toothed. Stems hairy, semierect or sprawling, often reddish. Fruit a tiny achene,
aggregated into rounded heads about ½ in. long. CT, MA,
ME, NH, VT

Geum rivale ROSACEAE
Purple avens, water avens
Spring and early summer, 1–2 ft., perennial.
Fens, swamps, and wet meadows.

Flowers yellow or purplish, ¾–1 in. wide, nodding, solitary or in few-flowered clusters; the pointed purple sepals
partially covering the petals. Leaves irregularly divided
and sharply toothed; the lower leaves with 3–7 leaflets,
the broad terminal leaflet 1½–3 in.
long, much larger than the laterals; the
upper leaves smaller, usually divided
into 3 narrow segments. Stems hairy.
Fruit a long-beaked, feathery achene
aggregated into heads. CT, MA, ME,
NH, RI, VT

*Allium vineale**   ALLIACEAE
Crow garlic, field garlic
Late spring to midsummer, 1–4 ft., perennial.
Fields and open, disturbed sites. Invasive.

Flowers purple, sometimes pink or white, ⅛ in. wide, on pinlike stalks, clustered in rounded umbels and stalked above sessile bulblets, ¼ in. long; the bulblets often tipped with green, needle-thin "tails" to 1 in. long. Leaves 8–24 in. long, linear, rounded in cross section, mostly hollow. Fruit a capsule with black seeds, ⅛ in. long. Native to Eurasia and North Africa. CT, MA, ME, NH, RI, VT

Sisyrinchium angustifolium   IRIDACEAE
Narrow-leaved blue-eyed grass
Late spring to midsummer, 6–20 in., perennial.
Fields, wet meadows, and river and lake shores.

Flowers blue or violet, ½ in. wide, in clusters of 1–5 at the tips of long stalks that branch from the base of an erect, narrow, leaflike bract on the upper stem. Leaves 4–10 in. long, grasslike. Stems ⅛–¼ in. wide, broadly winged, deep green. Fruit a rounded capsule, ¼ in. long. CT, MA, ME, NH, RI, VT (rare)

Sisyrinchium atlanticum   IRIDACEAE
Eastern blue-eyed grass
Late spring to midsummer, 8–24 in., perennial.
Fields, wet meadows, and marsh edges.

Flowers light blue or violet, ½–1 in. wide, in clusters of 1–5 at the tips of long stalks that branch from the base of an erect, narrow, leaflike bract on the upper stem. Leaves 4–10 in. long, grasslike. Stems less than ⅛ in. wide, scarcely winged, pale green. Fruit a rounded capsule, ⅛–¼ in. long. CT, MA, ME, NH, RI, VT (rare)

Sisyrinchium fuscatum (sandplain blue-eyed grass), a very rare species that grows only in dry, sandy grasslands on Martha's Vineyard and Nantucket, is similar in its flower and stem characteristics, but can be distinguished by the fibrous tufts at the leaf bases and its very stiff foliage. Summer. MA (rare)

Sisyrinchium montanum   IRIDACEAE
Strict blue-eyed grass, common blue-eyed grass
Spring and early summer, 6–20 in., perennial.
Fields, forest edges, and river and lake shores.

Flowers violet or blue, ½–1 in. wide, single or in
few-flowered clusters at the top of the stem; the flowers
overtopped by a short, erect, sharp-tipped bract. Leaves
3–6 in. long, ⅛ in. wide, grasslike. Stems ⅛ in. wide,
winged, unbranched. Fruit a rounded capsule, ¼ in. long.
CT, MA, ME, NH, RI, VT

Sisyrinchium mucronatum   IRIDACEAE
Slender blue-eyed grass, needle-tipped blue-eyed grass
Spring or early summer, 4–16 in., perennial. Fields,
forest edges, wet meadows, and edges of fens.

Flowers blue or violet, ½–1 in. wide, single or in
few-flowered clusters at the top of the stem; the flowers
overtopped by a short, erect, sharp-tipped bract. Leaves
1⁄16 in. wide or less, wiry, usually much shorter than
stems. Stems 1⁄16 in. wide, scarcely winged, unbranched.
Fruit a rounded capsule, ¼ in. long. CT, MA (rare), ME

Caulophyllum thalictroides   BERBERIDACEAE
Blue cohosh
Spring, 1–3 ft., perennial. Rich, rocky deciduous forests.

Flowers purple or greenish yellow, ¼ in. wide, stalked in
terminal clusters of 5–70 flowers, blooming at same time
as leaf emergence. Leaves smooth, grayish green, divided
into 3 long-stalked leaflets; the leaflets subdivided into
3 or more oval leaflet segments, 1–3 in. long, with lobed
margins. Stems smooth, often with a whitish bloom.
Fruits berrylike, ¼ in. long, at first green, becoming deep
blue. CT, MA, ME, NH, RI, VT

  Caulophyllum giganteum (early blue cohosh) is very
similar, but blooms earlier in spring, before its leaves
have fully emerged. It has larger, dark purple flowers, ½
in. wide, and the flower clusters generally have 5–18 flowers. CT, MA (rare), NH, VT

Ionactis linariifolia (*Aster linariifolius*) ASTERACEAE
Flax-leaved stiff aster, stiff aster
Late summer to fall, 4–20 in., perennial. Sandy fields, dry woodlands, ledges, and rocky river shores.

Flower heads one to several, erect, ½–1 in. wide, with 10–20 violet rays. Leaves ½–1½ in. long, linear, stiff, crowded, sharp-tipped, reduced below the flower heads to small bracts pressed against the stem. Stems clumped, wiry, finely hairy. CT, MA, ME, NH, RI, VT

Oclemena nemoralis (*Aster nemoralis*)
ASTERACEAE
Bog aster, bog nodding-aster
Midsummer to early fall, 6–36 in., perennial. Bogs and peaty shorelines.

Flower heads 1–15, erect, long-stalked, 1–1½ in. wide, with 13–27 violet rays. Leaves ½–2 in. long, crowded, lance-shaped, with inrolled edges and roughened surfaces, hairy underneath, reduced below flower heads to small bracts. Stems hairy and slightly sticky. CT (rare), MA, ME, NH, RI, VT (rare)

Symphyotrichum concolor (*Aster concolor*)
ASTERACEAE
Eastern silver American-aster, eastern silvery aster
Late summer to fall, 1–3 ft., perennial. Sandy grasslands and open, sandy woodlands.

Flower heads ½–1 in. wide, with 8–16 lilac-colored rays, arranged in narrow racemes; the whorled bracts beneath the heads silky, flat, with green tips. Leaves ½–1½ in. long, lance-shaped or oval, ascending, sessile, with silky hairs on both surfaces. Stems slender, very finely hairy. Currently known only in Nantucket. MA (rare)

Symphyotrichum dumosum *(Aster dumosus)*
ASTERACEAE
Bushy American-aster, bushy aster
Late summer to fall, 1–3 ft., perennial. Fields and
open woodlands, mostly in or near coastal plain.

Flower heads ½–¾ in. wide, with 13–30 pale blue or
white rays; the heads numerous, on wide-spreading
branches; the whorled bracts beneath the heads flat,
green, broadened near the tips. Leaves linear or narrowly
lance-shaped, the lower 1–4 in. long, the upper leaves
reduced to tiny, crowded, needlelike bracts. Stems slender, smooth or hairy. CT, MA, NH, RI

Symphyotrichum laeve *(Aster laevis)* ASTERACEAE
Smooth American-aster, smooth aster
Late summer to fall, 1–3 ft., perennial. Sandy fields,
sandy or rocky woodlands, and roadsides.

Flower heads ¾–1¼ in. wide, with 15–30 pale blue or violet rays; the heads few to many on spreading or ascending
branches; the whorled bracts beneath the heads smooth,
with green, diamond-shaped tips. Leaves 1–6 in. long,
smooth, thick, clasping, lance-shaped or oval, occasionally toothed; the uppermost leaves small and bractlike.
Stems smooth, often whitish. CT, MA, ME, NH, RI, VT

Symphyotrichum novae-angliae
(Aster novae-angliae) ASTERACEAE
New England American-aster, New England aster
Late summer to fall, 2–6 ft., perennial.
Moist fields, thickets, and roadsides.

Flower heads ¾–1½ in. wide, with 45–100 bright purple
or magenta rays; the heads several to many on spreading or ascending branches; the whorled bracts beneath
the heads slender, spreading, glandular-sticky, often
purple-tinged. Leaves 1¼–5 in. long, lance-shaped, very
crowded, deeply clasping. Stems densely hairy. CT, MA,
ME, NH, RI, VT

Symphyotrichum novi-belgii (Aster novi-belgii)
ASTERACEAE
New York American-aster, New York aster
Midsummer to fall, 1–4 ft., perennial. Wet meadows, thickets, river shores, and salt marshes.

Flower heads ¾–1¼ in. wide, with 20–50 light to medium blue rays; the heads several to many on spreading or ascending branches; the whorled bracts beneath the heads slender, green, glandless, with reflexed tips. Leaves 1½–6 in. long, narrowly lance-shaped, sessile or slightly clasping, sometimes toothed; the uppermost leaves smaller. Stems finely hairy. CT, MA, ME, NH, RI, VT

Symphyotrichum patens (Aster patens)
ASTERACEAE
Late purple American-aster, late purple aster
Late summer and fall, 1–3 ft., perennial. Sandy fields and woodlands.

Flower heads 1–1½ in. wide, with 15–25 blue-violet rays; the heads several to many on stiff, wide-spreading branches; the whorled bracts beneath the heads glandular-sticky, with green, reflexed tips. Leaves 1–6 in. long, oval, thick, occasionally toothed, with a heart-shaped, clasping base; the uppermost leaves small and bractlike. Stems smooth or finely hairy. CT, MA, NH (rare), RI

Symphyotrichum praealtum (Aster praealtus)
ASTERACEAE
Willow-leaved American-aster, willow aster
Late summer and fall, 1–4 ft., perennial. Wet meadows.

Flower heads ¾–1 in. wide, with 20–35 pale blue or violet rays; the heads often numerous on spreading and ascending branches; the whorled bracts beneath the heads slender, spreading, with dark green tips. Leaves 1–4 in. long, linear or narrowly lance-shaped, with slightly inrolled margins; undersurfaces intricately veined into a network of cell-like configurations. Stems usually smooth below, hairy above. CT, MA (rare in both)

336

Symphyotrichum subulatum (*Aster subulatus*)
ASTERACEAE
Annual saltmarsh American-aster, annual salt-marsh aster
Midsummer to fall, 1–3 ft., annual. Salt and brackish
marshes; occasionally inland along salted highways.

Flower heads ¼–½ in. wide, with 15–30 light blue or
white rays; the heads 10–50 or more on stiff, ascending or
erect branches; the whorled bracts beneath the heads flat,
lance-shaped, often purple. Leaves 1–8 in. long, linear or
lance-shaped, fleshy. Stems usually smooth. CT, MA, ME
(rare), NH, RI

Tragopogon porrifolius⁕ ASTERACEAE
Salsify, oyster-plant, purple goat's-beard
Spring and summer, 1–4 ft., biennial. Fields and roadsides.

Flower heads 2–4 in. wide, solitary; the heads underlain
by a spreading whorl of green bracts longer than the purple rays; the flowers close by early afternoon. Leaves 8–16
in. long, linear or lance-shaped, ascending; the broadened bases partially enfold stem. Stems smooth, hollow.
Fruit a silken-haired achene, aggregated into a feathery
dome. Native to Europe. CT, MA, ME, NH, RI

Echinacea purpurea⁕ ASTERACEAE
Eastern purple coneflower, purple cone flower
Summer and fall, 1–5 ft., perennial.
Fields and woodland edges.

Flower heads 2½–4 in. wide, with 6–25 drooping, purple rays and a large, conelike central disk; the large, solitary flower heads long-stalked. Leaves to 6 in. long and
4 in. wide, the lower broadly oval, toothed or occasionally entire. Stems smooth or hairy. Native to central and
southeastern United States, naturalized in New England.
MA, VT

Echinacea pallida (pale purple coneflower) is similar,
but the lower leaves are narrower (to 8 in. long and 1½ in.
wide) and usually entire. The drooping rays are light purple, and the stems densely hairy. Summer. Native to central and southeastern United States, naturalized in fields
in New England. CT, MA, ME

Eurybia macrophylla (Aster macrophyllus)
ASTERACEAE
Large-leaved wood-aster, large-leaf aster
Late summer and fall, 1–5 ft., perennial.
Deciduous and mixed forests.

Flower heads ½–1 in. wide, with 9–20 blue or violet rays, on glandular stalks, arranged in flattish, short-branched clusters; the whorled bracts beneath the heads hairy, glandular, flat, tipped with purple. Lower leaves 2–12 in. long, broadly oval, thick, rough-textured, long-petioled, notched at base; the upper leaves smaller, often sessile. Stems smooth or sparsely hairy. Often grows in large colonies of basal leaves with few flowering stems. CT, MA, ME, NH, RI, VT

Eurybia radula (Aster radula) ASTERACEAE
Rough-leaved aster, rough wood-aster
Midsummer to fall, 1–3 ft., perennial. Swamps, bogs, streambanks, and wet woods.

Flower heads 1–1½ in. wide, with 15–40 pale violet rays, the heads few, often long-stalked; the whorled bracts beneath the heads with broad, reflexed tips and finely hairy margins. Leaves 1–4 in. long, lance-shaped, sharply toothed, rough-textured, veiny. Stems smooth. CT (rare), MA (rare), ME, NH, RI, VT (rare)

Eurybia spectabilis (Aster spectabilis) ASTERACEAE
Purple wood-aster, showy aster
Late summer and fall, 6–30 in., perennial.
Sandy woodlands, fields, and roadsides.

Flower heads 1–2 in. wide, with 15–35 bright violet rays, arranged in a flattish, branching inflorescence; the whorled bracts beneath the heads blunt, spreading, sticky-glandular. Lower leaves 1–6 in. long, lance-shaped, long-petioled, slightly toothed or entire; the upper smaller and sessile. Stems hairy and often sticky-glandular. CT (rare), MA, RI

Symphyotrichum cordifolium (*Aster cordifolius*)
ASTERACEAE
Heart-leaved American-aster, heart-leaved aster
Late summer and fall, 1–4 ft., perennial. Forests
and forest edges, woodlands, and thickets.

Flower heads ½–¾ in. wide, with 10–20 pale blue or
violet rays; the whorled bracts beneath the heads flat,
lance-shaped, with darkened tips; the heads usually
numerous, on spreading, leafy branches. Lower and middle leaves 1½–6 in. long, heart-shaped, sharply toothed,
on long petioles; the uppermost leaves smaller, sessile.
Stems smooth or hairy. CT, MA, ME, NH, RI, VT
    Symphyotrichum ciliolatum (Lindley's American-aster,
northern heart-leaved aster) is much less common. The
flower heads are larger (1–1½ in. wide) and the inflorescences are sparser. Petioles of lower and middle leaves
are winged. Grows in woodlands and clearings. MA, ME,
NH (rare)

Symphyotrichum prenanthoides
(*Aster prenanthoides*) ASTERACEAE
**Crooked-stem American-aster, crooked-stem aster,
zigzag aster**
Late summer and fall, 1–3 ft., perennial.
Floodplain forests and wet thickets.

Flower heads 1–1½ in. wide, with 20–35 pale blue or violet rays; the whorled bracts beneath the heads green,
wide-spreading, blunt or acute; the heads in a spreading,
leafy inflorescence. Leaves 2½–6 in., long, lance-shaped,
entire on lower margins, narrowing to a broadly winged
petiole that strongly clasps the stem. Stems zigzag in
form, smooth below and finely hairy above. CT, MA (rare),
VT (rare)

Symphyotrichum puniceum (*Aster puniceus*)
ASTERACEAE
Purple-stemmed American-aster, purple-stemmed aster
Late summer and fall, 2–7 ft., perennial. Swamps,
marshes, wet meadows, and ditches.

Flower heads 1–1½ in. wide, with 30–60 light blue or
blue-violet rays; the whorled bracts beneath the heads
long, linear, spreading, sharp-tipped; the heads on spreading and ascending branches. Leaves 2½–6 in. long,
lance-shaped, toothed or occasionally entire, clasping at
base but not tapering to a winged petiole. Stems densely
hairy, often red or purple. CT, MA, ME, NH, RI, VT

Symphyotrichum undulatum (*Aster undulatus*)
ASTERACEAE
Wavy-leaved American-aster, wavy-leaved aster
Late summer and fall, 2–4 ft., perennial.
Dry woodlands, thickets, and fields.

Flower heads ¾ in. wide, with 8–20 light blue or violet rays; the whorled bracts beneath the heads flat, lance-shaped, green-tipped; the heads often numerous on spreading, leafy branches. Leaves 1½–6 in. long, heart-shaped, toothed or entire; the lower with clasping, winged petioles flared at the base, the upper clasping, without petioles. Stems stiff, usually hairy. CT, MA, ME, NH, RI, VT

Vernonia noveboracensis   ASTERACEAE
New York ironweed
Late summer and early fall, 2–6 ½ ft., perennial.
Wet meadows, streambanks, and ditches.

Flower heads ¼–½ in. wide; the purple rays actually aggregations of tiny, 5-petaled flowers; the bracts beneath the heads broad at base, tapering to tail-like tips; the heads forming a flattish, open inflorescence on ascending branches. Leaves 4–12 in. long, narrowly lance-shaped, crowded, sessile. Stems smooth or finely hairy. Native in CT, MA, RI; introduced in NH.

Anemone acutiloba (*Hepatica acutiloba*, *H. nobilis* var. *acuta*) RANUNCULACEAE
Sharp-lobed hepatica
Early spring, 2–8 in., perennial. Rich deciduous forests.

Flowers violet, white, or pink, ½–1 in. wide, solitary, with 5–12 petal-like sepals and bushy stamens; the 3 bracts below the sepals pointed at the tips. Leaves ½–3 in. long, leathery, long-petioled, with 3 sharp-pointed lobes, turning red in summer. Stems hairy. Fruit an oval achene, ⅛–¼ in. long. CT (rare), MA, NH, VT

Anemone americana (Hepatica americana, H. nobilis var. americana) RANUNCULACEAE
Blunt-lobed hepatica
Early spring, 2–7 in., perennial.
Deciduous and mixed forests.

Flowers blue, purple, white, or pink, ½–1 in. wide, solitary with 5–12 petal-like sepals and bushy stamens; the 3 bracts below the sepals rounded at the tips. Leaves ½–3 in. long leathery, long-petioled, with 3 rounded lobes, turning red in summer. Stems hairy. Fruit an oval achene, ⅛–¼ in. long. CT, MA, ME, NH, RI (rare), VT

Cichorium intybus* ASTERACEAE
Chicory
Summer to early fall, 1–4 ft., perennial. Fields, roadsides, and disturbed, open sites.

Flower heads 1–1½ in. wide, with 15–20 blue (occasionally white or pink) rays tipped with small teeth; the heads arranged in small, interrupted, almost sessile clusters on upper stem; the flowers usually open only in the morning. Lower leaves 3–10 in. long, lance-shaped, deeply divided into sharp-toothed segments; the upper leaves smaller, undivided. Stems hairy. Native to Europe. CT, MA, ME, NH, RI, VT

Lactuca biennis ASTERACEAE
Tall blue lettuce
Summer and fall, 3–15 ft., annual or biennial.
Fields, thickets, forest edges, and roadsides.

Flower heads ½–¾ in. wide, with 15–30 blue or whitish rays; the tips of the rays with 5 fine teeth; the heads crowded in a spirelike inflorescence. Leaves 4–12 in. long, lance-shaped, deeply divided into irregular segments with coarse teeth. Stems often towering, densely hairy, with milky sap. CT, MA, ME, NH, RI, VT

7 or more radial petals; leaves deeply divided, opposite, leaflets toothed or lobed

Petals indistinguishable; leaves simple, alternate, toothed or lobed

Petals indistinguishable; leaves simple, opposite, entire

Knautia arvensis✻   CAPRIFOLIACEAE
Bluebuttons, field scabiosa
Summer, 1–3 ft., perennial. Fields and roadsides.

Flower heads purple or lilac, ½–1½ in. wide, solitary on long, erect stalks; the "rays" actually aggregations of tiny 4-petaled flowers. Leaves to 10 in. long, lance-shaped, hairy, the middle leaves deeply divided into 7–13 narrow leaflets, the lower leaves usually toothed but not divided. Stems hairy. Fruit a hairy achene, ¼ in. long. Native to Eurasia. CT, MA, ME, NH, VT

Jasione montana✻   CAMPANULACEAE
Sheep's bit, sheepbit
Summer and fall, 4–20 in., annual or biennial. Sandy fields and roadsides.

Flower heads blue, ⅜–¾ in. wide, solitary on long, mostly leafless stalks; the rounded, bushy heads actually aggregations of tiny 5-petaled flowers. Leaves ½–1¼ in. long, linear or narrowly lance-shaped, shallowly toothed or entire, hairy. Stems hairy. Fruit a capsule, 1⁄16–⅛ in. long. Native to Eurasia. CT, MA, RI

Gentiana andrewsii   GENTIANACEAE
Andrew's bottle-gentian, prairie bottle-gentian
Late summer and fall, 1–3 ft., perennial. Wet meadows and thickets, often in high-pH soils.

Flowers blue, 1½ in. long, clustered at the top of the stem and sometimes the upper axils; the closed, 5-parted petal lobes tipped by a distinct white fringe; the finely fringed appendages between the petal lobes are distinctly taller than the lobes. Leaves 2–6 in. long and 1–1½ in. wide, oval or broadly lance-shaped. Stems smooth. Fruit an elliptical capsule, ⅜ in. long. CT, MA (rare), VT (rare)

342

Gentiana clausa   GENTIANACEAE
Meadow bottle gentian, closed gentian
Late summer and fall, 1–2 ft., perennial. Wet
meadows, thickets, and streambanks.

Flowers blue, 1½ in. long, clustered at the top of the stem
and sometimes the upper axils; the closed, 5-parted petal
lobes scarcely if at all fringed at the tip; the shallowly
toothed appendages between the petal lobes slightly
shorter than or just equal to the lobes. Leaves 2–6 in. long
and 1–1½ in. wide, oval or broadly lance-shaped. Stems
smooth. Fruit an elliptical capsule, ⅜ in. long. CT, MA,
ME, NH, RI, VT
  Gentiana rubicaulis (red-stemmed gentian), an
extremely rare species, is similar but the stems are reddish, the leaves are light green, and the flowers are pale
or reddish blue, and clustered only at the top of the stem.
Grows in wet meadows and marshes. ME (rare)

Gentiana linearis   GENTIANACEAE
Narrow-leaved gentian
Late summer and fall, 8–32 in., perennial.
Fens, wet meadows, and streambanks.

Flowers blue, 1½ in. long, clustered at the top of the stem
and sometimes the upper axils; the closed, 5-parted lobes
not fringed at the tip; the appendages between the lobes
much shorter than the lobes. Leaves 1½–3½ in. long and
¼–⅝ in. wide, linear or narrowly lance-shaped, dark
green. Stems smooth. Fruit an elliptical capsule, ⅜ in.
long. MA (rare), ME, NH, VT

Dipsacus fullonum* (D. sylvestris)
CAPRIFOLIACEAE
Fuller's teasel
Summer, 2–7 ft., biennial or perennial.
Fields and roadsides.

Flower heads lavender, 1¼–3½ in. long, spiny, cylindrical, solitary on long stalks; the heads underlain by long,
linear, spiny bracts. Leaves 4–16 in. long, lance-shaped,
usually toothed, prickly underneath; the leaf pairs fused
at the base. Upper stems prickly. Fruit an angular achene,
¼ in. long. Native to Europe. CT, MA, ME, NH, RI, VT
  *Dipsacus laciniatus** (cut-leaved teasel) is similar, but
the leaves are deeply cut into many sharp, narrow segments. Grows in fields and roadsides. Native to Eurasia.
MA, VT

Plantago rugelii PLANTAGINACEAE
Rugel's plantain, red-stemmed plantain
Late spring to fall, 2–20 in., perennial. Fields,
roadsides, and disturbed, open sites.

Flowers bluish or green, 1/16 in. long, densely clustered in
a long, pointed, pencil-thin spike. Leaves 1½–7 in. long,
broadly oval, long-petioled, with 3–7 prominent, parallel
veins; base of petioles red-purple. Stems hairy. Fruit oval,
capsulelike, about 1/8 in. long. CT, MA, ME, NH, RI, VT

Echium vulgare❋ BORAGINACEAE
Common viper's-bugloss, viper's-bugloss
Summer, 12–32 in., biennial. Fields,
roadsides, and open, disturbed sites.

Flowers bright blue, ½–¾ in. long, with red, protruding stamens; the flowers arranged in bristly, branching,
coiled racemes, opening 1 or 2 at a time on each raceme.
Leaves 1–4 in. long, hairy, sessile, lance-shaped or linear.
Stems bristly-hairy. Fruit capsulelike, 1/8 in. long. Native
to Eurasia. CT, MA, ME, NH, RI, VT

Lobelia kalmii CAMPANULACEAE
Brook lobelia, Kalm's lobelia
Summer, 2–8 in., perennial. Rich wet
meadows, fens, and seepages.

Flowers blue with white throat, ¼–½ in. long, the broad,
3-lobed lower lip larger than the erect, narrow, 2-lobed
upper lip; the flowers arranged in open, often one-sided
racemes. Stem leaves ½–2 in. long, linear or narrowly
lance-shaped. Fruit an oval capsule, 1/8–¼ in. long. CT
(rare), MA (rare), ME, NH (rare), VT

Commelina communis* COMMELINACEAE
Asiatic day-flower
Summer and fall, 12–32 in., annual. Moist,
shaded roadsides, fields, and thicket edges.

Flowers blue and white, ¾ in. long, the blue, upper petals
larger than the white lower petal; the flowers usually solitary, stalked above a folded, leaflike bract. Leaves 2–5 in.
long, glossy, oval or broadly lance-shaped, sheathing the
stem. Stems erect or sprawling, smooth. Fruit a rounded
capsule, ⅜ in. long. Native to Asia. CT, MA, ME, NH, RI, VT

Nuttallanthus canadensis (*Linaria canadensis*)
PLANTAGINACEAE
Old-field toadflax, blue toadflax
Spring to fall, 8–32 in., annual or biennial. Dry
fields, roadsides, and open, disturbed sites.

Flowers blue, ½ in. long, stalked, arranged in a tight
raceme, with a slender spur and a white, distinctly
double-ridged throat; the 3-lobed lower lip larger than the
erect, 2-lobed upper lip. Leaves ½–1¼ in. long, needlelike. Fruit an oval capsule, ⅛–¼ in. long. CT, MA, ME, NH,
RI, VT

Pontederia cordata PONTEDERIACEAE
Pickerelweed
Summer, 1–3 ft., perennial. Deep marshes
and pond and stream shallows.

Flowers purple, ¼ in. long, tubular, both the upper
and lower lips divided into 3 lobes; the flowers densely
crowded on a spike 2–6 in. long. Leaves 2½–8 in. long,
lance-shaped, long-petioled, heart-shaped at base; the
surface glossy, with fine, curving, parallel veins. Fruit a
ridged achene, ⅛–¼ in. long. CT, MA, ME, NH, RI, VT

Flowers bilateral; leaves
simple, alternate, entire

345

Lobelia inflata   CAMPANULACEAE
Indian-tobacco, bladder-pod lobelia
Summer and early fall, 6–36 in., annual.
Fields, thickets, ledges, and roadsides.

Flowers pale blue, ¼–⅜ in. long, arranged in 2 or more leafy, branching racemes; the lower lip with 3 spreading lobes, the upper with 2 pointed, ascending lobes; the calyx sac thick, veined, with linear, sharp-pointed sepals, prominently inflated in fruit. Leaves 1–3 in. long, oval, sessile or short-petioled. Stems hairy. Fruit a capsule, ¼–½ in., enclosed within the inflated calyx. CT, MA, ME, NH, RI, VT

Lobelia siphilitica   CAMPANULACEAE
Great blue lobelia, blue lobelia
Late summer and fall, 1–4 ft., perennial.
Calcareous fens, seepages, and wet meadows.

Flowers blue, 1–1½ in. long, often white-striped on the bottom, arranged in narrow, dense racemes; the lower lip 3-lobed, whitish at throat; the upper lip with 2 narrow, ascending lobes. Leaves 2–5 in. long, lance-shaped or oblong, sessile, slightly toothed. Stems thick, hairy. Fruit a capsule, ⅜–½ in. long. CT, MA (rare), NH (rare), VT (rare)

Lobelia spicata   CAMPANULACEAE
Spiked lobelia, pale-spiked lobelia
Summer and early fall, 1–3 ft., perennial.
Fields and roadsides.

Flowers pale blue, ¼–⅜ in. long, arranged in a spike; the lower lip with 3 spreading lobes, the upper with 2 pointed, ascending lobes; the calyx sac at base of flower small, only slightly thickened, with linear, sharp-pointed sepals, scarcely inflated in fruit. Leaves 1–4 in. long, lance-shaped or oval, sessile or short-petioled. Fruit a capsule, ¼ in. long, partly protruding from the short calyx tube. CT, MA, ME, NH, RI, VT

Veronica persica⁕   PLANTAGINACEAE
Bird's-eye speedwell, Persian speedwell
Spring and summer, 4–16 in., annual or biennial.
Fields, roadsides, and disturbed, open sites.

Flowers blue, whitish at center, ¼–½ in. wide, with 4 petals, the lower smallest; the flowers solitary on long, slender, axillary stalks. Leaves oval or rounded, ¼–1 in. long,
the lower opposite, the middle and upper alternate. Stems
hairy, semierect or sprawling. Fruit a heart-shaped capsule, ⅜ in. wide. Native to Southwest Asia. CT, MA, ME,
NH, RI, VT

Viola adunca   VIOLACEAE
Sand violet, hook-spurred violet
Early to late spring, ¾–6 in., perennial. Sandy
woodlands, fields, and roadsides.

Flowers violet, ¼–½ in. long, long-stalked from leaf axils,
with bearded lateral petals and a ¼-in.-long spur. Leaves
broadly oval or triangular, ½–1 in. long, short-hairy on
both surfaces, flat or bluntly rounded at base, with narrowly winged petioles; stipules at leaf bases linear or narrowly lance-shaped, with comblike teeth. Stems finely
hairy. Fruit an elliptical capsule, ¼ in. long. CT (rare), MA
(rare), ME, NH, VT

Viola labradorica (*V. conspersa*) VIOLACEAE
Dog violet, American dog violet, Labrador violet
Midspring to early summer, ¾–8 in., perennial. Forests,
fields, ledges, swamp edges, and mountain summits.

Flowers pale blue, ¼–½ in. long, long-stalked from leaf
axils, with bearded lateral petals and a ⅛- to ¼-in.-long
spur. Leaves ½–1½ in. long, broadly oval, heart-shaped
at base, smooth, or slightly hairy on upper surface only,
the petioles not winged; stipules at leaf bases broadly
lance-shaped, entire or irregularly toothed. Stems
smooth. Fruit an elliptical capsule, ¼ in. long. CT, MA,
ME, NH, RI, VT

   The introduced Eurasian species *Viola riviniana*, often
sold as *V. labradorica*, is very similar, but the stipules at
leaf bases have finely fringed teeth. The horticultural
form of *V. riviniana* has purple-tinged leaves. Escaped
from gardens and occasionally naturalized in fields and
woodlands. CT, MA, ME, NH, RI, VT

Viola rostrata VIOLACEAE
Long-spurred violet
Early to late spring, 2–8 in., perennial.
Rich deciduous forests.

Flowers pale lilac, ½–1 in. long, long-stalked from leaf axils, with beardless petals and a prominent, ½-in.-long spur. Leaves 1–1½ in. long, broadly oval, heart-shaped at

base; stipules at leaf bases with fine, comblike teeth. Stems smooth. Fruit an elliptical capsule, ¼ in. long. CT, MA (rare), NH, VT

Hedeoma hispida LAMIACEAE
Rough false pennyroyal
Summer to early fall, 4–16 in., annual. Dry fields, ledges, and open, disturbed sites in high-pH conditions.

Flowers light blue or purple, ¼ in. long, 2-lipped, whorled in leaf axils, with a hairy, sharp-toothed calyx. Leaves ⅜–1 in. long, linear, sessile. Stems hairy. Fruit capsule-like, less than 1/16 in. long. Native in CT, MA (rare), RI, VT; introduced in ME, NH.

Prunella vulgaris LAMIACEAE
Common selfheal, heal-all, self-heal
Late spring to fall, 4–20 in., perennial. Thickets, fields, woodland trails, and roadsides.

Flowers violet, ⅜–¾ in. long, hooded, with a drooping, fringed lower lip; the flowers and bracts densely crowded on a terminal spike ¾–2 in. long. Leaves 1½–3½ in. long, lance-shaped or oval, long-petioled, entire or sparsely toothed. Stems hairy. Fruit capsulelike, 1/16 in. long. CT, MA, ME, NH, RI, VT

348

Scutellaria parvula (*S. leonardii*) LAMIACEAE
Little skullcap, small skullcap
Spring to midsummer, 4–12 in., perennial.
Rocky woodlands, ledges, and rivershore
outcrops, usually in high-pH conditions.

Flowers violet, ¼–⅜ in. long, paired in the leaf axils,
short-stalked, with a hairy, hoodlike upper lip and spreading lower lip. Leaves ¼–¾ in. long, oval, occasionally
with a few blunt teeth, sessile or short-petioled. Stems
hairy. Fruit capsulelike, less than 1/16 in. long. CT, MA, VT
(rare in all)

Trichostema dichotomum LAMIACEAE
Blue curls, forked blue curls, bastard pennyroyal
Midsummer to fall, 8–16 in., annual. Sandy fields,
thickets, roadsides, and dry, disturbed sites.

Flowers bright blue, ¼ in. long, on long, branching
stalks; the flowers 4-lobed, with a prominent lower lip,
much longer than the other petals, and long, slender,
deeply curled stamens. Leaves ½–2½ in. long and ¼–1
in. wide, lance-shaped or oval. Stems hairy, branching.
Fruit capsulelike, ⅛ in. long. CT, MA, ME, NH, RI, VT
　　Trichostema setaceum (narrow-leaved blue curls) is very
similar, but the leaves are linear, 1/16–¼ in. wide. Grows
in dry sandy soils. Southwest CT
　　Trichostema brachiatum (pennyroyal bluecurls, false
pennyroyal) is similar, but the lower lip is equal to or
only slightly longer than upper and lateral petals, and the
stamens are straight. Grows in dry, open, stony sites on
high-pH rock. CT, MA (rare in both)

Lindernia dubia LINDERNIACEAE
Yellow-seeded false pimpernel, false pimpernel
Midsummer to early fall, 2–12 in., annual. Muddy or sandy
lake and river shores, freshwater estuaries, and ditches.

Flowers lavender, occasionally white, ¼ in., long,
2-lipped, in long-stalked, axillary pairs. Leaves ⅜–1¼ in.,
oval, entire or sometimes slightly toothed. Stems branching, finely hairy. Fruit a rounded capsule, ¼ in. long. CT,
MA, ME, NH, RI, VT

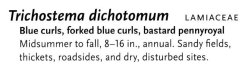

Neottia cordata (*Listera cordata*) ORCHIDACEAE
Heart-leaved twayblade
Spring to midsummer, 4–10 in., perennial. Coniferous swamps, mossy evergreen woods, and subalpine forests.

Flowers purplish or greenish, ⅛ in. wide, attached to rounded ovary sac, arranged in a raceme with 5–25 flowers; the lip protruding, deeply forked, ⅛–¼ in. long. Leaves a single pair midway up stem, ⅜–1 in. long, heart-shaped, with a pointed tip. Stems smooth, fleshy. Fruit a rounded capsule, ¼ in. long. CT, MA (rare), ME, NH (rare), VT

*Chaenorhinum minus** (*Chaenorrhinum minus*)
PLANTAGINACEAE
Dwarf snapdragon, lesser toadflax
Summer, 4–12 in., annual. Fields, roadsides, and disturbed, open sites.

Flowers lavender or whitish, ¼ in. long, long-stalked from leaf axils, 2-lipped, with a short spur; the upper lip 2-lobed and lower lip 3-lobed. Leaves ¼–1½ in. long, linear or narrowly oblong; the lower leaves opposite, upper leaves alternate. Stems hairy. Fruit an oval capsule, ⅛–¼ in. long. Native to Europe. CT, MA, ME, NH, VT

Veronica serpyllifolia PLANTAGINACEAE
Thyme-leaved speedwell
Spring and summer, 4–12 in., perennial. Forests, fields, and roadsides.

Flowers blue or white, ¼ in. wide, 4-lobed, the lowermost smallest, with blue or purple-lined interiors; the flowers arranged in short racemes. Leaves ⅜–1 in. long, oval, occasionally toothed. Stems finely hairy, with creeping bases. Fruit a notched capsule, ⅛–¼ in. wide. CT, MA, ME, NH, RI, VT

Agastache scrophulariifolia

(*A. scrophulariaefolia*) LAMIACEAE
Purple giant hyssop
Late summer and early fall, 2–5 ft., perennial. Rich, moist soils on floodplain terraces and deciduous forests.

Flowers purple, ½ in. long, arranged in dense spikes to 6 in. long; the flowers 2-lipped, with 4 protruding stamens and smooth green sepals. Leaves 2–5 in. long, lance-shaped or oval, green underneath, with petioles ¾–2 in. long; anise-scented when bruised. Stems angled, smooth or slightly hairy. Fruit capsulelike, 1/16 in. long. CT, MA (rare in both)

Agastache foeniculum* (lavender giant hyssop) is similar, but the leaves are whitened underneath and the petioles are ⅜–⅝ in. long. The sepals are blue-purple and finely hairy. Grows in fields. Native to north-central United States, an occasional garden escape in New England. CT, NH, RI

Ajuga reptans*   LAMIACEAE

Bugleweed, carpet bugle
Spring and summer, 4–12 in., perennial.
Fields and roadsides.

Flowers purple, ½–¾ in. long, arranged in whorls of 6 in erect, leafy spikes; the upper lip very short, the lower lip broad, notched at tip. Leaves ½–2½ in. long, oval or rounded, sessile, often purplish. Stems smooth or slightly hairy, creeping at base and often mat-forming. Fruit capsulelike, 1/16 in. wide. Native to Eurasia. CT, MA, ME, RI, VT

Ajuga genevensis* (standing bugle) is similar but much less common and its stems are densely hairy and all erect, not mat-forming. Native to Europe. CT, MA, ME, RI, VT

Blephilia ciliata   LAMIACEAE

Downy wood-mint
Spring and summer, 1–2 ft., perennial. Open thickets and ledges in high-pH conditions.

Flowers blue, lavender, or whitish, spotted with purple, ½ in. long, arranged in crowded, whorled spikes ¾–2 in. long. Leaves 1–3 in. long, lance-shaped or oval, sessile or short-petioled, narrowed to base, shallowly toothed or entire. Stems downy with short, curved hairs. Fruit capsulelike, less than 1/16 in. long. Western MA (rare)

Blephilia hirsuta   LAMIACEAE
Hairy wood-mint
Spring and summer, 1–3 ft., perennial.
Rich, deciduous forests.

Flowers pale purple or white, spotted with purple, ½ in. long, arranged in a spike of many-flowered whorls; the lower whorls usually separated from the crowded upper whorls. Leaves 1½–3 in. long, lance-shaped or oval, long-petioled, distinctly toothed, rounded at base. Stems usually densely hairy with spreading hairs, very occasionally smooth. Fruit capsulelike, less than 1/16 in. long. MA, VT (rare in both)

Glechoma hederacea❊   LAMIACEAE
Gill-over-the-ground, ground ivy
Spring to early summer, 4–16 in., perennial. Thickets, fields, and semiopen or shaded, disturbed sites. Invasive.

Flowers blue or violet, ½–1 in. long, whorled in the leaf axils, 2-lipped, with a short upper lip and a bearded lower lip. Leaves ⅜–1¼ in. long, rounded, long-petioled, with scalloped edges. Stems creeping, often forming extensive mats. Fruit capsulelike, 1/16 in. long. Native to Eurasia. CT, MA, ME, NH, RI, VT

Hedeoma pulegioides   LAMIACEAE
American false pennyroyal, American pennyroyal
Spring to midsummer, 4–16 in., annual.
Rocky woodlands, ledges, and fields.

Flowers light blue, ⅛–¼ in. long, 2-lipped, arranged in axillary whorls; the 3 upper calyx teeth broader than the 2 lower, linear, fringed teeth. Leaves ⅜–1¼ in. long, lance-shaped or oval, shallowly toothed, occasionally entire, the larger ones petioled. Fruit capsulelike, less than 1/16 in. long. CT, MA, ME, NH, RI, VT

Mentha canadensis (*M. arvensis* var. *canadensis*)
LAMIACEAE
American wild mint, wild mint
Summer, 12–24 in., perennial. Swamps, wet
meadows, and pond and river shores.

Flowers lavender, pink, or white, ¼ in. long, arranged
in sessile, dense, axillary whorls; the flowers 2-lipped,
with long, projecting stamens. Leaves 1–3 in. long,
lance-shaped or oval, sharply toothed, with a strong mint
fragrance. Stems downy or hairy, sometimes branching.
Fruit capsulelike, 1/16 in. long. CT, MA, ME, NH, RI, VT
    Closely related *Mentha arvensis** (ginger mint) is simi-
lar, but the leaves are more broadly oval and the uppermost leaves are very small. Native to Europe. CT, MA, ME,
RI, VT

Scutellaria galericulata (*S. epilobiifolia*)
LAMIACEAE
Marsh skullcap, hooded skullcap
Summer, 6–30 in., perennial. Marshes,
swamps, and lake and river shores.

Flowers blue or purple, ½–1 in. long, paired in the leaf
axils, the hoodlike upper lip arched above the spreading
lower lip. Leaves ¾–2½ in. long, lance-shaped or oval,
veiny; the petioles ⅛ in. long or less. Stems finely hairy.
Fruit capsulelike, 1/16–⅛ in. long. CT, MA, ME, NH, RI, VT

Scutellaria lateriflora   LAMIACEAE
Mad-dog skullcap
Summer, 1–3 ft., perennial. Marshes, wet
meadows, and lake and river shores.

Flowers blue or purple, ¼–⅜ in. long, with a hoodlike
upper lip arched above spreading lower lip; the flowers
arranged in one-sided racemes, 1–4 in. long, branching
from the leaf axils. Leaves 1–3 in. long, lance-shaped or
oval, veiny; the petioles ¼–1 in. long. Stems smooth or
hairy. Fruit capsulelike, 1/16 in. long. CT, MA, ME, NH, RI, VT

Euphrasia nemorosa (*E. americana*)
OROBANCHACEAE
Common eyebright
Summer, 4–16 in., annual. Fields, coastal headlands, and roadsides.

Flowers lavender or white, yellow at throat ¼–⅜ in. long, paired in the leaf axils; the upper lip short, 2-lobed, the lower lip with 3 notched, spreading lobes. Leaves ⅛–½ in. long, oval, sessile; the uppermost bracts spreading or ascending, with outwardly spreading teeth. Stems hairy. Fruit an oval capsule, about ¼ in. long. MA, ME, NH, VT

*Euphrasia stricta*** (strict eyebright) is very similar, but the uppermost bracts ascend or are erect, with upwardly ascending teeth. Grows in fields and roadsides. Native to Europe. MA, ME, RI, VT

Mimulus alatus   PHRYMACEAE
Winged monkey-flower
Summer, 1–4 ft., perennial. Streambanks, river floodplains, and wet meadows.

Flowers blue, ¾–1¼ in. long, arranged in short-stalked, axillary pairs, with a broadly 3-lobed lower lip. Leaves 2–4 in. long, lance-shaped or oval, tapering to the winged petiole. Stems square and narrowly winged. Fruit a capsule, ½ in. long. CT, MA (rare in both)

Mimulus ringens   PHRYMACEAE
Allegheny monkey-flower, monkey-flower
Summer, 1–4 ft., perennial. Wet meadows, marshes swamps, lake and river shores, and freshwater estuaries.

Flowers blue, ¾–1¼ in. long, arranged in long-stalked, axillary pairs, with a broadly 3-lobed lower lip. Leaves 1–4 in. long, lance-shaped or oval, sessile or clasping. Stems smooth, square, occasionally winged. Fruit an oval or rounded capsule, ½ in. long. CT, MA, ME, NH, RI, VT

Penstemon calycosus* (*P. laevigatus*)
PLANTAGINACEAE
Long-sepaled beardtongue, eastern beard-tongue
Summer, 2–4 ft., perennial. Fields,
roadsides, and clearings.

Flowers purple or lilac, whitish on the inside, ½–1¼
in. long, finely hairy, broadly tubular, open at throat,
abruptly constricted near base; the flowers clustered in
a narrowly branching, terminal inflorescence. Leaves
2–5 in. long, lance-shaped or oval, sessile, finely toothed.
Stems smooth or finely hairy. Fruit a capsule, ¼–⅜ in.
long. Native to central and southeastern United States.
CT, MA, ME, NH, RI, VT

Penstemon hirsutus PLANTAGINACEAE
Northeastern beardtongue, hairy beardtongue
Spring to midsummer, 16–32 in., perennial.
Dry woodlands, ledges, and fields.

Flowers violet or white, ¾–1¼ in. long, hairy, narrowly
tubular, closed at throat and tapering to base; the flowers clustered in a narrowly branching, terminal inflorescence. Leaves 2–5 in. long, lance-shaped or oval, sessile.
Stems densely hairy. Fruit a capsule, ⅜ in. long. CT, MA
(rare), ME, RI (rare), VT (rare)

Veronica americana PLANTAGINACEAE
American speedwell, American brooklime
Summer, 4–36 in., perennial. Streamsides,
seepages, and swamps.

Flowers blue or violet, ¼–½ in. wide, arranged in terminal and axillary racemes with 10–25 flowers. Leaves ¾–3
in. long, lance-shaped, with a short but distinct petiole,
broadest at base and pointed at tip. Stems fleshy, erect,
semierect, or sometimes creeping, growing in water or
mud. Fruit a rounded capsule, ⅛ in. long. CT, MA, ME,
NH, RI, VT

*Veronica beccabunga** (European speedwell) is similar,
but the short-petioled leaves are broadly oval, widest near
middle, and blunt or rounded at the tip. Grows in streamsides, seepages, and ditches. Invasive. Native to Eurasia.
CT, MA, ME

Veronica anagallis-aquatica⁎
PLANTAGINACEAE
Blue water speedwell, water speedwell
Summer, 4–36 in., perennial. Streamsides,
seepages, and ditches.

Flowers blue or violet, ¼–⅜ in. wide, arranged in terminal and axillary racemes with 20–50 flowers. Leaves 1–4 in. long, lance-shaped or oval, sessile or clasping, 1½–3 times as long as wide. Stems fleshy, erect or semierect. Fruit a capsule, ⅛ in. long. Native to Eurasia. CT, MA, ME, RI, VT

Veronica catenata (sessile water speedwell), a very rare native species, is similar, but the sessile leaves are narrowly lance-shaped, 3–5 (or more) times as long as wide, and the flowers are slightly smaller (⅛–¼ in. wide). Grows in streamsides and muddy pond shores. Western MA, VT (rare in both)

Veronica arvensis⁎   PLANTAGINACEAE
Corn speedwell
Spring and summer, 2–12 in., annual. Fields and roadsides.

Flowers blue, ⅛ in. wide, tucked singly in leaf axils. Middle and lower leaves ¼–¾ in. long, opposite, broadly oval, short-petioled or sessile, bluntly toothed; the upper leaves crowded, narrow, alternate, entire. Stems hairy. Fruit a rounded capsule, ⅛ in. long. Native to Eurasia. CT, MA, ME, NH, RI, VT

Veronica chamaedrys⁎   PLANTAGINACEAE
Germander speedwell, bird's-eye speedwell
Spring to midsummer, 4–12 in.,
perennial. Fields and roadsides.

Flowers blue, ⅜–½ in. wide, arranged in paired, long-stalked axillary racemes. Leaves ½–1½ in. long, oval, sessile or short-petioled, the larger with 5–11 teeth per side. Stems hairy, creeping at bases. Fruit a broad capsule, ⅛ in. long. Native to Europe. CT, MA, ME, NH, RI, VT

Veronica officinalis✳ PLANTAGINACEAE
Common speedwell
Spring to late summer, 4–12 in., perennial.
Woodlands, trail edges, fields, and roadsides.

Flowers light purple, ¼ in. wide, arranged in dense
axillary racemes. Leaves ¾–2 in. long, oval or elliptic,
short-petioled, the larger with 12–20 teeth per side. Stems
hairy, mostly creeping, the flower branches usually semierect. Fruit a broad capsule, ¼ in. long. Native to Europe.
CT, MA, ME, NH, RI, VT

Pinguicula vulgaris LENTIBULARIACEAE
Violet butterwort, butterwort
Early and midsummer, 2–6 in., perennial. Open,
moist subalpine ledges at high elevations.

Flowers violet, ⅜–¾ in. long, solitary, spurred, the
throat white and slightly hairy. Leaves ¾–2 in. long, oval,
sticky, yellow-green, with inrolled margins, arranged in a
rosette. Insects trapped on leaves are digested by plant's
enzymes. Stems finely hairy. Fruit an oval capsule, ¼ in.
long. ME, NH, VT (rare in all)

Liparis liliifolia ORCHIDACEAE
**Large-leaved twayblade, lily-leaf twayblade, lily-leaved
wide-lipped orchid**
Late spring to early summer, 4–10 in., perennial.
Deciduous and mixed forests and woodlands.

Flowers purple, ¾–1 in. long, arranged in an open
raceme; the lip fan-shaped, ⅜–½ in. long and wide; the 3
sepals green, narrow, wide-spreading; the 2 lateral petals
needle-thin, pointing straight down from the base of the
lip. Leaves 1½–7 in. long, oval, paired at the base. Stems
smooth, thick. Fruit an elliptical capsule, ½ in. long. CT
(rare), MA (rare), RI, VT (rare)

Viola affinis (*V. sororia* var. *affinis*) VIOLACEAE
Le Conte's violet
Early to late spring, 3–8 in., perennial. Swamps, wet meadows, streambanks, and floodplains.

Flowers violet, ¾–1¼ in. wide, solitary, short-spurred, the spreading lateral petals always and the lower petal sometimes bearded; the sepals entirely smooth. Leaves ¾–3 in., long, oval or triangular with a heart-shaped base, longer than wide. Stems smooth. Fruit an elliptical capsule, ⅜ in. long, smooth or slightly hairy (all other violets described here have smooth fruits). CT, MA, RI, VT

Viola sororia (woolly blue violet) is similar but has leaf blades as wide or wider than long and the sepals have fringed, marginal hairs.

Viola cucullata VIOLACEAE
Blue marsh violet, marsh blue violet
Spring, 4–10 in., perennial. Swamps, wet meadows, streambanks and seepages.

Flowers violet, darker towards the throat, ¾ in. wide, solitary, short-spurred, usually stalked well above the leaves; the lateral petals bearded with knob-tipped hairs (other violets described here have petals bearded with pointed hairs). Leaves 1–4 in. long and wide, heart-shaped; the margins bluntly toothed. Stems smooth. Fruit an elliptical capsule, ½ in. long. CT, MA, ME, NH, RI, VT

Viola nephrophylla VIOLACEAE
Northern bog violet
Spring to early summer, 4–6 in., perennial. Fens, wet meadows, and river shores, in high-pH conditions.

Flowers violet, ¾–1 in. wide, solitary, short-spurred, usually stalked slightly above leaves, the lateral petals angled forward; lateral petals and the lower petal bearded. Leaves 1–2½ in. long and at least as wide, broadly heart-shaped, sometimes purple-tinged underneath. Stems smooth. Fruit an elliptical capsule, ¼–⅜ in. long. CT (rare), MA (rare), ME, VT

Viola palustris VIOLACEAE
Northern marsh violet, alpine marsh violet
Summer, 1–6 in., perennial. Alpine seepages
and meadows at high elevations.

Flowers light purple or lilac-tinged, ½ in. wide, darker
towards the throat, solitary, short-spurred; the lateral
petals slightly bearded. Leaves ½–2 in. long and wide,
heart-shaped or oval, often creeping and clustered, the
margins bluntly toothed. Stems smooth. Fruit an elliptical capsule, ¼ in. long. ME, NH (rare in both)

Viola sagittata (V. fimbriatula) VIOLACEAE
Arrowhead violet
Spring, 2–8 in., perennial. Woodlands, fields,
and roadsides, in dry and moist soils.

Flowers violet, ¾–1 in. wide, solitary, short-spurred,
the lower 3 petals bearded. Leaves ½–4 in. long,
arrowhead-shaped, lance-shaped, oval, or triangular; leaf
bases often with coarse teeth or flared lobes. Stems often
finely hairy, sometimes smooth. Fruit an oval capsule,
¼–⅜ in. long. CT, MA, ME, NH, RI, VT
 Viola novae-angliae (New England violet), a rare species that grows only on river shore outcrops, also has
oval-triangular leaves but the leaves are shallowly and
evenly toothed, without coarse teeth or flared lobes.
Lower 3 petals bearded; the upper 2 petals also with scattered hairs. Stems hairy. ME

Viola selkirkii VIOLACEAE
Great-spurred violet, Selkirk's violet
Spring, 2–4 in., perennial. Rocky, moist deciduous forests.

Flowers light violet, ½–¾ in. wide, solitary, with a long,
thick, blunt-tipped spur ¼ in. long; all petals smooth.
Leaves ¾–1¼ in. long, oval or broadly heart-shaped,
notched at base; the basal lobes sometimes overlapping
above the notch. Stems smooth. Fruit an elliptical capsule, ¼ in. long. CT (rare), MA (rare), ME, NH, VT

Viola sororia (*V. papilonacea, V. septentrionalis*)
VIOLACEAE
Woolly blue violet, common blue violet
Spring, 2–8 in., perennial. Forests,
woodlands, thickets, and fields.

Flowers violet, ¾ in. wide, solitary, short-spurred, stalked
about as high as leaves; the 2 lateral petals bearded, the
lower petal smooth or occasionally hairy. Leaves 2–3 in.
long and wide, broadly heart-shaped; the margins bluntly
toothed. Stems hairy or occasionally smooth. Fruit an
elliptical capsule, ¼–⅜ in. long. Common and widespread. CT, MA, ME, NH, RI, VT

Viola affinis (Le Conte's violet) is similar but the leaves
are usually longer than wide and the sepals are entirely
smooth. The capsule is finely hairy; the capsules of the
other violet species described in this guide are smooth.

Amphicarpaea bracteata   FABACEAE
American hog-peanut, hog-peanut
Midsummer to fall, to 5 ft. long, annual
vine. Moist woodlands and thickets.

Flowers lilac or whitish, ½–¾
in. long, tubular, arranged in
stalked, axillary racemes; the
plant also produces inconspicuous flowers without petals along
the ground. Leaves long-petioled,
3-parted; the 3 leaflets ¾–3 in.
long, oval, rounded at base and pointed at tip. Stems twining, hairy, climbing or scrambling. Fruit an oblong, hairy
pod, ½–1½ in. long. CT, MA, ME, NH, RI, VT

*Baptisia australis**   FABACEAE
Blue wild indigo, blue false indigo
Spring and early summer, 1–4 ft.,
perennial. River banks and fields.

Flowers blue-violet, ¾–1¼ in. long, the 2 upper petals
round-tipped and erect, arranged in erect racemes, 8–16
in. long. Leaves 3-parted; the 3 leaflets ¾–3 in. long, oval,
broadest above middle. Stems smooth, thick. Fruit a thick
pod, 1¼–2½ in. long. Native to mid-Atlantic, central, and
southeastern United States. CT, MA, NH, VT

Lupinus perennis   FABACEAE
Wild lupine, sundial lupine
Spring and early summer, 8–24 in., perennial. Sandy or gravelly fields, woodlands, and open, disturbed sites.

Flowers blue or violet, occasionally pink or white, ½–¾ in. long, 2-lipped, arranged in racemes 4–8 in. long. Leaves long-petioled, palmately divided into 5–11 leaflets; the leaflets ¾–2 in. long, lance-shaped or narrowly oval. Stems smooth or finely hairy. Fruit a broad, hairy pod, 1¼–2 in. long. CT, MA (rare), NH (rare), RI (rare), VT (rare)

Lupinus polyphyllus⁎   FABACEAE
Blue lupine, garden lupine
Summer, 2–4 ft., perennial. Fields and roadsides.

Flowers blue or violet, sometimes pink or white, ¾–1 in. long, 2-lipped, arranged in racemes 8–24 in. long. Leaves long-petioled, palmately divided into 11–17 radiating leaflets; the leaflets 2½–5 in. long, lance-shaped. Stems smooth or finely hairy. Fruit a broad, densely hairy pod 1–1½ in. long. Native to western United States, naturalized in New England. CT, MA, ME, NH, VT

Vicia cracca⁎   FABACEAE
Cow vetch
Summer, 1–5 ft., perennial. Fields and roadsides.

Flowers blue, ¼–½ in. long, arranged in long-stalked, one-sided racemes of 20–50 downward-tilting flowers; the upper 2 sepals with broad, triangular tips. Leaves twining, pinnately divided into 12–30 leaflets; the leaflets ⅜–1¼ in. long, linear or narrowly lance-shaped. Stems finely hairy, trailing or climbing. Fruit a flattened, oval pod, ⅜–1 in. long. Native to Eurasia. CT, MA, ME, NH, RI, VT

Vicia tetrasperma FABACEAE
Four-seeded vetch, slender vetch
Late spring to late summer, 1–2 ft.,
annual. Fields and roadsides.

Flowers lilac or magenta, 1/8–1/4 in. long, long-stalked,
single or paired (sometimes 3) in leaf axils. Leaves twining, pinnately divided into 12–30 leaflets; the leaflets linear, 1/4–3/4 in. long and 1/8 in. (or less) wide. Stems slender, finely hairy, trailing or climbing. Fruit a flattened,
oval pod, 3/8–3/4 in. long. Native to Europe. CT, MA, ME,
NH, RI, VT

Vicia villosa FABACEAE
Hairy vetch
Summer, 1–5 ft., annual. Fields and roadsides.

Flowers 1/2–3/4 in. long, often bicolored blue and white,
occasionally pink, arranged in long-stalked, one-sided
racemes of 10–40 flowers; the upper 2 sepals with narrow
tips. Leaves twining, pinnately divided into 8–24 leaflets;
the leaflets 3/8–11/4 in. long, lance-shaped. Stems densely
hairy, trailing or climbing. Fruit a flattened, oval pod,
3/4–11/2 in. long. Native to Europe. CT, MA, ME, NH, RI, VT

Medicago sativa FABACEAE
Alfalfa, purple medick
Late spring to fall, 1–3 ft., perennial. Fields and roadsides.

Flowers blue or violet, 1/4–1/2 in. long, arranged in short,
stalked, axillary heads of 5–30 flowers. Leaves 3-parted;
the 3 leaflets linear or narrowly oval, 3/8–11/4 in. long,
finely toothed at the tip; the center leaflet tilted upward.
Stems branching, erect or semierect. Fruit a coiled pod,
about 1/4 in. long. A widely planted forage crop. Native to
Eurasia. CT, MA, ME, NH, RI, VT

Utricularia purpurea LENTIBULARIACEAE
Purple bladderwort, eastern purple bladderwort
Summer, 2–4 in., perennial, floating.
Pond and lake shallows.

Flowers 1–5, purple or pink-purple, yellow at center, ½ in. long; the upper lip cowl-like, the lower lip broad, 3-lobed, protruding. Leaves submerged, whorled, divided into filamentous, branching segments, with tiny bladders at the tips. Stems slender, floating. Fruit a capsule. CT, MA, ME, NH, RI, VT (rare)

Utricularia resupinata (resupinate bladderwort) is less common, the submerged leaves are alternately arranged, and the bladders are scattered along the leaves. Flowers solitary. CT (rare), MA (rare), ME, RI (rare), VT (rare)

Viola brittoniana VIOLACEAE
Coast violet
Spring to early summer, 2–8 in., perennial. Moist to wet meadows and upper floodplain terraces.

Flowers reddish violet, ¾–1¼ in. wide, solitary, short-spurred; the lateral petals bearded. Leaves 1½–4 in. long, deeply and variably divided into 5–15 irregular lobes; the uppermost lobe usually largest. Stems smooth. Fruit an oval capsule, ⅜– ¾ in. long. CT, MA (rare in both)

Viola pectinata (pectinate-leaved violet), a very rare species only in coastal areas, has triangular leaves, with long, sharp teeth, not deeply divided into narrow lobes. CT, MA

Viola palmata VIOLACEAE
Wood violet
Spring, 4–8 in., perennial. Forests, woodlands, and rocky slopes.

Flowers violet, ¾–1¼ in. wide, solitary, short-spurred; the lateral petals densely bearded, the lower bearded or smooth. Leaves 1–4 in. long, variably toothed and lobed, even on the same plant; the earliest emerging leaves often heart-shaped and unlobed, later leaves usually divided into 3–5 (sometimes more) irregular lobes. Stems hairy or smooth. Fruit an oval capsule, ½ in. long. CT (rare), MA, NH (rare), RI (rare), VT (rare)

Viola subsinuata (early blue violet) leaves are divided into 5–16 lobes. Western CT, MA (rare), VT (rare)

Viola pedata   VIOLACEAE
Bird-foot violet
Spring, 2–8 in., perennial. Sandy fields,
grasslands and dry woodland clearings.

Flowers lilac or violet, ¾–1½ in. wide, short-spurred, with
conspicuous orange stamens at center; all petals smooth.
Leaves 1–2 in. long, deeply divided into 9–15 narrow segments often toothed at the tip. Stems smooth. Fruit an
elliptical capsule, ⅜ in. long. CT, MA, NH (rare), RI

Aplectrum hyemale   ORCHIDACEAE
Puttyroot, Adam and Eve
Late spring to early summer, 12–24 in.,
perennial. Rich deciduous forests.

Flowers yellowish or greenish purple, about 1 in. long,
arranged in an open raceme; the 3 sepals spreading,
tipped with purple; the lip ⅜–1 in. long, white with purple spots. An oval, ribbed basal leaf, 4–8 in. long, develops in fall, after the blooming period, and withers the
following spring. Stems smooth, leafless except for several tiny bracts. Fruit an elliptical capsule, ⅝–1 in. long.
MA (rare)

Tipularia discolor   ORCHIDACEAE
Cranefly orchid
Mid- to late summer, 8–20 in., perennial.
Moist, deciduous forests and woodlands.

Flowers greenish purple, 1–1½ in. wide, arranged in an
open raceme, nodding and long-stalked, delicate, with
thin, spreading petals and sepals; the lip pale-purple, protruding, lobed at the base, with a long, slender spur ½–1
in. long. An oval basal leaf, 2–4 in. long, purple-veined,
develops in fall, after the blooming period, and persists
through the winter. Stems smooth. Fruit an oval capsule,
½ in. long. Southeastern MA (rare)

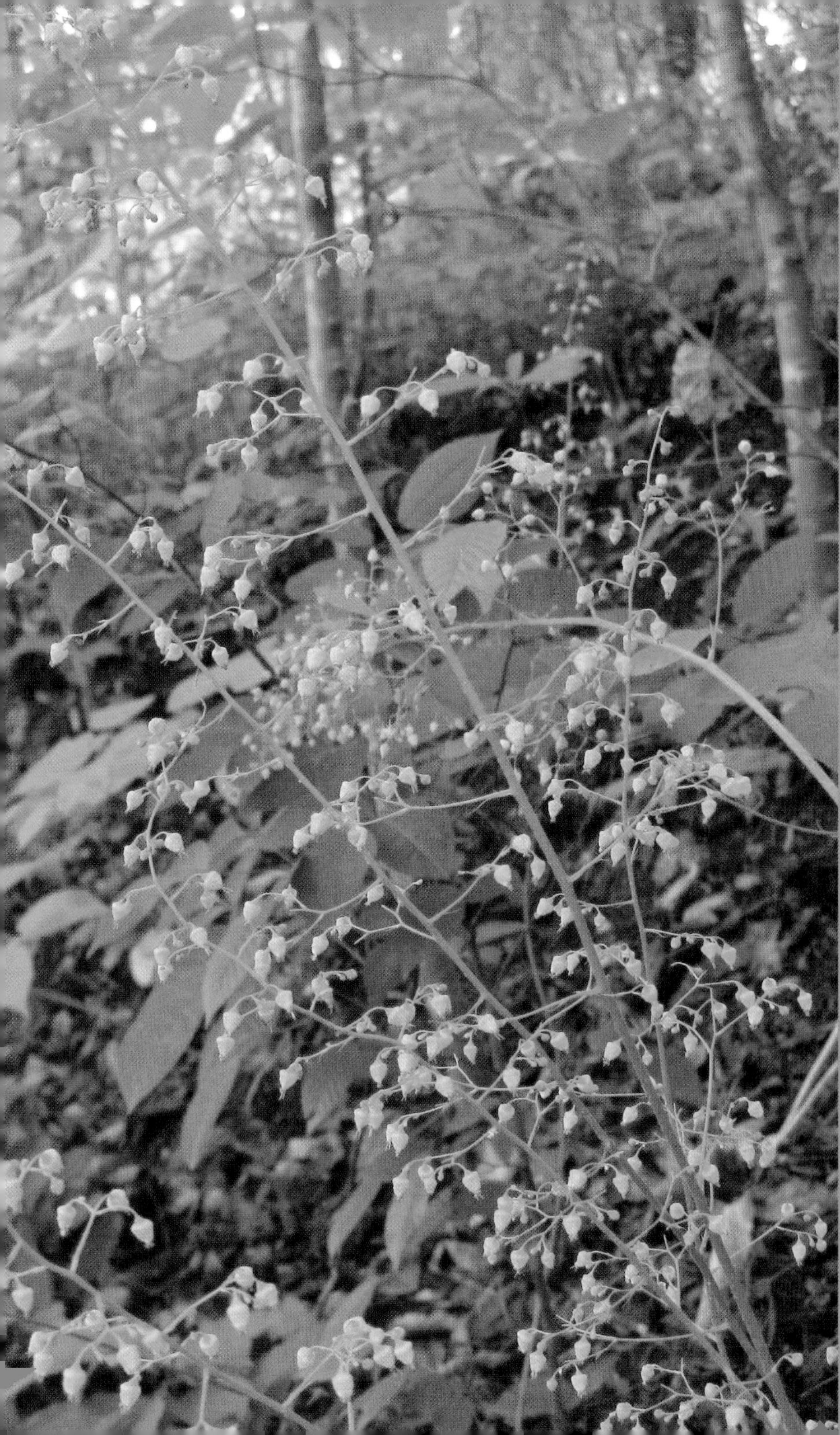

Veratrum viride   MELANTHIACEAE
American false hellebore, false hellebore, Indian poke
Late spring to midsummer, 2–6 ft., perennial.
Swamps, floodplains, and stream corridors.

Flowers yellowish green, ½–1 in. wide, arranged in a long, crowded, wide-branching panicle on upper stem. Leaves 6–14 in. long, oval or lance-shaped, clasping, strongly ribbed, emerging in early spring. Stems smooth or hairy. Fruit a narrowly oval capsule, about 1 in. long. The foliage and roots are poisonous. CT, MA, ME, NH, RI, VT

Smilax herbacea   SMILACACEAE
Carrion-flower
Spring to early summer, to 8 ft. long, perennial vine.
Moist woodlands, floodplains, and thickets.

Flowers yellowish green, ¼ in. wide, long-stalked, carrion-scented, densely clustered in long-stalked, round, axillary umbels. Leaves 2–5 in. long, oval or triangular, pointed at tip, long-petioled, with tendrils in the axils. Stems trailing or low-climbing, smooth. Fruit a blue berry, ⅜ in. long. CT, MA, ME, NH, RI, VT

Amaranthus cannabinus (*Acnida cannabina*)
AMARANTHACEAE
Saltmarsh water-hemp
Midsummer to fall, 2–7 ft., annual. Salt and brackish marshes, estuary shorelines.

Flowers green, ⅛ in. long, arranged in spikes at top of stem and in the leaf axils; the bracts beneath flowers tiny, shorter than the flowers. Leaves 2–6 in. long, linear or lance-shaped, long-petioled. Stems smooth, thick, ridged. Fruit an oval, black achene with a ridged surface, ⅛ in. long. A maritime species. CT, MA, ME, NH, RI

Amaranthus hybridus⁎   AMARANTHACEAE
Green amaranth, smooth pigweed
Late summer to fall, 2–6 ft., annual. Fields,
roadsides, and disturbed, open sites.

Flowers green, 1/16–1/8 in. long, clustered in slender terminal and axillary spikes; bracts under the flowers linear, sharp-pointed, slightly longer than the flowers.
Leaves 1–5 in. long, lance-shaped or oval, long-petioled,
hairy underneath. Stems hairy or smooth, often reddish
at base. Fruit an achene, 1/16 in. long. Native to tropical
America. CT, MA, ME, NH, RI, VT

Amaranthus retroflexus⁎   AMARANTHACEAE
Red-rooted amaranth, rough pigweed, redroot
Late summer to fall, 2–6 ft., annual. Fields,
roadsides, and disturbed, open sites.

Flowers green, 1/16–1/8 in. long, densely clustered in
short, thick, crowded terminal and axillary spikes; bracts
under flowers bristly, long-tapering to a sharp point,
twice as long as the flowers. Leaves 1–4 in. long, oval,
long-petioled, hairy underneath. Stems hairy, thick,
green or red. Fruit an achene, 1/16 in. long. Native to tropical America. CT, MA, ME, NH, RI, VT

Atriplex cristata (*A. arenaria, A. pentandra*)
AMARANTHACEAE
Seabeach orache, crested saltbush
Late summer to fall, 6–24 in., annual.
Sea beaches and salt marshes.

Flowers green, 1/8 in. long, arranged in short spikes
(male flowers) and in small, rounded, axillary clusters
(female flowers). Leaves silvery, 1/2–1 1/2 in. long, oval,
sessile or short-petioled, mostly entire, sometimes with
small, blunt teeth. Stems ascending or sprawling, widely
branched. Fruit a brown achene enclosed within a pair of
oval, toothed bracts, 1/8 in. long. CT, MA, RI

*Kochia scoparia** AMARANTHACEAE
Summer-cypress, kochia
Late summer to fall, 1–5 ft., annual. Fields, roadsides, beaches, and open, disturbed sites. Invasive.

Flowers yellowish green or reddish, 1/16 in. long, arranged in many crowded, leafy, hairy axillary spikes. Leaves 1/2–3 in. long, linear, crowded. Stems green or red, slightly hairy. Fruit a tiny, black-brown achene, enclosed within the 5 incurved sepals. Native to Eurasia. CT, MA, ME, NH, VT

Suaeda linearis AMARANTHACEAE
Annual sea-blite, tall sea-blite
Late summer to early fall, 8–36 in., annual.
Salt marshes and sea beaches.

Flowers green, 1/16 in. wide, closed, tucked in leaf axils; the 5 triangular sepals equal in size, keeled on upper surface. Leaves 1/8–3/4 in. long, linear, sharp-pointed, green. Stems erect or semierect, with many spreading or ascending branches. Fruit an achene less than 1/16 in. long. CT, MA, ME, NH, RI

Suaeda maritima AMARANTHACEAE
Herbaceous sea-blite, low sea-blite
Late summer to early fall, 2–24 in., annual.
Salt marshes and sea beaches.

Flowers green, 1/16–1/8 in. wide, closed, tucked in leaf axils; the 5 triangular sepals equal in size, flat, without keels. Leaves 1/8–1 in. long, linear, sharp-pointed, green with whitish bloom. Stems erect, semierect, or prostrate, with many branches. Fruits an achene, 1/16 in. long. CT, MA, ME, NH, RI

Suaeda calceoliformis (American sea-blite) is similar, but the 5 unkeeled sepals are unequal in size, and 1 or 2 of the sepals has a hornlike appendage. A rare species of salt marshes and sea beaches. CT, MA (rare), ME (rare), NH (rare), RI

*Persicaria hydropiper** *(Polygonum hydropiper)*
POLYGONACEAE
Water-pepper smartweed, common smartweed, water pepper
Summer to fall, 6–24 in., annual. Pond and river shores, swamps, and ditches.

Flowers whitish green, ⅛ in. long, closed, budlike, 4-parted and dotted with glands; the spikes 1–3 in. long, sparse, nodding, with scattered small leaves among the flowers. Leaves 1–4 in. long, lance-shaped, peppery to taste. Stems jointed, smooth, often red; the sheaths reddish or brown, with short bristles. Fruit a dull brown or black achene, 1/16 in. long. Native to Europe. CT, MA, ME, NH, RI, VT

*Persicaria perfoliata** *(Polygonum perfoliatum)*
POLYGONACEAE
Mile-a-minute vine
Summer, to 10 ft. long or more, annual vine. Woodlands, thickets, field edges, and disturbed, open sites. Invasive.

Flowers whitish green, ⅛ in. long, closed, budlike, clustered in short racemes borne above rounded bracts pierced by the stem. Leaves 1–3 in. long and wide, triangular, green or bluish green, with long, barbed petioles. Stems sharply barbed, climbing to 10 feet or more in trees and shrubs, often forming dense populations. Fruit a blue, berrylike achene, ⅛ in. long, aggregated in heads above the saucerlike bracts. Native to East Asia. CT, MA, NH, RI

Persicaria punctata *(Polygonum punctatum)*
POLYGONACEAE
Dotted smartweed
Summer to fall, 6–36 in., annual or perennial. Pond and river shores, swamps, and marshes.

Flowers whitish green, ⅛ in. long, closed, budlike, 5-parted and dotted with glands; the spikes 2–6 in. long, sparse, erect or ascending, without leaves among the flowers. Leaves 1½–6 in. long, lance-shaped. Stems jointed, smooth; the sheaths brown, smooth or hairy, with long bristles. Fruit a shiny brown or black achene, 1/16–⅛ in. long. CT, MA, ME, NH, RI, VT

Rumex britannica (*R. orbiculatus*) POLYGONACEAE
Greater water dock
Summer, 3–6 ft., perennial. Swamps, freshwater and tidal marshes, lake and river shores.

Flowers green, ¼ in. long, clustered in contiguous whorls on long, narrow racemes to 20 in. long. Leaves 8–24 in. long, lance-shaped, long-petioled, with flat or slightly wavy margins. Stems thick, ribbed, branched above. Fruiting head 3-valved, ¼ in. long, with rounded, entire edges and a flat base; the 3 slender grains much smaller than the valves. CT, MA, ME, NH, RI, VT

Rumex crispus⁎ POLYGONACEAE
Curly dock
Summer, 1–4 ft., biennial or perennial. Fields, roadsides, and open, disturbed sites.

Flowers green, ⅛ in. long, clustered in tight, contiguous whorls on long, narrow, branching racemes 6–18 in. long. Leaves 2–6 in. long, lance-shaped, with long petioles and strongly crisped, undulating margins. Stems thick, mostly smooth, often reddish, branched above. Fruiting head 3-valved, ⅛–¼ in. long, broadly oval, with entire edges; the 1–3 oval grains much smaller than the valves, and often unequal in size. Native to Eurasia. CT, MA, ME, NH, RI, VT

Rumex obtusifolius⁎ POLYGONACEAE
Bitter dock
Summer, 1–4 ft., perennial. Fields, roadsides, and open, disturbed sites.

Flowers green, ⅛ in. long, clustered in slightly separated whorls on long, narrow racemes. Leaves 4–16 in. long, broadly lance-shaped or oval, often red-veined, with a heart-shaped base and slightly wavy margins. Stems thick, ribbed, branched above. Fruiting head 3-valved, ⅛–¼ in. long, triangular, flattened, with spiny-toothed edges; the single slender grain much smaller than the valves. Native to Eurasia. CT, MA, ME, NH, RI, VT

Rumex pallidus POLYGONACEAE
Seabeach dock
Summer, 12–30 in., perennial. Sandy
and stony coastal beaches.

Flowers green, ⅛ in. long, clustered in contiguous or
slightly separated whorls on narrow racemes, 4–8 in.
long. Leaves 4–8 in. long, linear or lance-shaped, thick,
with a whitish bloom and flat margins. Stems erect, semierect, or sometimes sprawling. Fruiting head 3-valved, ⅛
in. long, oval, blunt-tipped, with entire edges; the 3 white,
oval grains almost as long as the valves. MA (rare), ME,
NH (rare)

Rumex triangulivalvis (*R. salicifolius*)
POLYGONACEAE
White dock, willow-leaved dock
Summer, 1–3 ft., perennial. Fields, roadsides,
shorelines, and disturbed, open sites.

Flowers green, ⅛ in. long, clustered in slightly separated
whorls on narrow racemes 4–12 in. long. Leaves 3–6 in.
long, narrowly lance-shaped, flat-margined, tapering
at both ends. Stems smooth, branching. Fruiting head
3-valved, ⅛ in. long, triangular, with entire edges; the 3
slender grains white, shorter than the valves. CT, MA, ME,
NH, RI, VT

Rumex verticillatus POLYGONACEAE
Swamp dock
Summer, 2–5 ft., perennial. Swamps and floodplains.

Flowers green, nodding, ⅛ in. long, clustered in stalked
(½ in. long), slightly separated whorls
on narrow racemes 8–16 in. long.
Leaves 2–12 in. long, lance-shaped,
flat-margined, narrowed at base. Stems
smooth. Fruiting head 3-valved, ⅛–¼
in. long, narrowly oval or triangular
with entire edges; the 3 slender grains
shorter than the valves. CT, MA (rare),
RI, VT

Scheuchzeria palustris   SCHEUCHZERIACEAE
Pod-grass, rannoch-rush
Spring, 8–16 in., perennial. Bogs and fens.

Flowers greenish, ¼ in. long, with spreading sepals (technically tepals) and 6 prominent purple stamens; the flowers arranged in loose, branching racemes, 1–4 in. long. Leaves 2–16 in. long, linear, grasslike, erect; the pointed tips with a tiny pore. Stems smooth, zigzag in form. Fruit a broadly oval, brown or yellow follicle, ¼ in. long, clustered in stalked groups of 2–4 (usually 3). CT (rare), MA (rare), ME, NH, RI (rare), VT (rare)

Parietaria pensylvanica   URTICACEAE
Pennsylvania pellitory, pellitory
Summer, 4–16 in., annual. Rocky forests and woodlands; occasionally in open, disturbed sites.

Flowers green, ⅟₁₆ in. long, clustered in small, sessile, axillary whorls, underlain by linear bracts slightly longer than the flowers. Leaves 1–3 in. long, lance-shaped, long-petioled, with fine hairs, tapering to tip. Stems hairy. Fruit an achene, less than ⅟₁₆ in. long, enclosed within the sepals. CT, MA (rare), NH, VT

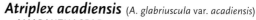

Atriplex acadiensis (*A. glabriuscula* var. *acadiensis*)
AMARANTHACEAE
Maritime orache
Summer to fall, 8–16 in., annual. Sea beaches, salt marshes.

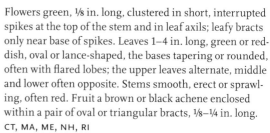

Flowers green, ⅛ in. long, clustered in short, interrupted spikes at the top of the stem and in leaf axils; leafy bracts only near base of spikes. Leaves 1–4 in. long, green or reddish, oval or lance-shaped, the bases tapering or rounded, often with flared lobes; the upper leaves alternate, middle and lower often opposite. Stems smooth, erect or sprawling, often red. Fruit a brown or black achene enclosed within a pair of oval or triangular bracts, ⅛–¼ in. long. CT, MA, ME, NH, RI

    Atriplex patula* (spearscale orache) is very similar, but the erect or sprawling stems are often longer (to 3 ft.), the stems and leaves are rarely tinged with red, and the plant occurs in weedy, disturbed habitats. Native to Eurasia. CT, MA, ME, NH, RI, VT

Atriplex prostrata   AMARANTHACEAE
Hastate-leaved orache, triangle orache
Summer to fall, 1–3 ft., annual. Sea beaches, salt marshes, and very occasionally in disturbed inland sites.

Flowers green, ⅛ in. long, clustered in short, interrupted spikes at the top of the stem and in leaf axils; leafy bracts only near base of spikes. Leaves similar in form and pattern to those of *Atriplex acadiensis*, but the leaf bases are more flattened, not tapered or round. Stems smooth, erect or sprawling. Fruit an achene, usually black, enclosed within a pair of triangular bracts ⅛–⅜ in. long. CT, MA, ME, NH, RI, VT

    Atriplex glabriuscula (bracted orache) has leafy bracts from the base to near the tip of the flower spikes. Stems widely branched. Fruit usually brown. CT (rare), MA (rare), ME, NH, RI (rare)

Chenopodium album⁎   AMARANTHACEAE
Lamb's-quarters, white pigweed
Summer to fall, 1–5 ft., annual. Fields, roadsides, and disturbed, open sites.

Flowers whitish green, 1⁄16 in. wide, closed, star-shaped, with 5 keeled sepals; the flowers densely clustered, in panicles 1–7 in. long. Leaves 1–4 in. long, oval or triangular, whitened underneath, long-petioled, the larger often coarsely toothed. Stems slightly hairy, branching. Fruit an achene, less than 1⁄16 in. wide, with a smooth surface. Widespread. Native to Europe. CT, MA, ME, NH, RI, VT

    Chenopodium berlandieri (pit-seeded goosefoot) is very similar, but the achene has a roughened surface. It is much less common. CT, MA, ME, NH, RI, VT

Chenopodium glaucum⁎   AMARANTHACEAE
Oak-leaved goosefoot
Summer to fall, 2–10 in. Roadsides and disturbed, open sites.

Flowers whitish green, 1⁄16 in. wide, closed, with 3 or 4 sepals; the flowers arranged on leafy axillary spikes 1–4 in. long. Leaves ¼–1½ in. long, lance-shaped or narrowly oval, the lower surfaces conspicuously whitened; larger leaves with several pairs of broad, shallow teeth. Stems erect or sprawling, branching from the base. Fruit a tiny black achene, less than 1⁄16 in. wide. Native to Eurasia. CT, MA, ME, NH, RI, VT

Chenopodium simplex (C. hybridum var.
gigantospermum) AMARANTHACEAE
Giant-seeded goosefoot, maple-leaved goosefoot
Summer to fall, 1–4 ft., annual. Woodlands,
rocky slopes, fields, and roadsides.

Flowers whitish green, 1/16–1/8 in. wide, closed, with 5
sepals; the flowers arranged in sparse, slender spikes
2½–6 in. long. Leaves 1½–6 in. long, triangular or oval,
long-petioled, bright green, tapering to a sharp point; the
margins with 1–4 pairs of coarse, widely separated teeth.
Stems smooth, branching. Fruit a black achene, 1/16 in.
wide. CT, MA, ME, NH, RI, VT

Dysphania ambrosioides* (Chenopodium
ambrosioides) AMARANTHACEAE
Mexican-tea
Summer to fall, 1–4 ft., annual. Roadsides
and disturbed, open sites.

Flowers green or reddish, 1/16 in. wide, closed, sessile,
with 5 sepals; the flowers clustered in leafy, ascending
or spreading spikes 1–3 in. long. Leaves 1–3 in. long,
lance-shaped, gland-dotted, with a kerosene-like smell;
the larger leaves sharply toothed. Stems sticky-hairy,
branching. Fruit a shining, dark brown achene, less than
1/16 in. wide. Native to tropical America. CT, MA, ME, NH,
RI, VT

Xanthium strumarium   ASTERACEAE
Rough cocklebur, clotbur
Midsummer to early fall, 1–6 ft. Beaches, dunes,
sandy river banks, fields, and disturbed, open sites.

Flowers green, tiny, clustered in rounded or cylindrical
heads at ends of stems (male flowers) and in leaf axils
(female flowers). Leaves 2–6 in. long, broadly oval or triangular, long-petioled, coarsely toothed, often with 3–5
broad lobes. Stems thick, branching, ridged. Fruiting
head a spiny, cylindrical bur, ½–1½ in. long, tipped by
2 straight or incurved beaks slightly thicker than the
spines. CT, MA, ME, NH, RI, VT

Acalypha gracilens   EUPHORBIACEAE
Slender three-seeded mercury
Summer to fall, 8–20 in., annual.
Thickets, fields, and roadsides.

Flowers yellowish green, ⅛ in. wide, tucked in
small clusters in leaf axils; the bracts under flowers
gland-dotted, green, hairy on the margins, with 9–15
sharp-pointed lobes. Leaves ¾–2 in. long, linear or narrowly lance-shaped, slightly toothed or entire; the petioles
of all leaves less than ¼ as long as the blades. Stems hairy
with short, incurved or pressed-in hairs. Fruit a 3-seeded
capsule, ¹⁄₁₆ in. long. CT, MA, NH, RI, VT (rare)

Acalypha rhomboidea   EUPHORBIACEAE
Common three-seeded mercury
Midsummer to fall, 8–24 in., annual.
Thickets, fields, and roadsides.

Flowers yellowish green, ⅛ in. wide, tucked in small
clusters in leaf axils; the green or reddish bracts
under the flowers mostly glandless, smooth, with 5–9
sharp-pointed lobes. Leaves 1–3 in. long, lance-shaped,
distinctly toothed; the petioles of the larger leaves usually more than ½ as long as the blades. Stems smooth or
finely hairy. Fruit a 3-seeded capsule, ¹⁄₁₆ in. long. CT, MA,
ME, NH, RI, VT

Acalypha virginica   EUPHORBIACEAE
Virginia three-seeded mercury
Late summer to fall, 4–20 in., annual.
Woodlands, thickets, fields, and roadsides.

Flowers yellowish green, ⅛ in. wide, clustered in very
small spikes in leaf axils; the bracts under the flowers
glandless, hairy, with 9–15 sharp-pointed lobes. Leaves
1–3 in. long, lance-shaped, with few, blunt teeth; the
petioles of the larger leaves usually ⅓–½ as long as the
blades. Stems usually hairy with incurved and spreading
hairs, occasionally smooth. Fruit a 3-seeded capsule, ¹⁄₁₆
in. long. CT (rare), MA (rare), RI

Petals indistinguishable; leaves simple, alternate, toothed or lobed

Proserpinaca palustris   HALORAGACEAE
Marsh mermaid-weed
Summer, 6–24 in., perennial. Pond and river
shallows, swamps, marshes, and fens.

Flowers green, ⅛ in. long, indistinctly 3-parted, usually
solitary in leaf axils. Leaves ¾–2 in. long, lance-shaped,
the above-surface leaves sharply toothed but not divided,
the subsurface leaves finely divided into 8–14 paired,
linear segments. Stems creeping at base, the flower
branches erect. Fruit an oval achene, ⅛ in. wide. CT, MA,
ME, NH, RI, VT (rare)

Laportea canadensis   URTICACEAE
Canada wood-nettle, wood-nettle
Summer, 1–4 ft., perennial. Rich, moist
forests and river floodplains.

Flowers whitish green, 1⁄16–⅛ in. wide, spreading in
loose, branching clusters from leaf axils; the upper clusters 1–4 in. long. Leaves 2–6 in. long, oval, long-petioled,
strongly veined, sharply toothed, with long-pointed tips;
the petioles with stinging hairs. Stems covered with
stinging hairs. Fruit an achene, 1⁄16–⅛ in. long. CT, MA,
ME, NH, RI, VT

Petals indistinguishable; leaves simple, opposite, toothed or lobed

Humulus japonicus⁕   CANNABACEAE
Japanese hops
Summer, 2–8 ft. long, annual vine. Thickets, fields,
stream corridors, and disturbed, open sites. Invasive.

Flowers yellowish green, ⅛ in. wide, clustered in open,
branching, erect inflorescences 1–8 in. long. Leaves 2–6
in. long, rough-surfaced; the larger leaves very broad,
with 5–9 lance-shaped lobes and petioles much longer
than the blades. Stems rough, prickly, trailing or climbing. Fruit an achene, ¼ in. long, aggregated in cylindrical heads about 1 in. long, partly covered by bristly bracts.
Native to East Asia. CT, MA, ME, NH, RI, VT

Humulus lupulus CANNABACEAE
Common hops
Summer, 3–30 ft. long, perennial vine. Stream corridors, thickets, fields, and disturbed, open sites.

Flowers yellowish green, ¼ in. wide, clustered in open, nodding, axillary inflorescences 2–6 in. long. Leaves 1½–6 in. long, with gland-dotted lower surfaces; the larger leaves very broad, with 3 (occasionally 5) broad lobes, and petioles shorter than the blades. Stems smooth or hairy and sparsely prickly, trailing or climbing. Fruit an oval achene, aggregated in cylindrical heads about 1 in. long, completely covered by blunt, smooth-margined bracts. CT, MA, ME, NH, RI, VT

Boehmeria cylindrica URTICACEAE
Small-spiked false nettle, false nettle
Summer, 1–3 ft., perennial. Swamps and floodplain forests.

Flowers green or whitish green, tiny, clustered in thin, axillary, ascending spikes 1–4 in. long. Leaves 1–6 in. long, oval, long-petioled, coarsely toothed, with 3 distinct, primary veins on the upper surface. Stems smooth or slightly hairy, without stinging hairs. Fruit an oval achene, ¹⁄₁₆ in. long. CT, MA, ME, NH, RI, VT

Pilea pumila URTICACEAE
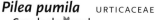
Canada clearweed
Midsummer to fall, 4–24 in., annual. Moist forests, floodplains, and seepages.

Flowers whitish green, tiny, arranged in drooping axillary clusters, ¼–1½ in. long. Leaves 1–5 in. long, oval, long-petioled, light green and translucent, coarsely toothed, tapering to a long point. Stems smooth, succulent, often colonial. Fruit a yellowish green achene, ¹⁄₁₆ in. long, sometimes with purple spots. CT, MA, ME, NH, RI, VT

    Pilea fontana (lesser clearweed) is very similar but much less common; the leaves are less translucent, and the achenes are a solid dark purple or black, with a thin, pale margin. CT, MA, RI (rare)

377

Urtica dioica (U. gracilis, U. procera) URTICACEAE
Stinging nettle
Summer, 2–8 ft., perennial. Floodplain
forests, thickets, fields, and roadsides.

Flowers whitish green, 1/16–1/8 in. wide, arranged in
spreading, axillary clusters 1–3 in. long; the flower clusters usually longer than leaf petioles. Leaves 2–7 in. long,
lance-shaped, tapering at tip, long-petioled, with stinging
hairs; paired stipules at the base of petioles 1/4–1/2 in. long,
erect, linear. Stems ridged, sparsely or densely covered
with stinging hairs. Fruit an achene, 1/16 in. (or less) long.
CT, MA, ME, NH, RI, VT

Urtica urens⁕ URTICACEAE
Burning nettle, dog nettle
Summer, 8–24 in., annual. Fields, roadsides,
and disturbed, open sites.

Flowers whitish green, 1/16–1/8 in. wide, arranged in axillary clusters 1/2–1 in. long; the flower clusters usually
shorter than the leaf petioles. Leaves 3/4–31/2 in. long, oval,
rounded at tip, long-petioled, with stinging hairs and
deep, sharp teeth; stipules at base of leaf petioles 1/8 in.
long, spreading or drooping, triangular. Stems ridged,
densely covered with stinging hairs. Fruit an achene, 1/16
in. long. Native to Eurasia. CT, MA, ME, NH, RI, VT

Heuchera americana SAXIFRAGACEAE
Common alum-root
Spring and early summer, 1–5 ft., perennial.
Deciduous forests and forest edges.

Flowers greenish, 1/4 in. long, arranged in an open panicle; the sepals green, longer than the purplish or pale petals; the protruding stamens with reddish orange anthers.
Leaves broadly oval or triangular,
11/2–41/2 in. long, long-petioled, with
5–9 lobes and prominent veins. Fruit
an oval, beaked capsule, 1/4 in. long. CT

Dysphania botrys* (*Chenopodium botrys*)
AMARANTHACEAE
Jerusalem-oak
Summer to fall, 8–24 in., annual. Roadsides
and disturbed, open sites.

Flowers green or reddish, 1/16 in. wide, closed, stalked,
with 5 densely glandular sepals; the flowers densely clustered in a leafless, branching inflorescence 4–9 in. long.
Leaves 1/2–1 1/2 in. long, lance-shaped, deeply cut into irregular lobes, glandular-hairy, aromatic. Stems sticky-hairy,
branching. Fruit a dull, blackish achene, less than 1/16 in.
wide. Native to Eurasia. CT, MA, ME, NH, RI, VT

Artemisia biennis*   ASTERACEAE
Biennial wormwood
Late summer to fall, 1–3 ft., annual or biennial.
Fields, roadsides, and disturbed, open sites.

Flower heads yellowish green, 1/8 in. wide, densely clustered along the stem in an erect, leafy, inflorescence 5–15
in. long. Leaves 2–6 in. long, crowded on stem, slightly
fragrant, deeply and finely divided into toothed, linear lobes. Stems smooth, green or reddish. Native to the
northwestern United States. CT, MA, ME, NH, RI, VT

Artemisia campestris (*A. cauduata*) ASTERACEAE
Field wormwood, tall wormwood
Midsummer to fall, 1–4 ft., biennial or perennial.
Cliffs, talus slopes, beaches, and dunes.

Flower heads yellowish green, 1/8 in. wide, arranged in
a branching, ascending, sparsely leafy inflorescence.
Leaves 1–5 in. long, hairy or smooth, crowded at base
(sparser on stem), slightly fragrant, deeply divided into
fine, linear, forking, toothless lobes. Stems smooth or
hairy, green or reddish brown. A variable species with 3
varieties in New England. CT, MA, ME, NH, RI, VT

Petals indistinguishable; leaves deeply
divided, alternate, leaflets toothed or lobed

379

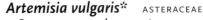

Artemisia vulgaris✻   ASTERACEAE
Common wormwood, mugwort
Midsummer to fall, 2–6 ft., perennial. Fields, roadsides, and disturbed, open sites.

Flower heads yellowish green, ⅛ in. wide, arranged in leafy, branching, ascending spikes. Leaves 1–5 in. long, green on upper surface, densely white-woolly on lower surface, strongly aromatic, divided into irregular, lance-shaped segments that are often toothed or lobed. Stems smooth or slightly hairy, often reddish brown. Widespread. Native to Eurasia. CT, MA, ME, NH, RI, VT

Proserpinaca pectinata   HALORAGACEAE
Comb-leaved mermaid-weed, coastal plain mermaid-weed
Summer, 8–20 in., perennial. Coastal plain pond shallows and shorelines and wet, peaty swales.

Flowers green, ⅛ in. long, indistinctly 3-parted, arranged in clusters of 1–3 in upper leaf axils. Leaves ½–1½ in. long, both the above and below-surface leaves deeply divided into 6–9 pairs of linear, comblike segments. Stems erect or creeping; the flowering branches erect. Fruit a 3-angled nutlet, ⅛ in. wide. Primarily coastal. CT, MA, ME (rare), RI (rare)

Thalictrum dioicum   RANUNCULACEAE
Early meadow-rue
Early to late spring, 12–30 in., perennial. Rich, rocky forests and floodplains.

Flowers about ¼ in. wide, with 4–6 greenish sepals and protruding, purple-yellow stamens (male plants) or white, digitlike pistils (female plants). Flower clusters branching and drooping on upper stem. Leaves long-petioled, smooth, pale or purplish green, twice divided into groups of 3–5 rounded or kidney-shaped leaflets, ½–1½ in. wide, with bluntly toothed or lobed margins. Stems smooth. Fruit an oval achene, ⅛ in. long. CT, MA, ME, NH, RI, VT

Ambrosia artemisiifolia ASTERACEAE
Common ragweed
Late summer to fall, 1–5 ft., annual. Fields,
roadsides, and disturbed, open sites.

Flower heads yellowish green, ⅛ in. wide, arranged in
erect, spikelike racemes 1–6 in. long. Leaves 1–6 in. long,
deeply divided into many lance-shaped or linear, lobed
segments; the lower leaves opposite, upper alternate.
Stems branching, usually hairy. Fruit a spiny achene,
⅛ in. long. Ragweed pollen is a major cause of hay fever;
in the words of American botanist Merritt Fernald, this
native species, now spread worldwide, is "a polymorphic
and despised weed." CT, MA, ME, NH, RI, VT

Ambrosia trifida ASTERACEAE
Giant ragweed
Late summer to early fall, 3–10 ft., annual. Fields,
roadsides, and disturbed, open sites.

Flower heads yellowish green, ⅛ in. wide, arranged in
erect, dense, spikelike racemes, 3–6 in. long. Leaves
2–8 in. long, long-petioled, all opposite; the larger leaves
broadly divided into 3–5 oval or lance-shaped, tapering
lobes. Stems green, hairy, often branching. Fruit a spiny
achene, ⅛–¼ in. long. CT, MA, ME, NH, RI, VT

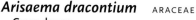

Arisaema dracontium ARACEAE
Green-dragon
Spring to early summer, 1–3 ft., perennial. Moist
forests and floodplains, often in high-pH soils.

Flowers tiny, aggregated in a thin, yellowish green spike,
2½–8 in. long, with an elongate, needlelike tip far sur-
passing the green, narrow spathe. Leaves usually solitary, long-petioled, divided into 5–15 lance-shaped leaflets in an apparent whorl; larger leaflets 4–8 in. long.
Fruit a berry, ¼–½ in. long, orange-red when ripe; the
berries clustered in a conical head. CT, MA (rare), NH
(rare), VT (rare)

Petals indistinguishable; leaves deeply divided, opposite, leaflets toothed or lobed

Petals indistinguishable; leaves deeply divided, basal, leaflets entire

381

Petals indistinguishable; leaves deeply divided, basal, leaflets entire

Arisaema triphyllum ARACEAE
Jack-in-the-pulpit, Indian turnip
Spring to early summer, 1–2 ft., perennial. Moist
forests, floodplains, and swamp edges.

Flowers tiny, aggregated in a thin green or yellow spike,
the "jack," 1½–3 in. long, covered by a broad, green- and
purple-mottled, white-striped, taper-pointed spathe (the
"pulpit"). Leaves 1 or 2, 3-parted, long-petioled; the 3 leaflets oval, 2–7 in. long. Fruit a berry, ¼ in. long, bright red
when ripe; the berries clustered in a conical head. CT, MA,
ME, NH, RI, VT

Petals indistinguishable; leaves absent, scaly, or needlelike

Salicornia ambigua (S. virginica)
AMARANTHACEAE
Perennial glasswort, woody glasswort
Late summer to fall, 4–12 in., perennial. Salt marshes.

Flowers green, ⅛ in. long, flattened, oval or triangular,
clustered in groups of 3, forming slender, jointed, branching spikes 1–2 in. long; central flower of each cluster at
same level as the lateral flowers. Bracts beneath the flowers scalelike, flattish or broad-tipped, usually slightly covering flowers. Stems creeping, woody and mat-forming at
base, about same width as spikes. Fruit an achene, 1/16 in.
long. CT, MA, ME, NH (rare), RI

Salicornia bigelovii AMARANTHACEAE
Dwarf glasswort
Late summer to fall, 2–16 in., annual. Salt marshes.

Flowers green, ⅛ in. long, flattened, oval, clustered in
groups of 3, forming thick, jointed spikes 1–4 in. long;
the central flower of each cluster elevated above the
lateral flowers. Bracts beneath the flowers scalelike,
sharp-tipped, partially or mostly covering flowers. Stems
succulent, erect, narrower than spikes, turning bright
red in fall. Fruit an achene, 1/16 in. long. CT, MA, ME (rare),
NH (rare), RI

Salicornia depressa (*S. europea*) AMARANTHACEAE
Common glasswort, slender glasswort
Late summer to fall, 2–20 in., annual. Salt marshes.

Flowers green, ⅛ in. long, flattened, oval, clustered in groups of 3, forming slender, jointed, branching spikes 1–4 in. long; the central flower of each cluster elevated above the lateral flowers. Bracts beneath flowers scalelike, blunt-tipped, usually slightly covering flowers. Stems succulent, mostly erect, sometimes creeping at base, about same width as spikes, turning bright red in fall. Fruit an achene, ⅟₁₆ in. long. CT, MA, ME, NH, RI

Coeloglossum viride (*Habenaria viridis* var. *bracteata*) ORCHIDACEAE
Long-bracted green orchid, long-bracted orchis, frog orchis
Late spring to summer, 8–20 in., perennial.
Moist forests, swamps, and fens.

Flowers green, sometimes purple-tinged, ¼–½ in. wide, with hoodlike petals and sepals and a long-protruding, notched lip, ¼–⅜ in. long; the spur very small and rounded. Inflorescence a single spike 2–8 in. long, with leafy, lance-shaped bracts much longer than the flowers. Primary leaves 2–5, oval, 2–5 in. long; the upper leaves much smaller. Stems smooth, with 1 or 2 sheaths at base. Fruit an oval capsule, about ½ in. long. CT (rare), MA (rare), ME, NH, RI, VT (rare)

Epipactis helleborine✳ ORCHIDACEAE
Broad-leaved helleborine, helleborine
Summer, 10–30 in., perennial. Forests, woodlands, and fields.

Flowers green or yellowish, often tinged with pink or purple, ¾–1 in. wide, with spreading to ascending petals and sepals, lacking a spur; the lip ⅜ in. long, heart-shaped at tip, with a pouchlike interior. Inflorescence a raceme, 4–12 in. long, often one-sided, with leafy bracts under the flowers. Leaves 1½–6 in. long, oval or lance-shaped, clasping, strongly veined. Stems leafy, the upper part hairy. Fruit an oval capsule, ½ in. long. Native to Eurasia and North Africa. CT, MA, ME, NH, RI, VT

Petals indistinguishable; leaves absent, scaly, or needlelike

Flowers bilateral; leaves simple, alternate, entire

Malaxis unifolia   ORCHIDACEAE
Green adder's-mouth
Midsummer, 3–10 in., perennial. Swamps,
bogs, and moist woodlands.

Flowers green, ⅛ in. wide, spreading or nodding, with
an angular, notched lip; the flower stalks ¼–⅜ in. long.
Inflorescence a raceme, with 10–100 flowers, densely
clustered at top, the lower flowers opening and wilting
first. Leaves 1 or occasionally 2, oval, 1–4 in. long, sheathing the stem. Stems smooth, thickened at base. Fruit
an oval capsule, ¼ in. long. CT (rare), MA (rare), ME, NH
(rare), RI (rare), VT (rare)
   Malaxis bayardii (Bayard's adder's-mouth), is an
extremely rare species limited to dry, sandy woodlands
and fields in eastern MA.

Platanthera aquilonis (*P. hyperborea*)
ORCHIDACEAE
North wind bog-orchid, northern green orchis
Summer, 6–24 in., perennial. Moist forests,
swamps, fens, and seepages.

Flowers whitish or yellowish green, ¼ in. wide, not fragrant, with hoodlike upper petals and sepal, spreading
or reflexed lateral sepals, and a narrow, yellow-green lip
⅛–¼ in. long; the spur shorter than the lip. Inflorescence
a raceme, 2–8 in. long, with a narrow, leafy bract below
each flower. Leaves 2–4, lance-shaped, 1½–8 in. long.
Stems smooth, thick. Fruit an oval capsule, ½ in. long.
CT, MA, ME, NH, RI (rare), VT (rare)

Platanthera clavellata (*Habenaria clavellata*,
Gymnadeniopsis clavellata)
ORCHIDACEAE
**Green woodland orchid, club-spur orchid, little club-spur
bog-orchid**
Summer, 4–16 in., perennial. Bogs, fens,
wet meadows, and swamps.

Flowers greenish white or yellowish, ¼–½ in., the lips
wedge-shaped, usually with several shallow lobes or
teeth at the tip; the flower spurs ⅜–½ in., with a dilated
"club-foot" tip. Inflorescence a loose raceme of 5–15 flowers; a number of the flowers are twisted so their spurs
are perpendicular or ascending relative to the stem axis.
Lower stem with 1 large leaf, lance-shaped or oval, 3–6
in.; other leaves much smaller. Fruit an oval capsule, ½
in. long. CT, MA, ME, NH, RI (rare), VT

Platanthera flava (*Habenaria flava*) ORCHIDACEAE
Northern tubercled bog-orchid, tubercled orchid
Midsummer, 6–24 in., perennial. Wet meadows
and thickets, floodplains, and seepages.

Flowers yellowish green, ¼ in. wide, with hoodlike upper
petals; the lip oval, ⅛–¼ in. long, with a small, round
protuberance at its crest; the spur slender, distinctly longer than the lip. Inflorescence a raceme, 2–8 in. long,
with a linear, sharp-tipped bract below each flower.
Larger leaves 2 or 3, lance-shaped, 2–12 in. long, near
middle of stem; the upper leaves much smaller. Stems
smooth. Fruit an oval capsule, ¼–½ in. long. CT, MA, ME,
NH, RI, VT (rare in all)

Platanthera huronensis (*P. hyperborea* var.
huronensis) ORCHIDACEAE
Lake Huron bog green orchid, green bog orchis
Summer, 6–36 in., perennial. Marshes,
fens, river and lake shores.

Flowers whitish green, ¼–½ in. wide, fragrant, with
hoodlike upper petals and sepal, spreading or reflexed lateral sepals, and a narrow, whitish green lip ¼–½ in. long;
the spur about equal in length to the lip. Inflorescence
a raceme, 3–10 in. long, with a narrow, leafy bract below
each flower. Leaves 2–4, lance-shaped, 2–12 in. long.
Stems smooth, thick. Fruit an oval capsule, ½ in. long.
CT, MA (rare), ME, NH, RI (rare), VT (rare)

Neottia convallarioides (*Listera convallarioides*)
ORCHIDACEAE
Broad-leaved twayblade
Summer, 4–12 in., perennial. Cool, mossy,
evergreen forests and forested swamps.

Flowers whitish green, pale, ½–⅝ in. long; the lip flattish, conspicuously protruding, ⅜ in. long, slightly
notched at tip, narrowing to a wedge-shaped base. Inflorescence an erect raceme with 5–20 flowers; the flower
stalks sticky with glandular hairs. The single pair of
stem leaves broadly oval, sessile, 1½–2 in. long. Stems
sticky-hairy above, smooth below. Fruit an oval capsule,
¼–⅜ in. long. ME, NH (rare), VT
  Neottia cordata (heart-leaved twayblade) is similar but
with blue flowers. CT, MA (rare), ME, NH (rare), RI, VT
  Neottia auriculata (auricled twayblade) is similar, but
the lip is rounded at the base and the tip is more deeply
notched. ME (rare), NH (rare), VT

Scrophularia lanceolata   SCROPHULARIACEAE
Lance-leaved figwort, American figwort
Late spring to midsummer, 2–6 ft., perennial.
Fields, thickets, and woodlands.

Flowers brownish green, shiny, ⅜–½ in. long, with an ascending, lobed upper lip and a drooping, blunt lower lip; the flower interior with 4 normal stamens and a yellowish green, sterile stamen just below upper lip. Inflorescence a panicle, 4–10 in. long and 1–3 in. wide, with ascending branches. Leaves 3–10 in. long, lance-shaped or oval, the larger sharply, coarsely, and deeply toothed, with winged petioles. Stems smooth, flattened or shallowly grooved. Fruit an oval capsule, ¼–⅜ in. long. CT, MA, ME, NH, RI (rare), VT (rare)

Scrophularia marilandica
SCROPHULARIACEAE
Eastern figwort, carpenter's-square
Mid- to late summer, 3–9 ft., perennial.
Woodlands, fields, and river banks.

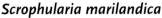

Flowers brownish or reddish green, dull, ¼–⅜ in. long, with an ascending, lobed upper lip and a drooping, blunt lower lip; the flower interior with 4 normal stamens and a dark purple or brown sterile stamen just below upper lip. Inflorescence a panicle, to 12 in. long and 3–6 in. wide, roughly pyramidal, with spreading branches. Leaves 4–6 in. long, sharply but evenly toothed; the petioles not winged. Stems hairy above, smooth below, prominently grooved. Fruit an oval capsule, ⅛–¼ in. long. CT, MA, NH, RI (rare), VT (rare)

Platanthera hookeri (*Habenaria hookeri*)
ORCHIDACEAE
Hooker's bog-orchid, Hooker's orchid
Late spring to midsummer, 8–16 in., perennial.
Rich, moist forests and forest edges.

Flowers green or yellowish, ½ in. wide, with reflexed lateral sepals, hoodlike upper petals and upper sepal, and a tapering, upwardly curving lip, ⅜–½ in. long; the spur conspicuous, descending, ½–1 in. long. Inflorescence a raceme, 4–10 in. long, with 2–25 flowers. Leaves 2, paired, broadly rounded, 2½–5 in. long, flat on the ground. Stems smooth. Fruit an oval capsule, ½ in. long. MA (rare), ME, NH, VT (rare)

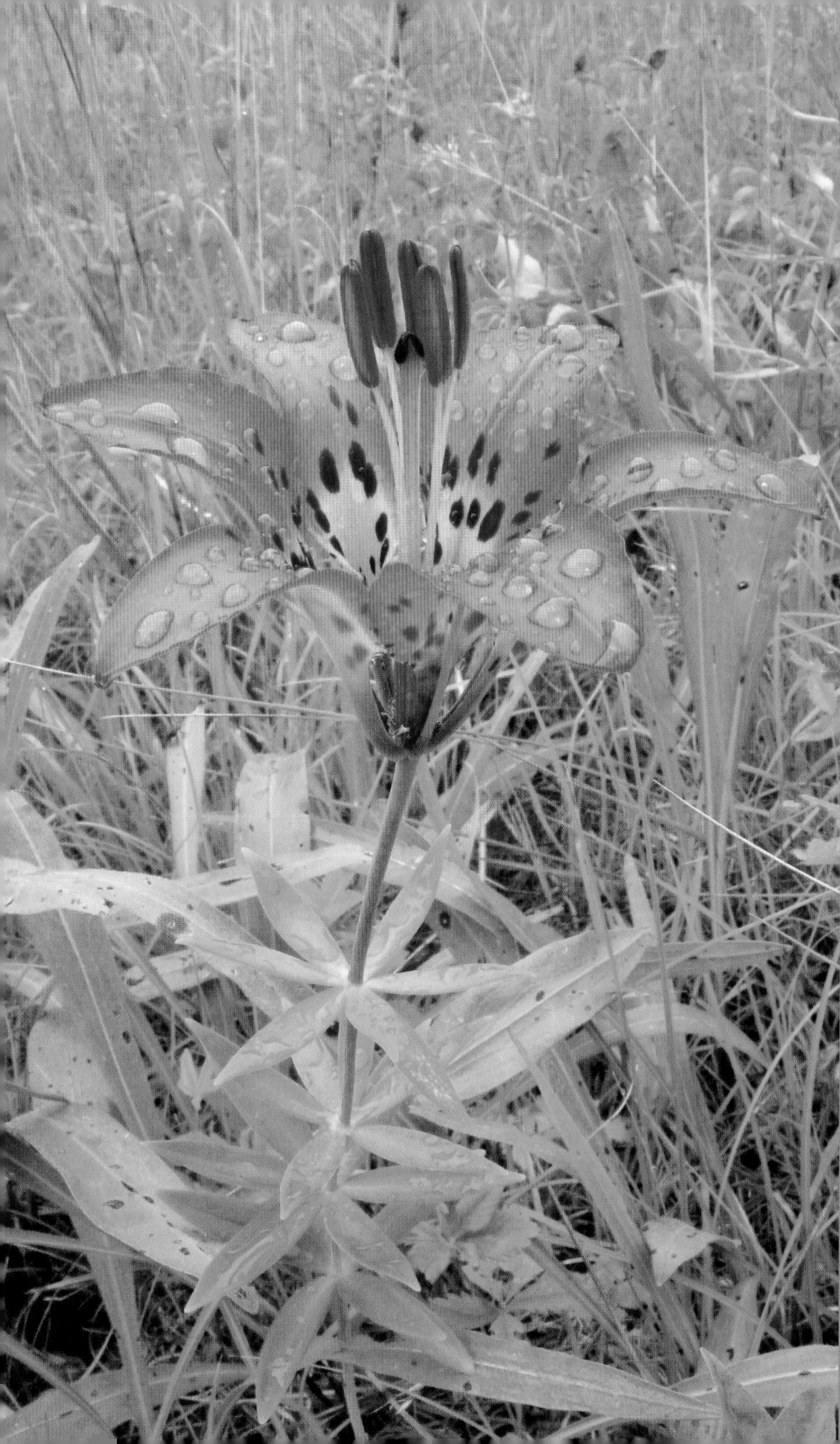

Asclepias tuberosa APOCYNACEAE
Butterfly milkweed, butterfly-weed, pleurisy-root
Summer, 12–30 in., perennial. Dry,
sandy fields and roadsides.

Flowers orange or yellowish orange, ½–¾ in. long, with
an upright, 5 parted-crown and 5 downward-curving petals beneath the crown; the flowers arranged in flattish
umbels 2–3 in. wide. Leaves 2–4 in. long, lance-shaped,
crowded, the upper leaves sometimes opposite. Stems
thick, hairy, often branching. Fruit a narrow, tapering,
upright follicle 3–5 in. long. Widely planted; naturally
occurring populations uncommon. CT, MA, NH (rare),
RI (rare)

Lysimachia arvensis (*Anagallis arvensis*)
MYRSINACEAE
Scarlet pimpernel, poor man's weather-glass
Summer, 4–12 in., annual. Fields, roadsides,
and disturbed, open sites.

Flowers reddish orange, occasionally blue, ¼ in. wide,
solitary on long, axillary stalks, closed on cloudy days.
Leaves ¼–1 in. long, oval, sessile. Stems semierect or
sprawling, wide-branching. Fruit a rounded capsule, ⅛
in. long. Native to Eurasia. CT, MA, ME, NH, RI, VT

Lilium lancifolium (*L. tigrinum*) LILIACEAE
Lance-leaved tiger lily, tiger lily
Summer, 2–6 ft., perennial. Fields, roadsides.

Flowers reddish orange, purple-spotted, 3–4 in. wide,
nodding, long-stalked, with strongly reflexed petals and
protruding stamens; the inflorescence a raceme of 3–25
flowers. Leaves 4–7 in. long, lance-shaped, sessile, the
upper with small, dark bulblets in the axils. Stem purple
or black, with whitish, cobwebby hairs. Fruit an elliptical
capsule, 1–3 in. long. Native to China. CT, MA, ME, NH,
RI, VT

Lilium superbum (Turk's-cap lily) is similar but has
whorled leaves.

Lilium philadelphicum   LILIACEAE
Wood lily
Mid- to late summer, 1–3 ft., perennial. Dry,
often sandy fields, thickets, and woodlands.

Flowers orange or reddish orange, purple-spotted, 1½–3
in. wide, erect, arranged in clusters of 1–5 at the top of
the stem. Leaves in whorls of 4–7, lance-shaped, 2–4 in.
long. Stems smooth. Fruit an elliptical capsule, 1–2 in.
long. CT, MA, ME, NH, RI (rare), VT (rare)

Lilium superbum   LILIACEAE
Turk's-cap lily
Mid- to late summer, 3–8 ft., perennial. Swamp edges,
and moist to wet woodlands, thickets, and meadows.

Flowers orange or reddish orange, purple-spotted,
2½–3½ in. wide, nodding, long-stalked, with strongly
reflexed petals and protruding stamens; the inflorescence a raceme of 1–12 flowers. Leaves in whorls of 3–20,
lance-shaped, 3–10 in. long. Stems smooth. Fruit an elliptical capsule, 1–2½ in. long. CT, MA, NH (rare), RI

Hemerocallis fulva*   LILIACEAE
Orange day-lily
Late spring to midsummer, 2–6 ft., perennial.
Fields, thickets, and roadsides.

Flowers reddish orange, unspotted, 3–4 in. wide, ascending or upright, arranged in clusters of 3–15 at the top
of the stem; individual flowers open only for 1 day.
Leaves in a basal cluster, 2–3 ft. long, linear or narrowly
lance-shaped. Stems smooth, often with a few small,
scaly bracts. Fruit an oval, 3-angled capsule, 1 in. long.
Native to East Asia. CT, MA, ME, NH, RI, VT

*Hieracium aurantiacum** ASTERACEAE
Orange hawkweed, devil's paintbrush
Summer, 5–15 in., perennial. Fields,
roadsides, and disturbed, open sites.

Flower heads deep orange, ¾ in. wide, with many
rays, arranged in compact clusters of 5–30 heads;
bracts beneath the flower heads covered with black,
gland-tipped hairs. Leaves in a basal rosette, 2–6 in. long,
lance-shaped, with bristly hairs. Stems densely hairy.
Native to Europe. CT, MA, ME, NH, RI, VT

Platanthera ciliaris (Habenaria ciliaris)
ORCHIDACEAE
Orange-fringed bog-orchid, yellow fringed orchis
Mid- to late summer, 1–3 ft., perennial. Sandy
and peaty meadows and thickets.

Flowers bright orange or yellow, ½–¾ in. long, with a
deeply fringed lower lip; the spur conspicuously elongated, ⅝–1½ in. long, exceeding the length of the lip.
Flowers arranged in a long, dense spike 2–6 in. long and
1½–2 in. wide, with 25–100 flowers. Leaves 2–8 in. long,
lance-shaped, the lower much larger than the upper.
Fruit a capsule, 1 in. long. CT (rare), RI (rare)
  Platanthera cristata (crested orange bog-orchid, yellow
crested orchis), a plant of wet, sandy or peaty soil, is similar, but the flower spur is shorter (¼–½ in. long), about
equal to the lip, and the flower spike is narrower (¾–1½
in. wide). Extremely rare, only near coast in MA.

Impatiens capensis BALSAMINACEAE
Jewelweed, spotted touch-me-not
Summer, 2–4 ft., annual. Swamps,
river and lake shores, ditches.

Flowers orange with red-brown spots, ¾–1¼ in. long,
suspended on slender, arching, axillary stalks; the body
funnel-shaped, with a deeply curving spur; the upper lip
hoodlike, the lower lip broad and deeply notched. Leaves
1–4 in. long, oval, fleshy, and bluntly toothed. Stems
smooth and succulent. Fruit a narrow capsule, ¾ in.
long, that explosively propels seed when touched. CT, MA,
ME, NH, RI, VT

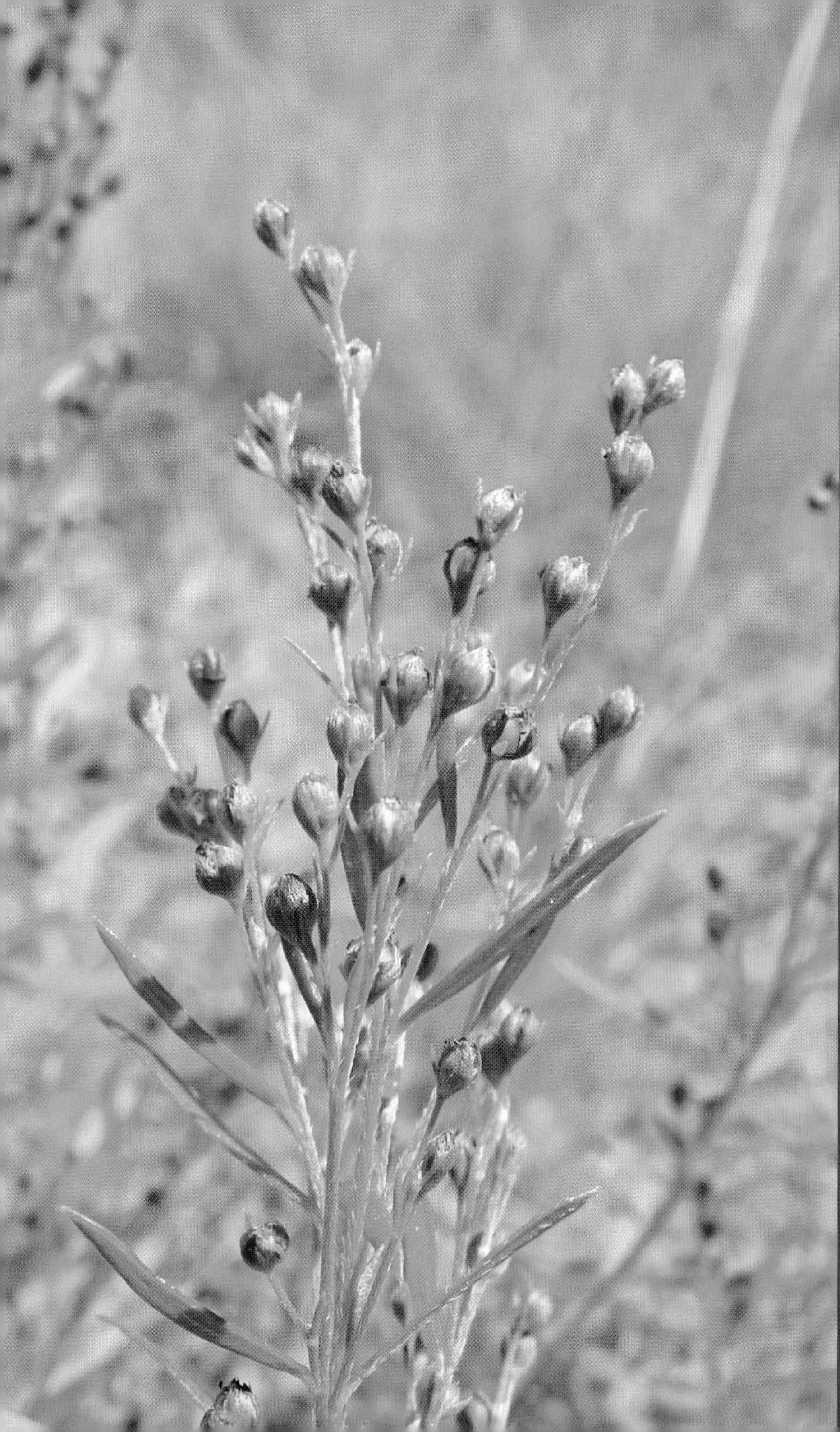

Salsola kali ⁕ AMARANTHACEAE
Saltwort
Midsummer to fall, 6–36 in., annual.
Sea beaches, salt marshes.

Flowers reddish brown or green, ¼ in. long, tucked in leaf axils, underlain by spiny bracts longer than the flowers. Leaves ½–1½ in. long, linear, fleshy, spine-tipped. Stems wide-branching, hairy, semierect or sprawling, often reddish. Fruit an achene, ¹⁄₁₆ in. long, enclosed in folded calyx lobes. Native to Eurasia and North Africa. CT, MA, ME, NH, RI

Endodeca serpentaria (*Aristolochia serpentaria*)
ARISTOLOCHIACEAE
Virginia serpentaria, Virginia snakeroot
Midspring to early summer, 6–24 in., perennial.
Rocky woodlands in high-pH soils.

Flowers greenish brown or purplish brown, ½–¾ in. long, solitary, with a broad, flaring mouth and a con-

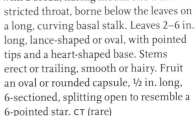

stricted throat, borne below the leaves on a long, curving basal stalk. Leaves 2–6 in. long, lance-shaped or oval, with pointed tips and a heart-shaped base. Stems erect or trailing, smooth or hairy. Fruit an oval or rounded capsule, ½ in. long, 6-sectioned, splitting open to resemble a 6-pointed star. CT (rare)

Gnaphalium uliginosum ⁕ ASTERACEAE
Brown cudweed, low cudweed
Midsummer to fall, 2–10 in., annual. Fields, roadsides, and disturbed, open sites.

Flower heads whitish brown, ⅛ in. long, aggregated in small, dense clusters at the top of the stem, usually overtopped by surrounding leafy bracts. Leaves ½–2 in. long, linear or lance-shaped, sessile, white-woolly on both sides. Stems branching, erect or sprawling, densely woolly. Native to Europe. CT, MA, ME, NH, RI, VT

Lechea intermedia CISTACEAE
Round-fruited pinweed, intermediate pinweed
Summer, 8–24 in., perennial. Sandy woodlands,
fields, roadsides, and dry, open clearings.

Flowers brown or reddish, 1/16 in. long, arranged on open,
ascending, axillary branches; the entire inflorescence
1/3–1/2 the height of the plant. Stem leaves 1/8–3/8 in. long,
linear or lance-shaped, the undersurface with scattered,
longish hairs on the margins and middle vein (sometimes smooth); basal leaf shoots to 3 in. long, prostrate,
hairy, crowded with small, whorled leaves. Stems with
pressed-in hairs. Fruit an oval capsule, 1/16 in. long. CT,
MA, ME, NH, RI, VT

Lechea maritima CISTACEAE
Beach pinweed, maritime pinweed
Summer, 4–16 in., perennial. Coastal beaches and
dunes; occasionally inland in open, sandy sites.

Flowers brown or reddish, 1/16 in. long, arranged in
spreading or ascending, axillary branches; the entire
inflorescence 1/2–2/3 the height of plant. Stem leaves 1/8–3/4
in. long, linear or lance-shaped, the undersurface covered
with fine hairs; basal leaf shoots to 8 in. long, ascending, with small, whorled, crowded, densely woolly-hairy
leaves. Stems covered with fine, ascending hairs. Fruit an
oval capsule, 1/16 in. long. CT, MA, ME, NH, RI, VT

Lechea mucronata (*L. villosa*) CISTACEAE
Hairy pinweed
Summer, 8–32 in., perennial. Woodlands,
fields, and roadsides.

Flowers brown or reddish, 1/16 in. long, densely clustered on short, ascending, axillary branches. Stem leaves
3/8–1¼ in. long, lance-shaped or oval, with long, spreading
hairs on margins and undersurface; basal leaf shoots to 4
in. long, with small, crowded, whorled, hairy, oval leaves.
Stems densely covered with spreading hairs. Fruit an oval
capsule, 1/16 in. long. CT, MA, ME, NH, RI, VT

Lechea tenuifolia CISTACEAE
Narrow-leaved pinweed
Summer, 4–12 in., perennial. Woodlands,
ridges, dry clearings, sandy fields.

Flowers brown or reddish, 1/16 in. long or less, arranged
on numerous, spreading, axillary branches; the entire
inflorescence about ½ the height of the plant. Stem leaves
¼–¾ in. long, needle-thin, more than 10 times as long
as wide, sparsely hairy on the undersurface; basal leaf
shoots to 3 in. long, mat-forming, crowded with linear
leaves. Stems with fine, ascending hairs. Fruit an oval
capsule, 1/16 in. long. CT, MA, NH (rare), RI

Typha angustifolia⁎ TYPHACEAE
Narrow-leaved cat-tail
Late spring to summer, 3–5 ft., perennial. Salt and
brackish marshes, inland ditches along salted roadways.

Flowers brown, minute, densely aggregated in elongate
male (upper) and female (lower) spikes separated by a
gap ½–3 in. long. Female spikes 4–8 in. long and ⅜–¾
in. thick. Leaves lance-shaped, 2–6 ft. long and ¼–½ in.
wide, usually taller than stem. Stems smooth, ¼–½ in.
thick. Fruit a tiny achene attached to long, bristly hairs.
Native to Eurasia. CT, MA, ME, NH, RI

Typha latifolia TYPHACEAE
Broad-leaved cattail
Late spring to summer, 3–8 ft., perennial. Marshes,
shallows of lakes, ponds, and rivers, ditches.

Flowers brown, minute, densely aggregated in elongate,
contiguous or scarcely separated male (upper) and female
(lower) spikes. Female spikes 4–6 in. long and 1–1½ in.
thick. Leaves lance-shaped, 3–8 ft. long and ½–1 in. wide,
equal to or shorter than stem. Stems smooth, ⅜–¾ in.
thick. Fruit a tiny achene attached to long, bristly hairs.
CT, MA, ME, NH, RI, VT

Epifagus virginiana   OROBANCHACEAE
Beech-drops
Late summer to fall, 4–20 in., perennial.
Forests, associated with beech trees.

Flowers purplish brown, ¼ in. long, tubular,
short-stalked, arranged in a slender raceme. Leaves tiny,
scalelike. Stems brown or yellowish, slender, branching
from near the base, persistent through winter. Fruit an
oval capsule, ⅛–¼ in. long. Plant lacks chlorophyll, parasitic on roots of beech. CT, MA, ME, NH, RI, VT

BIBLIOGRAPHY

Brandenburg, David M. 2010. *National Wildlife Federation Field Guide to Wildflowers of North America*. New York: Sterling Publishing.

Brumback, William E., and Jessica Gerke. 2013. Flora Conservanda: New England 2012. The New England Plant Conservation Program (NEPCoP) List of Plants in Need of Conservation. *Rhodora* 115: 313–408.

Clemants, Steven, and Carol Gracie. 2006. *Wildflowers in the Field and Forest: A Field Guide to the Northeastern United States*. New York: Oxford University Press.

Connecticut Botanical Society. 2014. *Native and Naturalized Vascular Plants of Connecticut Checklist*. Memoirs of the Connecticut Botanical Society, Number 5. New Haven, Connecticut.

Cullina, Melissa D., Bryan Connolly, Bruce Sorrie, and Paul Somers. 2011. *The Vascular Plants of Massachusetts: A County Checklist*. Westborough, Massachusetts: Natural Heritage and Endangered Species Program, Massachusetts Division of Fisheries and Wildlife.

DeGraaf, Richard M., and Mariko Yamasaki. 2001. *New England Wildlife: Habitat, Natural History, and Distribution*. Hanover, New Hampshire: University Press of New England.

Enser, Richard W., and Julie A. Lundgren. 2006. *Natural Communities of Rhode Island*. A joint project of the Rhode Island Dept. of Environmental Management Natural Heritage Program and the Nature Conservancy of Rhode Island. http://rinhs.org/wp-content/uploads/2012/05/ri_nat_comms_2006.pdf

Fernald, Merritt L. 1950. *Gray's Manual of Botany: A Handbook of the Flowering Plants and Ferns of the Central and Northeastern United States and Adjacent Canada*. 8th ed. New York: American Book Company.

Foster, David R., Brian M. Donahue, David B. Kittredge, et al. 2010. *Wildlands and Woodlands: A Vision for the New England Landscape*. Petersham, Massachusetts: Harvard Forest, Harvard University Press.

Gawler, Susan, and Andrew Cutko. 2010. *Natural Landscapes of Maine: A Guide to Natural Communities and Ecosystems*. Augusta, Maine: Maine Natural Areas Program.

Gleason, Henry A., and Arthur Cronquist. 1991. *Manual of Vascular Plants of Northeastern United States and Adjacent Canada*. 2nd ed. Bronx, New York: New York Botanical Garden.

Haines, Arthur. 2011. *The New England Wild Flower Society's Flora Novae-Angliae: A Manual for the Identification of Native and Naturalized Higher Vascular Plants of New England*. New Haven, Connecticut: Yale University Press.

Jorgensen, Neil. 1977. *A Guide to New England's Landscape*. Chester, Connecticut: Pequot Press.

Metzler, Kenneth J., and Juliana P. Barrett. 2006. *The Vegetation of Connecticut: A Preliminary Classification*. Hartford, Connecticut: State Geological and Natural History Survey of Connecticut.

Mittelhauser, Glen H., Linda L. Gregory. Sally C. Rooney, and Jill E. Weber. 2010. *The Plants of Acadia National Park*. Orono, Maine: University of Maine Press.

New England Wildflower Society. 2015. State of the Plants: Challenges and Opportunities for Conserving New

England's Native Flora. Framingham, Massachusetts.

Newcomb, Lawrence. 1977. *Newcomb's Wildflower Guide*. New York: Little, Brown and Company.

Peterson, Roger T., and Margaret McKenny. 1968. *A Field Guide to the Wildflowers of Northeastern and North-central North America*. New York: Houghton Mifflin Company.

Raymo, Chet, and Maureen Raymo. 1989. *Written in Stone: A Geological History of the Northeastern United States*. Chester, Connecticut: Pequot Press.

Sperduto, Dan, and Ben Kimball. 2011. *The Nature of New Hampshire: Natural Communities of the Granite State*. University of New Hampshire Press, University Press of New England.

Swain, Patricia C., and Jennifer B. Kearsley. 2011. *Classification of the Natural Communities of Massachusetts*. Version 1.4. Natural Heritage & Endangered Species Program, Massachusetts Division of Fisheries and Wildlife, Westborough, Massachusetts. http://www.mass.gov/eea/agencies/dfg/dfw/natural-heritage/natural-communities/classification-of-natural-communities.html

Thompson, Elizabeth, and Eric Sorenson. 2000. *Wetland, Woodland, Wildland: A Guide to the Natural Communities of Vermont*. Vermont Department of Fish and Wildlife and the Nature Conservancy. Hanover, New Hampshire: University Press of New England.

WEB RESOURCES

Atlas of the Flora of New England, http://neatlas.org/

Connecticut Botanical Society, http://www.ct-botanical-society.org/

E-floras (including the Flora of North America), http://www.efloras.org/

Go Botany (Native Plant Trust), https://gobotany.nativeplanttrust.org/

Invasive Plant Atlas of New England, http://www.eddmaps.org/ipane/

Salicicola—Eastern Massachusetts Vascular Plants, http://www.salicicola.com/photos/plantgallery/

NEW ENGLAND STATE NATURAL HERITAGE PROGRAMS WITH INFORMATION ABOUT RARE PLANTS

Connecticut Department of Energy and Environmental Protection. 2010. *Endangered, Threatened, and Special Concern Plants.* http://www.ct.gov/deep/cwp/view.asp?a=2702&q=323482

Maine Natural Areas Program. 2012. *Rare, Threatened, and Endangered Plant Taxa.* http://www.maine.gov/dacf/mnap/features/rare_plants/index.htm

Massachusetts Natural Heritage and Endangered Species Program. 2015. *List of Rare Species in Massachusetts.* http://www.mass.gov/eea/agencies/dfg/dfw/natural-heritage/species-information-and-conservation/rare-plants/

New Hampshire Natural Heritage Bureau. 2013. *Rare Plant List for New Hampshire.* http://www.nhdfl.org/about-forests-and-lands/bureaus/natural-heritage-bureau/about-us/rare-plants.aspx

Rhode Island Natural Heritage Program. 2007. *Rare Native Plants of Rhode Island.* http://www.rinhs.org/wp-content/uploads/ri_rare_plants_2007.pdf

Vermont Natural Heritage Inventory. 2014. *Rare and Uncommon Native Vascular Plants of Vermont.* http://www.vtfishand-wildlife.com/library/Reports_and_Documents/NonGame_and_Natural_Heritage/Rare_Threatened_and_Endangered_Species%20%20—%20lists/Rare_and_Uncommon_Native_Vascular_Plants_of_Vermont.pdf

GLOSSARY

achene A dry, usually one-seeded fruit that does not separate or split open at maturity

acidic Soils, rock, or water with a low pH, generally low in nutrients

alpine Plant community that occurs above timberline in high mountains

alternate Arranged singly along the stem.

annual A plant that lives for only one year

anther The pollen-bearing part of the stamen, usually at the tip

aquatic Living in fresh water, such as a pond, lake, river, or stream

ascending Diverging from the main stem at an upward angle

axil The point of junction of the leaf and the stem

axillary Position of a flower (or occasionally a very small leaf) that occurs at the junction of the leaf and the stem

basal At the base of the stem

basal rosette A cluster or whorl of leaves at the base of the stem

beak A narrowed, slender projection

bearded With tuft of hairs (on petals)

berry A fleshy fruit with a juicy or succulent wall that encloses two or more seeds

biennial A plant that lives for 2 years

bilaterally symmetrical A flower that can be divided into symmetrical halves along one plane, but not along both (horizontal and vertical) planes

blade (leaf) The expanded, outer part of the leaf

bloom 1) in flower; 2) a whitish coating on a stem

bog An acidic wetland habitat that forms on layers of peat and depends on precipitation for water inflow

brackish Intermediate between fresh and salt water, with some salinity

bract A small, modified leaf held under the flower or the inflorescence. (Members of the aster family have tight whorls of small, pointed bracts under the flower head.)

bristles Stiff, straight hairs

bulblet A small bulb, capable of growing into a new plant

calcareous Soils, rock, or water with a high pH, generally high in nutrients

calyx Collectively, all of the sepals of a flower

canopy The cover formed by the leafy upper branches in a woodland or forest

capsule A dry fruit that opens along 2 or more seams, pores, or teeth to release 2 or more seeds

circumneutral Soils, rock, or water with a moderate to high pH

clasping Closely surrounding the stem, as when the bases of a leaf almost meet on either side of the stem

cleft Deeply cut

climbing (vine) Growing high into shrubs, trees, buildings

compound (leaf) A leaf that is divided into 2 or more distinct, expanded segments called leaflets. A doubly or triply compound leaf has leaflets that are subdivided once or twice again into still smaller units

corolla Collectively, all of the petals of a flower

creeping Growing along the ground

cylindrical A fruit or a leaf with parallel sides and a rounded end, shaped like a cylinder

deciduous A nonpersistent leaf that falls off seasonally

disk flower The tiny flowers located in the center of a flower head in members of the aster family (Asteraceae)

downy With soft, fine hairs

drupe A fleshy fruit, such as a cherry, that usually encloses a single seed

elliptic Broadest in the middle and tapering to both ends

entire A leaf without teeth or lobes on the margins

estuary The tidally influenced, lower section of a river that empties into the ocean

evergreen Leaves that are green throughout the year

fen A wetland habitat that forms on peat in areas of groundwater seepages

field An open, upland habitat dominated by herbaceous plants

filament The stalk in the male part of the flower (stamen); supports the anther

floodplain A periodically flooded habitat, often forested, just above the banks of major rivers

follicle A fruit that splits along a single side to release the seeds

forest A habitat dominated by mature trees, with a canopy cover of 60 percent or higher

fringe Very fine hairs on the margin of a leaf or a petal

fruit The ripened part of the ovary that encloses the fertilized seed

gland A protuberance on an outer plant surface that secretes sticky oils

glandular A structure (such as a hair or leaf) that has glands

headland A steep coastal habitat with rock faces meeting the ocean

herbaceous A plant with a stem that dies after the growing season; not woody

indistinguishable A flower with extremely small or obscure petals and sepals

inflorescence Arrangement of flowers on a stem

inrolled Margin of a leaf that is folded under.

invasive A nonnative plant that infests and persists in natural habitats.

joint A swelling on the stem, often at the nodes (common in members of the buckwheat family)

krummholz A high elevation thicket of stunted spruce and fir just below the alpine zone

lance-shaped Broadest at or below the middle and tapering narrowly to the end, generally 4 or more times longer than wide

lateral On or to the side

leaflet One of the separate units of a compound leaf

linear Extremely narrow, with parallel sides

lip Upper or lower part of many bilaterally symmetrical flowers

lobe A projection of the leaf edge, broader and deeper than a tooth; often rounded, but can be angular or square-tipped

marsh A wetland habitat dominated by herbaceous plants; usually has standing water

midrib The middle, primary vein of the leaf

native A plant species that grows in the wild in New England, having naturally occurred in the area prior to the arrival of Europeans

needlelike Appearing similar to the thin, sharp-pointed leaf of an evergreen tree such as spruce or fir

node Point of attachment of a leaf to a stem

nonnative (introduced) A plant species that was accidentally or deliberately introduced to New England from outside the region

nut A dry fruit with a hard wall, usually containing only one seed; it does not split open at maturity

opposite Arranged in pairs along the stem

oval Broadest below middle and tapering to the tip; generally 1½–4 times longer than wide

ovary The enlarged, basal portion of the pistil where seeds are produced after fertilization

palmate A compound leaf broadly divided into radiating leaflets; like the fingers of a hand

panicle An elongated, branching inflorescence, roughly pyramidal in shape

parasite Living on and deriving nutrients from another organism, usually weakening that organism

peat A substrate of partially decayed vegetation, such as sphagnum moss in bogs, and sedges and grasses in fens.

perennial A plant that lives for more than 2 years

perfoliate The bases of a leaf or 2 opposite leaves join around a stem so that the stem appears to pierce the leaf or leaf pair

petal One of the inner whorl of flower lobes, usually pigmented and attracting pollinators

petiole The stalk of the leaf that holds the blade

pH A measure of the acidity or alkalinity of a solution (also soils and rock), on a scale of 0–14. A low pH (such as 3–5) indicates acidity; a higher pH (such as 6–8) indicates circumneutral or calcareous conditions

pinnate A compound leaf that is divided into distinct leaflets arranged on both sides of a central axis

pistil The female part of the flower, consisting of ovary, style, and stigma

pod A dry fruit enclosing a hollow space with one or more seeds; splits open at maturity

pollen Microscopic, sporelike male reproductive cells produced by the anther

prostrate Lying flat along the ground

raceme An elongated inflorescence in which the flowers are borne on short stalks along a central stem

radially symmetrical A flower that can be divided into symmetrical halves along more than one plane

ray flower The petal-like flowers that form the outer ring in many members of the aster family (Asteraceae)

reflexed Bent backward or downward

saline (salinity) Containing salt

salt marsh A coastal habitat inundated twice daily at high tide; dominated by salt-tolerant grasses, rushes, and wildflowers

saprophyte A plant that derives nutrients from dead or decaying organic matter

scale A tiny, modified, usually wedge-shaped leaf

scrambling Running along the ground and over low vegetation

sepal One of the outer whorl of flower lobes, often green

serrated (leaf) A leaf with toothed edges

sessile Without a stalk or petiole

sheath A tubular tissue where the leaf base encloses the stem

shrub A woody plant, usually shorter than 18 feet and with many stems at the base

silicle A fruit, less than 3 times as long as wide, that opens along 2 sides. This type of fruit is only in members of the mustard family (Brassicaceae)

silique A fruit, more than 3 times as long as wide, often elongate, that opens along 2 sides. This type of fruit is only in members of the mustard family (Brassicaceae)

simple (leaf) Undivided

sinus The indented or recessed area between 2 lobes

smooth Without hairs

spadix An unbranched, fleshy spike with flowers partially embedded in it, only in the arum family (Araceae)

spathe A large sheathing bract that surrounds the spadix, only in the arum family (Araceae)

spike An elongated inflorescence of unstalked flowers along a central stem

spine A very slender, straight, sharp-pointed structure

spoon-shaped (leaf) Broadly rounded at the tip and narrowed at the base

spreading Diverging more or less horizontally from the main stem

spur A hollow, tubular, tapering projection of a flower

stalk Slender, secondary, often short structure that holds the flower, fruit, or leaflet (note that the stalk of the leaf is called a petiole)

stamen The male, pollen-bearing part of the

flower, consisting of filament and anther

stem The main, central, supporting structure of the plant that holds all of the leaves, flowers, and other parts

stigma The tip of the pistil, which receives pollen

stipule An appendage, often paired, found at the base of the petiole in some species of plants, a part of the leaf

style The stalk of the pistil, below the stigma and above the ovary

subalpine Upper limit of spruce and fir stands, just below the alpine zone, at high elevations

swamp A wetland habitat that is dominated by trees or shrubs; usually has pockets of standing water

talus slope A steep, boulder-strewn slope, often located below sheer cliff faces

tendril Slender, twining or coiling structure used by vines for support and attachment

tepal Petals and sepals that are indistinguishable from each other, except by position, due to overall similarity

terminal The outermost portion (such as the top of the stem)

terrestrial Upland (forests and fields) and wetland (swamps and bogs) habitats; does not include aquatic (ponds, lakes, rivers) habitats

thicket A shrub-dominated upland habitat

thorn A short, stiff, acutely pointed structure (technically, it is a modified leaf)

throat The base of a tube-shaped flower

umbel A flattish or rounded inflorescence in which all the flower stalks originate from the same point, like the spokes of an umbrella

upland A habitat with dry to moderately moist soils. Most of New England's natural landscape consists of upland forests, thickets, and fields

veins Channels in a leaf which conduct fluids, sugars, and nutrients throughout the plant

vine A climbing or trailing plant that does not support its own weight

wetland A habitat with periodically or permanently saturated or inundated soils, such as a swamp, marsh, or bog

wet meadow A wetland habitat dominated by herbaceous plants, but without standing water

whorled Arranged in groups of 3 or more along the stem

wing (winged) A thin, flat extension along the edge of a stem, petiole, fruit, or so on.

woodland A habitat dominated by widely spaced trees, with an open canopy

ILLUSTRATION CREDITS

Steven Baskauf, www.bioimages.vanderbilt. edu: *Allium canadense, Ipomoea purpurea, Plantago rugelii*.

M. Batcher, Massachusetts Natural Heritage and Endangered Species Program (MNHESP): Image of a marsh on p. 40.

Luba Batuner, www.salicicola.com: *Lespedeza violacea* (flower close-up).

Jean Baxter: *Lilium lancifolium, Pseudognaphilum obtusifolium* (flowering stem).

Janet Bissell: *Iris pseudacorus*.

Merel Black: *Anemone cylindrica, Hackelia virginiana, Maianthemum racemosum, Physalis virginiana, Ranunculus hispidus, Viola renifolia*.

Frank Bramley: Image of *Oxalis violacea* on p. 16, *Isotria verticillata, Lathyrus palustris, Pseudognaphalium macounii* (inset), *Pseudognaphalium obtusifolium* (flowers), *Sagittaria graminea, Sanicula odorata, Sisyrinchium mucronatum, Trifolium aureum, Triadenum virginicum*.

Alan Bryan: Endpaper drawings.

John Burns: *Agrimonia gryposepala, Aralia nudicaulis, Aureolaria pedicularia, Chimaphila maculata, Chimaphila umbellata, Conopholis americana, Drosera rotundifolia, Gentianopsis crinita, Halenia deflexa* (habit and flower), *Osmorhiza longistylis, Sanguinaria canadensis, Sanicula marilandica, Scutellaria lateriflora, Sedum ternatum, Solidago squarrosa*.

Donald S. Cameron: *Sagittaria filiformis*.

Katy Chayka, www.minnesotawildflowers. info: *Acorus americanus, Apocynum androsaemifolium, Boehmeria cylindrica, Cryptotaenia canadensis, Gaultheria hispidula* (habit), *Gentiana andrewsii, Parietaria pensylvanica, Platanthera hookeri, Ranunculus abortivus, Sanicula canadensis* (habit),

Scrophularia lanceolata (habit), *Sium suave* (foliage).

Frances Clark: *Pterospora andromeda*.

Mareike Conrad: *Cynanchum rossicum, Viola brittoniana* (leaf).

Will Cook, www.carolinanature.com: *Cirsium horridulum, Cynoglossum virginianum*.

William Cullina: *Lythrum alatum, Mimulus moschatus* (habit), *Nelumbo lutea, Uvularia perfoliata*.

Nelson DeBarros, www.ct.gov/deep: *Asclepias purpurascens, Persicaria arifolia* (flower), *Pityopsis falcata, Polygala cruciata, Sabatia stellaris, Xyris torta*.

Dawn Dentzer: *Asclepias incarnata, Chamaecrista fasciculata, Dipsacus fullonum, Gentiana clausa, Hypopitys monotropa, Medeola virginiana, Medicago sativa, Polygala paucifolia, Ranunculus recurvatus, Viola pallens*.

Emil Doyle: Image of a pitch pine–scrub oak woodland on p. 37.

Bonnie Drexler: *Goodyera pubescens*.

Peter Dziuk, www.minnesotawildflowers. info: *Arabis pycnocarpa* (flower), *Cardamine parviflora, Cicuta bulbifera, Circaea canadensis, Claytonia caroliniana, Drosera intermedia, Eriocaulon aquaticum, Geum canadense, Geum laciniatum, Hydrophyllum virginianum, Lycopus virginicus, Malva neglecta, Panax trifolius, Persicaria virginiana, Platanthera obtusata, Ranunculus flabellaris, Rorippa palustris, Rorippa sylvestris, Sagittaria rigida, Sium suave* (flower), *Spiranthes romanzoffiana*.

Debbi Edelstein: *Cypripedium reginae*.

Ted Elliman: *Cardamine impatiens* (habit).

Anna Eshelman: Map, p. 31.

Jamie Fenneman: *Epilobium leptophyllum*.

Gary P. Fleming: *Dysphania botrys, Linum medium, Viola affinis.*

Gary P. Fleming, Virginia Natural Heritage Program, www.dcr.virginia.gov/natural_heritage: *Lechea tenuifolia, Ptilimnium capillaceum, Sanicula trifoliata.*

Deb Fountain: *Agastache scrophulariifolia, Allium tricoccum, Anemone americana, Apios americana, Artemisia stelleriana, Baptisia australis, Calopogon tuberosus, Cirsium vulgare, Erysimum cheiranthoides, Eupatorium perfoliatum, Helianthus strumosus, Linaria vulgaris, Lythrum salicaria, Oenothera biennis, Persicaria sagittata, Physostegia virginiana, Phytolacca americana, Polygonum articulatum, Pyrola americana, Silphium perfoliatum, Spiraea alba, Symphyotrichum novi-belgii, Tradescantia virginiana, Veratrum viride* (flower), *Verbena hastata, Veronicastrum virginicum, Viola pubescens.*

Jennifer Garrett: *Blephilia ciliata, Eriocaulon parkeri* (habit & close-up), *Eupatorium novae-angliae, Galium labradoricum* (flower), *Rumex verticillatus* (habit).

Steven C. Garske, Great Lakes Indian Fish and Wildlife Commission: *Humulus lupulus.*

Nancy Goodman: *Polygonum tenue.*

Elisabeth Green: *Mertensia virginica.*

Charles Grunden: *Nabalus serpentarius* (leaf).

D. Gumbart: Image of cordgrasses on p. 42.

John Gwaltney, www.southeasternflora. com: *Hydrocotyle umbellata, Onosmodium virginianum, Rumex verticillatus* (close-up), *Samolus valerandi.*

Arthur Haines: *Abutilon theophrasti, Acalypha gracilens, Acalypha virginica, Achillea millefolium, Aegopodium podagraria* (flower and leaf), *Agalinis maritima, Agalinis purpurea, Agrimonia striata, Ajuga reptans, Aletris farinosa, Allium schoenoprasum, Allium vineale, Amerorchis rotundifolia, Amphicarpaea bracteata* (flower), *Angelica atropurpurea, Angelica lucida, Antennaria howellii, Antennaria neglecta,* *Antennaria plantaginifolia, Anthemis cotula, Arabidopsis lyrata* (leaf), *Arabis pycnocarpa* (stem), *Arctium lappa, Arenaria serpyllifolia, Arnica lanceolata, Artemisia campestris, Asclepias quadrifolia, Asclepias syriaca, Asclepias verticillata, Atriplex cristata, Bartonia virginica, Bidens discoidea, Blephilia hirsuta, Boechera canadensis, Boechera laevigata, Boechera stricta, Caltha palustris, Calystegia spithamaea, Campanula rapunculoides, Capsella bursa-pastoris, Cardamine bulbosa, Cardamine maxima, Cardamine pratensis, Carum carvi* (flower and leaf)), *Centaurea nigra, Chamaedaphne calyculata, Chenopodium glaucum, Chenopodium simplex, Cichorium intybus, Cicuta maculata, Cirsium arvense, Clematis occidentalis, Clematis terniflora, Clematis virginiana, Collinsonia canadensis, Conium maculatum, Convolvulus arvensis, Coreopsis rosea, Cynanchum louiseae, Cypripedium parviflorum, Desmodium canadense, Desmodium ciliare, Diapensia lapponica, Draba reptans, Echium vulgare, Empetrum nigrum, Epifagus virginiana, Epigaea repens, Epilobium ciliatum, Epilobium palustre, Epilobium strictum, Erythronium americanum, Eupatorium hyssopifolium, Eupatorium pilosum* (flowering stem), *Euphorbia cyparissias, Euphorbia polygonifolia, Euphrasia nemorosa, Euthamia caroliniana, Eutrochium dubium* (leaf), *Eutrochium fistulosum* (flower), *Eutrochium maculatum* (habit and leaf), *Fallopia scandens, Floerkea proserpinacoides, Galium lanceolatum* (habit), *Galium mollugo* (flowering stem), *Galium tinctorium, Gaultheria hispidula* (fruit), *Geocaulon lividum, Geranium bicknellii, Geranium carolinianum, Geranium robertianum, Geum fragarioides, Geum peckii, Geum rivale* (leaf), *Glaucium flavum, Glechoma hederacea, Goodyera repens* (flower and leaf), *Goodyera tesselata* (leaf), *Harrimanella hypnoides, Hedeoma pulegioides, Heracleum maximum* (flower and leaf), *Hibiscus moscheutos, Honckenya* peploides, *Houstonia caerulea, Houstonia longifolia, Hudsonia tomentosa, Hydrastis canadensis, Hydrophyllum canadense* (leaf), *Hypericum ascyron, Hypericum canadense, Hypericum ellipticum, Hypericum perforatum, Hypochaeris radicata* (leaf), *Impatiens pallida, Kalmia procumbens, Krigia virginica, Lactuca canadensis* (leaf), *Lactuca serriola* (leaf), *Lamium galeobdolon, Laportea canadensis, Lathyrus japonicus, Lathyrus latifolius* (flower and leaf), *Lechea maritima, Leonurus cardiaca, Lepidium campestre, Lespedeza stuevei, Ligusticum scoticum, Limosella australis, Liparis liliifolia, Liparis loeselii, Lobelia siphilitica, Ludwigia alternifolia, Lunaria annua, Lychnis flos-cuculi, Lysimachia ciliata, Lysimachia hybrida* (leaf), *Lysimachia quadrifolia, Lysimachia thyrsiflora, Malaxis monophyllos, Matricaria chamomilla, Mentha spicata, Mertensia maritima, Micranthes pensylvanica* (habit), *Minuartia michauxii, Mitella diphylla, Moehringia macrophylla, Mollugo verticillata, Monarda fistulosa, Moneses uniflora, Myosotis sylvatica, Myosotis verna, Myosoton aquaticum, Neottia cordata, Nepeta cataria, Oligoneuron album, Origanum vulgare, Osmorhiza claytonii, Oxalis violacea* (leaf), *Packera aurea* (flower), *Panax quinquefolius, Paronychia argyrocoma, Pedicularis canadensis, Pedicularis lanceolata, Penthorum sedoides, Persicaria careyi, Persicaria hydropiper, Persicaria orientalis, Petasites frigidus, Phlox paniculata, Phlox subulata, Phyllodoce caerulea, Physalis grisea, Physalis heterophylla, Platanthera aquilonis, Platanthera ciliaris, Platanthera flava, Platanthera grandiflora, Platanthera huronensis, Platanthera lacera, Platanthera orbiculata, Polemonium reptans, Polygala nuttallii, Polygala senega, Polygala verticillata, Polygonatum pubescens, Polygonum glaucum, Polymnia canadensis, Potentilla canadensis, Potentilla indica* (flower and habit), *Primula mistassinica, Proserpinaca palustris, Proserpinaca pectinata, Prunus pumila, Pycnanthemum muticum, Pycnanthemum virginianum, Pyrola asarifolia* (flower and leaf), *Pyrola elliptica, Ranunculus bulbosus, Ranunculus pensylvanicus, Ranunculus repens, Rhexia virginica, Rhododendron lapponicum, Rubus dalibarda, Rubus pubescens* (flower and leaf), *Rumex triangulivalvis, Sagina nodosa, Sanguisorba canadensis* (flower and leaf), *Sanicula canadensis* (close-up), *Saxifraga rivularis, Scrophularia lanceolata* (flower), *Securigera varia, Senna hebecarpa, Sicyos angulatus, Sisyrinchium angustifolium, Sisyrinchium atlanticum, Solidago odora* (leaf), *Solidago puberula, Solidago simplex, Solidago ulmifolia, Sparganium eurycarpum, Spiranthes lacera, Spiranthes lucida, Stachys hispida, Stachys hyssopifolia, Stellaria media, Strophostyles helvola* (flower and leaf), *Symphyotrichum cordifolium, Symphyotrichum ericoides* (flowering stem), *Symphyotrichum laeve, Symphyotrichum lanceolatum, Symphyotrichum novae-angliae, Symphyotrichum praealtum* (leaf), *Symphytum officinale, Symplocarpus foetidus, Taenidia integerrima, Taraxacum laevigatum, Teucrium canadense, Thalictrum revolutum, Thymus pulegioides, Triantha glutinosa, Trichostema dichotomum, Trifolium repens, Triodanis perfoliata, Triosteum aurantiacum* (flower), *Triphora trianthophora, Urtica dioica, Vaccinium pallidum, Vaccinium uliginosum, Verbascum blattaria, Verbena simplex, Veronica americana, Veronica persica, Vicia sativa, Vinca minor, Viola adunca, Viola blanda, Viola nephrophylla, Viola palmata, Viola palustris, Viola primulifolia, Viola rostrata* (habit), *Xanthium strumarium.*

John Hilty, www.illinoiswildflowers.info: *Agrimonia pubescens* (flower and leaf), *Anemone virginiana, Anthemis arvensis, Cerastium nutans, Desmodium perplexum* (flower and leaf), *Dioscorea villosa* (flower and leaf), *Euthamia graminifolia, Medicago lupulina, Opuntia humifusa, Penstemon pallidus, Persicaria coccinea, Zizia aurea.*

Becky Hrdy: *Rotala ramosior.*

Dan Jaffe: *Agrimonia parviflora, Alisma subcordatum, Baptisia tinctoria, Chelidonium majus, Lilium superbum, Lobelia cardinalis, Monarda punctata, Monotropa uniflora, Nymphaea odorata, Penstemon calycosus, Saururus cernuus, Scrophularia marilandica* (habit).

J. Jenkins: Images of an open wet meadow on p. 11, an oak-hickory glade forest on p. 36, a deep marsh on p. 39.

Donna Kausen: *Andromeda polifolia, Anemone quinquefolia, Atriplex prostrata, Campanula rotundifolia, Chelone lyonii, Galium triflorum, Geum aleppicum, Hieracium kalmii, Lilium canadense, Lilium philadelphicum, Lysimachia borealis, Malaxis unifolia, Matricaria discoidea, Oxalis montana* (flower), *Ranunculus cymbalaria, Rumex obtusifolius, Solidago juncea, Sonchus asper* (leaf), *Tussilago farfara, Typha angustifolia, Utricularia intermedia, Xyris difformis.*

Ben Kimball: Image of a glacial cirque on p. 32, a subalpine spruce-fir forest on p. 35, Philbrick-Cricenti Bog on p. 41, *Adlumia fungosa, Amaranthus cannabinus, Asclepias amplexicaulis, Bidens laevis, Gentiana linearis, Isotria medeoloides, Menyanthes trifoliata, Minuartia groenlandica, Streptopus lanceolatus.*

George Kocur: *Polygonum douglasii.*

Louis-Marie Landry: *Hieracium lachenalii, Pseudognaphalium macounii* (flowers).

William Larkin: *Mimulus moschatus* (flower close-up).

Glen Lee, Regina, Saskatchewan, Canada: *Bidens beckii.*

Ben Legler, www.biology.burkemuseum. org/herbarium/imagecollection.php: *Butomus umbellatus, Calypso bulbosa, Crepis capillaris* (leaf), *Malva sylvestris, Myosotis arvensis, Ranunculus acris.*

Max Licher, www.swbiodiversity.org/portal/ index.php: *Tragopogon porrifolius.*

Deborah Lievens: *Desmodium rotundifolium, Eutrochium fistulosum* (leaf).

Dorothy Long: *Trillium erectum, Phlox maculata.*

Marilee Lovit: Image of Mt. Katahdin cliff on p. 38, *Alisma triviale, Anaphalis margaritacea, Artemisia vulgaris* (habit and leaf), *Bidens cernua, Brasenia schreberi, Cakile edentula, Calystegia sepium* (flower close-up), *Capnoides sempervirens* (flower and leaf), *Chelone glabra, Comarum palustre, Corema conradii, Galeopsis tetrahit, Galium aparine* (flower and fruit), *Galium verum, Gaylussacia baccata, Hieracium aurantiacum, Hudsonia ericoides, Hypericum gentianoides, Iris versicolor, Lepidium virginicum, Limonium carolinianum, Linnaea borealis, Lupinus polyphyllus, Maianthemum trifolium, Malva moschata, Melampyrum lineare, Moehringia lateriflora, Nabalus altissimus* (leaf), *Nuttallanthus canadensis, Nymphoides cordata, Oclemena acuminata, Orthilia secunda, Oxalis montana* (habit), *Packera schweinitziana* (flower), *Pogonia ophioglossoides, Primula laurentiana, Prunella vulgaris, Raphanus raphanistrum, Rhodiola rosea, Rumex pallidus, Sarracenia purpurea, Silene latifolia, Spergula arvensis, Suaeda linearis, Trifolium hybridum, Utricularia cornuta, Utricularia vulgaris, Uvularia sessilifolia, Veronica serpyllifolia, Viola cucullata.*

John Lynch: *Hydrophyllum canadense* (flower), *Polemonium vanbruntiae, Pyrola chlorantha, Pyrola minor, Salicornia ambigua, Spiranthes vernalis, Tradescantia ohiensis, Viola brittoniana* (habit), *Viola rostrata* (flower close-up).

Lisa Mattei: *Lupinus perennis, Maianthemum stellatum.*

Cathryn McDonough: *Echinacea purpurea.*

Douglas McGrady: *Calla palustris, Kummerowia striata, Lachnanthes caroliniana, Pycnanthemum incanum, Tephrosia virginiana.*

Leslie J. Mehrhoff, University of Connecticut, www.bugwood.org: *Humulus japonicus, Onopordum acanthium, Persicaria perfoliata, Trapa natans.*

Glen Mittelhauser: Image of Mt. Katahdin on p. 1, *Actaea rubra, Agalinis paupercula, Aquilegia canadensis* (flower close-up), *Amaranthus retroflexus, Amphicarpaea bracteata* (leaf), *Anemone canadensis, Aralia hispida, Arctium minus, Argentina egedii, Arisaema triphyllum, Artemisia biennis, Asparagus officinalis, Atriplex acadiensis, Barbarea vulgaris, Bartonia paniculata, Bidens connata, Brassica juncea, Brassica rapa, Calystegia sepium* (habit), *Campanula aparinoides, Cardamine impatiens* (leaf), *Cerastium arvense, Chamaepericlymenum canadense, Chenopodium album, Clintonia borealis, Conioselinum chinense* (flower and leaf), *Crepis capillaris* (flower), *Cuscuta gronovii, Daucus carota, Erechtites hieraciifolius, Erigeron canadensis, Fallopia convolvulus, Galium asprellum* (flower), *Galium labradoricum* (habit), *Galium mollugo* (leaf), *Galium palustre, Galium trifidum, Gaultheria procumbens, Gnaphalium uliginosum, Helianthus tuberosus, Heracleum mantegazzianum* (flower and leaf), *Hylotelephium telephium, Kalmia polifolia, Lactuca biennis* (leaf), *Lechea intermedia, Lobelia kalmii, Lycopus uniflorus, Lysimachia arvensis, Lysimachia maritima, Maianthemum canadense, Melilotus albus, Mentha canadensis, Myosotis laxa, Myosotis scorpioides, Nabalus trifoliolatus, Oclemena nemoralis, Oenothera fruticosa, Oxalis stricta, Packera schweinitziana* (leaf), *Pastinaca sativa* (flower and leaf), *Persicaria amphibia, Persicaria arifolia* (habit), *Persicaria lapathifolia, Persicaria punctata* (flowering stem and leaf), *Plantago major* (flower and leaf), *Plantago maritima, Platanthera clavellata, Platanthera psycodes, Polygala sanguinea, Polygonum aviculare, Potentilla norvegica, Ranunculus aquatilis, Ranunculus flammula, Rhinanthus minor, Rumex britannica* (habit and fruit), *Rumex crispus* (habit and fruit), *Salicornia depressa, Salsola kali, Scutellaria galericulata, Senecio vulgaris, Sibbaldiopsis tridentata, Sisymbrium officinale, Sonchus oleraceus* (flower and leaf), *Sparganium americanum, Sparganium emersum* (fruit), *Stellaria alsine, Stellaria borealis, Suaeda maritima, Thalictrum pubescens, Trifolium arvense, Trifolium campestre, Trifolium dubium, Trifolium pratense, Utricularia radiata, Vaccinium myrtilloides, Vaccinium oxycoccos, Vaccinium vitis-idaea, Veronica arvensis, Veronica chamaedrys, Veronica officinalis, Viola lanceolata, Xyris montana.*

Keir Morse, www.keiriosity.com: *Fragaria vesca, Galium boreale, Geum macrophyllum, Grindelia squarrosa, Hedeoma hispida, Lythrum hyssopifolia, Urtica urens, Verbena stricta, Veronica peregrina, Vicia villosa.*

Maile Neel: *Agalinis acuta.*

M. N. Nelson, Massachusetts Natural Heritage and Endangered Species Program: Image of a floodplain forest on p. 41.

Lawrence Newcomb: *Neottia convallarioides, Sparganium androcladum, Triosteum aurantiacum* (stem).

Allen Norcross, www.nhgardensolutions. wordpress.com: *Dianthus armeria, Epipactis helleborine, Hesperis matronalis, Lobelia spicata, Veratrum viride* (habit).

North Carolina Native Plant Society, www. ncwildflower.org, Tom Harville: *Heuchera americana* (flower and leaf).

Bruce Patterson: Image of *Sium suave* on p. 13, *Actaea pachypoda, Actaea racemosa, Arethusa bulbosa, Asclepias exaltata, Bidens hyperborea, Boechera missouriensis, Cardamine concatenata, Cardamine diphylla, Cirsium pumilum, Cypripedium acaule, Draba verna, Drymocallis arguta, Erigeron annuus, Eupatorium pilosum* (leaf), *Euphorbia corollata, Fallopia japonica, Fragaria virginiana, Geum rivale* (flower), *Lactuca canadensis* (flower), *Lespedeza capitata, Lespedeza virginica, Lindernia dubia, Lycopus americanus, Lysimachia hybrida* (flower), *Micranthes virginiensis, Mikania scandens, Mimulus ringens, Mirabilis nyctaginea, Orontium aquaticum, Penstemon hirsu-*

tus, *Ranunculus fascicularis, Rhododendron canadense, Rhododendron groenlandicum, Sagittaria latifolia, Sericocarpus asteroides, Sericocarpus linifolius, Silene caroliniana, Solidago canadensis, Solidago odora* (flower), *Solidago speciosa, Spergularia marina, Spergularia rubra, Stellaria graminea, Symphyotrichum racemosum, Symphyotrichum undulatum, Thlaspi arvense, Trillium undulatum.*

Douglas Payne: *Platanthera dilatata.*

Walt and Louiseann Pietrowicz: *Dicentra cucullaria, Tiarella cordifolia, Trillium cernuum.*

Adelaide Pratt: *Nabalus altissimus* (flower).

Karan A. Rawlins, University of Georgia, www.bugwood.org: *Sclerolepis uniflora* (habit and flower).

Daniel Reed, www.2bnthewild.com: *Cardamine douglassii.*

Anton A. Reznicek, www.michiganflora.net: *Fallopia cilinodis, Packera paupercula.*

Rob Routledge, Sault College, www.bugwood.org: *Symphyotrichum boreale.*

Jason Sachs: *Aureolaria virginica, Cardamine pensylvanica, Desmodium marilandicum, Galium lanceolatum* (flower close-up), *Gaylussacia bigeloviana, Nabalus boottii, Paronychia canadensis, Potentilla robbinsiana, Rubus chamaemorus* (flower and leaf), *Streptopus amplexifolius.*

Réal Sarrazin, www.fleurssauvages.ca: *Desmodium canescens.*

Eleanor Saulys: *Corallorhiza odontorhiza, Gentianella quinquefolia, Mimulus alatus, Platanthera blephariglottis, Scutellaria parvula, Spiranthes tuberosa, Triosteum perfoliatum.*

David G. Smith, www.delawarewildflowers.org: *Aplectrum hyemale, Eupatorium rotundifolium, Lycopus rubellus, Sisymbrium altissimum.*

R. W. Smith, www.michiganflora.net: *Phryma leptostachya.*

Richard Snellgrove: *Alliaria petiolata, Asarum canadense, Caulophyllum thalictroides,*

Centaurea stoebe, Cirsium discolor, Comandra umbellata, Desmodium paniculatum, Dicentra canadensis, Eurybia radula, Geranium maculatum, Hottonia inflata, Kalmia angustifolia, Liatris novae-angliae, Pontederia cordata, Potentilla simplex, Sabatia kennedyana, Scorzoneroides autumnale (flower and leaf), *Silene vulgaris, Solidago bicolor, Solidago sempervirens, Spiraea tomentosa, Thalictrum dioicum, Thalictrum thalictroides, Utricularia gibba, Uvularia grandiflora, Vaccinium macrocarpon.*

Paul Somers: *Coptis trifolia, Symphyotrichum puniceum.*

Bruce Sorrie, Massachusetts Natural Heritage and Endangered Species Program: *Arisaema dracontium.*

Will Stuart: *Claytonia virginica.*

Patricia Swain, Massachusetts Natural Heritage and Endangered Species Program (MNHESP): Image of storm-eroded dunes on p. 43, *Viola rotundifolia.*

Arieh Tal: www.nttlphoto.com: Images of *Solidago simplex* on p. 14, *Ambrosia artemisiifolia* on p. 21, *Agalinis tenuifolia, Ageratina altissima, Amaranthus hybridus, Ambrosia artemisiifolia, Anemone acutiloba, Aquilegia canadensis* (habit), *Arabidopsis thaliana* (habit and flower), *Arctostaphylos uva-ursi, Asclepias tuberosa, Bidens frondosa, Brassica nigra, Centaurea jacea, Chaenorhinum minus, Chamaecrista nictitans, Chrysosplenium americanum, Cirsium muticum, Clinopodium vulgare, Commelina communis, Convallaria majalis, Crocanthemum bicknellii, Crocanthemum canadense, Desmodium cuspidatum* (habit and leaf), *Dianthus deltoides, Diodia teres, Doellingeria infirma, Doellingeria umbellata, Epilobium hirsutum, Erigeron philadelphicus, Erigeron strigosus, Eupatorium sessilifolium, Euphorbia maculata, Eurybia divaricata, Eurybia macrophylla, Eurybia schreberi, Eurybia spectabilis, Eutrochium dubium* (flower), *Eutrochium purpureum, Galearis spectabilis, Gratiola neglecta, Hele-*

nium autumnale, Helianthus annuus, Helianthus decapetalus, Helianthus divaricatus, Hibiscus trionum, Hieracium caespitosum, Hieracium flagellare, Hieracium paniculatum, Hieracium piloselloides, Hieracium scabrum, Hieracium venosum, Hylodesmum glutinosum (habit), Hypericum mutilum, Hypericum punctatum, Hypochaeris radicata (flower), Hypoxis hirsuta, Impatiens capensis, Inula helenium, Ionactis linariifolia, Lactuca biennis (flowering stem), Lactuca serriola (flower), Lapsana communis, Lechea mucronata, Leucanthemum vulgare, Linum usitatissimum (habit and flower detail), Linum virginianum, Lobelia inflata, Lotus corniculatus, Lysimachia nummularia, Lysimachia terrestris, Melilotus officinalis, Micranthes pensylvanica (flowering stem detail), Mitchella repens, Monarda didyma, Mycelis muralis (flower and leaf), Myosotis stricta, Nabalus albus, Nuphar variegata, Oenothera perennis, Oligoneuron rigidum, Orobanche uniflora, Packera aurea (leaf), Packera obovata, Parnassia glauca, Penstemon digitalis, Persicaria hydropiperoides, Persicaria longiseta, Persicaria maculosa, Persicaria pensylvanica, Pilea pumila, Plantago aristata, Plantago lanceolata, Pluchea odorata, Potentilla argentea (habit and leaf detail), Pycnanthemum tenuifolium, Rubus hispidus, Rudbeckia hirta, Rumex acetosella, Saponaria officinalis, Silene antirrhina, Silene dioica, Sisyrinchium montanum, Smilax herbacea, Solanum carolinense, Solanum dulcamara, Solanum ptycanthum, Solidago altissima, Solidago arguta, Solidago caesia, Solidago flexicaulis, Solidago gigantea, Solidago hispida, Solidago latissimifolia, Solidago leiocarpa, Solidago macrophylla, Solidago nemoralis, Solidago patula, Solidago rugosa, Solidago uliginosa, Sonchus arvensis (flower), Sonchus asper (flower), Spiranthes cernua, Symphyotrichum concolor, Symphyotrichum dumosum, Symphyotrichum ericoides (flower detail), Symphyotrichum lateriflorum, Symphyotrichum patens, Symphyotrichum pilosum, Symphyotrichum praealtum (flower), Symphyotrichum prenanthoides, Symphyotrichum subulatum, Symphyotrichum tenuifolium, Symphyotrichum tradescantii (flower and leaf), Tanacetum vulgare, Taraxacum officinale, Tragopogon pratensis, Turritis glabra (habit and flower), Verbascum thapsus, Verbena urticifolia, Vernonia noveboracensis, Vicia cracca, Vicia tetrasperma, Viola canadensis, Viola labradorica, Viola sagittata, Viola sororia.

Dan Tenaglia, www.missouriplants.com: Agastache nepetoides, Barbarea verna, Castilleja coccinea, Crotalaria sagittalis, Endodeca serpentaria (flower and leaf), Galium pilosum (habit and flower), Helenium flexuosum, Hylodesmum nudiflorum, Lespedeza hirta, Lespedeza procumbens, Potentilla recta, Scrophularia marilandica (flower), Silene stellata, Tipularia discolor.

John Thayer, www.minnesotawildflowers. info:, Hydrocotyle americana.

Lou Wagner: Lepidium latifolium.

Rebekah D. Wallace, University of Georgia, www.bugwood.org: Aureolaria flava, Trifolium incarnatum.

Beverly S. Walters, www.michiganflora.net: Acalypha rhomboidea.

Jill Weber: Corallorhiza trifida, Galinsoga quadriradiata, Lysimachia vulgaris.

Pete Westover: Vaccinium angustifolium.

Steve Ziglar: Cypripedium arietinum, Trillium grandiflorum.

Dale A. Zimmerman Herbarium, Western New Mexico University: Euphorbia vermiculata.

Alexey Zinovjev, www.salicicola.com: Apocynum cannabinum, Cerastium fontanum, Drosera filiformis, Dysphania ambrosioides, Epilobium coloratum, Ficaria verna, Fumaria officinalis, Galium asprellum (stem), Geum virginianum, Goodyera tesselata (stem), Hemerocallis fulva, Lespedeza frutescens, Lespedeza violacea (habit), Lycopus amplectens, Nasturtium officinale, Petasites hybridus, Polygala polygama, Salicornia bigelovii, Stachys palustris, Utricularia purpurea, Viola pedata.

Flickr, Creative Commons Attribution 2.0 Generic license: Col Ford and Natasha De Vere, Hemerocallis lilioasphodelus.

Flickr, Creative Commons Attribution-Share Alike 2.0 Generic license: J. Brew, Goodyera oblongifolia. Matt Lavin, Kochia scoparia. Udo Schmidt, Impatiens glandulifera.

Wikimedia, Creative Commons Attribution 3.0 Unported license: Molekuel, Berteroa incana. Fritz Flohr Reynolds, Arabidopsis lyrata (flower), Hylodesmum glutinosum (flower), Nabalus serpentarius (flower), Rubus flagellaris.

Wikimedia, Creative Commons Attribution-Share Alike 2.5 Generic license: Júlio Reis, Portulaca oleracea.

Wikimedia, Creative Commons Attribution-Share Alike 3.0 Germany license: Jörg Hempel, Pinguicula vulgaris.

Wikimedia, Creative Commons Attribution-Share Alike 3.0 Unported license: Alvesgaspar, Heliopsis helianthoides. Denis Barthel, Veronica anagallis-aquatica. Dalgial, Anthriscus sylvestris. Jan Eckstein, Calluna vulgaris. Christian Fischer, Centaurium pulchellum, Scheuchzeria palustris. Hans Hillewaert, Coeloglossum viride, Lithospermum officinale. Hiuppo, Jasione montana. Icerge, Hieracium pilosella. Lazaregagnidze, Cynoglossum officinale. Ivar Leidus, Knautia arvensis. 4028mdk09, Lamium album.

Wikimedia, Creative Commons Attribution-Share Alike 4.0 International license: Hans Hillewaert, Sparganium angustifolium.

Wikimedia, GFDL and Creative Commons Attribution 3.0 Unported license: Hajotthu, Omalotheca sylvatica, G.-U. Tolkiehn, Sparganium emersum (flower).

Wikimedia, GFDL and Creative Commons Attribution-Share Alike 2.5 Generic license: Derek Ramsey, Chenopodium capitatum.

Wikimedia, GFDL and Creative Commons Attribution-Share Alike 3.0 Unported license: Aiwok, Sedum acre. Antti Bilund, Viola selkirkii. Bjoertvedt, Tripleurospermum maritimum. Enrico Blasutto, Ranunculus sceleratus. Ffaarr, Oenothera laciniata. Hermanhi, Silene acaulis. Kallerna, Chamerion angustifolium. Kenraiz, Arnoseris minima, Circaea alpina. Le.Loup.Gris, Ambrosia trifida. Typha latifolia. Ilona Loser, Oxalis violacea (flower). Meneerke bloem, Ornithogalum umbellatum. Jerzy Opioła, Saxifraga paniculata. Pethan, Armoracia rusticana, Euphorbia esula. Pleple2000, Lamium purpureum. Rasback, Chenopodium rubrum, Jacobaea vulgaris. Riyosha, Rudbeckia laciniata. Anneli Salo, Sonchus arvensis (leaf). Walter Siegmund, Corallorhiza maculata. Taka, Datura stramonium. TeunSpaans from nl, Lamium amplexicaule, Nymphoides peltata.

Wikimedia, public domain: Devin Rodgers and Mason Brock, Iris prismatica. Hermann Schachner, Euphorbia nutans. Velociraptor, Podophyllum peltatum.

INDEX

Main species entries are in **bold type.** Species only mentioned in the descriptions are in roman type.

ABOUT THE AUTHORS

ANN ELLIMAN

TED ELLIMAN is a highly regarded New England botanist. Since retiring from the conservation department at Native Plant Trust, his consulting and teaching have focused on botanical inventories, natural habitat surveys, and invasive species management. Previously, he worked as a contract ecologist for the National Park Service, doing rare plant searches and forest community studies on lands managed by the Appalachian Trail Park Office in much of the Northeast. Since the mid-1990s, he has led natural history tours to the high mountain regions of western China, where he spent two years working as a teacher and plant ecologist. Ted has an undergraduate degree from Southern Connecticut State University and a master's degree from Yale School of Forestry and Environmental Studies.

Founded in 1900, **NATIVE PLANT TRUST** (formerly the New England Wild Flower Society) is the nation's oldest plant conservation organization and a recognized leader in native plant conservation, horticulture, and education. The organization's headquarters, Garden in the Woods, is a renowned native plant botanic garden in Framingham, Massachusetts, that attracts visitors from all over the world. From this base, 25 staff and more than 700 volunteers work throughout New England to monitor and protect rare and endangered plants, collect and preserve seeds to ensure biological diversity, detect and control invasive species, conduct research, and offer a range of educational programs. Native Plant Trust also operates a native plant nursery at Nasami Farm in western Massachusetts and has seven sanctuaries in Maine, Massachusetts, New Hampshire, and Vermont that are open to the public. See nativeplanttrust.org.

LEAF FORM

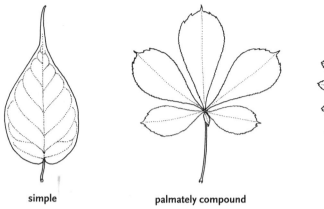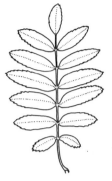

simple   palmately compound   pinnately compound

LEAF SHAPE

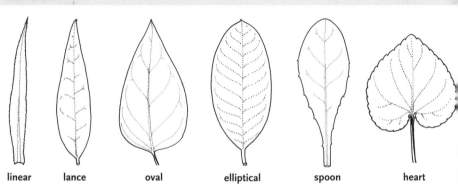

linear   lance   oval   elliptical   spoon   heart

LEAF MARGINS

LEAF ARRANGEMENT

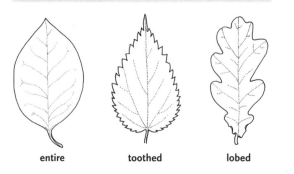

entire   toothed   lobed   alternate